TCM TURNER CLASSIC MOVIES

REWINDING THE '80s

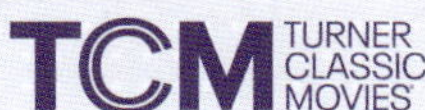

REWINDING THE '80s

CINEMA UNDER THE INFLUENCE OF MUSIC VIDEOS, ACTION STARS, AND A COLD WAR

JOHN MALAHY

RUNNING PRESS
PHILADELPHIA

Running Press
Hachette Book Group
1290 Avenue of the Americas, New York, NY 10104
www.runningpress.com
@Running_Press

First Edition: October 2025

Published by Running Press, an imprint of Hachette Book Group, Inc. The Running Press name and logo are trademarks of Hachette Book Group, Inc.

Print book cover and interior design by Amanda Richmond
Front cover illustration by Doaly

Library of Congress Cataloging-in-Publication Data has been applied for.

ISBNs: 978-0-7624-8966-4 (hardcover), 978-0-7624-8967-1 (ebook)

Printed in China

TLF

10 9 8 7 6 5 4 3 2 1

Contents

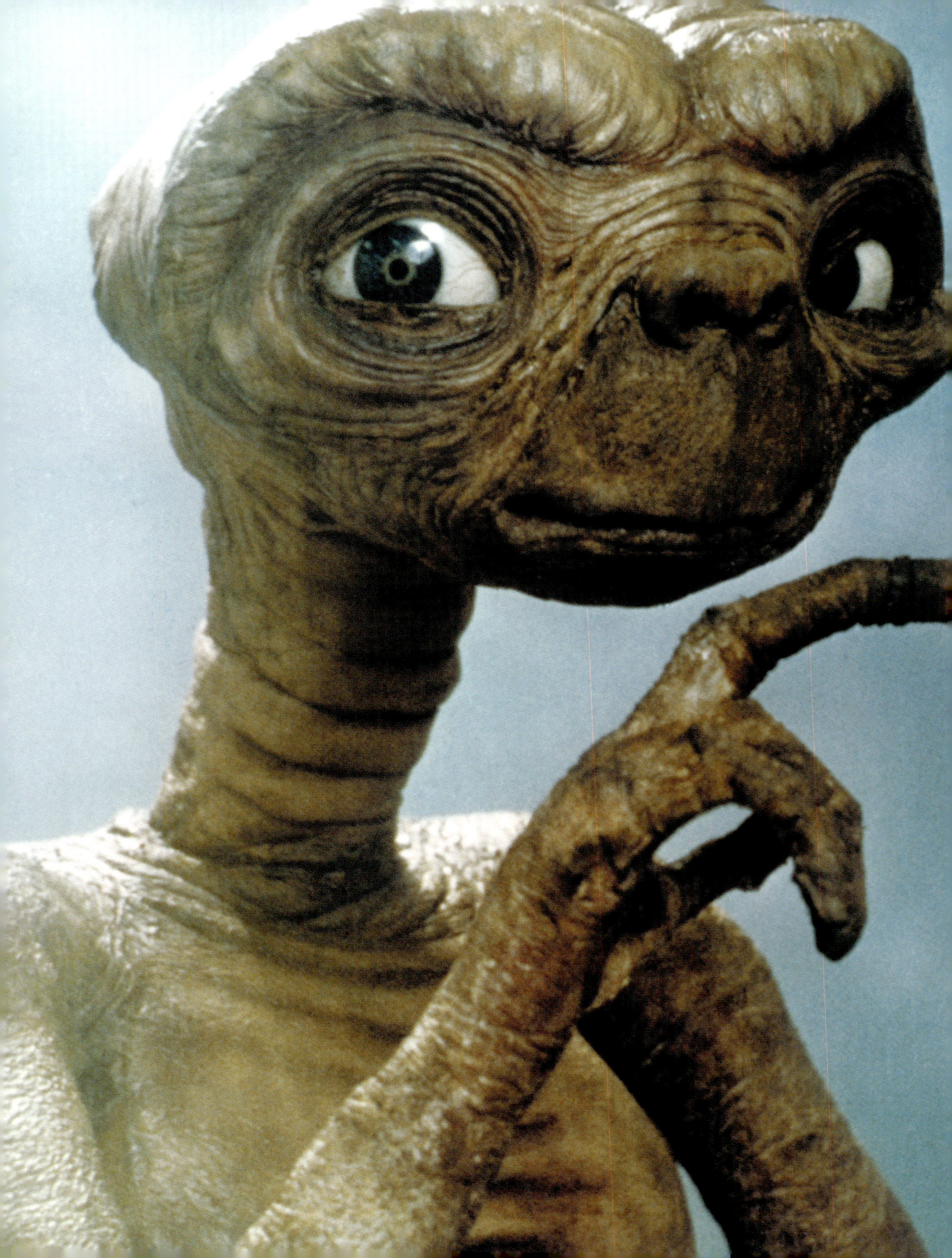

Introduction

THE NEW CLASSIC CINEMA

"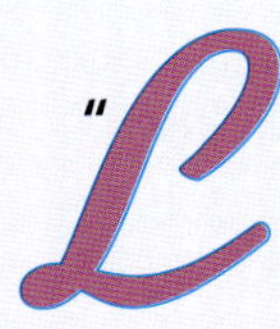**ET'S FACE A SAD FACT SQUARELY; THIS WAS ONE OF THE SORRIEST** decades yet in the annals of film. What good there was was very very good, but there was not a lot of it, and what you had to wade through to reach it was, at times, unspeakable."

Sheila Benson had been the chief critic for the *Los Angeles Times* since 1981 and knew as well as anyone the cinematic highs and lows of the previous ten years. On Christmas Eve 1989, she began her end-of-decade roundup with these lines, which captured the consensus view of film critics and movie buffs: the '80s were a poor imitation of the "New Hollywood" 1970s—those halcyon days when artists made original, challenging, rule-breaking movies like *The Conversation* (1974) and *Nashville* (1975) and *Taxi Driver* (1976). Yet for those of us who cherish *Blade Runner* (1982), *The Breakfast Club* (1985), and *Do the Right Thing* (1989), there is plenty of reason to take this attitude with a grain of salt.

Some say the decade's films were products of crass commercialism, that art had vanished, that individual filmmakers weren't supported by

E.T. the Extra-Terrestrial was the highest-grossing movie of the 1980s.

the studios, but it would be a mistake to think the '80s stood alone as a unique period of artistic struggle. Film historian Joseph McBride once described his job as a journalist in the "golden age" of the '70s: "When I covered that period as a reporter and reviewer for *Daily Variety*, I felt American movies were in a perilous state of decline, mired in a coarsening process thrown into stark relief by filmmakers' occasional success in slipping masterpieces through the system. For every *Chinatown* and *Godfather*, I had to sit through dozens of schlocky car-chase movies, brutal revenge fantasies, misogynistic buddy pictures, and bloated disaster epics."

The film industry was not in a state of existential crisis as it had been in the mid-'60s, when young filmmakers were given free rein to invigorate the system. But the naturally risk-averse studios had discovered new ways to make money, and they leaned into them—franchises, product placement, merchandising, pop soundtracks. To some, the accompanying shift of creative power to producers was seen as regressive, to others a return to normalcy. Entertainment writer Peter Biskind put it succinctly: "Everything that had been turned upside down in the 1970s was set right side up again."

For one thing, the culture had changed, and Hollywood had changed with it. Matching the anxieties of their time, New Hollywood films were critical of societal ills, suspicious of power, distrustful of standards that they had been taught to respect. The major films of the '80s weren't as cynical and didn't make a habit of questioning authority. *Jaws* (1975) juxtaposed a flag-waving Fourth of July at the beach with a boastful mayor who cared solely about profits and a lethal terror that lurked below the surface. Eleven years later, the patriotism of *Top Gun* (1986) was not in question.

The way Hollywood operated was shifting, too. In October 1984, *Daily Variety* identified seven major film studios. Columbia, Metro-Goldwyn-Mayer (UA), Paramount, 20th Century–Fox, Universal, and Warner Bros. were joined by Walt Disney Studios, newly added thanks to a momentous change of executives and an expansion of its film offerings beyond the family market. (Several years later, the decline of MGM reduced the majors to a "Big Six" once more.) For many of these, film production was one piece of a diverse portfolio—like Disney, which had a major parks division—and others were now owned outright by corporations like News Corp and Coca-Cola.

Home video was becoming a major factor, as VCR use rose from 1 percent of US homes in 1980 to 67 percent in 1990. Rather than hurting the movie industry as studios feared, it became a boon by providing a big source of ancillary revenue. Cable television and premium channels like HBO were providing additional outlets for studio product. Talent agencies were gaining power by brokering larger-scale deals that grouped actors and filmmakers in "packages." At the same time, interest rates were sky-high in the early '80s, and studios were ever more reluctant to borrow money to fund nonsurefire hits.

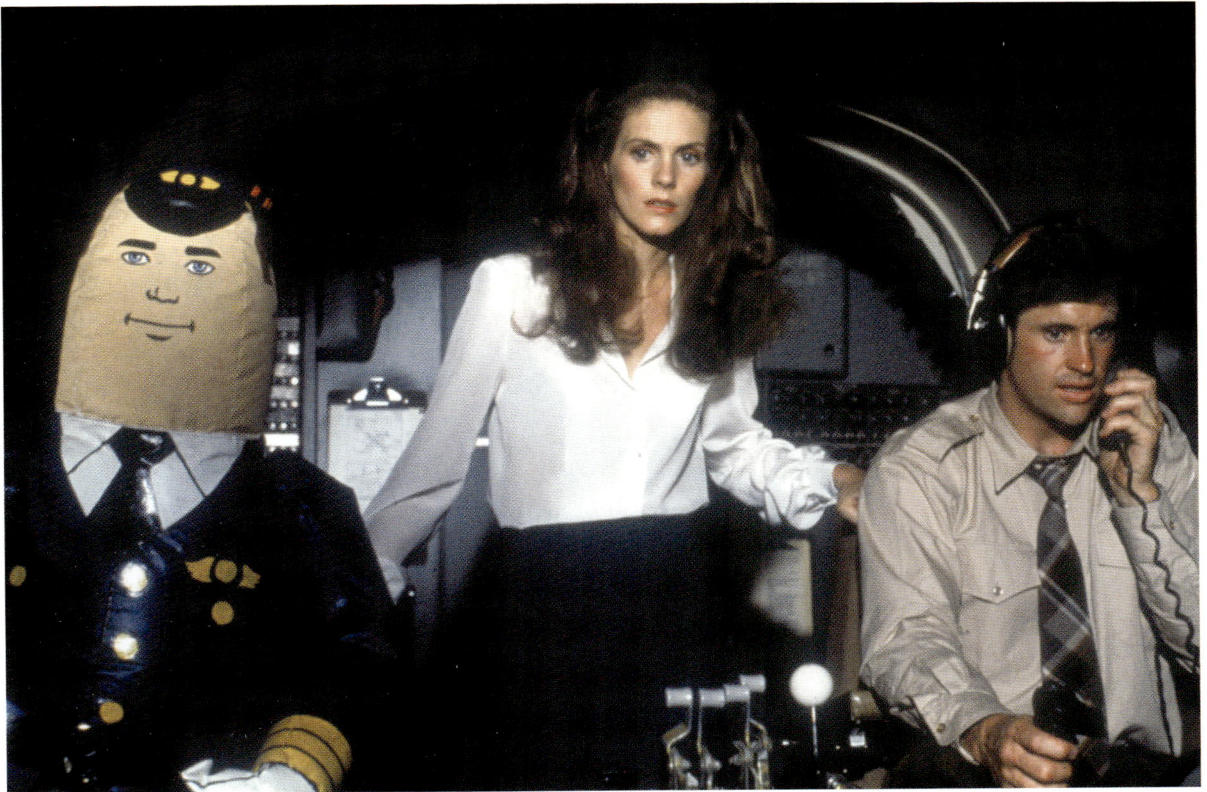

"Otto," Julie Hagerty, and Robert Hays in *Airplane!*

Changes in industry drove changes in style. For example, the robust market for soundtrack albums led to the increased use of pop tunes in movies—and the casting of pop artists in those movies. A film was more likely to get made if its characters could also be marketed as action figures, its story turned into video games, or its art plastered on Happy Meal boxes.

People were also changing—the ones in front of the camera, the ones behind it, and the ones who paid for tickets. Baby boomers, born from 1946 to 1964 and raised on television, were in their prime moviegoing ages here: sixteen to thirty-four when the decade began and twenty-six to forty-four when it ended. Steven Spielberg was thirty-four in 1980, James Cameron twenty-six, Spike Lee twenty-three. These folks supplanted the older New Hollywood auteurs, whose prospects dimmed during the decade—Francis Ford Coppola was forty-one; Martin Scorsese was thirty-eight. On their heels came Generation X. These two groups constituted a prime audience for Hollywood product—especially in the teen comedy and horror genres. Theatrical movies were starting to meet them where they lived, with suburban multiplexes being built at a rapid pace. The decade saw the average ticket price rise from $2.69 to $3.99, about a 50 percent increase, but still a quaint figure by today's standards.

We're now more than thirty years past the point at which Benson made her assessment,

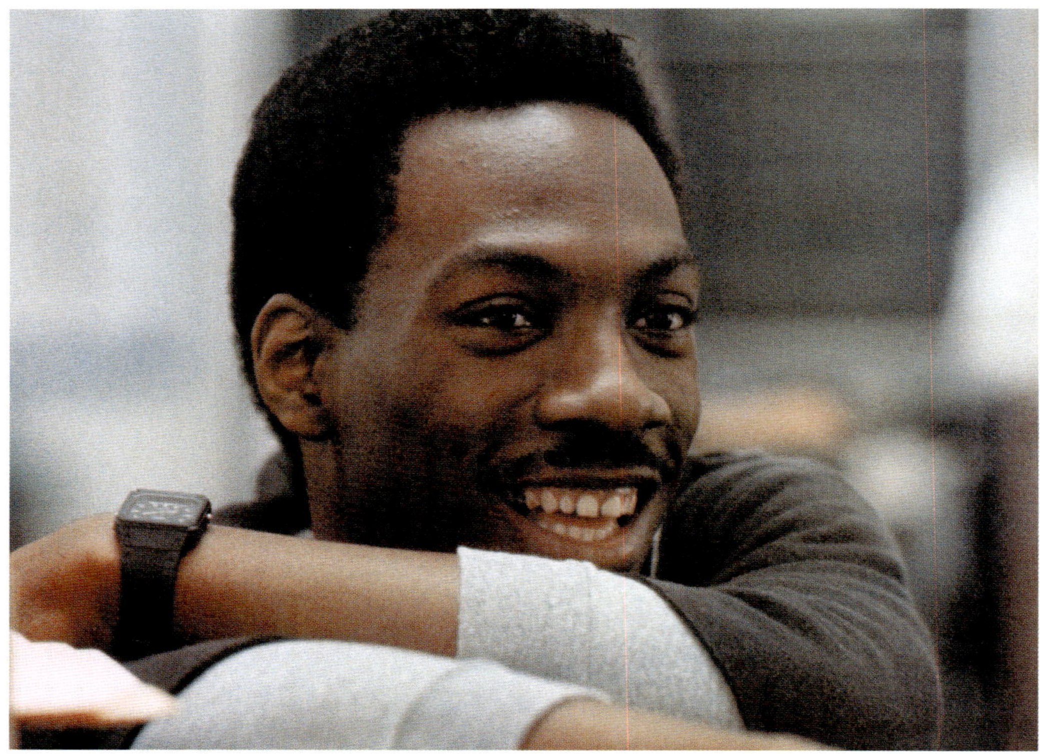

Eddie Murphy solidified his box office power in *Beverly Hills Cop.*

and with many cinematic hits and misses and industrial changes in the interim, it's time for a reassessment. Plenty of people already view '80s movies as beloved classics—especially those for whom the decade's teen cinema defined their youth. Beyond nostalgia, we can safely look back at these movies without the hype of studio marketing, the groupthink of awards season and top-ten lists, or the box-office figures that tend to warp our understanding of "good" and "bad."

Most significantly, we can now appreciate these movies (good *and* bad) as pieces of art locked in time, viewable in the context of a larger trajectory of culture and industry. Even mundane films from 1983 or 1987 acquire new value when watched decades in the future. (That's what people wore? That's what was on the radio? That's what Times Square looked like?) In some cases, trash turns magically to camp, and what was once derided in the pages of the *Los Angeles Times* becomes the stuff of art-house movie theaters and boutique home-video labels.

In some cases, the decade represents a definitive break from the past. In April 1980, Alfred Hitchcock died. In November, he was joined by Mae West and Steve McQueen. The preceding years had seen the losses of Charlie Chaplin, Howard Hawks, Joan Crawford, Elvis Presley, Mary Pickford, and John Wayne. Of course, plenty of legends remained and kept working throughout the '80s—like John Huston, who showed up to the 1986 Oscars with an oxygen tank, or Katharine Hepburn, who

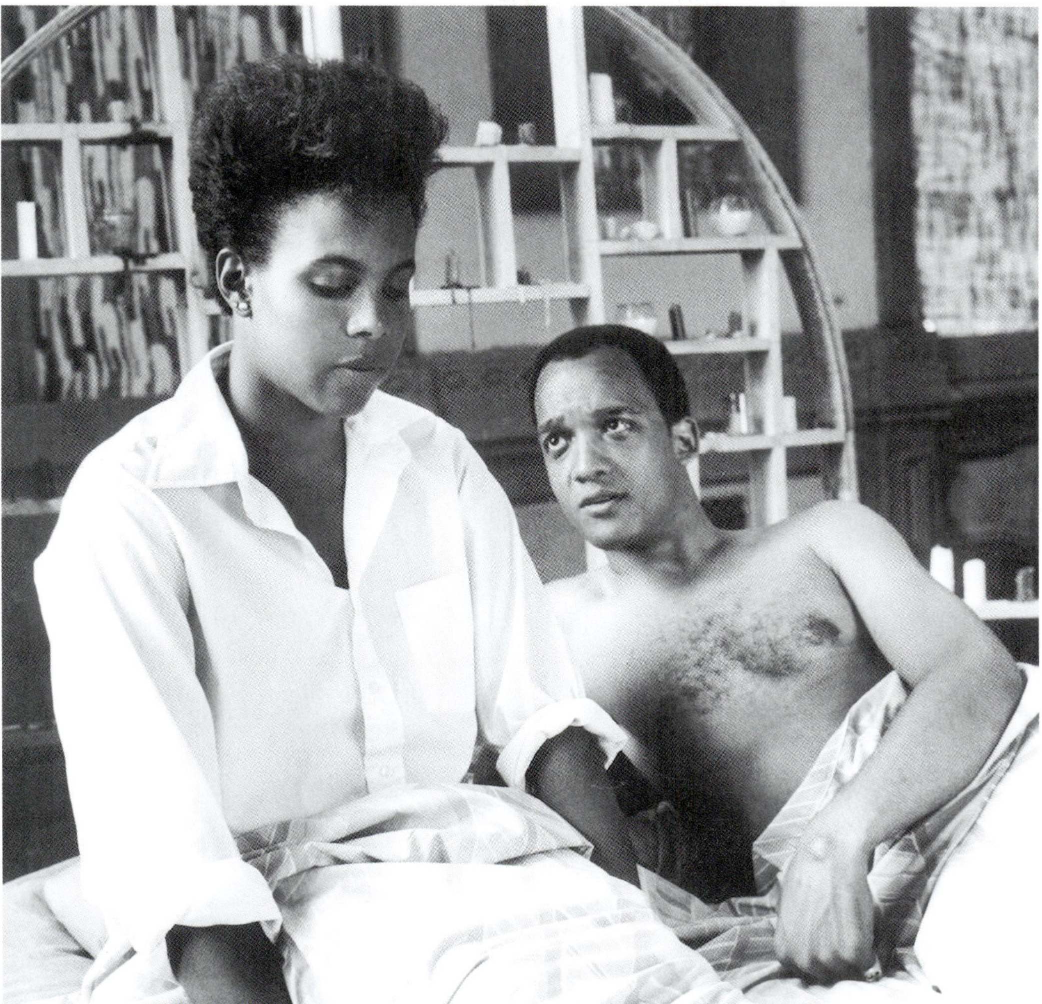

Tracy Camilla Johns and Tommy Redmond Hicks in *She's Gotta Have It.*

didn't bother attending when she won a fourth statuette in 1982.

In their wake came new icons. The '80s saw the reemergence of the everyman actor—from Tom Hanks and Michael Douglas to Steve Guttenberg and Judge Reinhold—as well as extraordinary action stars like Arnold Schwarzenegger, Sylvester Stallone, and Jean-Claude Van Damme. Mononymous pop musicians Madonna, Prince, and Cher competed at the box office with *Saturday Night Live* alumni like Eddie Murphy, who not only became a top action-comedy star but also drew huge crowds for theatrical stand-up films like *Raw* (1987). Meanwhile, multitalented actresses like Meryl Streep and Whoopi Goldberg worked effortlessly across genres.

It was the decade of the teen comedy, the New Wave soundtrack, and the gross-out creature feature. It was the decade of

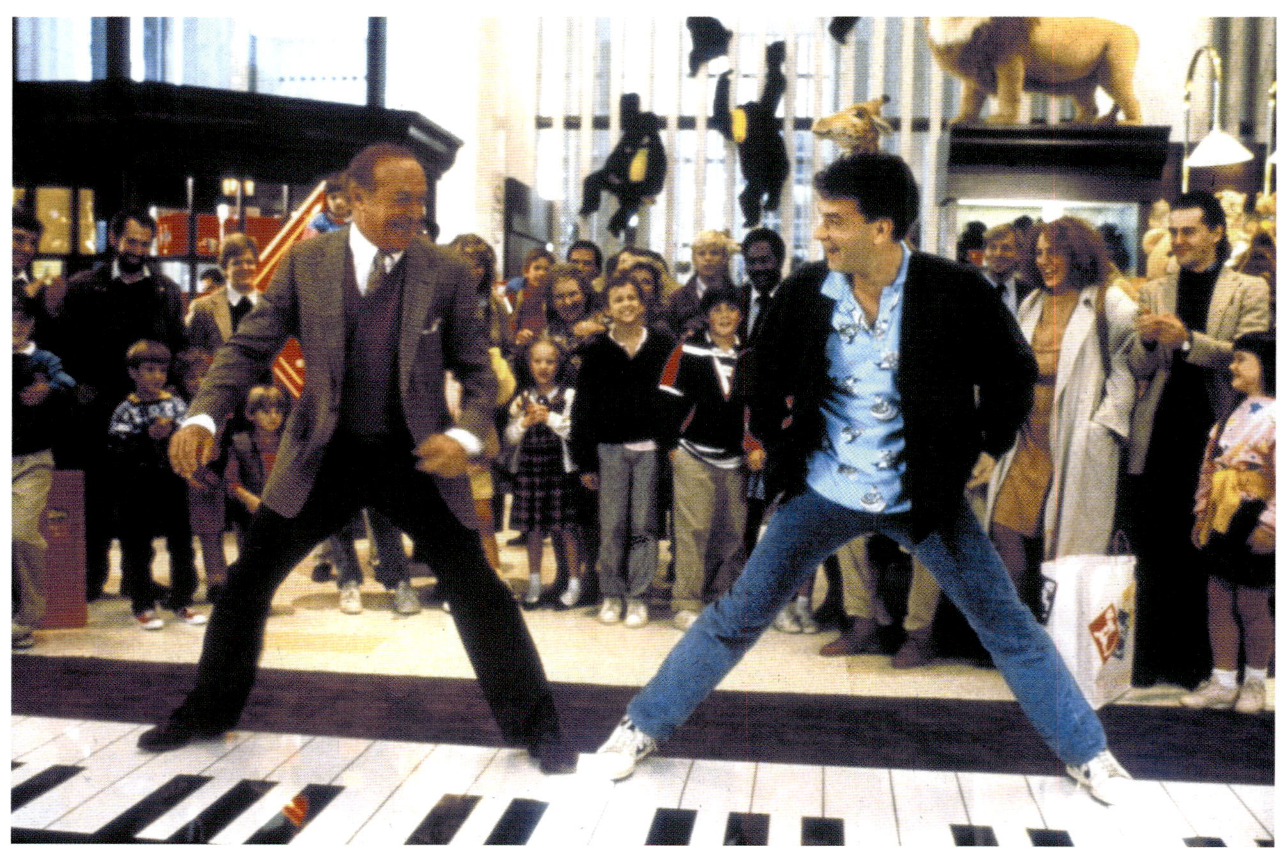

The indelible duet by Robert Loggia and Tom Hanks in *Big*.

Gordon Gecko and Clark Griswold, of Mozart and Salieri, of E.T. and Yoda. It saw the dawn of MTV and the twilight of the Cold War. It ushered in modern modes of animation and independent filmmaking and offered new opportunities to women directors and filmmakers of color.

This book tells a variety of stories about movies in the '80s. It begins with a focus on major directors—an imperfect but convenient way to talk about filmmaking in any era. The first two chapters tell a downbeat story and an upbeat one, respectively, about the shifting dynamics of the industry and the alternating fortunes of its leading figures. Some adapted well; some did not. Where creative gaps formed, new talents came to fill them. Other chapters survey genres and cultural topics that preoccupied Hollywood, from horror to music (broad categories like comedy and drama run throughout each section). The book concludes with alternatives to the mainstream system: independent filmmakers and underrepresented groups.

A quick IMDb search tells us that somewhere north of forty thousand feature films were released in the 1980s. Clearly, this book can't talk about all of them. Nor, in the age of Wikipedia and Letterboxd, should it. We have sadly not found room for Louis Malle's *Atlantic*

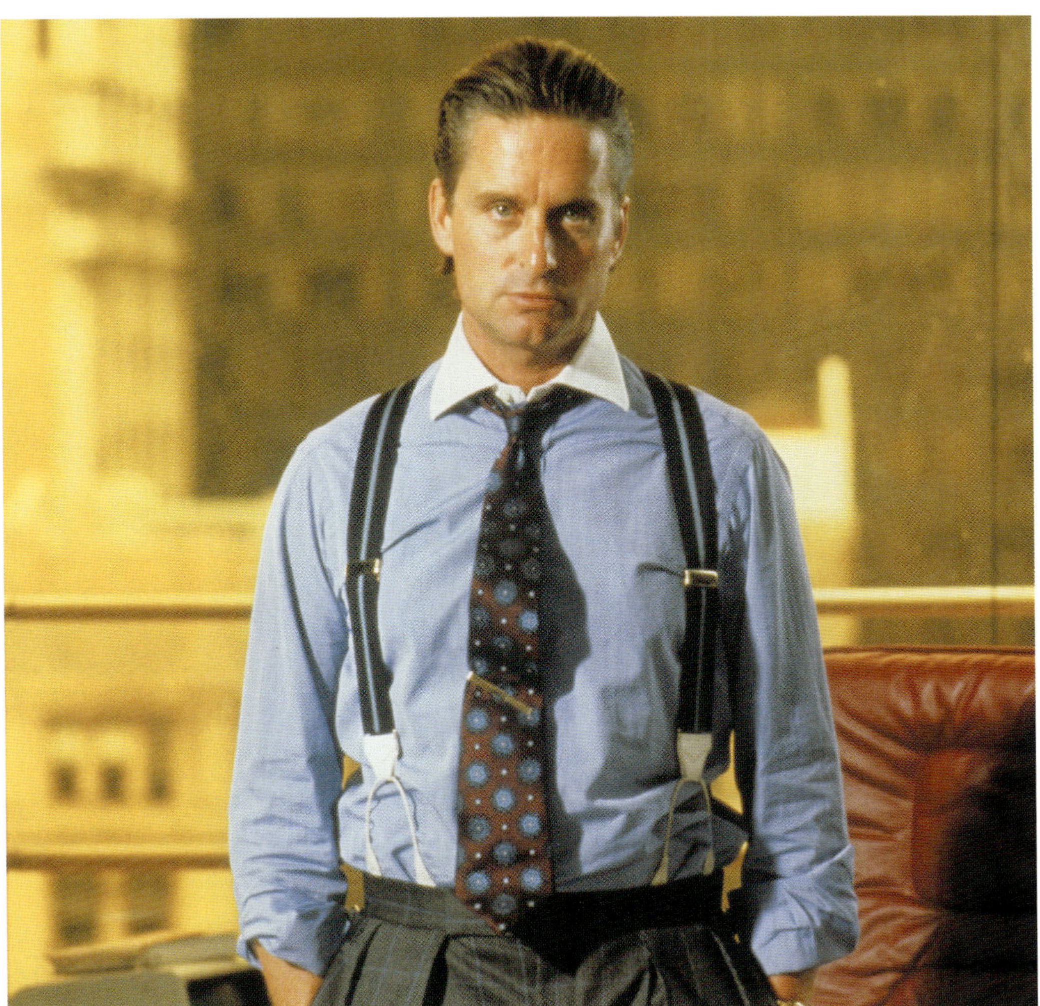

Michael Douglas as Gordon Gecko in *Wall Street*.

City (1980), Juzo Itami's *Tampopo* (1985), Patricia Rozema's *I've Heard the Mermaids Singing* (1987), or David Zucker's *The Naked Gun* (1988). Riches overflow. At the same time, it aims to do more than string together a list of superior movies, as some best-of books have done, nor will it be limited to this author's personal favorites. (Who would care for that, anyway?)

The hope for this book is that it might lead to new ways of thinking about classic cinema—of which the '80s are now a part. Let's dust off the masterpieces, reassess the flops and failures, and shine a light on some forgotten gems. More people should watch *The Long Good Friday* (1980), *Diva* (1981), *Losing Ground* (1982), *Rumble Fish* (1983), *Starman* (1984), *The Legend of Billie Jean* (1985), *Matador* (1986), *La Bamba* (1987), *Dead Ringers* (1988), and *Tongues Untied* (1989), to name just a few. A renewal of these films in their historical and artistic contexts is overdue.

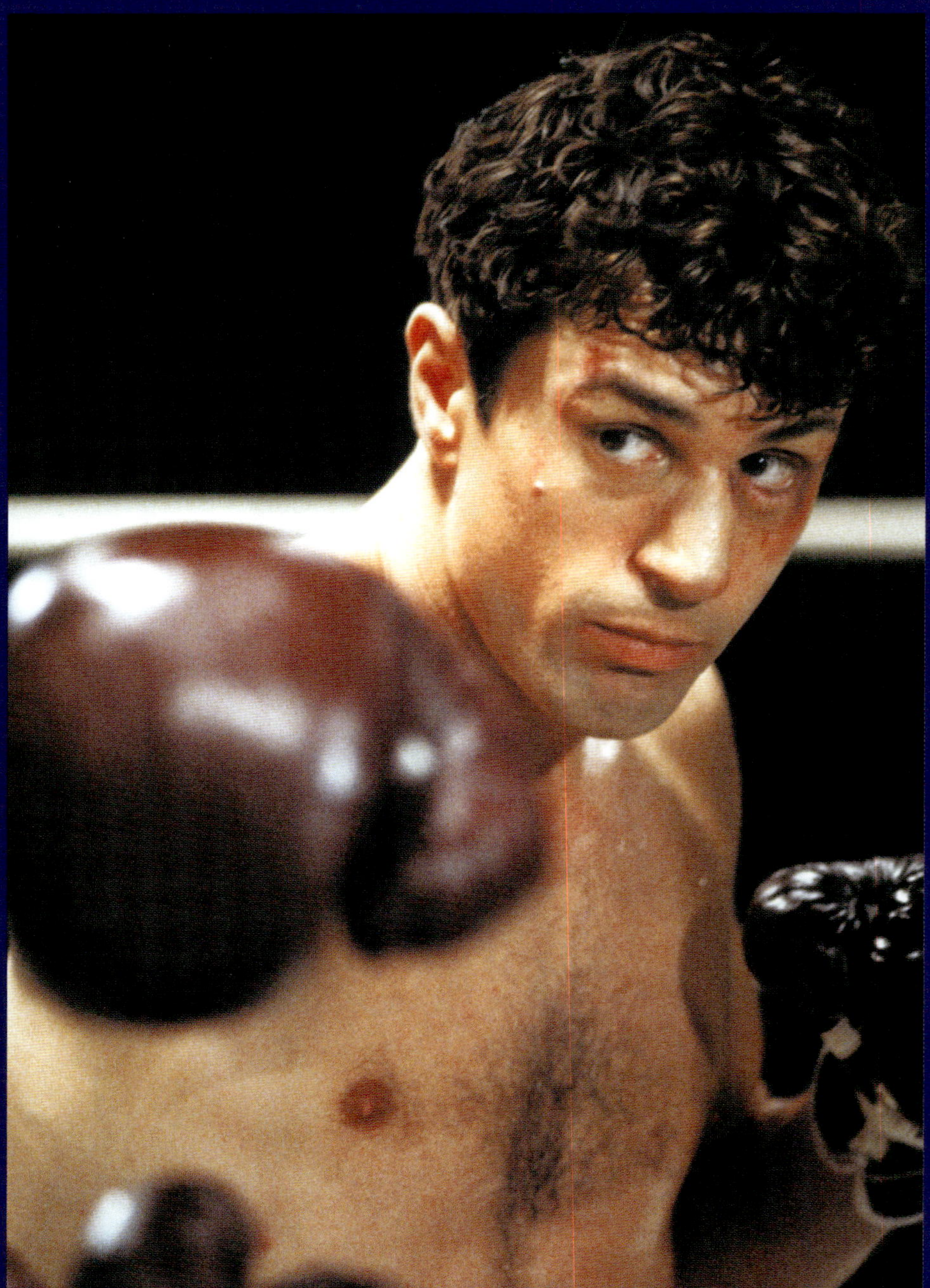

Raging Bull

CHAPTER ONE

Old NEW HOLLYWOOD

CHICAGO FILM CRITICS GENE SISKEL AND ROGER EBERT DEDICATED their January 5, 1982, episode of *Sneak Previews* to "the dogs" of 1981, the worst movies they saw all year. At the bottom of the pack, Ebert chose the "enormously ambitious" western drama *Heaven's Gate*, the third film from acclaimed New Hollywood director Michael Cimino, which Ebert called "stunningly boring, disconnected, uninvolving, impossible to follow." Siskel picked the Jack Lemmon–Walter Matthau comedy *Buddy Buddy*—the last gasp of an Old Hollywood stalwart, legendary writer-director Billy Wilder—"an astoundingly bad film. . . . I still don't believe it." He added, "If we can find something that runs through all of these pictures, I think the word 'ego' applies. . . . Ego of the comic filmmaker, or the comic actor, who says 'anything I do is funny'; the director, who will build a set and forget the elements of a story. Ego."

Tough words from America's two most admired film critics. But they were also offering a clear-eyed observation of the challenges facing two celebrated generations of filmmakers in the opening years of a new decade—one that brought with it economic and cultural challenges that would forever alter the movies. Despite the election of classical Hollywood actor Ronald Reagan to the White House, the film industry was moving on from its old guard and shrugging off the edgier styles and adventurous content that had dominated just a few years earlier. With financial disappointments like *Heaven's Gate* and Robert Altman's *Popeye* (1980), personal filmmaking was quickly becoming an endangered species.

Martin Scorsese's *Raging Bull* (1980) was arguably the last of its kind—a major achievement of New Hollywood cinema—and it makes a fitting prologue to a new chapter in the careers of Francis Ford Coppola, Altman, William Friedkin, and other revered directors who faced unprecedented artistic and financial challenges. "The 1980s were a difficult decade for some of the industry's most ambitious and talented filmmakers," wrote film historian Stephen Prince. "In the 1960s and 1970s, these directors achieved significant critical, and sometimes great commercial, success, yet in the 1980s they struggled to obtain financing for productions and several careers foundered."

There's no single reason for New Hollywood's decline. It had to do with style, distribution models, and audience tastes. Some of it probably had to do—as Siskel suspected—with ego. Were these directors hard to work with? Would their sense of self-importance not allow them to kowtow to corporate Hollywood interests? Were they unwilling to compromise their artistic vision or way of doing things?

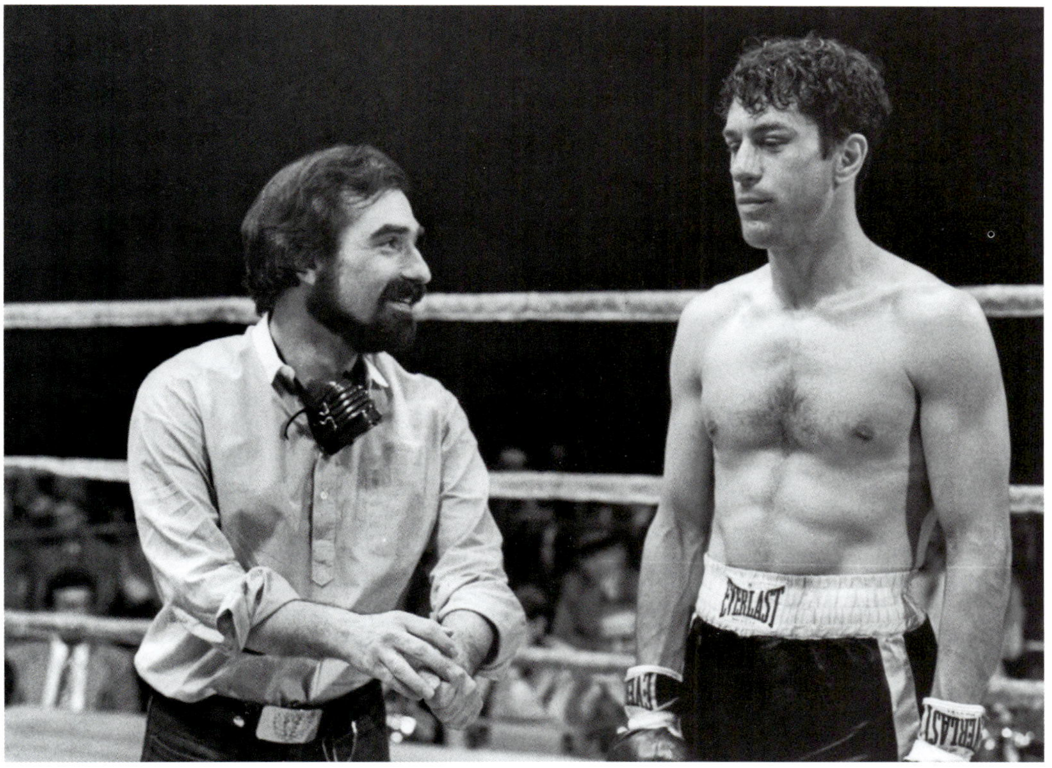

Martin Scorsese directs Robert De Niro in one of *Raging Bull's* visceral fight scenes.

Had they simply run out of creative juice? Only one thing is clear. While the films in this chapter might be financial mishaps, there are some truly great ones in the bunch and they deserve the spotlight.

SCORSESE: ON THE ROPES

Raging Bull is one of the most atmospheric of Martin Scorsese's films, its black-and-white portrayal of 1940s New York somehow both nostalgic and devastating. It took years to bring to the screen, partially because Scorsese wasn't naturally drawn to boxing as a subject.

The celebrated young director was in a rough patch. His latest major movie, the musical *New York, New York* (1977), had flopped. He was struggling through a divorce and a drug problem. He had overdosed on cocaine in 1978 and almost lost his life, and he wasn't sure he would ever even work again. When he took on *Raging Bull*, at the urging of its star, Robert De Niro, he assumed the movie would be his last. He pulled no punches and made the movie he wanted.

De Niro had come across the biography of champion middleweight boxer Jake LaMotta while making *The Godfather, Part II* (1974). The story follows the fighter from his early days in the ring through his marriage and decline. Structurally, it's bookended by scenes of LaMotta as a nightclub owner, older and heavyset. The film begins in medias res, freeing it from the trappings of a traditional Hollywood biopic. While it flows chronologically, it avoids a strict cause-and-effect plot—which struck Scorsese as old-fashioned—and allows the characters and their emotions to dictate the flow. The role was a tour de force for De Niro, who physically transformed, putting on sixty pounds for his sequences as the older LaMotta. He is transfixing even when quiet, often charming, sometimes paranoid, and quick to violence.

Perhaps it's not a surprise that the film began in an earlier, more fertile time for this type of antiheroic storytelling. De Niro would take home a second Oscar for his performance, but his win by then was an exception to the rule. LaMotta was a brute among a string of sympathetic characters that drew tears and admiration from their audiences: Jon Voight's paraplegic veteran in *Coming Home* (1978), Dustin Hoffman's divorced father striving for custody of his young son in *Kramer vs. Kramer* (1979), Henry Fonda's aging patriarch with onsetting dementia in *On Golden Pond* (1981), Ben Kingsley's principled revolutionary in *Gandhi* (1982). LaMotta was a creature from another era.

Raging Bull didn't make huge sums of money—it would be a mistake to assume that the artistic triumphs of New Hollywood were all hits with audiences—but it is full of captivating moments, bravura boxing sequences, and emotional turmoil. Today it is heralded as one of the greatest films ever made, and what it lacks in traditionally appreciated qualities of popular cinema, it makes up for in soul.

It also reunited Scorsese with editor Thelma Schoonmaker, whom he met at New York University (NYU) in the '60s. From that point on, Scorsese's films gained an urgency that can be attributed, at least in part, to Schoonmaker's contribution. She has argued that his films are made in the editing room and that his distinct style as a director becomes apparent only through the way the images are connected. She insists that the film won the Best Editing Oscar because of its fight sequences, which were constructed the way they were thanks to Scorsese's careful advanced planning.

Raging Bull wound up being personally resonant for Scorsese, who was working through his own demons during its production. His films can often be read as explorations or extrapolations of his personal struggles. *The King of Comedy* (1983) is about the perils of celebrity and obsessive fandom. *After Hours* (1985) puts a man in a nightmare he can't escape. *The Color of Money* (1986) shows a veteran hustler dealing with a new generation of talent. *The Last Temptation of Christ* (1988) follows a hero who feels unworthy and questions his stated destiny. Anxiety and uncertainty ripple throughout these films.

The King of Comedy again starred De Niro as a wannabe stand-up comedian who craves the attention and approval of his idol, a late-night host played by Jerry Lewis. Made shortly after an assassination attempt was made on President Reagan by an obsessed Jodie Foster fan, it is a

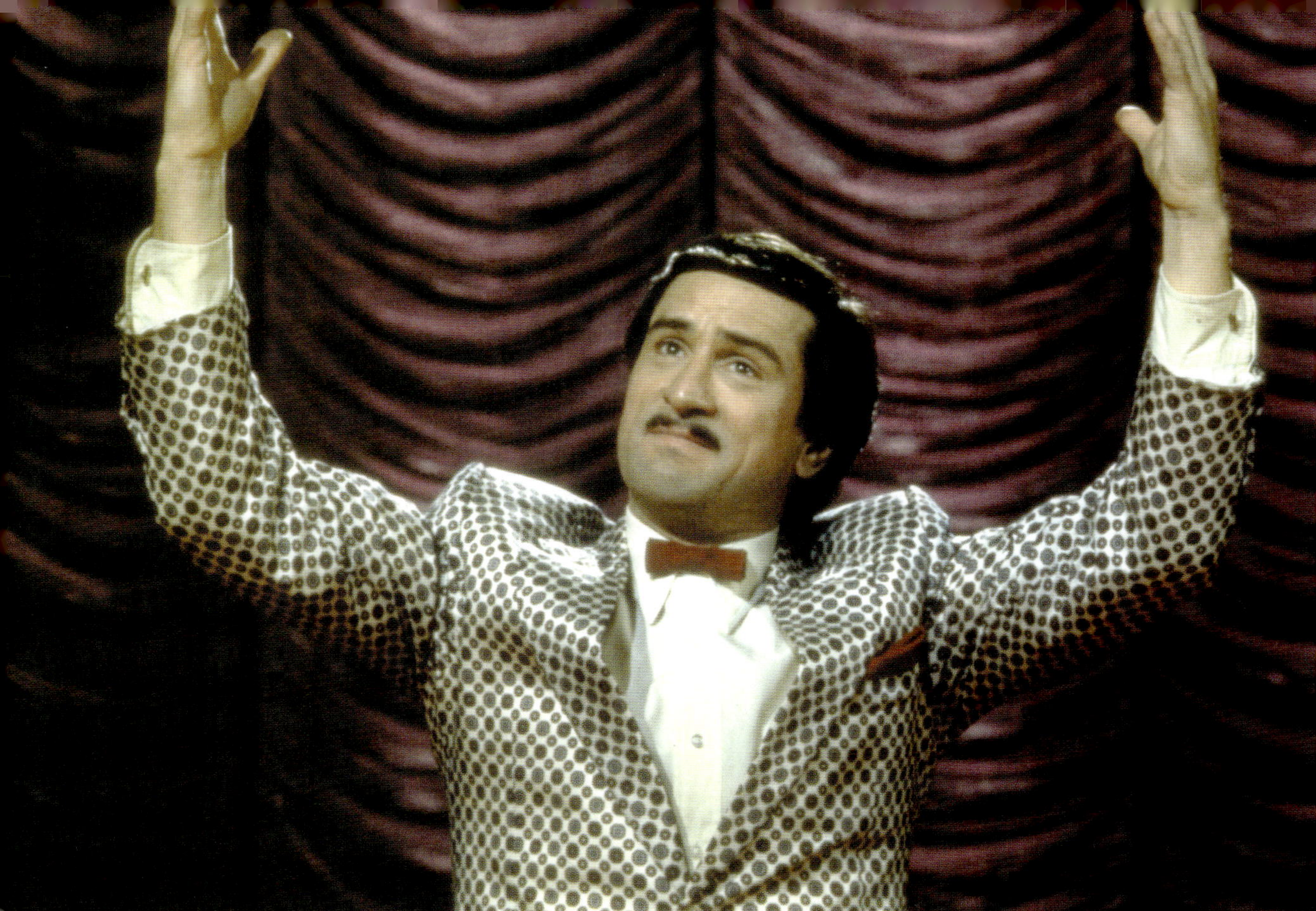

Robert De Niro in *The King of Comedy*.

trenchant look at toxic fandom and the unique culture of celebrity in America. As with *Raging Bull*, De Niro brought the project to Scorsese, and the actor gives one of his most interesting, complex performances. His history of violent characters adds an undertone of menace to the character of Rupert Pupkin.

By that point, audiences may have expected a Scorsese–De Niro film to be something other than a dark comedy. (Are we supposed to laugh at Rupert or recoil from him?) *The King of Comedy* was underappreciated at the time—"the flop of the year," acknowledged Scorsese—but its unsettling story has become more relevant in the ensuing decades. Famously, it was an inspiration, along with *Taxi Driver* (1976), for the 2019 film *Joker*.

The King of Comedy earned just $2 million against a budget of $20 million. Scorsese's next movie was set to be *The Last Temptation of Christ*, a true passion project with a script by Paul Schrader, who had written *Raging Bull*. Paramount was financing the $15 million production, sets were built in Israel and Morocco, and the cast was in place. But the failure of *The King of Comedy*, along with other high-profile commercial disappointments like the Warner Bros. space-race epic *The Right Stuff* (1983), made Paramount wary. The final straw came when religious groups organized protests against Gulf and Western, the studio's parent company, and the film was canceled shortly before production was to begin. *Last Temptation* was put on the back burner for several years, but in Scorsese's view, with one high-profile failure leading to another, this moment marked the end of an era of director-led, personal filmmaking.

DIRECTORS DEPOSED

But when had that era begun? And why do we talk about '70s cinema in these terms?

The "auteur theory" got its start in the pages of the French film journal *Cahiers du Cinéma* and was championed in the United States by film critic Andrew Sarris in the early '60s. It assumes the basic premise that a director is the "author" of a film and goes on to suggest that, over time, a pattern develops across their work that can be attributed to their distinctive style and vision. If that isn't yet controversial, it can be taken a step further: to call a filmmaker an "auteur" is, essentially, a statement of quality. Martin Scorsese is an *auteur* because one can draw thematic connections among his many great films—take the alienated protagonists of *Taxi Driver* and *The King of Comedy*, for example—but perhaps the director of the latest teen comedy is not.

The praise of the director-as-artist came from the newfound admiration among young postwar critics for major filmmakers of the past—John Ford, Orson Welles, Howard Hawks, Alfred Hitchcock—whose work they were rewatching and holding up as a yardstick for new films. It led to several of the French critics becoming filmmakers themselves, people still spoken of with reverence today like Jean-Luc Godard, François Truffaut, and Éric Rohmer, and in Hollywood it coincided with an industrial downturn in the '60s that led studios to hand the reins over to many young filmmakers to make the kinds of movies they wanted. New styles were valued because audiences were eating them up. This "New Hollywood" period that ran through the 1970s was a time when directors "initiated their own projects and completed them with the studios' blessings and without their interference," recalled Arthur Penn, director of *Bonnie and Clyde* (1967). "I can't think of a situation during that decade where there was a film I wanted to make that I couldn't make."

Unfortunately for Penn, Scorsese, and others like them, the priorities of studios were shifting in the '80s, partly because the studios themselves were in flux. The industry was being reshaped thanks to a series of corporate takeovers. In 1981, 20th Century–Fox was sold to Denver petroleum magnate Marvin Davis, who in turn sold it to Rupert Murdoch's News Corp in 1985. Las Vegas investor Kirk Kerkorian, who had owned MGM since 1969, purchased the struggling United Artists from Transamerica in 1981 to form MGM/UA; in 1986 the MGM assets were sold to—and later purchased back from—media mogul Ted Turner.

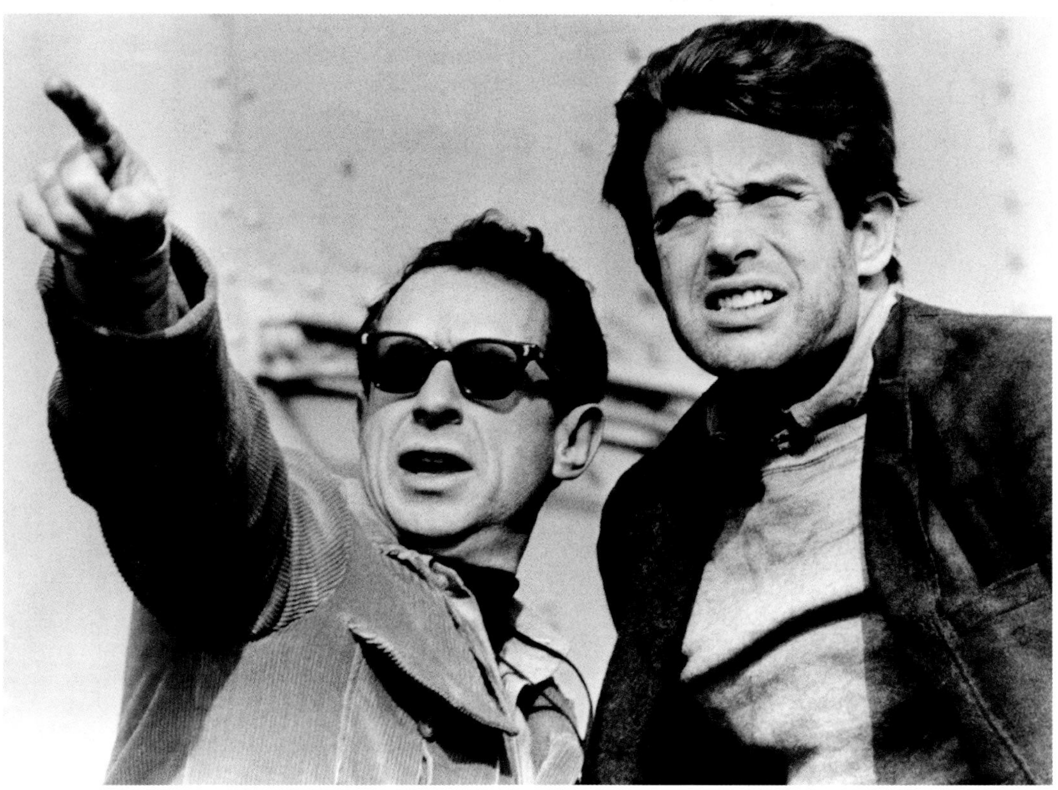

Arthur Penn directs Warren Beatty on the set of 1965's *Mickey One*.

One of the most infamous studio acquisitions was that of Columbia by the Coca-Cola Company in 1982. Atlanta-based Coke had a long history in Hollywood, having set up an office in LA in the '60s to support its relationship with the industry. Academy Awards host Johnny Carson poked fun at this development in his opening monologue at the 1982 ceremony: "Don't worry about Columbia, they're going to be just fine. They're collecting a nickel deposit on every film can." That same year, the studio launched Tri-Star Pictures, in partnership with HBO and CBS.

Columbia went through several leadership changes during this time, reflecting shifts in priorities. Head of production Frank Price resigned in 1983; former talent agent Guy McElwaine took over until 1986, after green-lighting *Ishtar* (1987); British producer David Puttnam focused on developing up-and-coming talent for a year, with mixed results; merchandising and marketing executive Dawn Steel closed out the decade. Coca-Cola, in a reversal of its earlier diversification efforts, sold Columbia to Japanese electronics company Sony in 1989. The next year, Warner Communications (parent company of Warner Bros.) and Time Inc. formally merged to create the massive Time Warner media conglomerate.

After the box-office smashes of *Jaws* (1975) and *Star Wars* (1977), as well as the ancillary revenue provided by home-video sales, Hollywood's

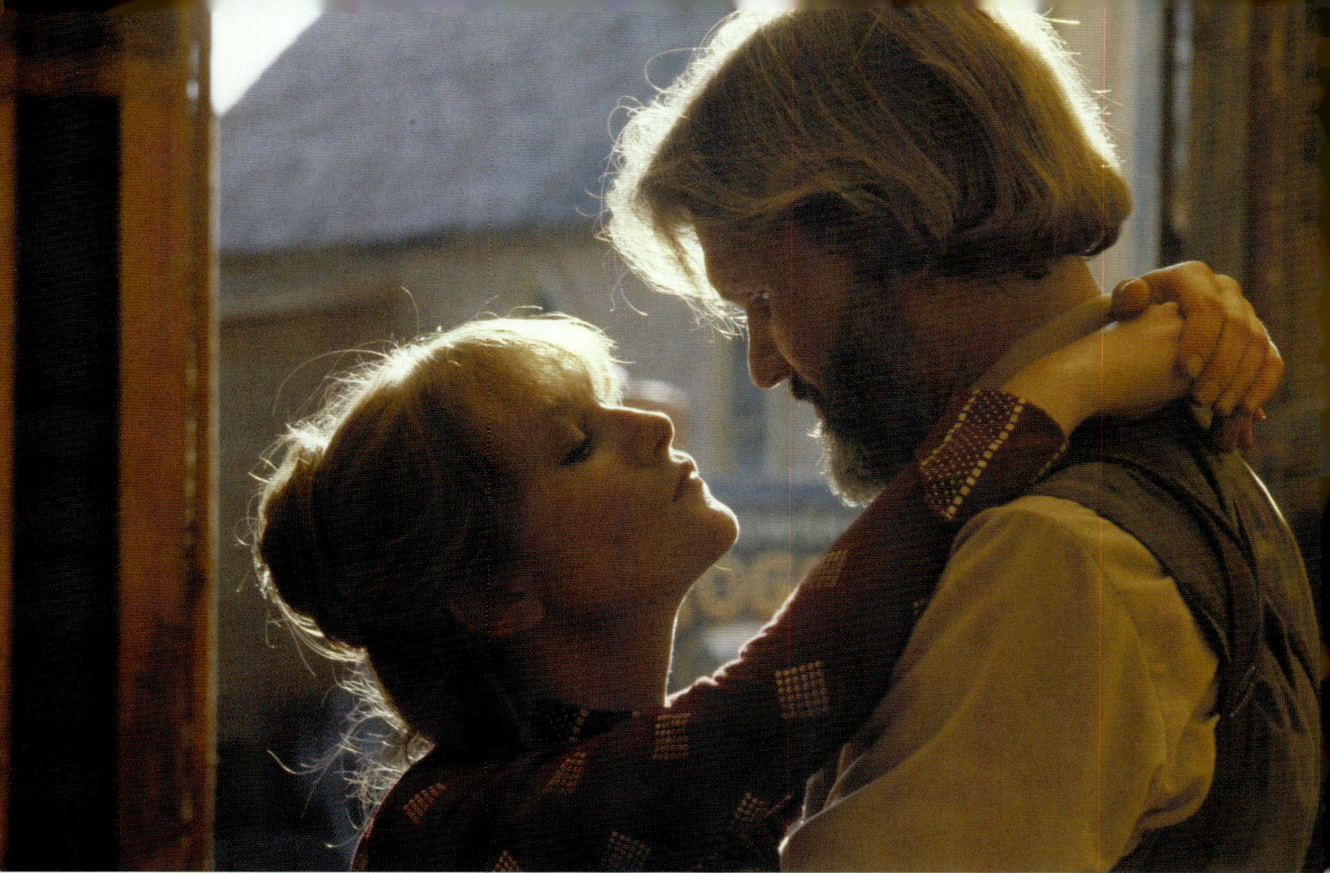

Isabelle Huppert and Kris Kristofferson in *Heaven's Gate.*

corporate-controlled studios were still willing to spend big money on top-tier productions, along with huge marketing campaigns to support them. The trouble was, with inflation on the rise, the cost of films had skyrocketed, creating unease in corporate boardrooms. A United Artists executive confirmed for the *Washington Post* in November 1980, "Inflation, just in the last four years, has pushed the cost of even ordinary films to steep levels." United Artists and its parent company, Transamerica, were feeling the pain, as one of their big fall releases found itself at the center of the storm.

OH, HEAVENS

Five days separated *New York Times* film critic Vincent Canby's reviews of *Raging Bull*, which premiered in New York on November 14, 1980, and *Heaven's Gate*, director Michael Cimino's epic western about the Johnson County War, on the nineteenth. Both films were United Artists releases, but Canby's reactions to them could not have been more different. Whereas Scorsese's film was "unusually intelligent . . . breathtaking . . . an achievement," the new film from the director of *The Deer Hunter* (1978) was "something quite rare in the movies these days—an unqualified disaster."

Canby wasn't alone in his dismissal of the nearly four-hour cut of *Heaven's Gate*, but his review—printed on opening day in the most respected newspaper in America—is cited as the catalyst for the movie's downfall, taking with it (so the legend goes) the solvency of United Artists, and ultimately the end of directorial freedom in Hollywood. Hours after the review's publication, with the studio "in chaos," the film was pulled from theaters, reportedly at Cimino's request, and sent back to the editing room. It would not reemerge until April 1981, in a severely truncated form.

The impact of the film's poor reception and swift closure was felt immediately, and far beyond the halls of UA. The industry was shocked at the final cost of the project—an elephantine $44 million, all in—that would have required blockbuster numbers to turn a profit. (It ended up making about $3.5 million.) The film's wild cost overruns have been attributed to Cimino's perfectionism, which at one point included dismantling a large street set so that it could be moved over several feet and reconstructed. Hundreds of hours of film were shot, with some scenes being reportedly filmed fifty times or more. UA executive Steven Bach later reported that everyone involved in the production, from Cimino, to the costume designer, to the actors, to the studio executives themselves, had thought they were making the next grand epic, a surefire hit. A few days after the disastrous New York premiere, the *Times* quoted an unnamed head of a rival studio: "There but for the grace of God go I."

There had been other films in recent months that had greatly exceeded their budgets and took time to become profitable, but they had at least proved popular with audiences. Among them are a few that might sound surprising today: *Apocalypse Now* (1979), *Star Trek: The Motion Picture* (1979), and *The Blues Brothers* (1980). What made *Heaven's Gate* unique was its obscure historical subject matter, coupled with the bad press that tempered any potential popular interest. Were audiences in the age of *Star Wars* and *Dallas* really that interested in long-winded art films about Wyoming?

Heaven's Gate opened Hollywood's eyes to the realization that nothing is guaranteed in their business. Transamerica, able but not willing to weather the financial storm, spun off the dispirited United Artists in 1981 and sold it to Kerkorian, who combined it with MGM. Other studios, scared out of their wits, tightened the reins on their productions.

The film can be watched today in a fuller three-and-a-half-hour running time and—if one so chooses—divorced from its reputation of profligacy. It was lovingly restored in 2012, with its stuffy sepia tones replaced by a more sumptuous color palette. (Roger Ebert had called it "one of the ugliest films I have ever seen" in 1981.) It exists now, for those open to its message, as a grandiose rumination on manifest destiny and the conflict between the immigrants who seek a better life in America and the moneyed interests who seek to make a profit. It is at times a stunningly beautiful film with period

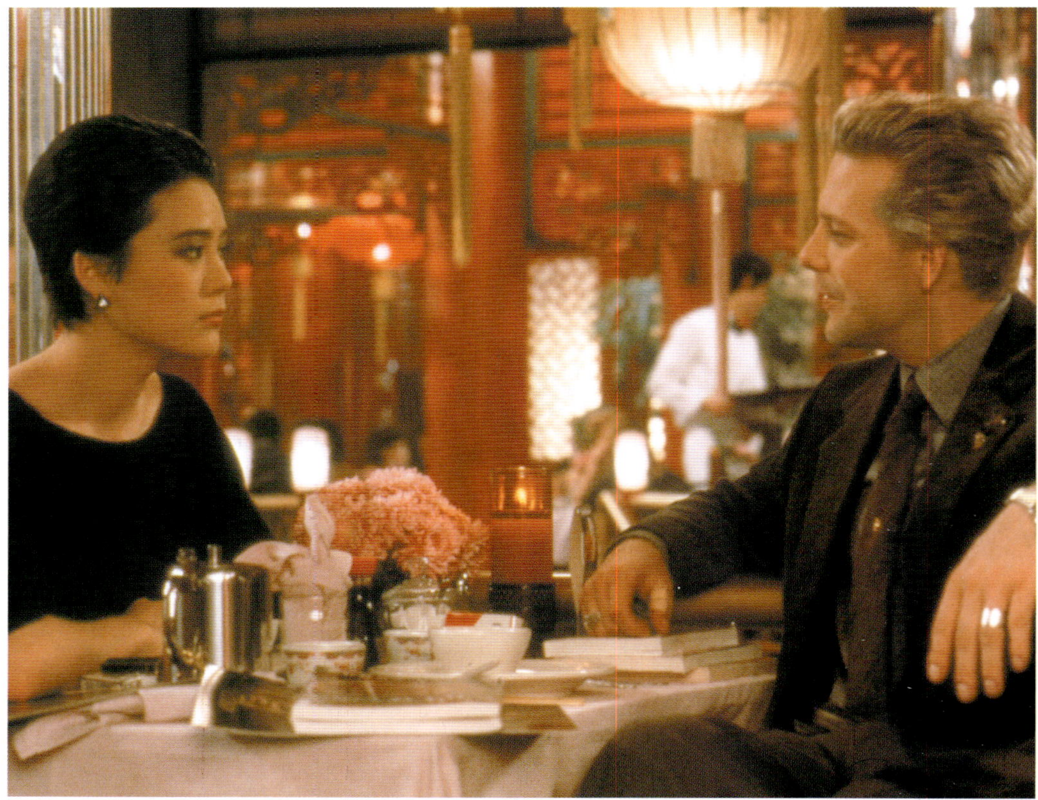

Ariane Koizumi and Mickey Rourke costar in *Year of the Dragon*.

detail that may be impossible to outdo and a cast that includes Kris Kristofferson, Christopher Walken, John Hurt, and Isabelle Huppert. Some viewers today see *Heaven's Gate* as an unrecognized masterpiece and its director a singular artist that bitter Hollywood executives made an example of. They might echo Kristofferson, who said the film was "used by powers that be to stop a way of filmmaking, where the author was the director and was in control of the money." Other viewers, bored by its sheer length and lack of involving narrative, may wonder why they bothered restoring it in the first place.

Either way, *Heaven's Gate* very nearly ended Cimino's career. The director had talent, the proof of which was his Oscar for *The Deer Hunter*. "I think what happens . . . when you win an Oscar as Best Director," stated Gene Siskel in 1982, trying to discern what went wrong, "maybe you lose control, the control of striving to please. You think that you can please by your nature, and of course no one can."

Cimino's next movie, *Year of the Dragon*, wouldn't come out until 1985, just weeks after the release of Steven Bach's tell-all book *Final Cut*, which detailed the startling behind-the-scenes drama on the *Heaven's Gate* set and the studio's complicity in the director's runaway production. *Year of the Dragon* was a historical crime film starring Mickey Rourke and John Lone, set in New

York's Chinatown but filmed—with incredible detail and cost—in North Carolina. It had been financed by the adventurous, risk-taking—some might say wild-eyed, some might say heroic—Italian producer Dino De Laurentiis. This time, the *New York Times*' Janet Maslin wrote, "Michael Cimino has a distinctive way of making things look and sound, but he could never be accused of having a style." Rather, the film was accused by Asian American groups of playing up racial stereotypes, necessitating a disclaimer in the opening credits. Like *Heaven's Gate*, the film has lately been reassessed and praised as a taut thriller by fans like Quentin Tarantino.

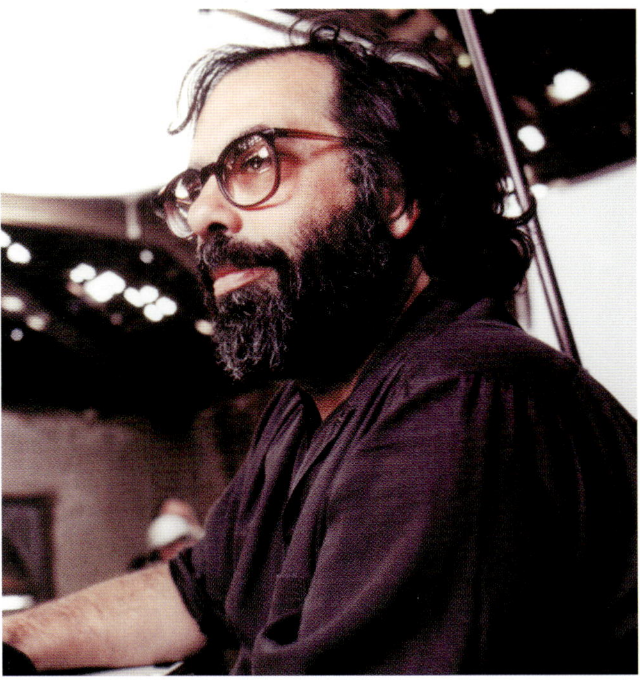

Francis Ford Coppola on the set of *The Outsiders*.

HURRICANE FRANCIS

Few filmmakers have ever had a run like Francis Ford Coppola did in the 1970s. With just four directing credits, he helped shape American cinema with daring and provocative work that looked deep into the soul of the nation during a turbulent era. The short list—*The Godfather* (1972), *The Conversation* (1974), *The Godfather, Part II*, *Apocalypse Now*—is a rare set of cultural landmarks, rivaling filmmakers like Charlie Chaplin for preeminence. Beyond the directing chair, he wrote screenplays for *Patton* (1970) and *The Great Gatsby* (1974) and produced *American Graffiti* (1973) for his friend George Lucas.

Visionary artistry aside, the production of *Apocalypse Now* had almost killed him. The Vietnam-set film was shot on location in the Philippines over 238 days, during which leading man Martin Sheen suffered a heart attack, a local insurgency diverted military helicopters that were being used in production, and a typhoon destroyed most of the sets. Coppola also had to contend with an untamable Marlon Brando. Seemingly stuck in a Kafkaesque world that wasn't helped by reported alcohol and drug abuse on set, the director recalled, "Little by little we went insane." The film was made for just over $30 million, received some divisive early reactions, and could have easily gone the way of *Heaven's Gate* if not for its successful debut at the Cannes Film Festival in May 1979, where it screened as a "work in progress" and won the Palme d'Or. When postproduction finally wrapped, its theatrical release that August was a critical and commercial success, although it took a while to recoup its high costs.

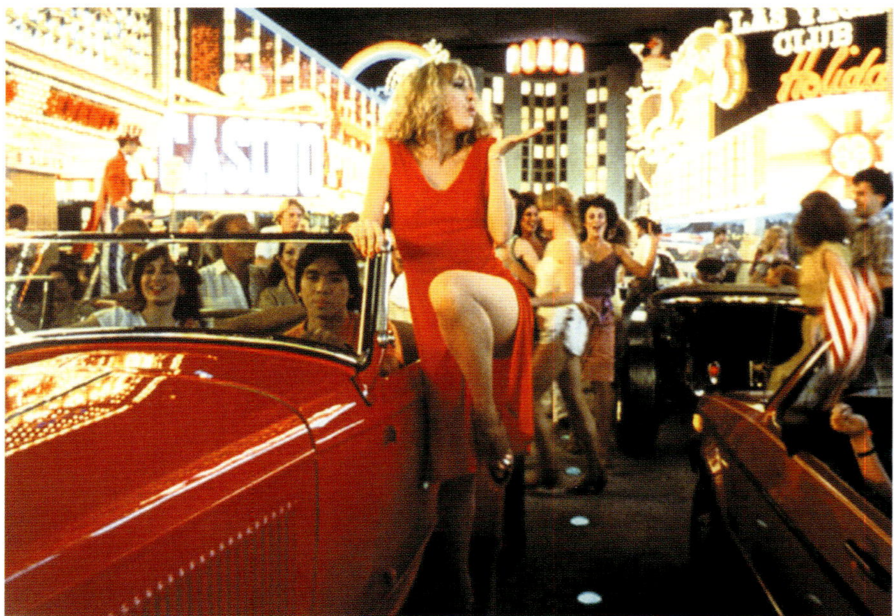

Teri Garr shines in *One from the Heart.*

Coppola was at heart an innovator, a dreamer of big dreams. Part of the mystique of *Apocalypse Now* was its technological achievement, specifically the Dolby Stereo 70mm Six Track surround-sound design. His blue-sky fantasy was to have the film play solely at a purpose-built theater located in the geographic center of the nation, not unlike the Festspielhaus built by Richard Wagner, the revolutionary German opera composer whose "Ride of the Valkyries" underscores an iconic scene in Coppola's film. Not content with just making movies, he wanted to forever change the way films were made and experienced.

The making of *One from the Heart* (1982) can be read as an attempt to mitigate the out-of-control nature of the *Apocalypse Now* shoot, and the film represents a definite shift in tone and style. It is a pop musical that leans into artificiality with the spirit of a classic studio picture of the Busby Berkeley variety—complete with over-the-top set design and visual and emotional extravagance. The film plays a key role in the story of Coppola's production company, American Zoetrope, and of the short-lived Zoetrope Studios.

The new studio was located on the former Hollywood General Studios lot, whose soundstages once hosted Harold Lloyd, Mae West, and the first two seasons of *I Love Lucy*. Coppola purchased the ten-acre property in 1980 for $6.7 million and attempted to re-create an old-fashioned "dream factory" where everything was done in house with talent under contract. He invested in a research department that pioneered the use of electronic equipment and video editing to instantaneously view and manipulate footage as it was being shot—housed in an Airstream trailer known as "the Silverfish." In addition to being a custom space for film production and technological experimentation, Zoetrope Studios offered Coppola that rarest of things in Hollywood: total creative freedom. As long as the money was there.

Nine soundstages were used in the production of *One from the Heart*, which swelled to a cost of $23 million. The highly stylized Las Vegas–set musical was marketed as "a new kind of old-fashioned romance" and tells the simple story of a pair of lovers (Teri Garr and Frederic Forrest) who quarrel, meet new partners (Raul Julia and Nastassja Kinski), and later return to each other. The film is set over the Fourth of July and comments on the dreams and illusions that we uphold in relationships and as Americans—romantic constructs that are echoed by the audacious, expressionistic set design.

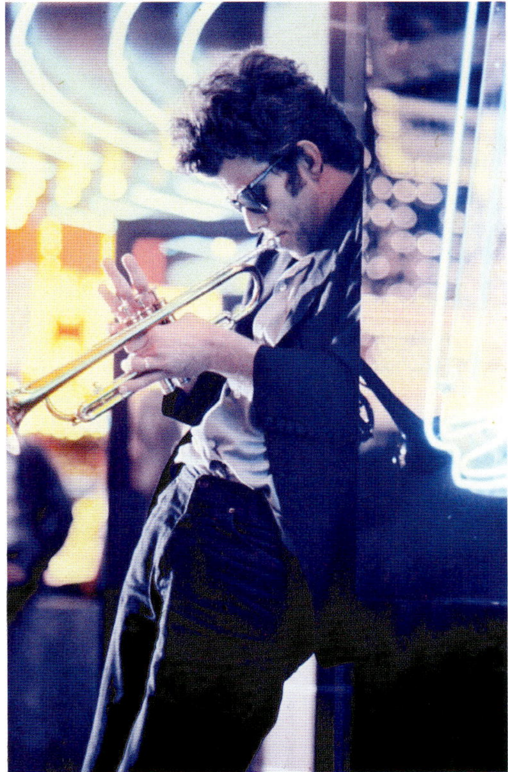

Tom Waits provided the original score for *One from the Heart*.

Unfortunately, the incredible design tends to overwhelm the substance of the film. "*One From the Heart* has so little in the way of story or tension," wrote Janet Maslin, "that the effect of Mr. Coppola's dazzling technical feats is almost superfluous. . . . It's as if Rembrandt were painting Easter eggs." The film was screened to exhibitors in the fall of 1981 while still in post-production, and Coppola personally organized a preview at Radio City Music Hall on January 15, 1982, for the public. The much-anticipated follow-up to *Apocalypse Now* failed to live up to the hype. The film tanked, and by April, Zoetrope Studios was put up for sale.

The other studios were practically gleeful when the Zoetrope went under, seeming proof that Coppola's revolutionary methods were naive and that the wannabe mogul was getting too big for his britches. Suddenly, the diversified corporations that ran Hollywood weren't looking so bad. Coppola suffered not only from the animosity of the establishment, but from bad timing as well, having launched Zoetrope in the era of 20 percent interest rates. The failure of *One from the Heart* was another hit against artist-led filmmaking in Hollywood, and the movies Coppola would go on to make throughout the decade were done so in an effort to pay back his debts.

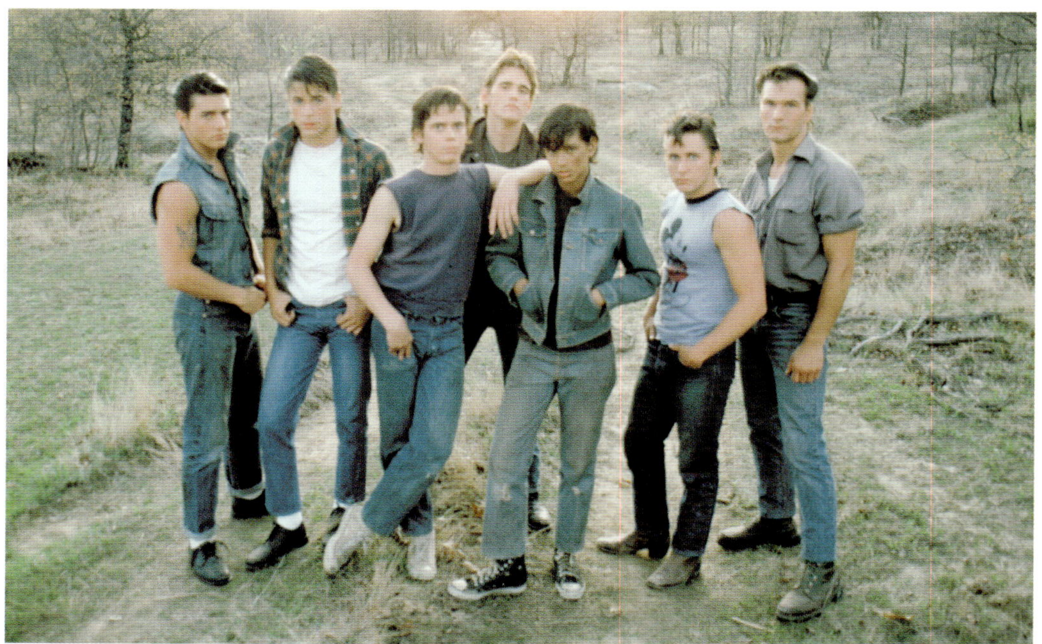

The promising young cast of *The Outsiders*.

STAY GOLD, PONYBOY

The idea for his next project came to him from a California school librarian named Jo Ellen Misakian, who had sent him a paperback of *The Outsiders* several years earlier. S. E. Hinton's popular novel had a built-in audience, and Coppola relished the chance to make a movie with a young cast, who were both fun to work with and cheap to hire. (He later noted with irony that the actors from *The Godfather* were by that point big stars and thus unaffordable to him.)

The story of a group of lower-class teenagers known as "greasers" and the rival, well-off "socs" was set in '60s-era Tulsa, Oklahoma, and filmed there in the spring of 1982. The main character is the orphan "Ponyboy," played by fifteen-year-old C. Thomas Howell. A quick glance at the cast list reveals an ensemble of young actors that today is remarkable in its continuing fame and influence: Matt Dillon, Patrick Swayze, Ralph Macchio, Rob Lowe, Diane Lane, Emilio Estevez, and, perhaps most notably, Tom Cruise, who would soon become a huge star with *Risky Business* (1983).

The Outsiders proved popular with audiences when it was released in March 1983, a relief for Coppola and the distributor, Warner Bros. Meanwhile, just two weeks after wrapping *The Outsiders*, the production team began work on a second Hinton adaptation, *Rumble Fish* (1983). This time, Matt Dillon was cast in the lead role as the teenage head of a local gang, paired with Mickey Rourke as his older and wiser brother, "Motorcycle Boy."

Coppola called *Rumble Fish* an "antidote" to *The Outsiders*, a black-and-white, avant-garde answer to the color and sentiment of the previous film. If *The Outsiders* was akin to *Gone with the Wind* (1939) in its warm landscapes and emotional scope, in his view, *Rumble Fish* was "an art film for teenagers." The two films are like a cinematic A/B test, released the same year with the same crew and similar source material, populated by many of the same actors, produced at the same budget, shot by the same cinematographer (Stephen H. Burum), but stylistically 180 degrees apart.

The choice to shoot in black-and-white was driven by the colorblindness of Rourke's character, but Coppola ultimately went much further: "My attitude, and I'm sure I encouraged all my collaborators—we wanted to do everything. And I would do anything that was perverse and different and seemed to be leading in a new direction. You feel like a pioneer." Using the passage of time as a unifying theme, he explored ways to express it visually, from images of ticking clocks to beautiful time-lapse transitions of downtown Tulsa in the setting sun, fast-moving clouds, and shadows of fire escapes drifting across brick walls. The film contains several fantastical sequences, such as one in which Dillon's character has an out-of-body experience and floats through an alleyway.

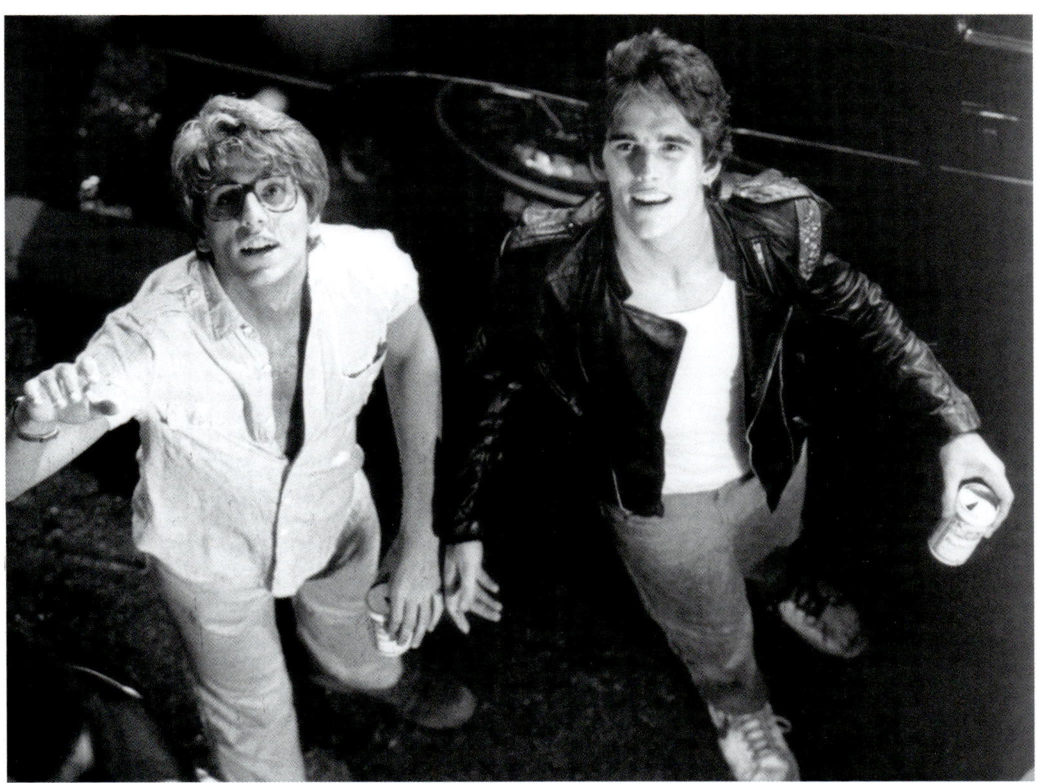

Vincent Spano and Matt Dillon in *Rumble Fish*.

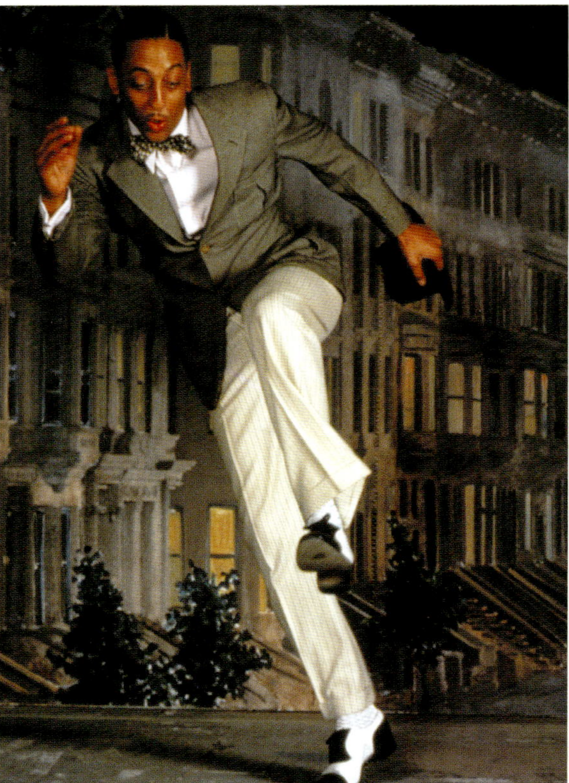

Gregory Hines displays his multiple talents in *The Cotton Club*.

Experimentation continued behind the scenes. Preproduction storyboards were made on an "electronic chalkboard" that recorded the images, and to preview the look of the film, the actors were shot on video using a blue-screen process. Coppola invited French filmmaker Chris Marker to shoot second-unit footage of Tulsa. (Marker apparently found the city ugly and promptly went back home: "I don't see one image, and I can't do it.") He also hired Stewart Copeland, drummer for the Police, to compose an experimental score.

Warner Bros. had financed *The Outsiders* but declined to produce the second film. *Rumble Fish* was distributed by Universal in October 1983 and performed badly at the box office. "Coppola simply will not behave," wrote Richard Corliss in *Time*. "*Rumble Fish* is Coppola's professional suicide note to the movie industry, a warning against employing him."

STORMY WEATHER

Coppola's next movie, *The Cotton Club* (1984), was a labor of love for its producer, the colorful Robert Evans, under whose leadership as production chief of Paramount came classics like *Love Story* (1970), *The Godfather*, and *Chinatown* (1974). Now an independent producer, he saw great potential in the story of the legendary Mob-owned nightclub in Harlem, where white patrons were entertained by Black performers like bandleader Duke Ellington, singers Lena Horne and Ethel Waters, and dancer Bill "Bojangles" Robinson. The material was "a fuckin' natural!" Evans wrote in his memoir. "Violence, sex, music, I'm holdin' *The Godfather* with music. Look out, eighties—here I come!"

Although a number of characters are introduced—both historical and fictional—the film primarily follows cornet player Dixie Dwyer (Richard Gere) who gets in the good graces of the club's bootlegger owner (Bob Hoskins), falls in love with a gangster's girlfriend (Diane Lane), and later makes his break in Hollywood. Originally, it also followed the story of Black dancer Sandman Williams (Gregory Hines). But in postproduction, the distributors mandated a restructuring of the narrative, complaining that

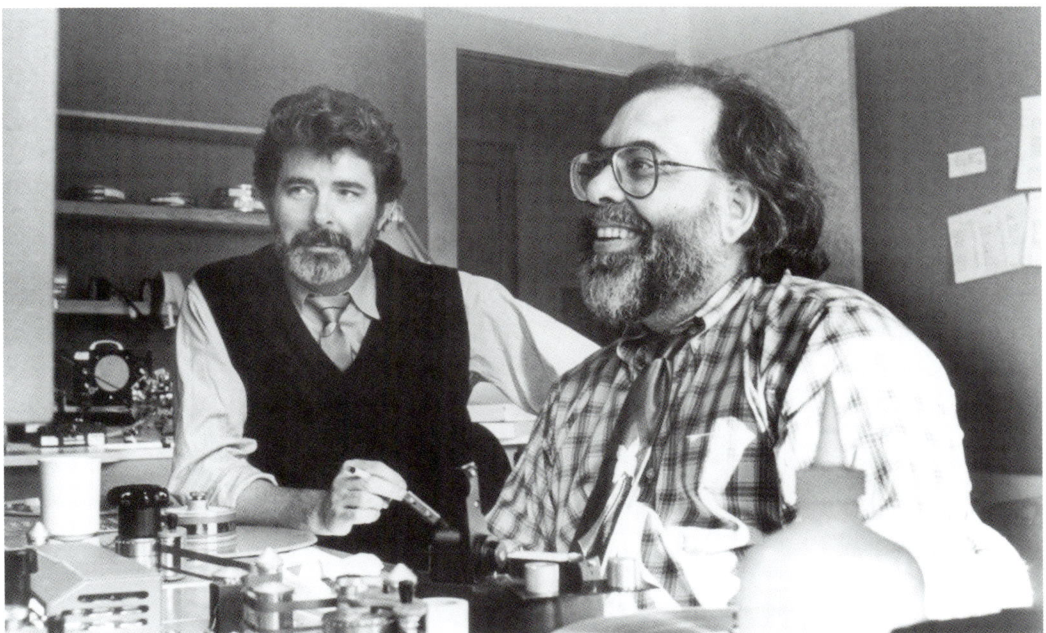

George Lucas and Coppola behind the scenes of *Tucker: The Man and His Dream.*

"it's too long, there's too much tap dancing, too many Black people," according to Coppola.

The director was initially hired to work on the screenplay, drafts of which had already been written by *Godfather* author Mario Puzo and novelist William Kennedy. First Robert Altman, and then Evans himself, planned to direct, but Coppola was eventually offered that job as well, despite an antagonism that tended to plague his working relationship with Evans.

In fact, the entire production was rife with scandal, from Evans's cocaine-possession charge to the murder of one of the film's investors, to another set of investors using Mob intimidation to force Evans to cede control of production, and yet another investor suing all the other partners for breach of contract, resulting in Evans being barred from postproduction.

On top of that, the final budget landed somewhere around $58 million. When finally released in December 1984, it had little chance of financial success. Its shortened format, moreover, left many of its Black characters and even their musical numbers on the cutting-room floor. In 2019, Coppola released *The Cotton Club Encore*, a new edit that restored more than half an hour of original content, resulting in a more equal balance between Gere's and Hines's plotlines. Most significantly, the new cut allows for performances like Lonette McKee's showstopping "Stormy Weather" to truly shine.

Coppola was busy on other projects during this time, as his company American Zoetrope continued to produce other directors' work. As executive producer, he received credits on Godfrey Reggio's *Koyaanisqatsi*, Wim Wenders's *Hammett* (both 1982), and Paul Schrader's

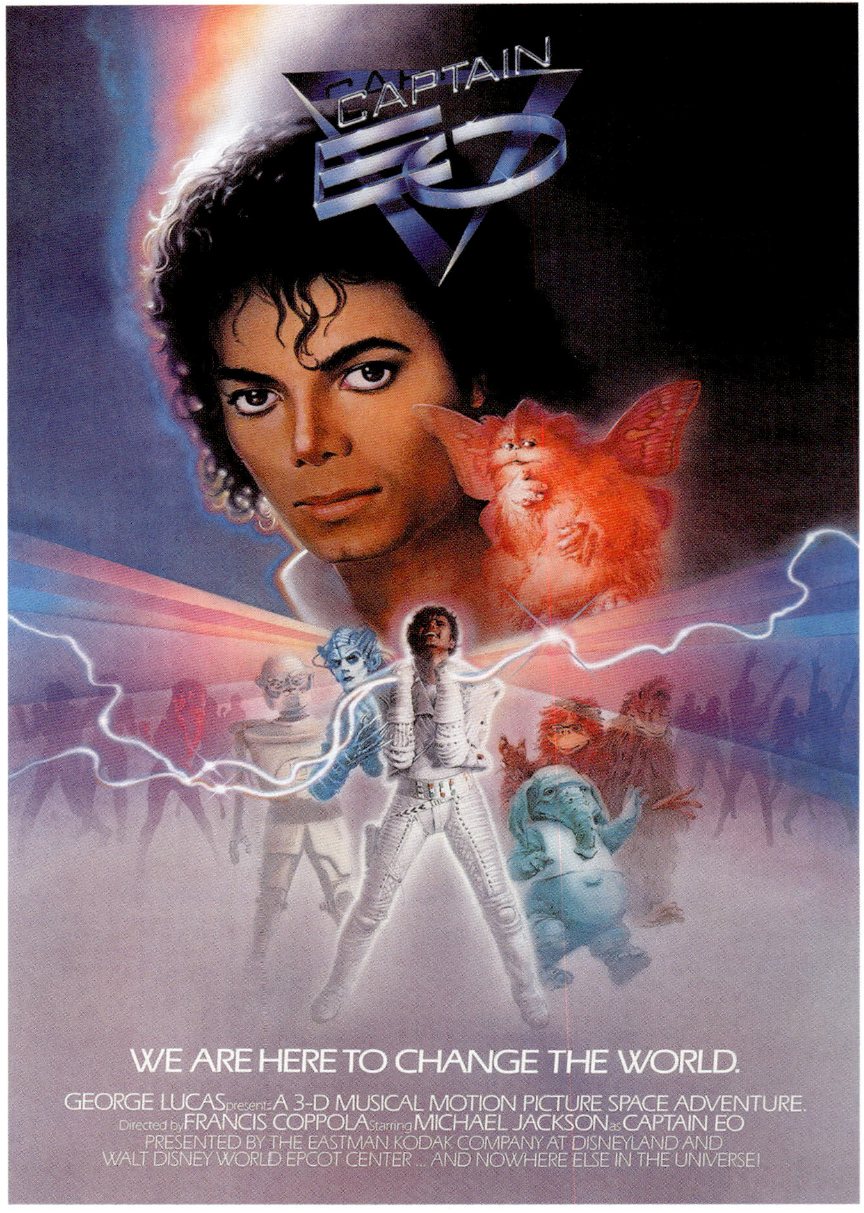

The King of Pop Michael Jackson starred in Coppola's seventeen-minute *Captain EO*.

Mishima: A Life in Four Chapters (1985), among others. He even directed an hour of television for Shelley Duvall's *Faerie Tale Theatre*, hiring his sister, Talia Shire, to star alongside Harry Dean Stanton as Rip Van Winkle. Most notably, he joined producer George Lucas and Walt Disney Imagineering on a $23 million short film, which was shot in 3-D and starred the biggest entertainment icon of the decade, Michael Jackson. The musical space adventure *Captain EO* featured two new songs by Jackson and opened in September 1986 at EPCOT Center in Florida and at Disneyland in California. It was a cultural sensation and likely remains Coppola's most widely seen directorial effort of the decade.

A month later, Coppola had another popular hit with *Peggy Sue Got Married* (1986), a time-traveling romance in which Kathleen Turner's character revisits her high school days and falls back in love with her (future) husband, played by Coppola's nephew Nicolas Cage. Coppola was a director-for-hire on the project, coming on after the script was complete and Turner was cast, but these limitations don't seem to have adversely affected his work. The film is an intelligent exploration of midlife regret and ultimately an entertaining and reassuring film for viewers. Turner earned her only Oscar nomination for Best Actress for her performance.

The next year saw the release of his second film on the Vietnam War, *Gardens of Stone* (1987), starring James Caan as a veteran assigned to the ceremonial honor guard for the funerals of fallen soldiers. (The title refers to the fields of headstones at Arlington National Cemetery.) The film is unfortunately remembered today for the tragic death of his twenty-two-year-old son, Gian-Carlo "Gio" Coppola, in a boating accident that occurred during production—adding a level of poignancy to a story that was already burdened with a profound sense of loss. Coppola has said he remembers little about the making of the film, but that he kept working on the movie to keep himself busy. "I always tell my kids . . . Let your films be personal," he told *GQ* in 2022. "Always make it as personal as you can because you are a miracle, that you're even alive. Then your art will be a miracle."

One more passion project was realized in the 1980s thanks to his friend George Lucas, who agreed to produce *Tucker: The Man and His Dream* (1988), a biopic of carmaker Preston Tucker—an innovator who had attempted to disrupt the American automobile industry in the 1940s but was done in by powerful interests. If this sounds like what happened to Coppola and his Zoetrope Studios, that would not be a misinterpretation. It was a plot that he knew intimately, and with it he crafted a compelling film about a loving father and shrewd businessman (played by Jeff Bridges) whose Tucker 48 sedan was designed to be the "car of tomorrow."

"In his salute to a 'failed' American visionary, Francis Coppola was actually making a tribute to the loners and dreamers of the world, whether they make paper clips, vast flying machines or, perhaps, vast unruly films which do or do not fly, according to your viewpoint," wrote film critic Sheila Benson in the *Los Angeles Times* in 1989, placing *Tucker* in her top-ten movies of the decade. Perhaps Coppola's biggest lesson of the 1980s was the importance of friends—like Lucas, who had shepherded *Tucker* through production and to commercial viability—and the love of family, around which his life revolved. Coppola dedicated *Tucker* to his late son Gio, "who loved cars."

DIRECTORS ADRIFT

William Friedkin was another major New Hollywood figure who won an Oscar for his New York–set cop movie *The French Connection* (1971) and released the horror classic *The Exorcist* (1973). Following those landmarks, he made the 1977 thriller *Sorcerer*, an update of the 1953 French film *The Wages of Fear* that flew under the radar when it was released in theaters one week after *Star Wars*. Rightly or wrongly, the bad timing is often cited for its failure and is a convenient example of how studio blockbusters were beginning to overshadow more challenging work by established auteurs. (One review referred to Friedkin's "belligerent iconoclasm" when explaining the film's commercial fate.)

Friedkin courted controversy in 1980 with his gritty exploration of the underground New York gay scene with *Cruising*. Al Pacino stars as an undercover police officer who infiltrates this world—with eye-popping scenes filmed at actual clubs—to find a serial killer who is preying on the queer community. The film found an audience in theaters but also sparked outrage among gay rights groups who accused it of further marginalizing LGBTQ+ Americans. Today, now that gay representation in film and TV has expanded and improved, some viewers have

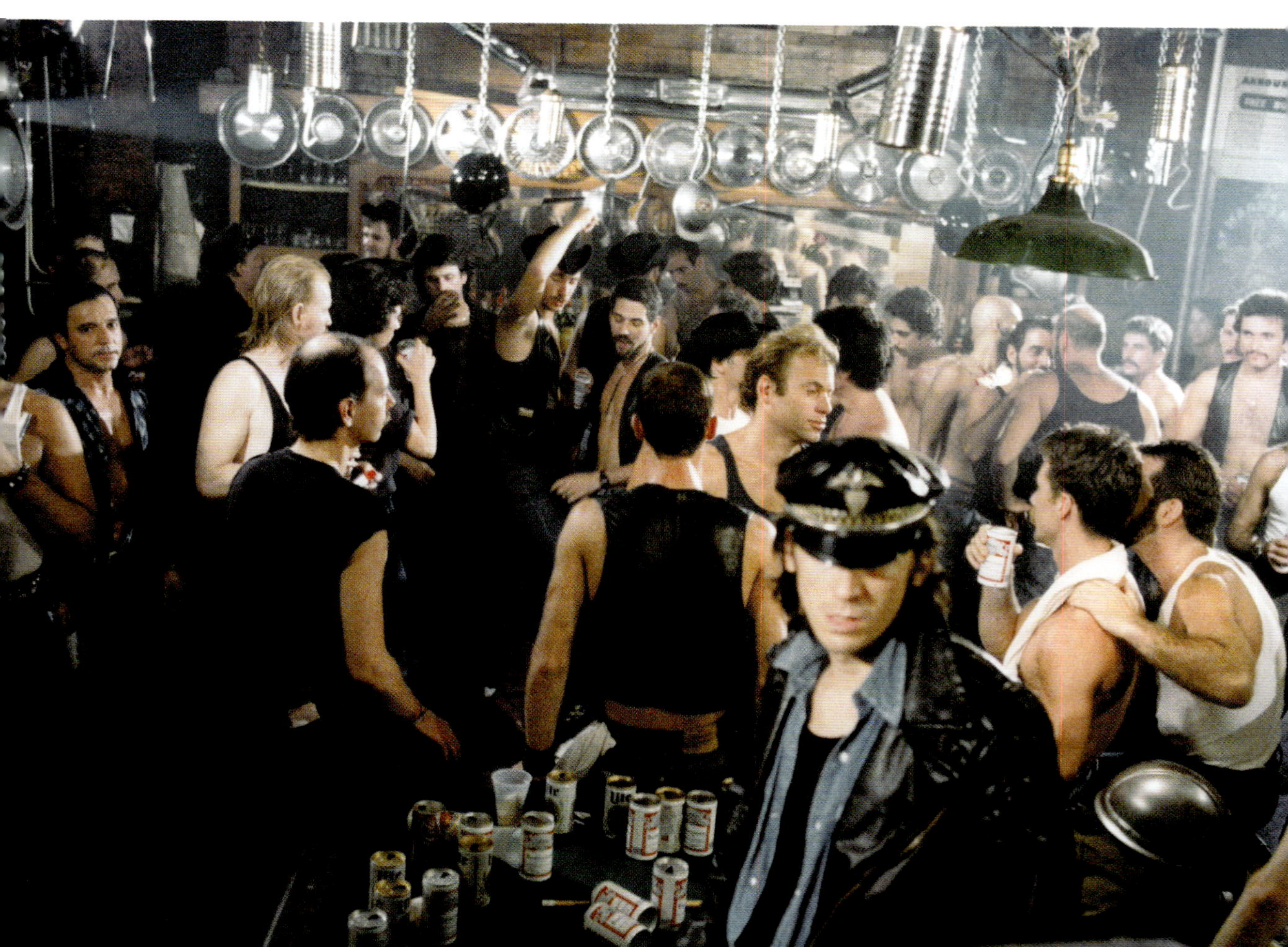

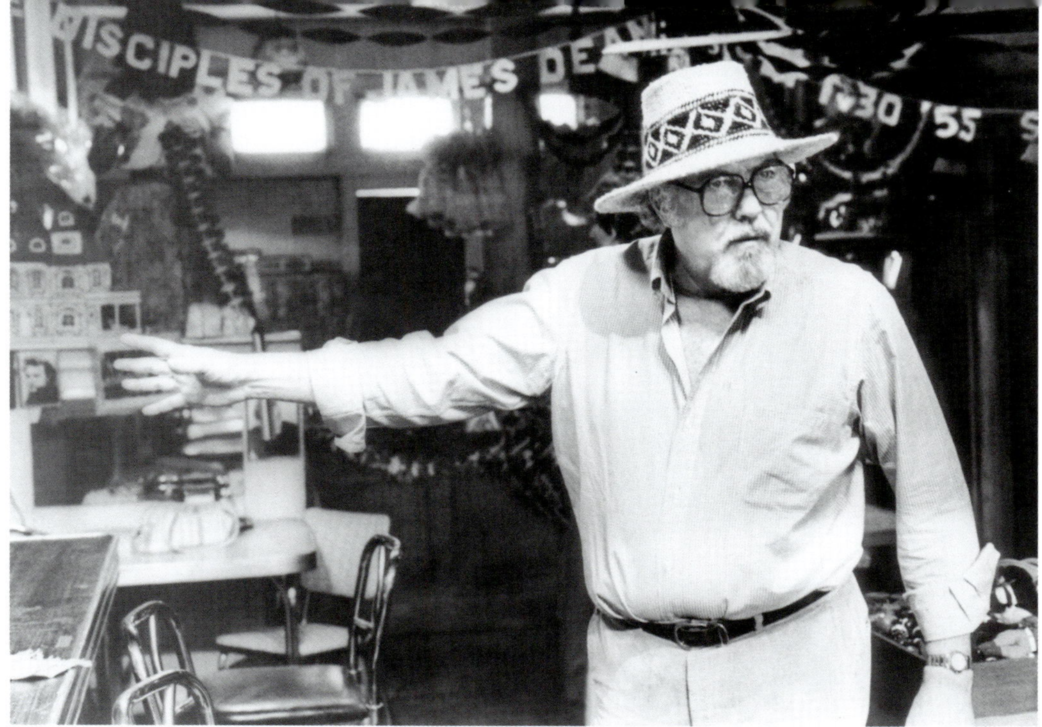

Robert Altman directs *Come Back to the Five and Dime, Jimmy Dean, Jimmy Dean.*

reassigned *Cruising* as a provocative but significant document of pre-HIV gay culture.

Friedkin suffered a heart attack in 1981 on the Warner Bros. lot. "I remember thinking, 'Oh my God, I'm dying, and I've accomplished nothing in my life,'" he told the *Los Angeles Times*. But he still had at least one marvel up his sleeve. The crime film *To Live and Die in L.A.* (1985) was hailed as a return to the style and form of *The French Connection*, including a harrowing freeway car-chase sequence that Roger Ebert described as "a long, dazzling ballet of timing, speed and imagination."

Robert Altman had been the darling of film critics in the 1970s after films like *M*A*S*H* (1970), *McCabe & Mrs. Miller* (1971), and *Nashville* (1975) but had released a string of misfires by 1980 when his musical comedy *Popeye* came out that December. The highly anticipated adaptation of a beloved cartoon character—played by comedian Robin Williams in his film debut—failed to ignite the box office and ultimately doomed Altman's career for the rest of the decade.

Perhaps his heart wasn't in it. In an interview with Ebert the previous summer about the state of the film industry, the director lamented, "We are adrift. There is nobody at the helm. There is no rudder. The bridge is cut off from the rest of the ship." As for the major studios, "You don't negotiate with them anymore. You plea bargain."

Popeye had begun its life with Robert Evans at Paramount, after the studio lost a bidding war for the Broadway musical *Annie* (1982). In response, Evans chose a property whose theatrical rights Paramount already owned and

William Friedkin shot *Cruising* on location in New York's Meatpacking District.

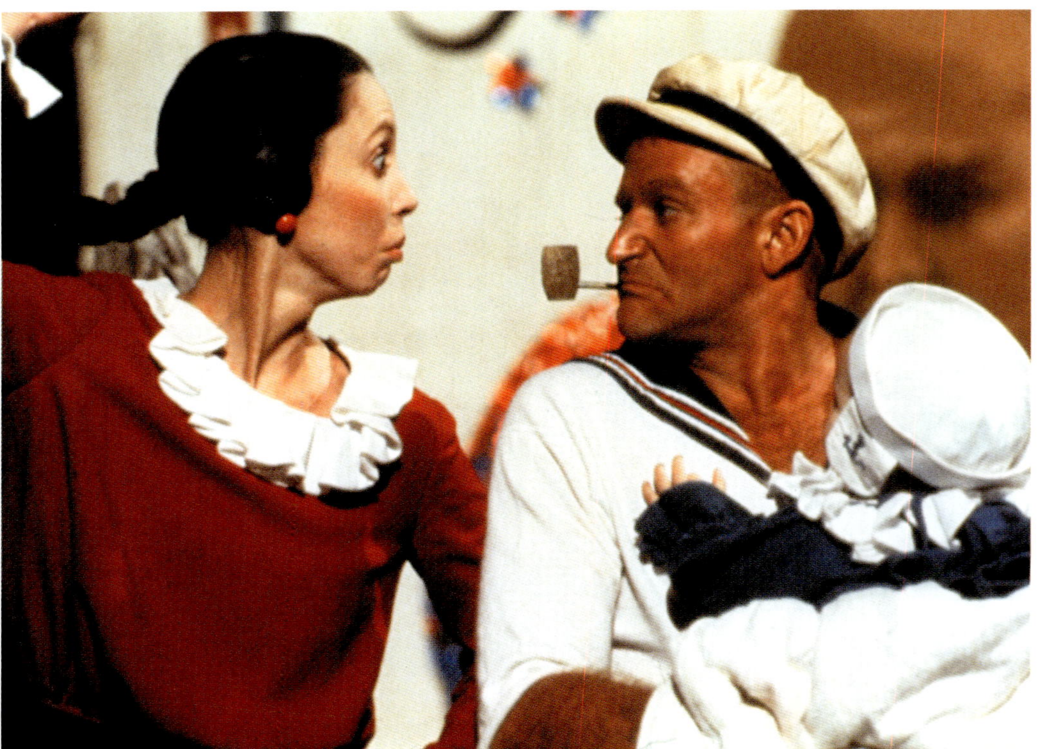

Shelley Duvall and Robin Williams brought classic cartoon characters to life in *Popeye*.

planned a major production, with an elaborate fishing-village set built on the coast of Malta that was used for both exterior and interior filming. ("Popeye Village" still stands today, having become a local tourist attraction.)

Evans's suggestion to hire Altman, after Hal Ashby and others passed on the script, wasn't warmly received. "People in the corporate suite went white when I mentioned his name," Evans recalled. "'He's uncontrollable' they said. 'We can't deal with his irreverence.'" In his memoir, *The Kid Stays in the Picture*, the legendary producer recounted further troubles. He begged his friend Henry Kissinger to intercede with the antagonistic leader of Malta, persuaded Disney to split distribution duties for the first time in their history, and was charged with cocaine possession that June.

Popeye was shot with verve and wit, true to the spirit of the original comics, but while the studios had planned for a major hit, it became only a modest success. Though its popularity has grown in the years since, the unusual production failed to live up to expectations. "Tune in a couple hours' worth of Max Fleischer cartoons instead," recommended critic Leonard Maltin. "You'll be much better off." Altman's supporter at 20th Century–Fox, Alan Ladd Jr., left that studio in 1979, and he was having trouble getting them to release the film he had shot a year before. *Health* (1980) is a political satire set at a Florida health-food conference and was designed to align with the presidential conventions in the summer of 1980. Altman personally took *Health* on the festival circuit, and Fox eventually gave it limited theatrical runs in Los Angeles and New York. Ronald Reagan called it "the world's worst movie" when he screened it in June 1982.

Never one to work well with studio interference, Altman sold his production company and spent the rest of the decade in independent film, television, and live theater. The one movie he did make for a major studio, the teen comedy *O.C. and Stiggs*, was shot in 1983 but not distributed by MGM until 1987. In frustration, Altman left Los Angeles for New York, and ultimately Paris.

One interesting Altman film from this period is *Come Back to the Five and Dime, Jimmy Dean, Jimmy Dean* (1982), shot on 16mm and independently distributed. Based on a play by Ed Graczyk, the film concerns a group of Texas women who learn of the death of actor James Dean and reunite twenty years later to commemorate the anniversary. It starred Cher in her debut film role alongside Karen Black and Sandy Dennis—the same cast Altman had directed in the play's Broadway staging. Several of his '80s films deal with queer characters, from *Jimmy Dean*'s Joe to the outed Vietnam veteran in *Streamers* (1983), to the bisexual character in *Beyond Therapy* (1987). Two politically oriented projects are also noteworthy: *Secret Honor* (1984), a one-man show about Richard Nixon, and the satirical HBO miniseries *Tanner '88*, for which he won an Emmy.

Altman always worked in a way that was at odds with the system and the traditional mode of filmmaking, which started with a strong script and conveyed easy emotions and identifiable heroes. He often threw scripts out, encouraged improvisation, recorded competing dialogue tracks, and knitted together a story after the fact. Many of his best movies, like *Nashville*, don't even have a single main character. Perhaps it isn't surprising that he returned with a vengeance in 1992 with *The Player*, an independent film about the dark side of Hollywood and the studios that chew people up and spit them out.

Like Altman, director Terrence Malick had produced a pair of unconventional films in the '70s—*Badlands* (1973) and *Days of Heaven* (1978). Unlike Altman, Malick played nice with the studios. *Days of Heaven* had the good fortune of costing less than—and opening in theaters two years before—*Heaven's Gate*. It was shot in Canada with a small crew and a modest budget, and though expenses mounted and production ran well past schedule, it drew less scrutiny from Paramount than more worrying shoots like Friedkin's *Sorcerer*. The finished film's warm reception—including an Oscar for Best Cinematography—helped mitigate any charges of irresponsibility on the director's part.

Among Malick's admirers was Charles Bluhdorn, head of Paramount's corporate parent, Gulf and Western, who told him, "I don't care if your films never make a nickel. You'll always make movies for me." Tragically, Bluhdorn died of a sudden heart attack in 1983.

Malick began work on a follow-up immediately after the release of *Days of Heaven*, tentatively titled "Q," but Paramount grew impatient with his slow writing process. He abruptly left for Europe and became what *Vanity Fair* writer Peter Biskind called "a cinematic Salinger." Had he given up? Was he ever a real filmmaker, or just a philosopher with a camera? While living in Paris, he reportedly worked on a spec script for *The Elephant Man*, before learning of the concurrent David Lynch project. He was attached to a script for French filmmaker Louis Malle and attempted adaptations of the Walker Percy novel *The Moviegoer* and Larry McMurtry's *The Desert Rose*. "He just got waylaid for twenty years," reported his longtime production designer Jack Fisk. But when they did collaborate, "it was nice to work on a film that you thought was being guided artistically by one strong person." Malick wouldn't get a film off the ground until 1998's *The Thin Red Line*, and his long absence from Hollywood became as much a part of his legacy as his completed films.

Peter Bogdanovich had made a name for himself as a Hollywood prodigy when he produced the era-defining film *The Last Picture Show* (1971) at age thirty-two, reminiscent of earlier boy wonder Orson Welles. He also developed an actual relationship with Welles and other classical-era filmmakers, earning a reputation as an important chronicler of Hollywood history. The late '70s had not been kind to him, and his films regularly failed to find an audience. By any measure, the '80s were worse.

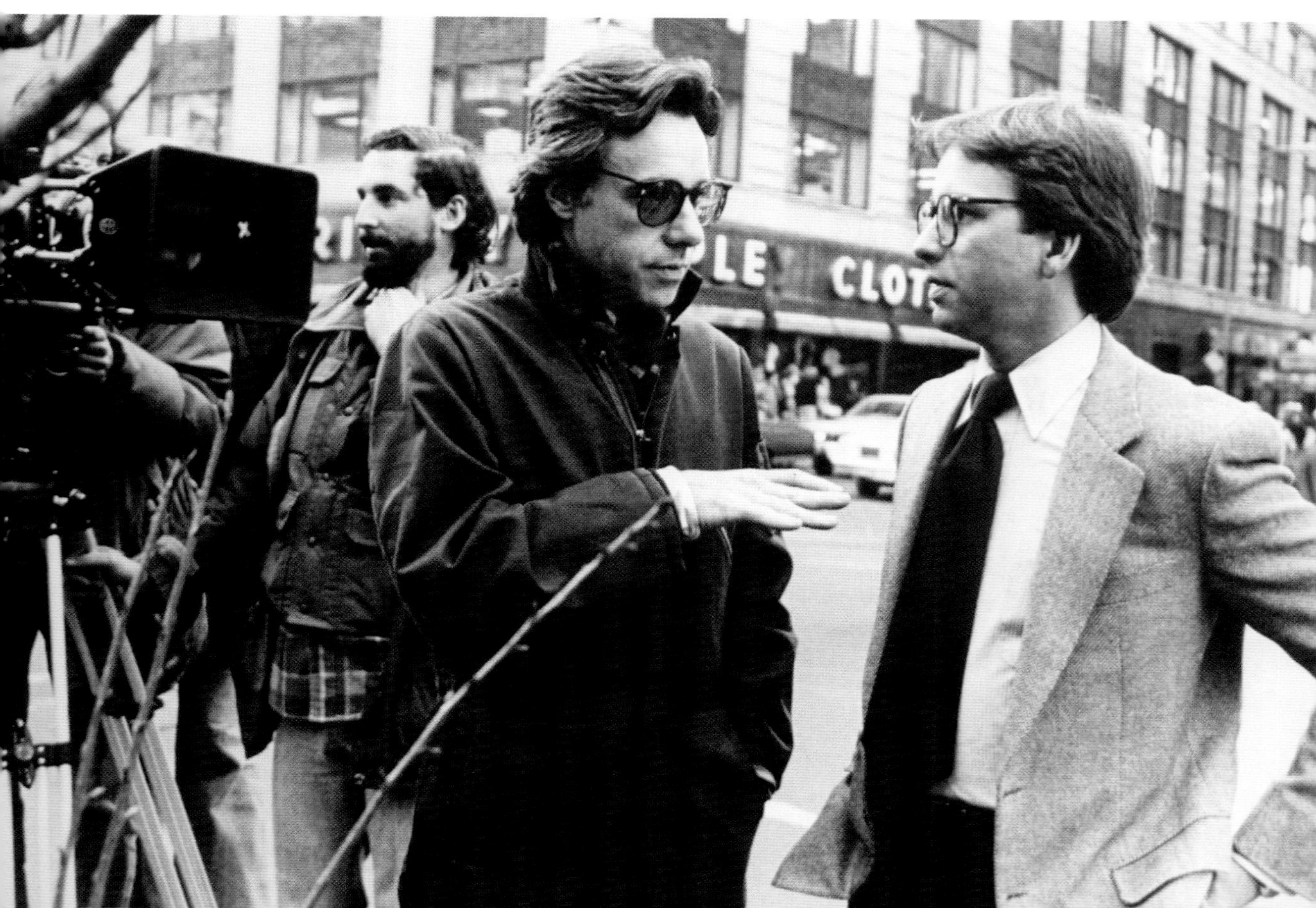

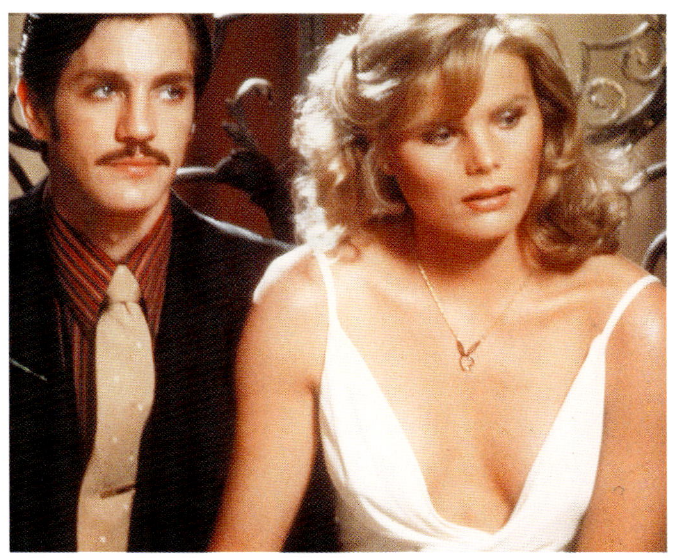

Eric Roberts and Mariel Hemingway in *Star 80.*

They All Laughed (1981) is a lighthearted New York–set romance about private detectives who fall in love with the women they investigate—including a financier's wife, played by Audrey Hepburn in her final lead role. Although the film was named by Bogdanovich as a personal favorite, its production was marked with tragedy. After completing her scenes, Bogdanovich's then girlfriend, Dorothy Stratten (1980's *Playboy* Playmate of the Year, with a supporting role in the film), was murdered by her estranged husband. Working through his grief, Bogdanovich released a 1984 book about the events, *The Killing of the Unicorn*, that was highly critical of *Playboy* and led to a very public feud with Hugh Hefner. In 1988, he married Dorothy's younger sister, Louise, causing yet more tabloid publicity.

To rub salt in the wound, 20th Century–Fox test-marketed *They All Laughed* to mixed results and shelved the project. Bogdanovich then bought the movie back from the studio and personally took over distribution. He wound up losing millions of dollars, which eventually led to his bankruptcy. After several years away from filmmaking, he returned with *Mask* (1985), starring Cher as the mother of a boy with lionitis, which won the Best Actress award at the Cannes Film Festival, and *Illegally Yours* (1988), a screwball comedy with young star Rob Lowe. Where *Mask* had drawn a wide audience, *Illegally Yours* failed to launch—which unfortunately would remain the case for the remainder of Bogdanovich's career.

Legendary Broadway choreographer and Oscar-winning director Bob Fosse used the Dorothy Stratten murder as the subject of his final film, *Star 80* (1983). Mariel Hemingway and Eric Roberts play Stratten and her husband in an exploration of the dark underbelly of show business—not unlike Fosse's previous behind-the-scenes films *Cabaret* (1972), *Lenny* (1974), and *All That Jazz* (1979). "He put forth a dark vision because he was a dark man," said biographer Sam Wasson. About *Star 80*, which had a poor box-office performance, "It's one of the darkest movies ever to have a major studio's logo on its opening credits. Which alone is an achievement."

If there's anyone who perfectly embodies the '70s–'80s artistic divide, it's Hal Ashby. He had started as a skilled editor and won an Oscar for his work on *In the Heat of the Night* (1967). He

Peter Bogdanovich directs John Ritter in *They All Laughed.*

began directing features in the 1970s and had a run of creative successes that today makes him a darling among film buffs: *The Landlord* (1970), *Harold and Maude* (1971), *The Last Detail* (1973), *Shampoo* (1975), *Bound for Glory* (1976), *Coming Home*, and *Being There* (1979). Those same buffs might be hard-pressed to name one of his '80s films, though: The much-delayed *Second-Hand Hearts* (1981) with Robert Blake? *Lookin' to Get Out* (1982), starring and written by Jon Voight, most notable for its debut of his daughter, Angelina Jolie? The Neil Simon–scripted *The Slugger's Wife* (1985)? Or perhaps the neo-noir thriller *8 Million Ways to Die* (1986), with Jeff Bridges and Rosanna Arquette? His last film remains infamous not for its significant financial losses but because the beloved director had been unceremoniously fired at the end of principal photography.

As a documentarian of American counterculture in the 1960s and '70s—*Bonnie and Clyde* (1967), *Alice's Restaurant* (1969), *Little Big Man* (1970)—Arthur Penn had artistic aspirations that were perhaps incompatible with Reagan-era audiences and the priorities of the Hollywood establishment. His 1976 western, *The Missouri Breaks*, an ill-fated pairing of post–*Last Tango in Paris* (1972) Marlon Brando and prime-era Jack Nicholson, had been a head-scratcher for audiences and a box-office disappointment. His later work didn't fare much better. "It's quite possible that Penn simply lost his touch, because his 1980s films are curiosities at best," wrote the *Los Angeles Times* upon his death in 2010.

Penn's *Four Friends* (1981) is, appropriately, a look back at the 1960s, told through the experiences of high school classmates who navigate the turbulent era together. It was a well-reviewed film, landing on some critics' year-end best-of lists, but not in moviegoers' hearts. The mystery-thriller *Target* (1985) was shot in Europe and reunited Penn with *Bonnie and Clyde* and *Night Moves* (1975) star Gene Hackman, opposite up-and-coming actor Matt Dillon. *Dead of Winter* (1987) is a neo-noir with a triple role for Mary Steenburgen. His last theatrical release was *Penn & Teller Get Killed* (1989), a comedy starring the famous magician team. "Today, you get pretty much the same response from all the studios. Essentially, the same breed of executives are running all of them," Penn reflected. "They are corporate smart. . . . They just don't know how to make movies."

After starting as a producer, Alan J. Pakula directed what is commonly referred to today as a "paranoia trilogy" in the 1970s, culminating in the landmark *All the President's Men* (1976). His films were largely successful, sometimes wildly so, but the '80s represent a low point. The first reunited him with his *Klute* (1971) star, Jane Fonda. *Rollover* (1981) paired her with Kris Kristofferson in a political thriller about a banking crisis that "works neither as love story nor as satire, and it isn't even the thriller it sets out to be," complained the *New York Times*. "The cleverness and proficiency of Mr. Pakula's other work are astonishingly absent here."

His standout film of the decade is *Sophie's Choice* (1982), an adaptation of the US National Book Award–winning novel by William Styron about a Polish concentration-camp survivor who makes a new life for herself in late-1940s Brooklyn. This devastating premise is made watchable by the film's skilled performers, including stage actor Kevin Kline in his screen debut and an Oscar-winning Meryl Streep, in what has gone down as a performance for the ages. The role established her as both the premier actress of her generation and a skilled deliverer of non-American accents. "I think he really laid a map of integrity for artists, and that, more than anything, is his legacy for me," Streep said of Pakula. "He was such a moral filmmaker. It's like an old-fashioned idea, but he was. He was a moral man and he had a backbone."

Sophie's Choice was a critical hit, but his follow-up projects were duds. *Dream Lover* (1986) with Kristy McNichol was described by film critic Patrick Goldstein as "a sloggy zonker that has all the energy of a sleepy St. Bernard and the clarity of your Aunt Emma after she's popped a few Valiums." *Orphans* (1987) starred Albert Finney as a Chicago gangster who is kidnapped by streetwise brothers played by Matthew Modine and Kevin Anderson. *See You in the Morning* (1989) showed Jeff Bridges as a divorcé navigating a new relationship with a widow and her kids. All were box-office flops. Pakula did, however, bounce back later, directing a series

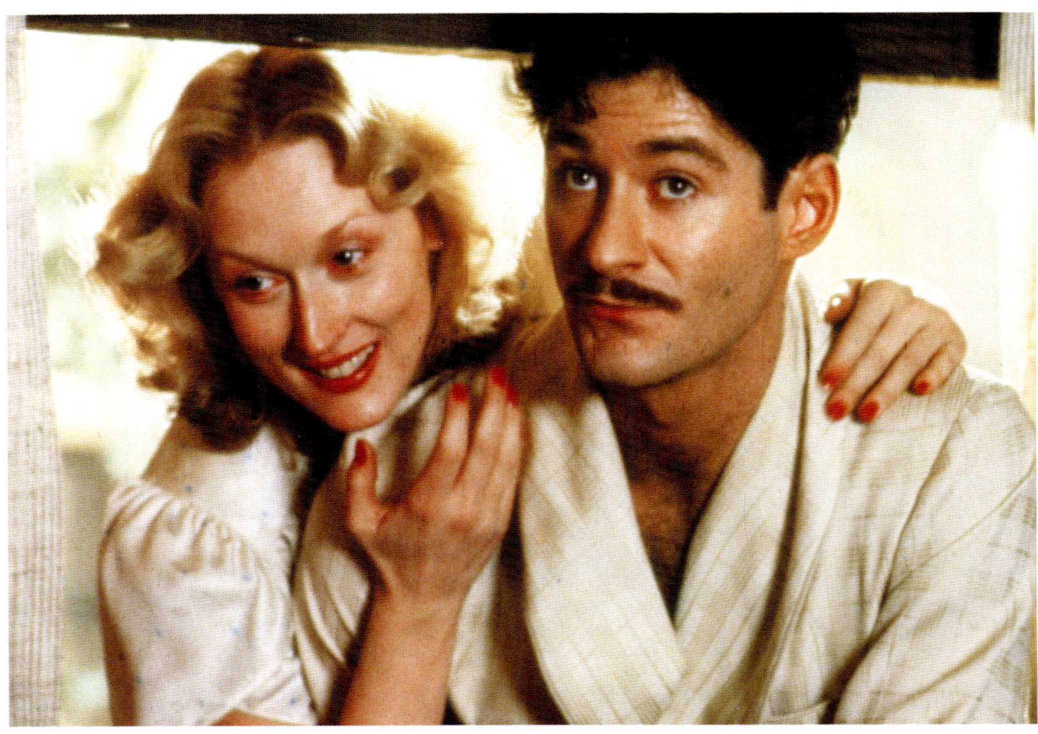

Meryl Streep and Kevin Kline play tumultuous lovers in *Sophie's Choice*.

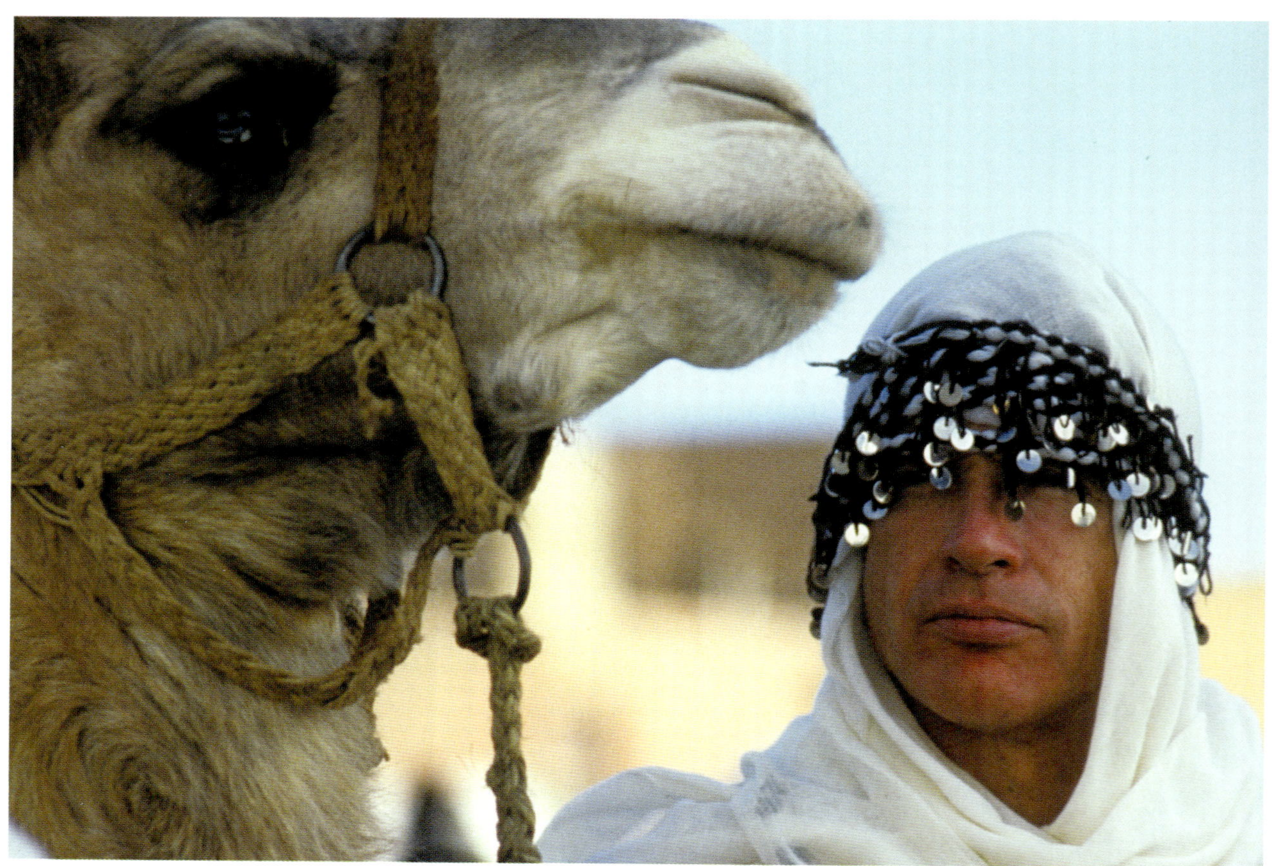

Warren Beatty (right) produced and costarred in *Ishtar*.

of hit thrillers: *Presumed Innocent* (1990), *The Pelican Brief* (1993), and *The Devil's Own* (1997).

Comedian, writer, and film director Elaine May had spent the '80s as merely an uncredited script doctor (*Reds* [1981]; *Tootsie* [1982]) when she tackled the 1987 comedy *Ishtar*. Her longtime friend Julian Schlossberg remembers getting a call one day: "Do you know that Bob Hope and Bing Crosby made movies together?" she asked him. "I'm thinking that there might be a movie in this." *Ishtar* was conceived by May as an update of Hope and Crosby's popular "Road to . . ." series, featuring two bumbling musicians who get in over their heads in a foreign land. Did this concept, workable in classic Hollywood, translate to the 1980s? Not successfully, according to critics and audiences.

Producer and star Warren Beatty spearheaded the project, allowing May to have control as a rare female writer-director in the studio system; her earlier films *A New Leaf* (1971), *The Heartbreak Kid* (1972), and *Mikey and Nicky* (1976) were unicorns within the male-dominated New Hollywood. *Ishtar* was shot primarily in Morocco, in part because Coca-Cola, the corporate owner of Columbia Pictures at the time, had money in the country that couldn't be repatriated. Unfortunately, the film went way over budget due to a variety of production difficulties and May's perfectionist habit of excessive shooting—much like Beatty himself, to be fair (see *Reds*). The $51 million comedy (before marketing costs) grossed only $14 million in the United States, supposedly causing Coca-Cola to rethink its entire venture in the movie business; it sold Columbia to Sony two years later. With echoes of the *Heaven's Gate* affair—a director gone rogue, a runaway shoot, a box-office disappointment, the fate of its studio in the balance—the film has gone down in popular lore as one of the worst films of all time.

"I think the first act of *Ishtar* is perfection," said May's biographer Carrie Courogen. "She gets great performances out of her actors. That's what she cared about, not whether they were losing light in the desert. Her attitude was, 'It's not my money, I don't give a shit.' That didn't exactly endear her to the studios."

In recent years, the film's story of two untalented songwriters (Beatty and Dustin Hoffman) who unwittingly become embroiled in a Middle East political conspiracy has been reclaimed by some viewers—including filmmakers Edgar Wright and Quentin Tarantino—who are drawn to the film's conscious absurdity and political commentary. Another of the admirers is Martin Scorsese: "In 1987, a lot of people claimed that *Ishtar* wasn't funny—it was as if they couldn't allow themselves to laugh. . . . [May] is fearless, absolutely independent, and a great artist, and I wish she would step behind the camera again."

New Hollywood was adapting to the changing dynamics in the industry with decidedly mixed results. Provocative action director Sam Peckinpah made his last movie, *The Osterman Weekend* (1983), before his death in 1984. *Variety* called the Burt Lancaster film "competent, professional but thoroughly impersonal." George Roy Hill, director of enduring classics with Paul Newman and Robert Redford, finished his career with a few highlights, such as the adaptation of John Irving's *The World According to Garp* (1982), an entertaining Robin Williams vehicle with noteworthy supporting performances by John Lithgow and Glenn Close. John Schlesinger (an Oscar winner for *Midnight Cowboy* [1969]) had an enormous box-office bomb with 1981's *Honky Tonk Freeway*, followed by mild successes like *The Falcon and the Snowman* (1985). Iconoclast Bob Rafelson—who gave the world the Monkees and *Five Easy Pieces* (1970) and was notoriously fired from *Brubaker* (1980) after allegedly assaulting the head of Fox—actually fared better than most with his high-profile, erotically charged update of *The Postman Always Rings Twice* (1981), starring Jack Nicholson and Jessica Lange. "Like the whole film," reported the *New York Times*, "they stand just this side of the absurd."

Best Picture

The Oscars had rewarded New Hollywood auteurs in the '70s like Francis Ford Coppola and William Friedkin for their daring work, but by the time the '80s rolled around, a more traditional air of "prestige" began to dominate the top awards once again. Historical epics had a great run, punctuated by the occasional modern-day drama that struck a chord with audiences. The decade also featured one of the oldest groups of acting winners ever, from Henry Fonda to Jessica Tandy, as nostalgia for Old Hollywood took hold in the Reagan era. Here are the decade's esteemed winners of Best Picture:

1980—*Ordinary People* (Paramount, directed by Robert Redford)

1981—*Chariots of Fire* (20th Century–Fox, directed by Hugh Hudson)

1982—*Gandhi* (Columbia, directed by Richard Attenborough)

1983—*Terms of Endearment* (Paramount, directed by James L. Brooks)

1984—*Amadeus* (Orion, directed by Miloš Forman)

1985—*Out of Africa* (Universal, directed by Sydney Pollack)

1986—*Platoon* (Orion, directed by Oliver Stone)

1987—*The Last Emperor* (Columbia, directed by Bernardo Bertolucci)

1988—*Rain Man* (MGM/UA, directed by Barry Levinson)

1989—*Driving Miss Daisy* (Warner Bros., directed by Bruce Beresford)

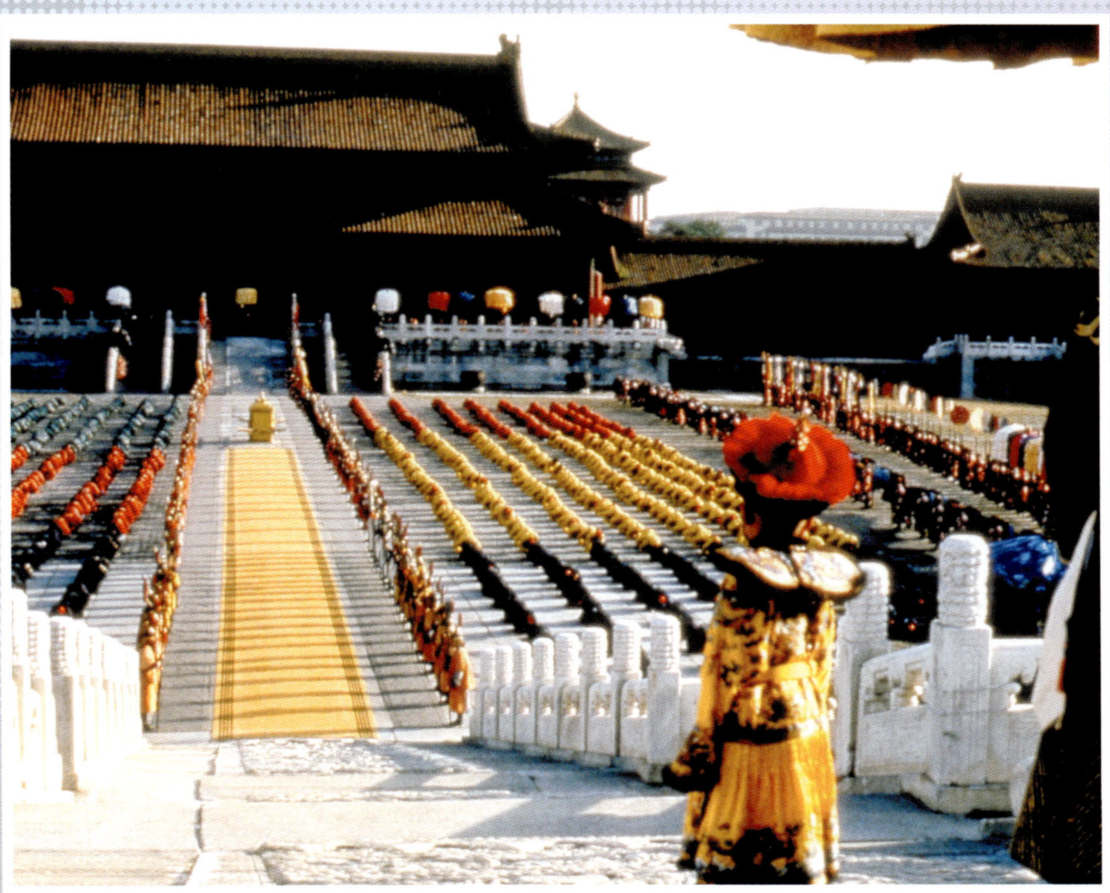

The Last Emperor was the first Western production to be filmed inside the Forbidden City in Beijing.

THE EDGE OF MADNESS

England is where you would have found American director Stanley Kubrick in the 1980s. He lived and worked full-time in the United Kingdom and rarely left the country, usually filming at Elstree Studios in London. Kubrick made only thirteen features in his career, and while few of them can be considered "lesser" works, his later films tend to divide critics and audiences to a degree that his midcareer masterpieces (*Dr. Strangelove* [1964]; *2001: A Space Odyssey* [1968]) do not. His two '80s films cover wildly different terrain, but both explore the nature of evil through portraits of men in psychological crisis.

The Shining (1980) originated as a 1977 best-seller by Stephen King. In the process of adapting the book to screen, Kubrick kept the basic plot but excised much of the main character's struggles—alcoholism, career crisis, sense of fatherly inadequacy—that gave the book its allegorical heft. What remains is a pure and untarnished descent into madness, played with maniacal perfection by Jack Nicholson, whose character, Jack Torrance, spends a long winter holed up in a mountain resort hotel with only

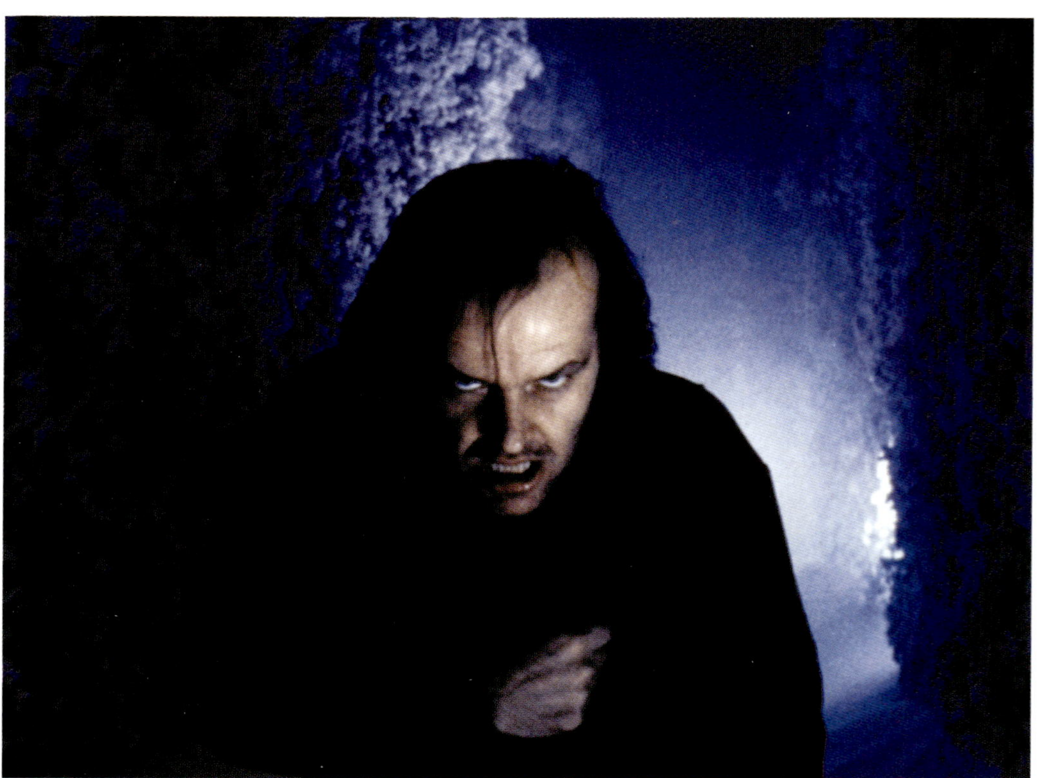

Jack Nicholson wanders the hedge maze in *The Shining*.

his wife and young son. The results are boldly cinematic, and much of the appeal of the film is its visual precision, aided by the use of Steadicam photography as the characters roam the vast hotel, the perfectly composed images contrasting with the very imperfect emotional state of Jack and his family.

The film offered none of the standard-issue frights or jump scares of recent horror films like *Halloween* (1978), and critics struggled to categorize it. Part of the issue was its grandiosity. "It's as if Kubrick wanted to go all the way back to the pure entertainment of *The Killing* (1956) without returning to the modest scale that made that film work so well," wrote Kevin Thomas in the *Los Angeles Times*. "Consequently, *The Shining* comes across as a kind of horror epic." Kubrick got the usual charges of wasteful spending that were familiar to the era, with the $15 million budget resulting in what Gary Arnold of the *Washington Post* called "a peerlessly wrong-headed finished product," six months before the *Heaven's Gate* premiere. He was even nominated for a Razzie for Worst Director and costar Shelley Duvall as Worst Actress. (The latter nomination was rescinded in 2022, after reports surfaced of the psychological torment Kubrick put her through on set.)

The Shining is largely a mood piece, a style exercise, with a wildly drawn central character whose motivations are open to interpretation. The things that made it disorienting in 1980 are what make it special today. "There are no creaking doors, no skeletons tumbling out of closets; none of the paraphernalia of the standard horror film," Kubrick said upon its release. "It's just the story of one man's family quietly going insane together."

Insanity also lives at the heart of *Full Metal Jacket* (1987)—a Vietnam War film whose structure, along with its personality, is split in two. Critic Vincent Canby wrote that its first and second acts are "so different in tone, look and method that they could have been made by two different directors working with two different cameramen from two different screenplays. Only the actors are the same."

Based on the book *The Short-Timers* by Marine Corps veteran Gustav Hasford, the film opens stateside at the Parris Island training center, where seasoned drill instructor Sergeant Hartman (R. Lee Ermey) memorably dehumanizes the new recruits, including central characters played by Matthew Modine and Vincent D'Onofrio. After a pivotal explosion of violence, the film transitions to Vietnam, a surreal environment where the strict discipline of the first half quickly fades away into meaninglessness.

Siskel and Ebert famously disagreed about it on their popular television show. A big fan of the recent Vietnam film *Platoon*, which had been praised for its realism, Ebert was not impressed with Kubrick's latest effort. He called it clichéd and routine, drawing comparisons to the low-budget Republic Studio war films of the 1940s and '50s. "I don't think it's going to hold up that well. It's not one of his great films." (Siskel, for his part, called Ebert's thumbs-down review "a gross mistake.")

Anthony Swofford, Marine Corps veteran and author of the 2003 Iraq-set memoir *Jarhead*, reported on seeing the film in 1987 with his friends: "What we saw felt beautiful and profane and dangerous—normal American kids transformed into war-ready combatants through barbarism and violence. . . . It was both terrifying and thrilling to watch." His subsequent boot-camp experience came complete with drill instructors who mimicked Sergeant Hartman, a testament to the film's influence, no doubt, but one that later filled Swofford with misgivings. "He handed us a romantic idea of what masculinity and warriorism looked like: Self-sacrifice, mission before man, victory at all costs—these were the slogans that effortlessly built the ranks of American ground-combat units and made it easy for our leaders to send young men and women to war."

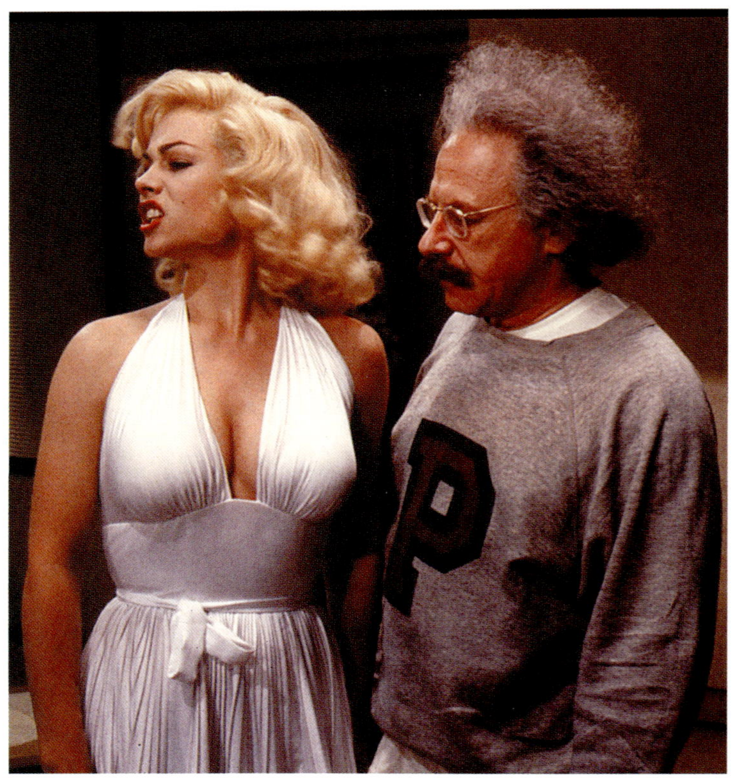
Theresa Russell and Michael Emil in *Insignificance*.

British filmmaker Nicolas Roeg began his career as a cinematographer before directing *Performance* in 1970, with Rolling Stones frontman Mick Jagger in the lead role. By 1980, he added other musicians to his repertoire. David Bowie took the lead in *The Man Who Fell to Earth* (1976) and then Art Garfunkel in 1980's *Bad Timing*. Like his celebrated 1973 Venice-set mystery *Don't Look Now*, Roeg's psychosexual thriller follows two Americans (Garfunkel and Theresa Russell) who meet in Vienna and embark on an obsessive affair. Roeg "brought me to the edge of madness and violence," Garfunkel later claimed.

Meanwhile, Roeg married Russell and cast her in four more of his movies. In *Eureka* (1983), a film that was initially rated X because of its graphic violence, she plays the daughter of a paranoid millionaire (Gene Hackman). In *Track 29* (1988), she gives what *Variety* called a "3-D performance" opposite Christopher Lloyd and Gary Oldman, whose character claims to be the child she once gave up for adoption. *Insignificance* (1985) casts her as Marilyn Monroe, who crosses paths one fanciful night with Albert Einstein (Michael Emil), Joe DiMaggio (Gary Busey), and Joseph McCarthy (Tony Curtis), finding them to be kindred spirits. With all these films, Roeg continued the trend he had begun with his 1970s masterpieces of exploring human psychology to an often visceral degree.

Chinatown director Roman Polanski had not been working in the United States since 1978, when he fled to France after being charged with the sexual assault of a minor. He continued to produce films in Europe, however, and his 1979 film *Tess* (released in the United States in 1980) was a critical success, even winning four Oscars (with Polanski nominated as Best Director). It remains a beautifully shot, engaging adaptation of Thomas Hardy's nineteenth-century novel *Tess of the d'Urbervilles*, starring a teenage Nastassja Kinski. But it is also, as critic Janet Maslin noted, "a film about a young girl's seduction by an older man."

Polanski's output in the '80s consists of only two lackluster releases, starting with the adventure film *Pirates* (1986) with Walter Matthau. Polanski had begun work years earlier on what would become a huge production, inspired by classic adventure tales and—reportedly—Disneyland's Pirates of the Caribbean attraction. Due to a number of factors, including a costly location shoot on the coast of Tunisia, the budget ballooned to an unrecoverable $40 million. "You're only as good as your last movie, and mine was a flop," he admitted to an interviewer in 1988. He followed it with *Frantic* (1988), a Paris-set suspense film starring Harrison Ford as an American doctor who comes to France on business and gets embroiled in a Hitchcock-like political conspiracy. It's a gripping thriller about alienation and "jet lag," according to the director, and the plot hinges on a miniature souvenir of the Statue of Liberty—a pointed symbolic gesture.

AU REVOIR, LES AUTEURS

In the '70s, several art-house auteurs from Europe had cinephiles lining up around the block to see their latest releases. Their films—*Cries and Whispers* (1972), *Day for Night* (1973), *Amarcord* (1973)—got major Oscar nominations and remain acknowledged classics today. But like their American counterparts, their influence was waning.

French New Wave icon François Truffaut made the wartime film *The Last Metro* (1980) out of a desire to depict the Nazi occupation of Paris and the French Resistance, in which his own family had participated. Set in the world of live theater that draws parallels between the idea of performance onstage and off-, the film also gave Catherine Deneuve a richly drawn and, in his words, "responsible" female role, as the wife of a Jewish actor whom she hides from the authorities within the theater. The title refers to the Nazi-enforced curfew and the importance of Parisians not to miss the last metro train of the evening. The film was well received in France and abroad but proved to be the last hit of Truffaut's career. He completed two more films—*The Woman Next Door* (1981) and *Confidentially Yours* (1983)—before his death in 1984 from a brain tumor, at the age of fifty-two.

During a decade in which Italian master Federico Fellini made movies about his attitudes toward feminism, an aging pair of Fred Astaire and Ginger Rogers impersonators, and a personal history of the famous Cinecittà Studios, his most successful film was arguably *And the Ship Sails On* (1983), a highly stylized satire about the mourning of a famous opera singer. The film is set just prior to World War I, aboard a ship chartered to spread the late singer's ashes at sea. It features a cast of eccentric and broadly written characters, the kind for which Fellini had become famous in his prime.

Acclaimed Swedish filmmaker Ingmar Bergman had been working in television for a decade before making *Fanny and Alexander*, which premiered in a three-hour theatrical version in December 1982, with a five-hour cut airing on TV the following year. Though it wasn't Bergman's final work, it was the last one to be released in theaters in Sweden, and it remains one of the most cherished movies of his career. Opening with an elaborate Christmas celebration in

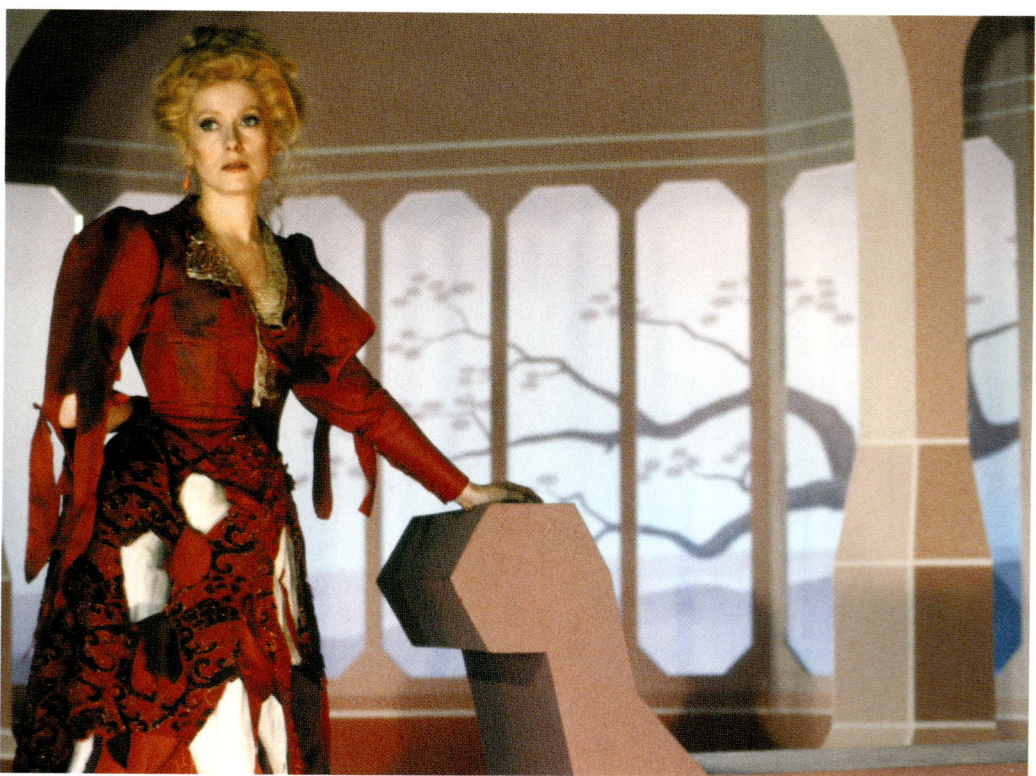

Catherine Deneuve in *The Last Metro*.

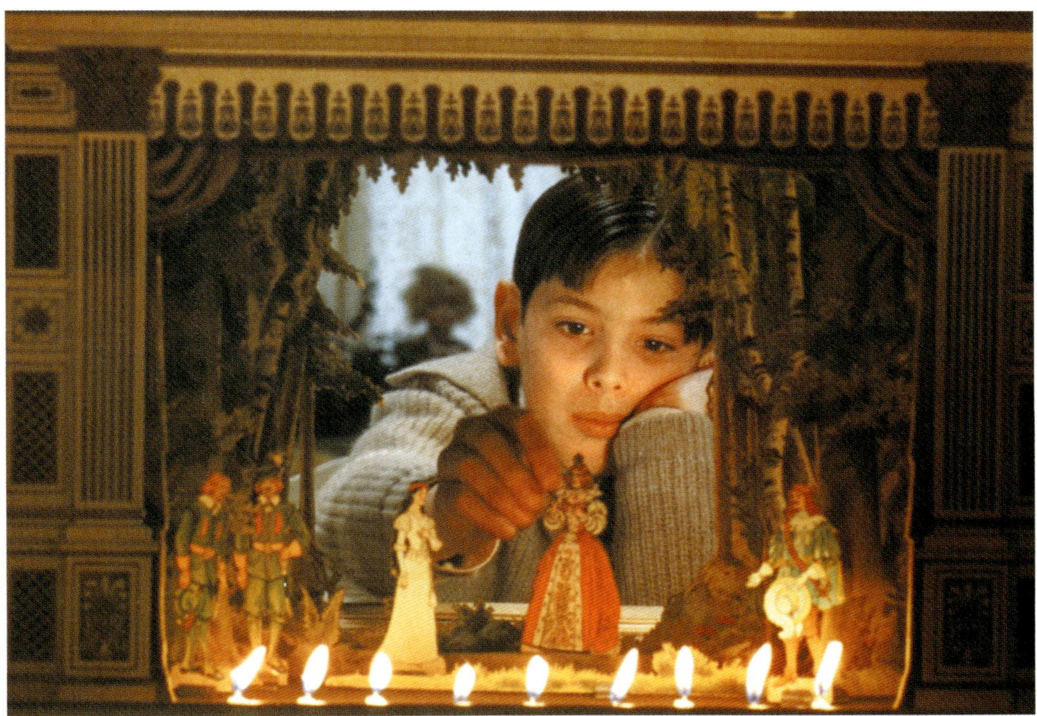

Bertil Guve portrays Alexander of the titular pair, *Fanny and Alexander*.

1907, it tells a Dickensian story about the two title characters whose lives are turned upside down after the death of their father. *Los Angeles Times* critic Sheila Benson named *Fanny and Alexander* her favorite film of the decade, calling it "generous, ribald, reflective, and radiantly life-affirming."

THE TV GENERATION

Looking beyond the 1970s to earlier generations of filmmakers, there were still a number of classic-era directors working in the '80s, some with a great deal of fanfare and critical acclaim. A few started their careers in the then new medium of television in the 1950s and were still making great films, several even nominated for Oscars. These are directors who adapted well to changing climates in the industry and in the culture at large, simply because they knew how to tell a good story. Norman Jewison crafted the romantic comedy *Moonstruck* (1987) to be as authentic to its Brooklyn setting as possible, and the charm of its Italian American family is part of the reason the film—starring Cher and Nicolas Cage—has been so enduring. Sidney Lumet was a master of "social problem" films and ensemble performance, having debuted with *12 Angry Men* (1957). His sprawling New York crime drama *Prince of the City* (1981), with Treat Williams as an NYPD detective turned informant, was followed by the murder mystery *Deathtrap* (1982), the Paul Newman courtroom drama *The Verdict* (1982), and *Running on Empty* (1988), in which a fugitive family is tracked by the FBI.

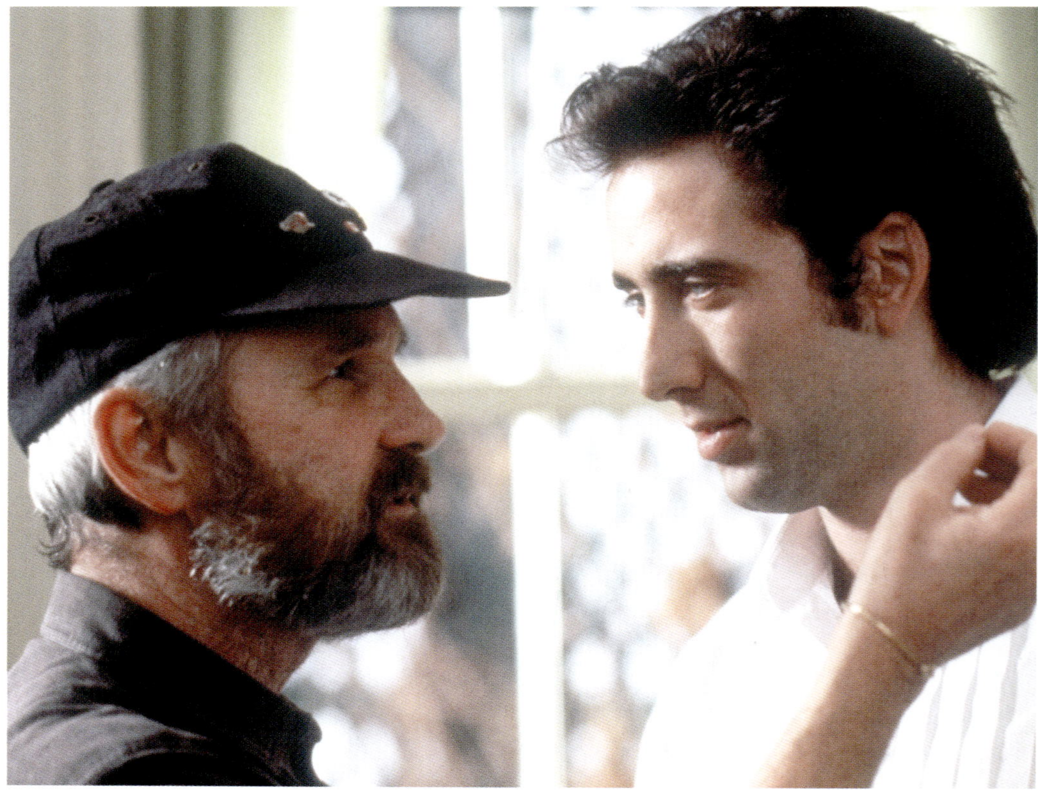

Norman Jewison directs Nicolas Cage in *Moonstruck*.

Franklin J. Schaffner, the director of *Patton* and *Papillon* (1973), served as the president of the Directors Guild of America (DGA) in the late '80s, but the several films he made that decade were critical and financial disappointments. These include the Luciano Pavarotti vehicle *Yes, Giorgio* (1982) and the historical adventure *Lionheart* (1987). The next DGA president was journeyman director Arthur Hiller, who worked steadily in the '80s and produced a couple of box-office successes—*Outrageous Fortune* (1987) with Bette Midler and Shelley Long and *See No Evil, Hear No Evil* (1989) with Richard Pryor and Gene Wilder—but nothing to rival his 1970 touchstone *Love Story*. At the far end of the spectrum was *The Manchurian Candidate* (1962) director John Frankenheimer, whose most accomplished film in the 1980s may have actually been on television: the 1982 HBO film version of *The Rainmaker*, starring Tommy Lee Jones and Tuesday Weld.

TOUGH GUYS

Now in his seventies and entering his fifth decade behind the camera, *The Maltese Falcon* (1941) writer-director John Huston took a rare break from his largely cynical, male-centric filmography with the 1982 family musical adaptation *Annie*. Thanks to its inherent appeal, the film was one of the big moneymakers of Huston's career—though given its high production costs, it didn't turn a profit. A much smaller film followed; *Under the Volcano* (1984) gave star Albert Finney a meaty role as an alcoholic diplomat in pre–World War II Mexico. *Prizzi's Honor* (1985) was a popular Mob comedy starring Jack Nicholson and Kathleen Turner, earning Huston his final Oscar nomination for Best Director. His daughter, Anjelica Huston, was named Best Supporting Actress and followed up her win with a major role in *The Dead* (1987), an adaptation of a James Joyce short story long believed to be unfilmable, which became the director's heralded swan song.

Samuel Fuller, "who never saw or heard of a war without having his creative antennae agitated," according to writer David Thomson, returned to the screen after a long absence with the World War II drama *The Big Red One* (1980). The film was a personal one for Fuller, based on his own war diaries as an infantryman, but in postproduction the studio chopped the film down to half of his intended length. "Those desperate men at the top with their endless meetings . . . ," complained Fuller to the *New York Times*. "If 'moneymaking' is the one and only target, you're heading for catastrophe. They are men with no background in film and

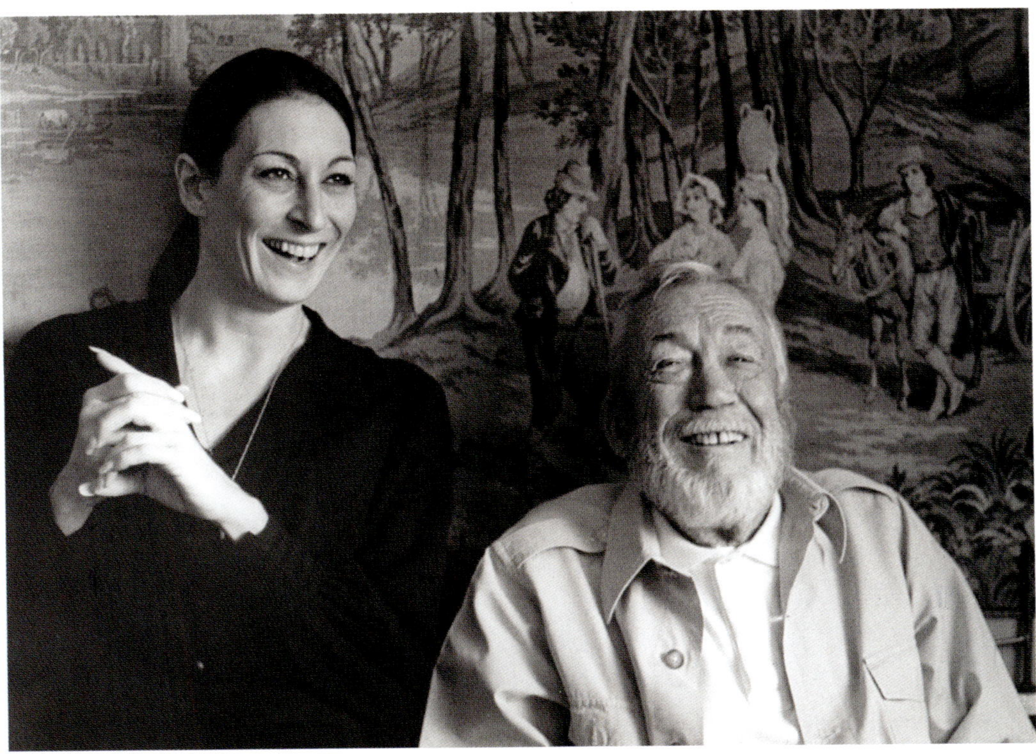

Anjelica Huston and her father, director John Huston, on the set of *Prizzi's Honor*.

with no family name like Warner or Selznick to protect." *The Big Red One* was later reassembled and premiered at the 2004 Cannes Film Festival to much acclaim. His next film was *White Dog* (1982), a drama about a German shepherd who had been trained to attack people of color. When the movie courted boycotts from the NAACP, who deemed the film inflammatory, it was shelved by Paramount until finally being screened in the United States in 1991.

A TRIO OF EPICS

The following three international filmmakers have little in common other than their legacy of excellence and their age. Yet they each turned in an expansive, late-career epic that speaks to the culture in which they were working.

David Lean's *A Passage to India* (1984) is a brilliant adaptation of the classic E. M. Forster novel about the British Raj and its many inequities. At the center is the friendship between a young English woman (Judy Davis) and an Indian doctor (Victor Banerjee) that is shattered by an alleged assault and further drives a wedge between the two cultures. The script was written by the *Lawrence of Arabia* (1962) director himself, who persuaded King's College, Cambridge, to give him the film rights to Forster's work. "Look," he told them, "I'm going to make a movie, which, with luck, will be remembered for two or three

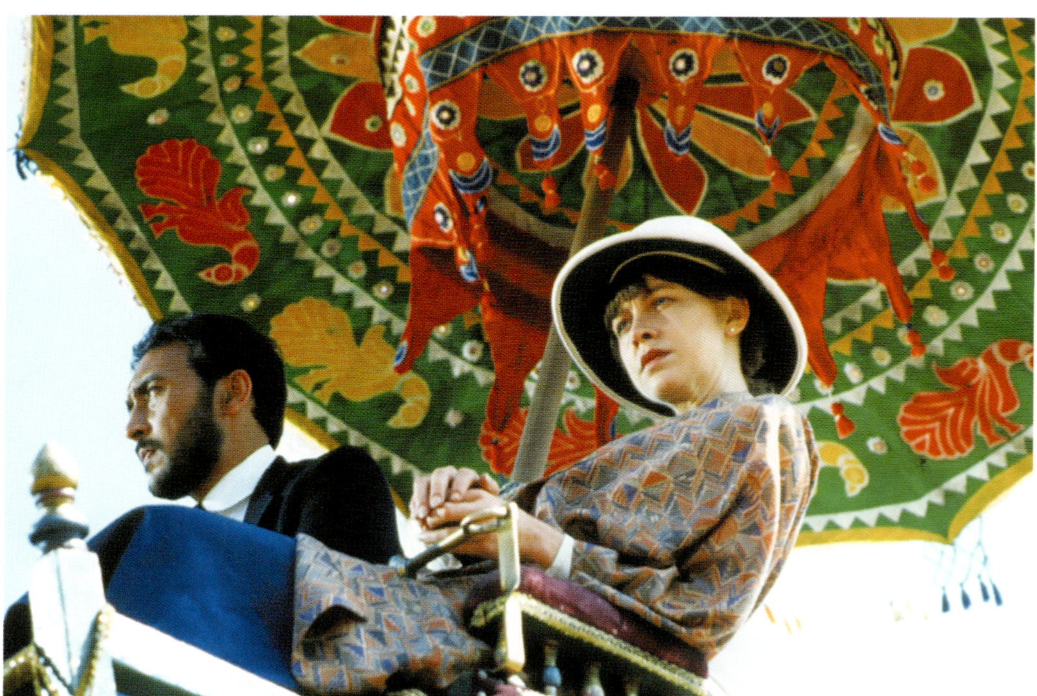

Victor Banerjee and Judy Davis in *A Passage to India*.

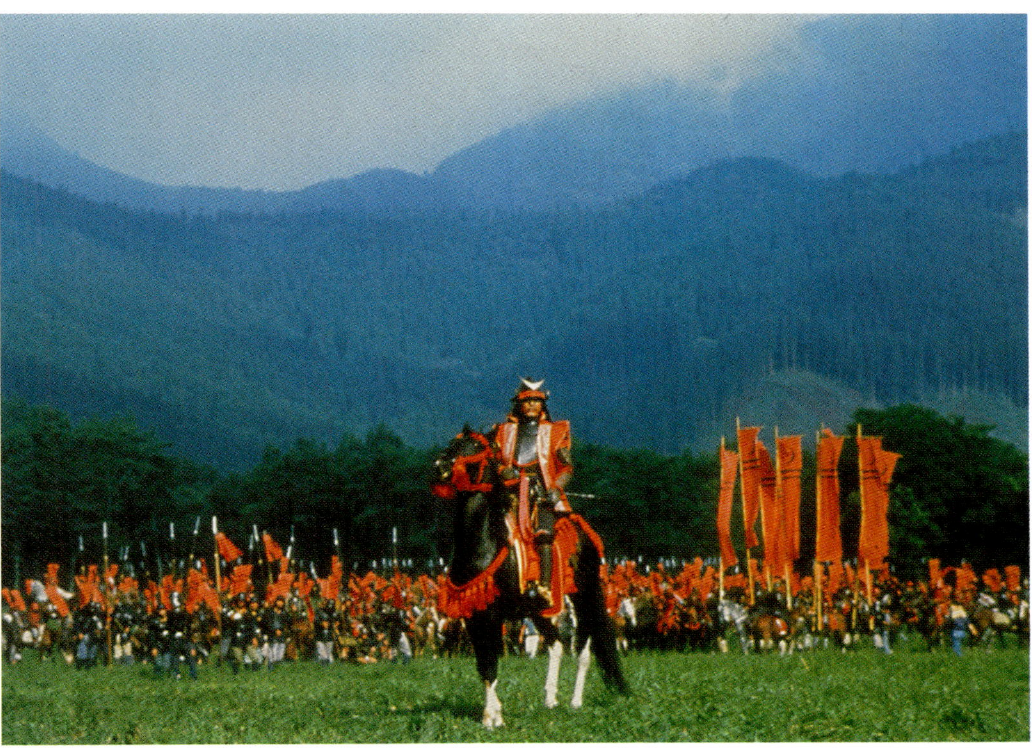

Ran was director Akira Kurosawa's last historical epic.

years. There's always the book. And those who are offended by the idea of making a movie don't have to see it. . . . I can't damage the book. I can only damage myself." The film was a success and was nominated for eleven Oscars.

Italian director Sergio Leone was filming his own final epic at Cinecittà Studios and a variety of locations around the world, including an iconic scene in Brooklyn in the shadow of the Manhattan Bridge. *Once Upon a Time in America* (1984) tells of childhood friends turned gangsters (Robert De Niro and James Woods) whose fortunes fade with the end of Prohibition. The film took years to produce and was released in cuts of varying lengths: 229 minutes in Europe, 139 minutes for its American wide release (which Leone disavowed). Decades after its failure at the box office, it was restored for home video and given a positive critical reappraisal.

Finding it difficult to get financing in his native Japan, the legendary Akira Kurosawa turned to foreign investors to help produce films in the 1970s and '80s. Hollywood studio 20th Century-Fox rescued his 1980 feature *Kagemusha* (with help from George Lucas and Francis Ford Coppola), and his next film was funded by successful French producer Serge Silberman. *Ran* (1985) is based on William Shakespeare's *King Lear* and set in feudal Japan, where an elderly ruler is betrayed by two of his sons. Though not Kurosawa's final film—he made three more, thanks in part to the success of *Ran*—it is one of his grandest spectacles.

The Razzies

Silly, bloated, melodramatic, and overproduced major Hollywood films got their comeuppance when the Golden Raspberry Awards arrived in 1981 to recognize the worst of the previous year's cinematic blunders. In its quaint early years, founder John Wilson would host the "ceremony" in his living room after the Oscars telecast, but the event grew in stature so that, by 1990, it had 275 voting members across two continents, its nominees and winners were picked up by major publications, and its ceremony was held at the Hollywood Roosevelt Hotel (the site of the inaugural Academy Awards). Often controversial, sometimes mean-spirited, always funny, the Razzies continue to keep Hollywood's self-importance in check. Here are the first ten winners for "Worst Picture."

1980—*Can't Stop the Music* (Associated Film Distribution)

1981—*Mommie Dearest* (Paramount)

1982—*Inchon* (MGM/UA)

1983—*The Lonely Lady* (Universal)

1984—*Bolero* (Cannon Films)

1985—*Rambo: First Blood Part II* (TriStar)

1986—(tie) *Howard the Duck* (Universal); *Under the Cherry Moon* (Warner Bros.)

1987—*Leonard Part 6* (Columbia)

1988—*Cocktail* (Buena Vista)

1989—*Star Trek V: The Final Frontier* (Paramount)

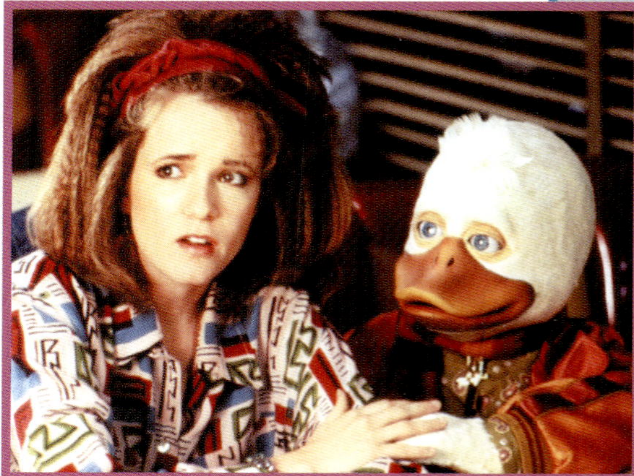

Lea Thompson has an unlikely romance in *Howard the Duck*.

ELDER STATESMEN

Like John Huston, there were several notable classical-era filmmakers whose careers stretched into the 1980s. Unlike Huston, they didn't receive much late-career acclaim. George Cukor's last movie was *Rich and Famous* (1981) with Jacqueline Bisset and Candice Bergen, an adaptation of the 1940 play *Old Acquaintance* that had been previously filmed in 1943 by Vincent Sherman. Fred Zinneman's *Five Days One Summer* (1982), starring Sean Connery as a mountain climber in a controversial love affair, was filmed in the Swiss Alps; Stanley Donen's *Blame It on Rio* (1984) starred Michael Caine as a rich lothario and was made on location in Brazil. Billy Wilder ended his career with the poorly received *Buddy Buddy*. "People say, 'It wasn't your year,'" he acknowledged. "Well, it hasn't been my decade."

SCORSESE: PURGATORY TO PARADISE

As shown in all the examples above, when faced with the realities of a changing industry, veteran filmmakers were forced to sink or swim. At this point it might be instructive to take a further look at one such director and his example of creative resilience.

After the financial failure of *The King of Comedy* and the shelving of his biblical epic, Martin Scorsese changed gears. "After *The Last Temptation* was cancelled . . . I had to get myself back in shape," he told *Film Comment* magazine. "First

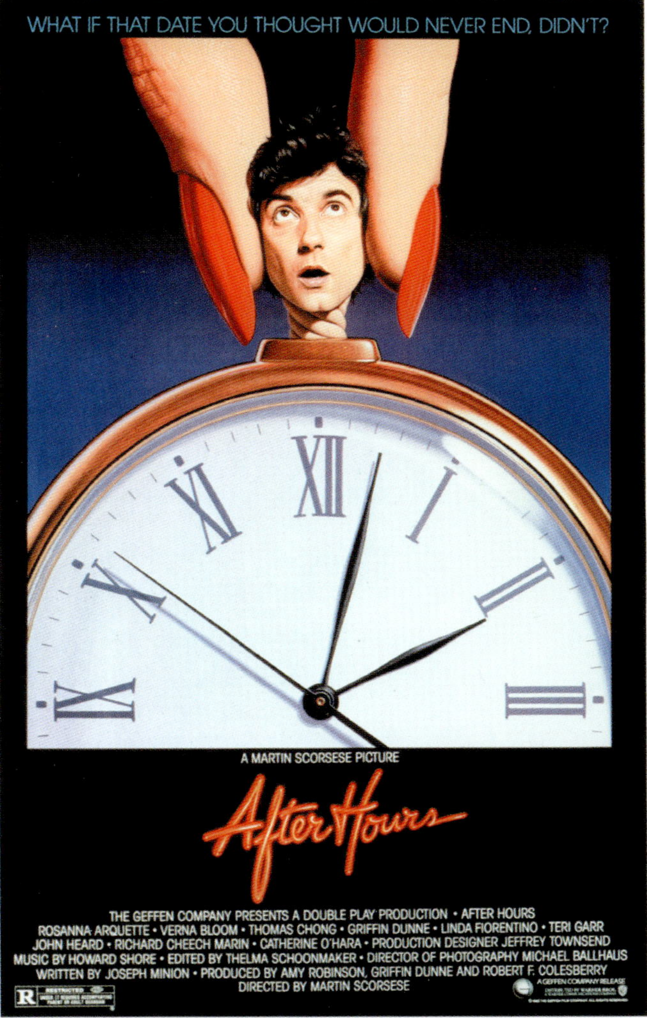

Marvin Mattelson created the illustrated theatrical poster for Scorsese's *After Hours*.

After Hours, on a small scale. The idea was that I should be able, if *Last Temptation* ever came along again, to make it like *After Hours*, because that's all the money I'm gonna get for it." The dark comedy about a Manhattan office dweller who has a terrible night out was made for just $4.5 million by producers Amy Robinson and Griffin Dunne (who also starred). The film had been written by Joe Minion, who had studied at Columbia under Yugoslav filmmaker Dušan Makavejev, which may help explain the film's surreal plot. It was also Scorsese's first film with German cinematographer Michael Ballhaus, whose roving camera would become a staple of the director's works going forward. Overall, Scorsese's situation in 1985 seemed to mimic the frustrations of his hero: a man who has lost control of his own life and is tossed around by fate.

Though *After Hours* came to the director through its producers, it has always been understood as a thoroughly "Martin Scorsese" film. It even earned him honors at the Cannes Film Festival and the newly launched Independent Spirit Awards. Still, the era of the director-as-dictator was rapidly coming to a close, and creative filmmakers had to learn to work within or around the corporate film industry if they hoped to make their dream projects. The auteur theory had its day in the sun, but esteemed filmmakers like Jean-Luc Godard were recognizing its limits, even as he was one of the original group of French critics who had developed it in the first place. "We did it to protect ourselves, and it has done a lot of damage to the brains of some young boys now filming," Godard told press at the 1980 New York Film Festival. "Movies are made by teams."

Part of what sustained Scorsese's career in this decade was his ability to work with others and try new approaches. He directed an episode of Steven Spielberg's *Amazing Stories* anthology television series for NBC, a commercial for Armani, and music videos for Michael Jackson's "Bad" and Robbie Robertson's "Somewhere Down the Crazy River." He even had a cameo in Bertrand Tavernier's film *Round Midnight* (1986). When Paul Newman came calling with the offer to direct a sequel to *The Hustler* (1961), Scorsese said he was interested. "With *The Color of Money*, working with two big stars, we tried to make a Hollywood movie. Or rather, I tried to make one of my pictures, but with a Hollywood star: Paul Newman. That was mainly making a film about an American icon. That's what I zeroed in on. I mean, Paul's face!"

The other star, of course, was twenty-four-year-old Tom Cruise, whose film *Top Gun* was in postproduction when *The Color of Money* began shooting in the spring of 1986. By the time Scorsese's film was released in October, Cruise was a superstar. The appeal of these two actors, combined with Scorsese's smaller but loyal following, brought audiences to the theater for the continuing story of pool shark "Fast Eddie" Felson. The film was a hit and earned Newman his elusive Academy Award.

The Color of Money was shot quickly and came in $1.5 million under budget, "the stuff sainthood is made of in Hollywood," said Scorsese. "The industry is now run by businessmen, and if I want to continue to make personal films, I have to show them I have some sort of respect for money." In another fortuitous business decision, he switched management to Michael Ovitz at Creative Artists Agency (CAA), who had become famous for "packaging" his talent into film projects that were then sold to studios. Ovitz

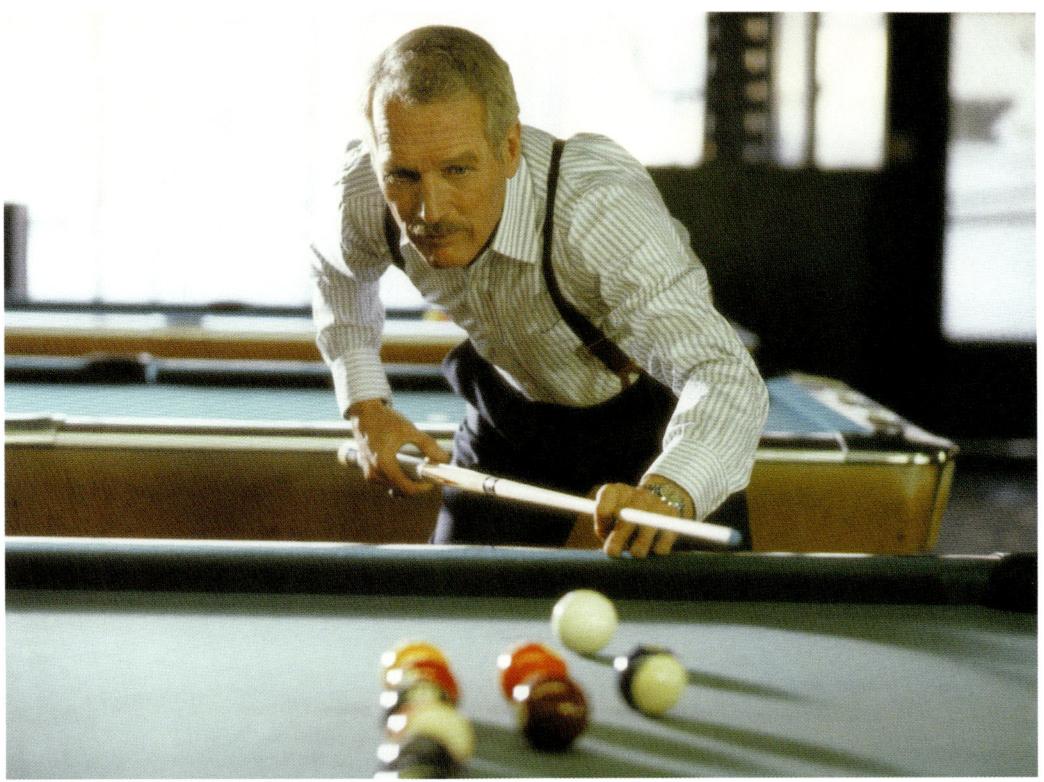

Paul Newman reprises the role of "Fast Eddie" Felson in *The Color of Money*.

was Paul Newman's agent, and Scorsese had seen firsthand his work behind the scenes on *The Color of Money*; it suddenly looked like his dream project might be possible again. *Last Temptation* "had been the laughingstock of cocktail parties in Hollywood until the minute I signed with CAA," he said. "Then it was made!"

Scorsese, who as a boy had wanted to enter the priesthood, had long wanted to make spiritual films, but "religion kept getting in the way." Dealing with these particular images and themes head-on was a challenge he hadn't faced with his other movies. Perhaps it helped, then, that *The Last Temptation of Christ* was the story of Jesus by way of another author's vision and interpretation. The film's opening credits make it clear that the book is based not on the gospels, but rather on the 1955 novel by Greek writer Nikos Kazantzakis, which details the life of Jesus as both fully divine and fully human—complete with doubts, fears, and ideas of what his life could be like if he turned away from his sacrificial destiny.

Scorsese had been given the book by Barbara Hershey—whom he later cast as Mary Magdalene—on the set of his 1972 film *Boxcar Bertha*. The novel wasn't readily adaptable into a film and had to be greatly condensed. The resulting movie features many of the same scenes as a traditional biblical film like *The King of Kings* (1927), but with a notable twist. The film's antagonist is not the Roman Empire, or Judas, or Satan, but

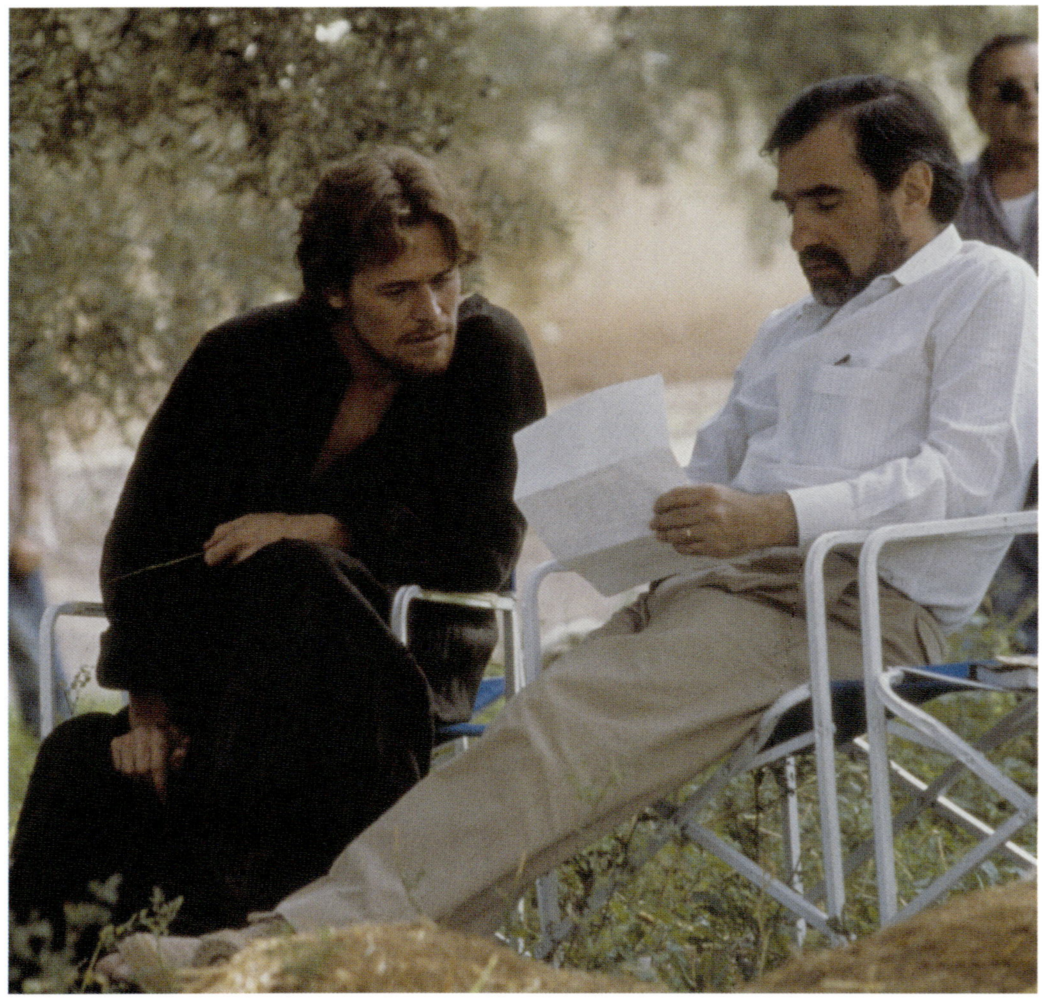

Willem Dafoe and Scorsese on the set of *The Last Temptation of Christ*.

Jesus's own divinity, which he resists for much of the movie. Screenwriter Paul Schrader envisioned Jesus (played by Willem Dafoe) lying on a rocky hill with a splitting migraine: "God as the ultimate headache."

Scorsese's movie is populated with working-class characters—Jesus and the apostles included—and that understanding informed both the casting process and individual performances. Harvey Keitel (as Judas) retains his own Brooklyn accent, rather than adopting a British one as had often been done in biblical films. "The apostles, most of them, were tough guys who worked with their hands," explained Scorsese, who didn't want language or mannerism to distance today's audience from the story. "It should be Jesus on 8th Avenue and 43rd Street." Jay Cocks, who wrote later drafts of the screenplay, noted how famous lines from scripture were rephrased to retain their immediacy and emotion. Thus, "Let he who is without sin cast the first stone" became "Who has never sinned? Who? Which one of you people has never sinned?"

The film was shot in Morocco for a mere $7 million. While its production values may not blow away viewers, the boldness of its ideas, the directness of its language, the handheld camerawork, and the score by Peter Gabriel all work together to create a compelling and intimate experience. "To scale down made it more realistic," said Scorsese. "The simplest, most direct way is usually the most heartfelt way."

Well before its theatrical release, *The Last Temptation of Christ* began to receive staunch criticism from religious groups, who (sight unseen) declared it blasphemous and a threat to the faith. MCA chairman Lew Wasserman, whose company controlled the film's distributor, Universal, even saw his home picketed in July 1988. Rather than waiting for a film-festival debut as originally planned, Universal chose to release the film early, "to make it available to the American people and allow them to draw their own conclusions based on fact, not fallacy," according to a press statement. Despite massive protests outside Universal Studios and theaters showing the film, it opened in nine US theaters on August 12. Scorsese was glad for the wait to be over. "I've had it," he said. "There were so many accusations, so much confusion. I just want people to see the film."

Controversy continued to dog the film in America and in overseas markets. Some theater chains refused to screen the film, and later, when it was released on home video, rental stores like Blockbuster Video declined to carry it. Scorsese received an Oscar nomination for Best Director in 1989, due in no small part to his image as a beleaguered artist:

> I came out of the '70s where a lot of directors were the boss. By 1980, with *Heaven's Gate*, that all ended. And so, in a sense I had to be pushed back, right back to number one and start all over again. And I think it was kind of fitting that it was this particular project that did that, because I had to see if I could survive, quite honestly. And I think that was part of the process of making this film. You had to be humbled to the state of barely able to walk again, and still see if you could do it.

Beyond Hollywood: China

The People's Republic of China had undergone momentous change since the repressive Cultural Revolution came to a close in 1976. For cinema, this included the reopening of the Beijing Film Academy, which saw its first class matriculate in 1978.

Filmmaking had continued during the Cultural Revolution, albeit under tight censorship. Theater attendance was strong, reaching a peak in the late '70s. A reported seven hundred million tickets were sold for the folktale adaptation *Legend of the White Snake* (1980), an all-time world record. Now a wave of "scar dramas," encouraged by the government, depicted the excesses of the Cultural Revolution and criticized those who led it. *Hibiscus Town* (1986), from director Xie Jin, follows a roadside food vendor who is declared to be a "rich peasant" and has her home and business taken from her.

The first wave of students from the academy graduated in 1982, and soon they were popularly termed the "Fifth Generation" of Chinese filmmakers. (The First Generation worked in the silent era, the Second in the 1930s and '40s, the Third after Mao took power in 1949, and the Fourth during the Cultural Revolution.) These young filmmakers, who had not known life before communism, were for several years given relative latitude to make the films they wanted, which turned out to be largely historical in nature and excelled at revealing the personal humanity so often lost in political rhetoric.

One and Eight (1983), about the soldiers in the communist Eighth Route Army in the Second Sino-Japanese War, saw the collaboration of classmates Zhang Junzhao as director and Zhang Yimou as cinematographer. Chen Kaige's landmark *Yellow Earth* (1984) features a soldier who travels the country collecting folk songs to use as propaganda. It was also shot by Zhang Yimou, who would later direct his own feature, *Red Sorghum* (1988), the story of a young woman (Gong Li) who takes over her new husband's sorghum wine distillery after his mysterious death. It won the Golden Bear at the Berlin International Film Festival and launched Zhang's storied career.

Tian Zhuangzhuang's *The Horse Thief* (1986) was made in Tibet using nonprofessional actors and tells the simple story of a man forced to steal in order to take care of his family. The film, full of beautifully photographed landscapes and meditative in its pacing, was famously praised by Martin Scorsese: "*The Horse Thief* was a real inspiration to me. It's that rare thing—a genuinely transcendental film."

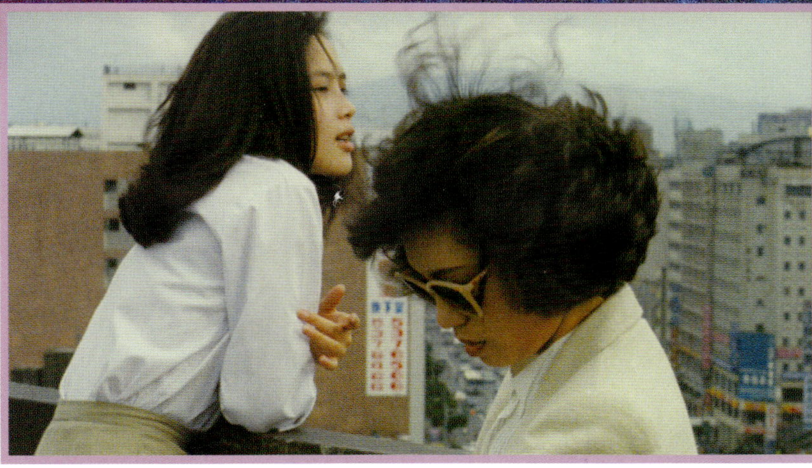

Lin Hsiu-Ling and Tsai Chin in *Taipei Story*.

Chinese-language film outside of the mainland also experienced a creative renewal brought on by fresh talent. Taiwan, which was under martial law for much of the decade, began to see a loosening of restrictions on subject matter that had kept criticism of contemporary society off the menu for many years. The omnibus film *In Our Time* (1982) announced the arrival of director Edward Yang, who went on to make the features *That Day, on the Beach* (1983) and *Taipei Story* (1985). Where Yang focused on urban drama, Hou Hsiao-hsien—the lead actor of *Taipei Story*—was a poet of small-town life. His international breakthrough *The Time to Live and the Time to Die* (1985) followed a young man whose coming of age in Taiwan separates him from the experience of older family members who had fled the mainland. *A City of Sadness* (1989) covered previously taboo historical topics and used Taiwanese dialect rather than the standard Mandarin, which had been strictly imposed for decades.

In addition to its long history of action and martial arts cinema, the Hong Kong film industry was seeing innovations in other genres. Ann Hui depicted the plight of Vietnamese refugees as seen through the eyes of a Japanese photojournalist in *Boat People* (1982). Tsui Hark, producer of John Woo's action films *A Better Tomorrow* (1986) and *The Killer* (1989), also made the popular horror comedy *A Chinese Ghost Story* (1987). New York University graduate Mabel Cheung made a series of films about Chinese immigration to America, including the romantic drama *An Autumn's Tale* (1987). Stanley Kwan's *Rouge* (1988) is about a woman who follows through on a suicide pact with her lover, only to discover that he remained alive. Critical darling Wong Kar-wai also made his directorial debut in the '80s with the crime film *As Tears Go By* (1988).

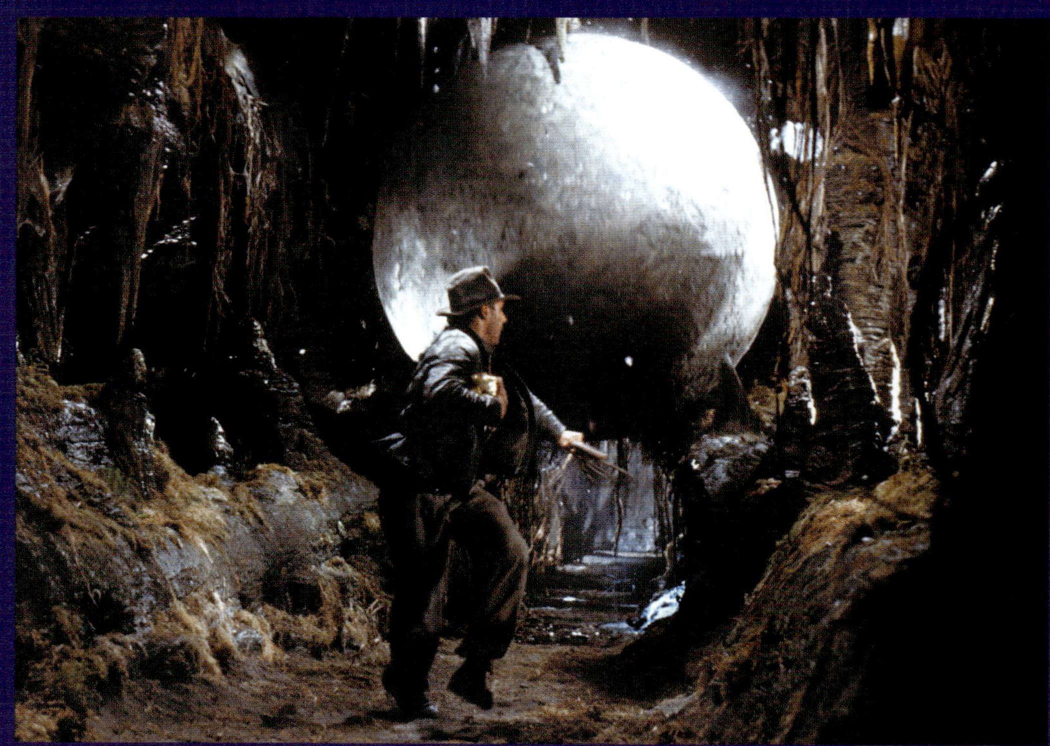

Raiders of the Lost Ark

CHAPTER TWO

New STUDIO AUTEURS

"IT'S HERE! HOLLYWOOD'S NINTH ERA!" DECLARED *ESQUIRE* MAGAZINE in February 1975. In the pages of that issue, actor and writer L. M. Kit Carson delineated the various historical phases of American movies. It culminated in an exciting new wave of filmmakers that included Steven Spielberg, George Lucas, and others who would continue to blossom in the next decade (and some, like Hal Ashby, who would not). The article was prescient, for just a few months later, Spielberg's summer suspense film *Jaws* opened to unprecedented commercial success and created a frenzy among Hollywood decision-makers.

In 1992, after having worked on scripts for *Breathless* (1983) and *Paris, Texas* (1984), Carson returned to update the timeline. "What started out as a thrust of auteurship turned into being enslaved by what they thought were the tricks of the making of a hit." The ninth wave had given way to a tenth, in which Hollywood lawyers and bean counters determined the creative direction for studios, leading to impersonal blockbusters and endless sequels. Yet, while Francis Ford Coppola and Martin Scorsese struggled, some filmmakers were able to endure and even thrive—financially, artistically, or both—through the 1980s. Call them the new studio auteurs.

Spielberg and Lucas had proved themselves, generating massive hits with audiences and heralding a new way forward for Hollywood, but they were only the tip of the iceberg. To be successful in the industry meant rewriting the rules for an American population that was, by 1980—five years removed from Vietnam and now entering the nation's third century—less introspective and hungering for renewed national pride. Many of the decade's premier directors either met that spirit head-on or cleverly undermined it.

The era of New Hollywood formal experimentation was largely over—to the dismay of some film lovers. While Coppola was opening his own studio and attempting to create a new "electronic cinema," established studio filmmaking largely shifted back to classical forms. *Star Wars* (1977) was a postmodern sci-fi serial; *Jaws* was a Vietnam-era *King Kong* (1933). Old genres were revived: *Raiders of the Lost Ark* (1981) was a classic action-adventure tale with cardboard-cutout Nazi villains; *Body Heat* (1981) was a moody, muggy neo-noir. It was a nostalgic era in which older actors like Don Ameche and Geraldine Page were winning Oscars and the US president was a grandfatherly former actor.

Audiences were still able to get their dose of darkness with horror movies, which experienced a boon in the '80s, but in mainstream Hollywood, antiheroes and narrative ambiguity were out. If moviegoers were more willing to embrace

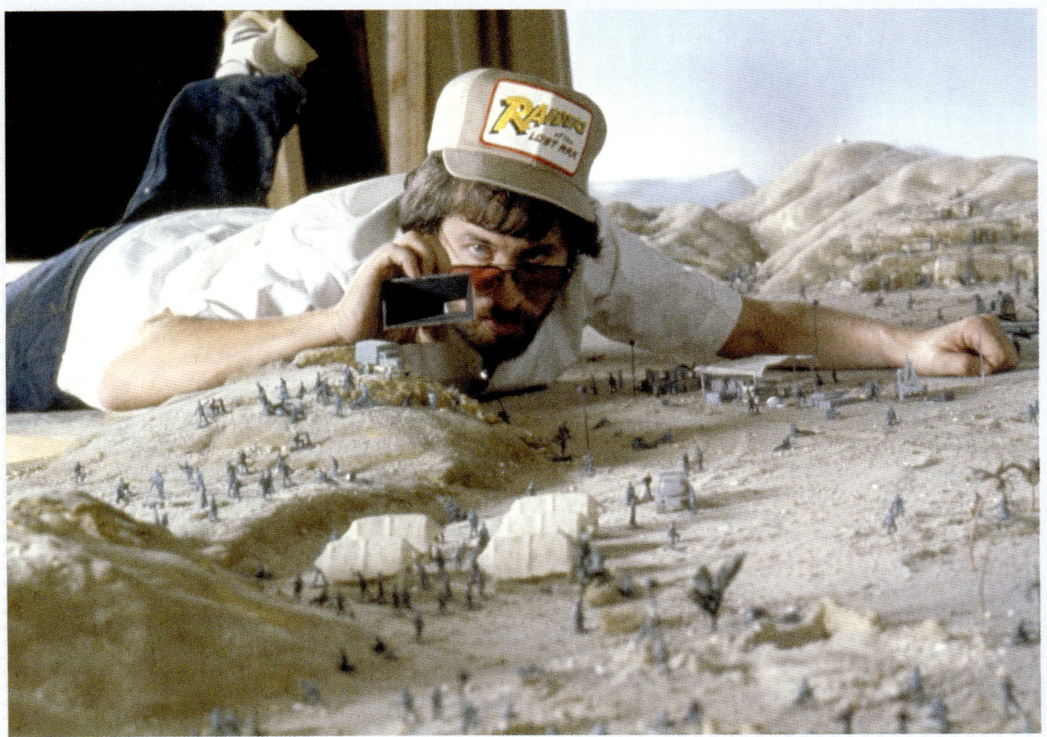

Steven Spielberg plans a sequence for *Raiders of the Lost Ark*.

classic forms of storytelling, with tales of clearly defined heroes and villains, smart filmmakers followed their lead by foregrounding inspiring characters.

The history of Hollywood is the story of the push and pull between artistry and the box office. It is popularly understood that pursuit of profits reigned supreme in the '80s, whereas the artists had run the show a decade before. Such an argument is so simplistic that it's impossible to repudiate, but it's clear that artistic success continued in the '80s just as it had before. The style and content of movies had simply evolved to fit the times. The films discussed in this chapter could be Exhibit A for why '80s cinema should be taken seriously. These directors were working at the top their game, dipping in and out of popular genres, tapping into the culture, and pushing studio filmmaking to its limits.

HOLLYWOOD WUNDERKIND

Steven Spielberg is the greatest storyteller of the '80s. His early films had played in the New Hollywood sandbox, taking advantage of risk-taking within the studio system to make a name for himself, but his inspiration came from iconic moviemakers of the past like Cecil B. DeMille and John Ford. The director who emerged from *Close Encounters of the Third Kind* (1977) was reassuring and openly embraced sentiment. If Richard Dreyfuss played its tortured protagonist, he was still a loving dad—not a sociopath on the level of Robert De Niro in *Taxi Driver* (1976). *Close Encounters* was not about the

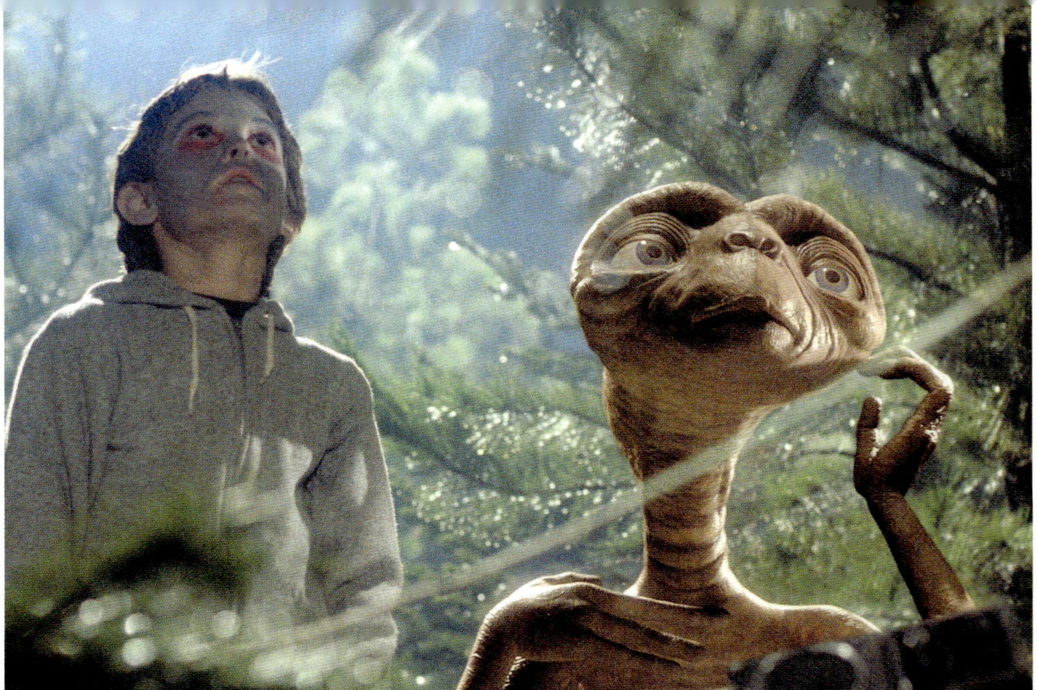

Henry Thomas stars as Elliott in *E.T. the Extra-Terrestrial.*

impending doom of an alien attack, but about the awe of connecting with a larger universe, not an allegory on Vietnam or communism, but what Spielberg called "a seductive alternative for a lot of people who no longer have faith in anything." In terms of a big-screen experience, it dazzled.

The year 1979 brought a rare misfire—the zany wartime comedy *1941* with Dan Aykroyd, Ned Beatty, and Jim Belushi—that inspired Pauline Kael to quip, "It was like having your head inside a pinball machine for two hours." But Spielberg was still able to use his incredible leverage in the next decade to direct and produce—through his company, Amblin Entertainment, named after his 1968 short film—a series of era-defining movies. As always, financial success in the '80s led to greater creative freedom, and Spielberg was a creative master.

The story of *Raiders of the Lost Ark* originated with George Lucas, who envisioned a new take on classic adventure serials like *Flash Gordon Conquers the Universe* (1940). After help from writer-director Philip Kaufman, who added a storyline about the search for the biblical Ark of the Covenant, the characters were brought to full life by screenwriter Lawrence Kasdan, and Harrison Ford and Karen Allen were hired to play the hero and his leading lady. The concept is simple—an American archaeologist races the Nazis to find the Ark—but the experience is that of a thrill ride, set in exotic locales, littered with intriguing characters, and given an earworm of a musical score by John Williams. *Raiders* was a smash, and its $363 million worldwide gross made it the biggest-ever hit for Paramount at that time. "I took the movie as seriously as I took a barrel of buttered popcorn," said Spielberg. But its success allowed him to make a much more meaningful project.

E.T. the Extra-Terrestrial (1982) is the product of a broken home. When its ten-year-old hero, Elliott (Henry Thomas), finds and forms a close bond with a childlike space alien left behind in a California forest, the film transcends its supernatural trappings to become a personal story about family and belonging. Though it bore similarities to Indian director Satyajit Ray's unproduced film *The Alien* and developed from the darker script *Night Skies* by John Sayles, *E.T.* spoke directly to Spielberg's own upbringing. "If E.T. had not come into Elliott's life and without Elliott having a father around, Elliott would have gone down a dark road," he said about the film's underlying paternal dynamic. "That's probably the most important aspect of the movie for me, personally." Meanwhile, he became an on-set father figure to the film's young actors, including Robert MacNaughton and seven-year-old Drew Barrymore.

E.T.—full of mystery, heart, and thrills—became the decade's box-office champion. But it wasn't the only Spielberg film to come out in the summer of 1982, as *Poltergeist* (produced by Amblin and directed by Tobe Hooper) also proved popular with audiences. The story of a little girl who is carried off by the ghosts who haunt her suburban home is sort of an anti-*E.T.* in which the visitors do *not* come in peace. "*Poltergeist* is like a thoroughly enjoyable nightmare, one that you know that you can always wake up from," wrote Vincent Canby in the *New York Times*. Comparing its sense of dread to a Hitchcock film, he noted, "I can't think of many other directors who could raise goose bumps by playing 'The Star-Spangled Banner.'"

Spielberg sent the script for *Gremlins* (1984), a horror film about cuddly little creatures who turn violent when exposed to water, to horror director Joe Dante, whose werewolf movie *The Howling* (1981) had been a minor hit. While *Gremlins* was in development, he invited Dante to make one of the four segments of the anthology film *Twilight Zone: The Movie* (1983), based on the popular TV series. Spielberg, John Landis, and George Miller were the other contributors. The film is remembered today primarily for the tragic on-set death of actor Vic Morrow and two children, rather than any artistic accomplishments. "This has been the most interesting year of my film career," Spielberg told the *Los Angeles Times* in April 1983. "It has mixed the best, the success of *E.T.*, with the worst, the *Twilight Zone* tragedy. A mixture of ecstasy and grief."

He returned to a proven character with *Indiana Jones and the Temple of Doom* (1984), a rip-roaring Asian-set prequel that saw Harrison Ford's Dr. Jones team up with a young orphan named Short Round (Ke Huy Quan) and an American cabaret singer (Kate Capshaw). Arguably inferior to *Raiders*, it nonetheless became a big hit and led to a third entry, *Indiana Jones and the Last Crusade* (1989), which introduced Sean Connery as Jones's father. Beyond directing, Spielberg was busy producing additional projects through Amblin, including Robert

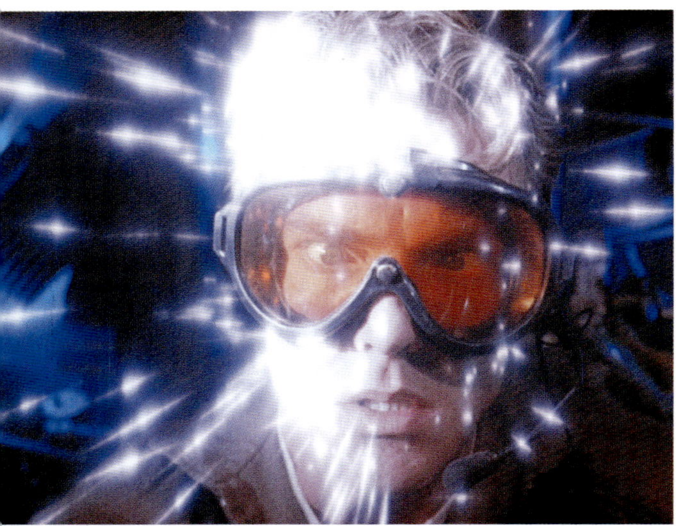

Amblin Entertainment produced director Joe Dante's *Innerspace*.

Zemeckis's *Back to the Future* (1985), Don Bluth's *An American Tail* (1986), and Dante's fantasy film *Innerspace* (1987). On occasion, such as the filming of *The Goonies* (1985), his executive producer credit downplays the extensive role he actually performed on set. Additionally, his fantasy anthology series on NBC, *Amazing Stories* (1985–1987), spanned two seasons and forty-five episodes. Many of these were directed by an impressive roster of filmmakers like Clint Eastwood, Martin Scorsese, and Zemeckis, plus outside-the-box contributors like Paul Bartel, Bob Balaban, and Danny DeVito. Spielberg developed the stories for many of the episodes and personally directed two. Asked if he would do a spin-off series, he replied, "I'm not ready to be Aaron Spelling."

The last half of the '80s marked a shift into dramatic territory. *The Color Purple*, an adaptation of Alice Walker's Pulitzer Prize–winning novel about the life of a poor, uneducated Black woman (played by Whoopi Goldberg) in early-twentieth-century Georgia, was announced in May 1985 by Warner Bros. It was filmed that summer in North Carolina and released in December. Few were more skeptical of the idea of a white male tackling a story told from an African American woman's perspective than the director himself. But producer Quincy Jones, who lobbied for Spielberg's involvement, asked him, "Did you have to be an alien to direct *E.T.*?"

"We all hope that we write for the world, not just that little corner that's like us," Walker recalled years later. "But for someone like Steven—so unlike me and everyone in the story—to feel what I was offering, that was unusual. And Quincy understood the culture immediately. He said, 'Celie is the blues.' Perfect! I felt safe in their hands." She remained on hand as a project consultant, and her contract stipulated that the production team be diverse in race and gender.

Though critically praised—it was Roger Ebert's top film of 1985—there was mounting criticism of the film's representation of various minorities. While some took offense to its negative portrayal of Black male characters, others objected to the whitewashing of the book's queer overtones. When Academy Award nominations were announced, *The Color Purple* received eleven—but Spielberg was conspicuously absent in the directing category. The "snubbing" of the industry's most successful commercial filmmaker was the talk of Hollywood over the ensuing weeks, with the *Los Angeles Times* plainly stating, "There is the scent of referendum in the air." The Directors Guild promptly awarded him its top prize.

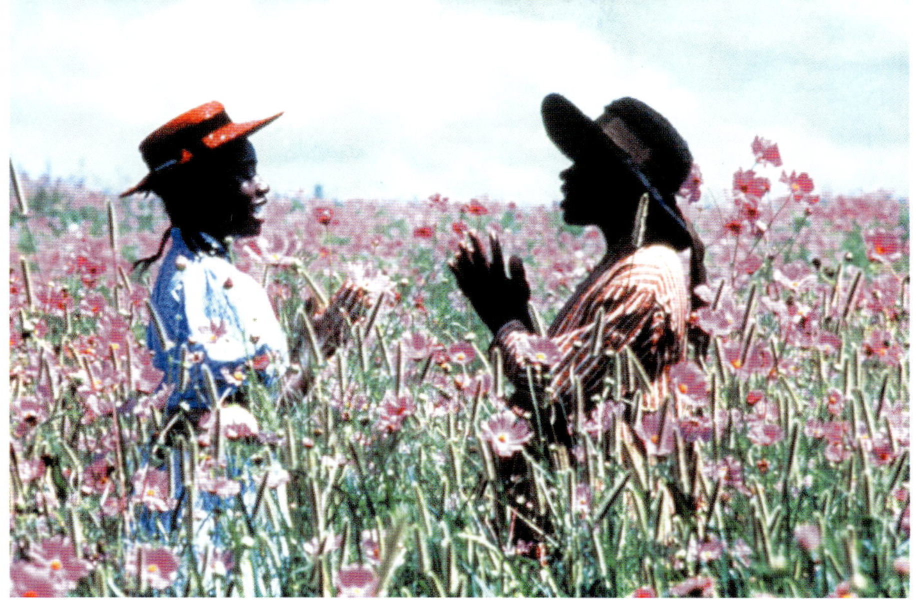

Akosua Busia and Desreta Jackson in *The Color Purple*.

The next year, the Academy's Board of Governors selected him to receive the Irving G. Thalberg Memorial Award for a life's achievement in producing. At age thirty-nine, Spielberg was one of the award's youngest recipients, but he had already racked up an impressive résumé.

He rounded out the decade with a pair of wartime dramas. *Empire of the Sun* (1987) is the story of a British boy (Christian Bale) living in 1930s China, who spends the war in a Japanese internment camp. Before directing, Spielberg had been attached as a producer for British director David Lean, whose epic *The Bridge on the River Kwai* (1957)—one of Spielberg's favorites—had told a similar prisoner-of-war camp story. The inspiration for *Always* (1989) was more personal: the 1943 film *A Guy Named Joe*, about a pilot who dies in the war and returns to tell his widow that she should let herself love again—a film that he first saw while his parents were going through their divorce. Starring Richard Dreyfuss, Holly Hunter, and John Goodman, and with a small part for Audrey Hepburn as an angel, *Always* was a bit too sentimental for many critics' tastes. "There's more drag than lift," wrote the *Washington Post*. "What was perhaps a comfort to the widows of World War II evolves today as a fable for the sensitive male." But this series of historical dramas, with Spielberg leaning into the emotional more than the commercial, was an important period of transition for America's hottest filmmaker, paving the way to his first Academy Award win for *Schindler's List* (1993).

MARIN COUNTY MAVERICK

George Lucas was similarly playing with old forms. He and Spielberg blew up Hollywood in the late '70s and dominated it in the '80s, but Lucas largely worked behind the scenes as a semi-independent producer and technical innovator. He had made three films as a writer-

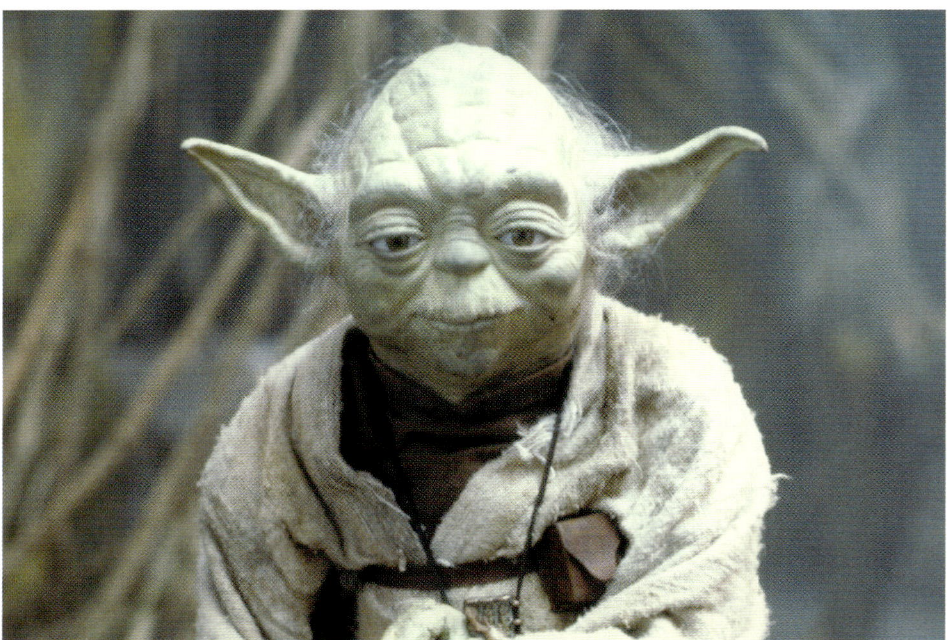

Frank Oz voiced and puppeteered the character of Yoda in *The Empire Strikes Back*.

director in the 1970s: *THX 1138* (1971), *American Graffiti* (1973), and *Star Wars*, and these would remain his sole directing credits for the next twenty years.

"In person he's no self-promoter—Robert Altman in reverse," wrote the *Los Angeles Times* of the thirty-three-year-old director before the release of *Star Wars*. He explained his thinking behind the sci-fi fantasy. "I never bank on anything. I think this movie will break even." In developing it, he was simply after "pure entertainment" for a modern audience that craved fairy tales. "There's a whole generation today with a great need for fantasy. The Lone Ranger and Long John Silver. *Star Wars* is hopefully a feeble attempt to make up for that lack."

The film, of course, was one of the biggest game changers in the history of Hollywood. When it came time to make a sequel, however, Lucas took a step back. While filming commenced on *The Empire Strikes Back* (1980) in Norway—for the sequences on the ice planet Hoth—and Elstree Studios in England, he stayed behind in California to focus on the film's elaborate visual-effects work. He is credited for the film's story and as an executive producer. "I hate directing," Lucas told *Rolling Stone* in 1980. "You go to work knowing just how you want a scene to be, but by the end of the day, you're usually depressed because you didn't do a good enough job. . . . It was easy to let go of directing." In his place was Irvin Kershner, to whom he granted creative independence. "Kersh," twenty years Lucas's senior, had started his career in documentaries and television and had met Lucas as a lecturer at the University of Southern California (USC) film school.

Empire was designed to be different in tone and psychologically richer than the first film. "I wanted everyone to reveal their emotional side—robots included," said Kershner. It also introduces the beloved character of Yoda—an elderly Jedi master portrayed by a puppet that was voiced and controlled by Franz Oz. The plot sees the main characters separated from each other and each facing trials that do not entirely resolve; its cliff-hanger ending was quietly revolutionary.

Lucas's decision to place Kershner's name in the end credits so as not to detract from the film's dynamic opening sequence got him into hot water with the Directors Guild. In response, Lucas resigned from the DGA. He also closed the LA office of his production company, Lucasfilm, and moved all operations north to Marin County. "I don't have to work for a living anymore," he said. In Hollywood, "for every honest true filmmaker trying to get his film off the ground, there are a hundred sleazy used-car dealers trying to con you out of your money." For the third *Star Wars* film, *Return of the Jedi* (1983), he hired English director Richard Marquand, who was likewise not a member of the DGA.

Lucasfilm's base of operations, just north of San Francisco, was home to his visual-effects company Industrial Light & Magic (ILM), which had been formed in 1975 for *Star Wars* and, in the '80s, served as a state-of-the-art effects shop for major productions across the various studios. Lucasfilm's computer division, known as the Graphics Group, was a pioneering digital graphics team—later sold to Steve Jobs and renamed Pixar—while Sprocket Systems (later Skywalker Sound) provided sound engineering and other postproduction facilities.

After *Return of the Jedi* and *Indiana Jones and the Temple of Doom*, Lucasfilm released a series of highly creative films, including Paul Schrader's *Mishima: A Life in Four Chapters* (1985), Jim Henson's *Labyrinth* (1986), the Marvel Comics adaptation *Howard the Duck* (1986), Ron Howard's fantasy adventure *Willow* (1988), and (along with Amblin) Don Bluth's animated epic *The Land Before Time* (1988). In many ways, Lucasfilm was a more pragmatic version of Coppola's Zoetrope Studios venture. In a twist of fate, Lucas, whose *American Graffiti* had been made possible by Coppola's involvement, wound up producing the struggling director's 1988 project *Tucker: The Man and His Dream*.

MAJOR PRODUCERS

The 1980s saw the rise of the producer as a major creative force in big-budget studio filmmaking. Several of these figures became recognizable names in their own right. Paramount executive Don Simpson and advertiser turned producer Jerry Bruckheimer had been friends for a decade before they collaborated on *Flashdance* (1983). With "high-concept" films like *Beverly Hills Cop* (1984) and *Top Gun* (1986), they showed a knack for appealing to a wide film audience, and their films became some of the era's most successful hits.

Jon Peters started as a hairdresser before producing then girlfriend Barbra Streisand's film *A*

Star Is Born (1976). With former Columbia executive Peter Guber, he launched PolyGram Pictures and, later, the Guber-Peters Company, which produced a variety of films like *Clue* (1985), *The Color Purple*, and *Rain Man* (1988). Their biggest production was the Warner Bros. blockbuster *Batman* (1989), which they had shepherded though development for more than a decade.

Italian producer Dino De Laurentiis had gotten his start with postwar neorealist films and 1950s works by Federico Fellini and Roberto Rossellini. After working on several Hollywood productions in Italy, he relocated to the United States and even briefly ran a studio facility in North Carolina in the mid-'80s. His output was eclectic. After establishing his name with the big-budget remake of *King Kong* (1976), his company produced *Flash Gordon* (1980), *Halloween II* (1981), *Conan the Barbarian* (1982), *Dune* (1984), *Blue Velvet* (1986), and dozens of other films.

After stepping down as head of production at 20th Century–Fox, Sherry Lansing partnered with former Paramount and Columbia exec Stanley R. Jaffe to produce *Fatal Attraction* (1987), *The Accused* (1988), and Ridley Scott's *Black Rain* (1989). The prolific Joel Silver produced *48 Hrs.* (1982), *Predator* (1987), *Die Hard* (1988), and more with onetime Fox president Lawrence Gordon; *Lethal Weapon* (1987) and *Lethal Weapon 2* (1989) with Richard Donner; and—by himself—*Weird Science* (1985), *Commando* (1985), and *Road House* (1989).

Some producers were known primarily for their work with specific directors, including Frank Marshall and Kathleen Kennedy (Steven Spielberg), Debra Hill (John Carpenter), and Gale Anne Hurd (James Cameron). Meanwhile, the "most powerful man in Hollywood" was talent manager Michael Ovitz of Creative Artists Agency. In addition to representing major talent, Ovitz pioneered the phenomenon of "package" deals, in which CAA would connect actors and directors on film projects before bringing the full packages to studios.

A number of smaller production companies were operating during this time as well. One of the most successful was Orion, which had launched in 1978 by a group of former United Artists executives, including chairman Arthur Krim. Initially partnering with Warner Bros. for distribution, the company had a mixed track record at the box office and, though it rapidly scored four Best Picture Oscar wins (from 1984's *Amadeus* to 1991's *The Silence of the Lambs*), filed for bankruptcy in the early 1990s. At the other end of the spectrum, indie production company Cannon Films was purchased by Israeli film producer-cousins Menahem Golan and Yoram Globus in 1979. Cannon began specializing in exploitation and B-movies, from Chuck Norris and Charles Bronson action films to teen sex films like *The Last American Virgin* (1982) and low-budget musicals like *Breakin'* (1984). Carolco Pictures was responsible for major action films like *First Blood* (1982) and *Red Heat* (1988).

Product Placement

When Coca-Cola purchased Columbia in 1982, it kicked off a cinematic soda war that saw Marty McFly say, "All I want is a Pepsi!" in *Back to the Future Part II* (1989) and a vending machine in the Pentagon emblazoned with Dr. Pepper in *Godzilla 1985*. Product placement became big business in the '80s, with companies like Associated Film Promotions popping up to provide representation for brands that wanted to get their products on-screen.

This practice could sometimes get out of hand, as in the Jerry Lewis comedy *Hardly Working* (1980), which featured everything from the Budweiser Clydesdales to the Goodyear blimp, with little care for how they were worked into the story. The sci-fi film *Mac and Me* (1988) has been derided for essentially being a wall-to-wall McDonald's ad (among other reasons), while the video-game competition in *The Wizard* (1989) was used to shamelessly plug Nintendo's new Power Glove, the upcoming release of *Super Mario Bros. 3*, and Universal Studios Hollywood.

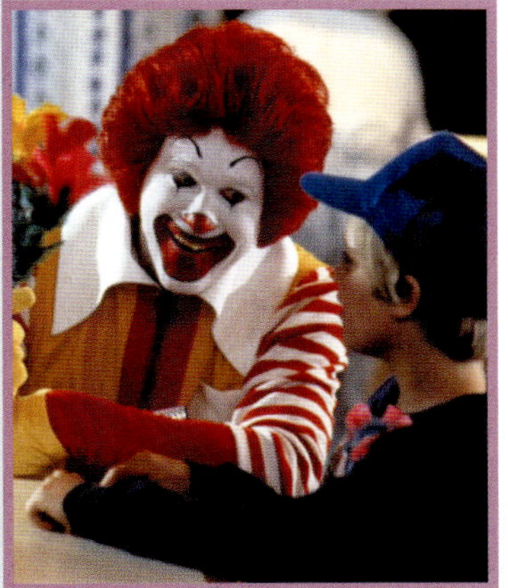

McDonald's looms large in *Mac and Me.*

Some films have become intrinsically linked to certain products, as in Hershey's placement of Reese's Pieces in *E.T. the Extra-Terrestrial* (1982). Ray-Ban saw interest in its Wayfarer sunglasses soar after *Risky Business* (1983) and partnered again with Tom Cruise on *Top Gun* (1986), this time with its Aviators getting a 40 percent sales bump. Car companies like Aston Martin and Lotus continued to sponsor James Bond films, and the DeLorean brand remains in the popular consciousness today solely because of *Back to the Future* (1985).

In 1988, *Return of the Killer Tomatoes* spoofed the concept when the film runs out of money in the middle of shooting. "We've been avoiding it, but it's the '80s," says George Clooney's character. "I think it's time for product placement." One can of Pepsi, a Nestle Crunch Bar, two beers, a tube of Crest, and a box of Corn Flakes later, the story resumes.

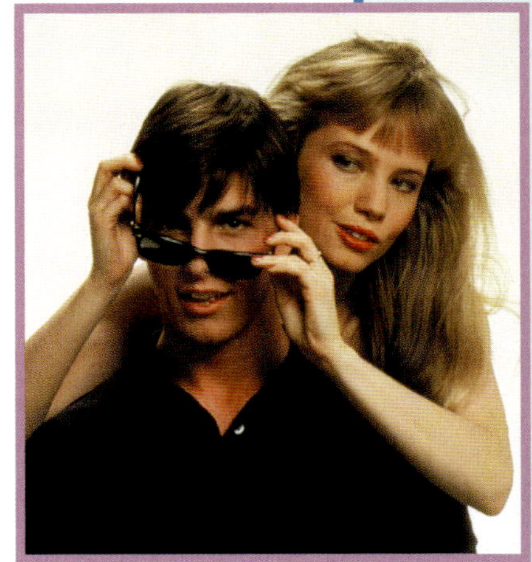

Rebecca De Mornay fools around with Tom Cruise's *Risky Business* Ray-Bans.

PROVOCATEURS AND ICONOCLASTS

Brian De Palma's career had exploded with his 1976 adaptation of Stephen King's *Carrie*, but the next decade was his most fertile creative period. It was, though, not without its challenges, many of which were brought on by De Palma's choices of subject matter and public attitude. With ostentatious stories of violence, crime, and sex, his films often felt antithetical to the demure moral climate of the Reagan era, and he could be combative about it.

De Palma is a movie buff's director, sort of an American Jean-Luc Godard who embraces playful techniques like the use of split diopter lenses and slow-motion shots while making overt and loving references to classic filmmakers like Alfred Hitchcock and Sergei Eisenstein. His joy of making movies spills over and pours off the screen, making it difficult to not appreciate his boldness—even if his movies stretch the bounds of reason or believability. His films contain, in addition to elements that are pulpy and controversial, set pieces of incredible virtuosity.

Because of *Carrie*, De Palma entered the 1980s with a reputation as a horror director. So when *Dressed to Kill* (1980) was released, that was the lens through which the film was viewed. With a nod toward *Psycho* (1960), he tells the story of a woman (Angie Dickinson) who is murdered by a mysterious patient of her psychiatrist (Michael Caine) and the call girl (Nancy Allen) who becomes embroiled in the crime. The film drew criticism for its controversial depiction of a transgender character and reputed misogyny, but at the same time many critics praised its stylistic prowess. "Has any other moviemaker mastered new skills with each picture the way Brian De Palma has?" asked Pauline Kael. "Now, in his thirteenth feature film, he has become a true visual storyteller."

His next film was a tour de force. *Blow Out* (1981) is about a movie sound designer (John Travolta) who intervenes in a car crash and later discovers—thanks to his audio recording—that it may not have been an accident. The film is an homage to *Blow-Up* (1966) by Italian director Michelangelo Antonioni, in which a photographer believes he shot a murder, and follows in the tradition of political paranoia films of the Watergate era. Politics is on the surface in *Blow Out*, with the hero's obsession echoing the frame-by-frame analysis of the Zapruder film and the car crash suggestive of the Chappaquiddick affair. Set on "Liberty Day" in Philadelphia, the film climaxes with fireworks and a pair of grisly deaths.

Scarface (1983), meanwhile, played into domestic paranoia about dangerous immigrants flooding American shores, with its saga of Cuban mobsters, cocaine, and murder. An opening title card references the mass migration of the 1980 Mariel boatlift, during which the film's antihero Tony Montana (Al Pacino) arrives in Miami. "Of the 125,000 refugees that landed in Florida, an estimated 25,000 had criminal records." The opportunistic Tony rises from obscurity to become a ferocious drug kingpin, through what

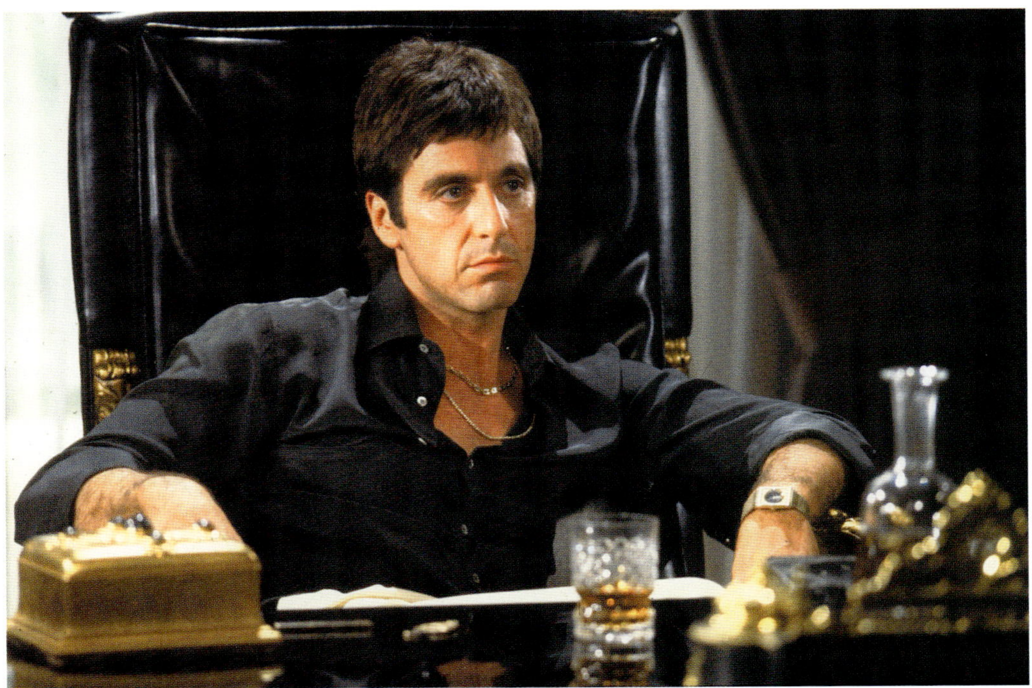

Al Pacino in *Scarface*.

producer Martin Bregman called "operatic, over-the-top" sequences of shocking violence. Throughout, De Palma and writer Oliver Stone spin a dark tale about the American dream and society's relationship to crime. "You need people like me," Tony growls to a restaurant full of rich clientele, "so you can point your fucking fingers and say, 'That's the bad guy!'" The film inspired Martin Scorsese to tell Steven Bauer, one of the film's actors, "They're going to hate it in Hollywood . . . because it's about them."

After the Motion Picture Association of America (MPAA) threatened his gangster epic with an X rating, De Palma told *Esquire*, "As soon as I get this dignity from *Scarface* I'm going to go out and make an X-rated suspense porn picture. . . . I'm sick of being censored. . . . So if they want an X, they'll get a real X. They wanna see suspense, they wanna see terror, they wanna see SEX—I'm the person for the job." And so came *Body Double* (1984), a murder mystery set in the shadowy world of adult entertainment, starring Bauer's wife, Melanie Griffith. The film's study of voyeurism borrowed liberally from Hitchcock's *Rear Window* (1954) and *Vertigo* (1958), and certain scenes of violence rivaled that of *Scarface*. But whereas the gangster film had been a hit, *Body Double* failed to find a wide audience. The same was true for his Mob comedy *Wise Guys* (1986), an example of a CAA package film where the services of actors Danny DeVito and Joe Piscopo, along with De Palma, the writer, and the producer, were sold to MGM collectively.

Again, De Palma found success with a gangster drama, *The Untouchables* (1987), which chronicled the pursuit of Al Capone (Robert De Niro) by FBI agent Eliot Ness (Kevin Costner) in Prohibition-era Chicago. The script was written by playwright and Windy City native David Mamet, but the film's most iconic scene was a De Palma contribution. Mimicking the iconic "Odessa Steps" sequence in the Soviet landmark *Battleship Potemkin* (1925), a baby stroller bounces dangerously down a staircase in Union Station in the midst of gunfire. "Eliot Ness has to get the guy and protect the innocent simultaneously. And suddenly, somehow, *Potemkin* popped into my head," explained De Palma. "*The Untouchables* is essentially about how the innocent get slaughtered in the conflict of the gangsters."

When his next film *Casualties of War* opened in 1989, the *New York Times* proclaimed De Palma "a director who, by all the available evidence, is at the height of his career." The new Vietnam-set film would disappoint at the box office, as would a higher-profile flop, *The Bonfire of the Vanities*, in 1990. But the director had made his mark with a series of daring and provocative movies that wore their film literacy on their sleeve like few others in the 1980s. "I never went out to be famous," he told *Esquire*. "If you just want to be famous, it's better to go out and shoot somebody.... I want to be *infamous*. I want to be *controversial*. It's much more colorful."

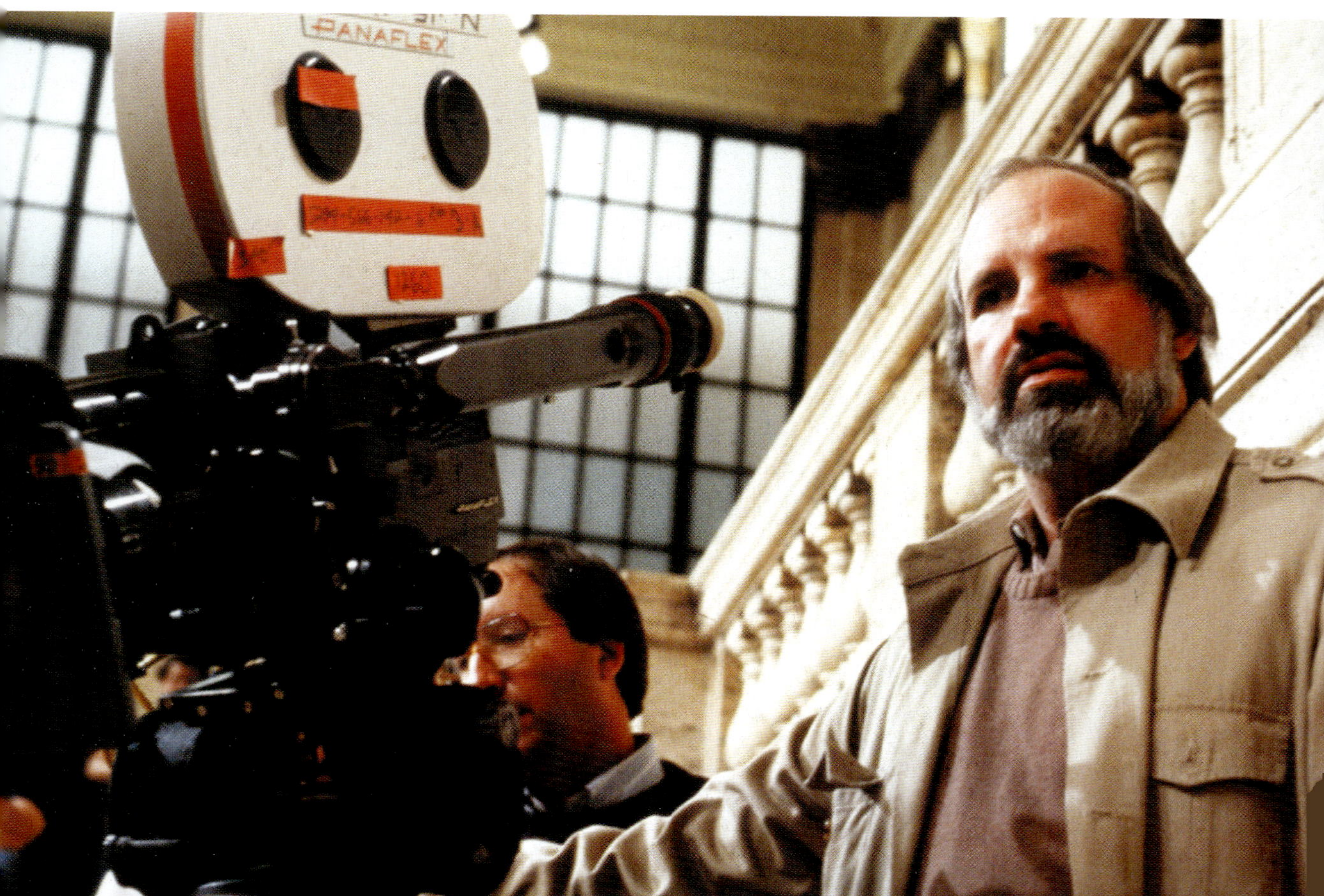

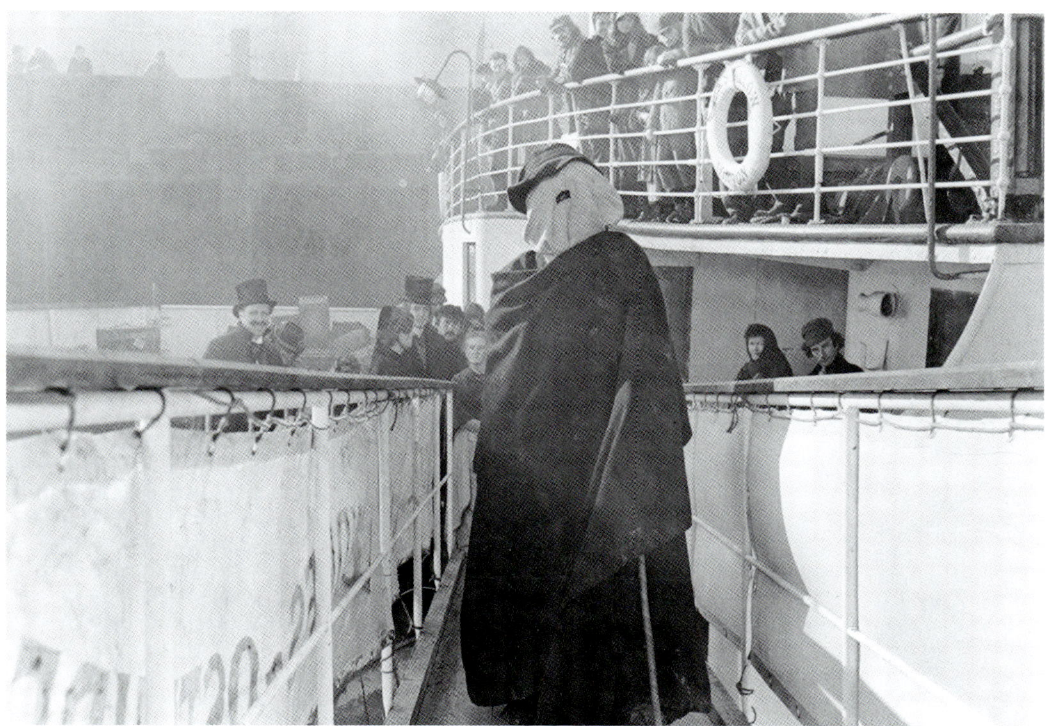

John Hurt portrayed the title role in *The Elephant Man.*

David Lynch's low-budget black-and-white surrealist film *Eraserhead* (1977) is not your average movie. But when Mel Brooks saw it, he thought the director of the "odd little picture" might be ideal for his new project. "My films, even if they're comic, they're about: 'Let's accept the bizarre. Let's learn more about these creatures, or these Jews,'" Brooks said in 2008. "I know the Elephant Man wasn't Jewish, but, to me, the story had all the aspects of antisemitism."

The Elephant Man (1980) was an atmospheric, brooding, sometimes carnivalesque depiction of Victorian London. With a sympathetic main character in the physically deformed John Merrick (John Hurt), it's one of Lynch's most emotionally resonant films, with a "triumph of the human spirit" narrative that overcomes its German Expressionist influences. Mel Brooks's wife, Anne Bancroft, plays a key supporting role, along with venerable British actors Anthony Hopkins, John Gielgud, and Wendy Hiller, though Brooks removed his name from the credits so as not to confuse audiences about what kind of movie they were about to see.

Dune came to Lynch through producer Dino De Laurentiis, who offered him the epic sci-fi project after several failed attempts at adapting Frank Herbert's celebrated 1965 novel had already been made. The story of young Paul Atreides (Kyle MacLachlan) who becomes a messianic figure for a resource-rich desert planet was a sprawling, visually striking, and ultimately campy film that failed to impress critics or audiences. Lynch, to his deep regret, did not ask for

Director Brian De Palma on the set of *The Untouchables.*

final-cut privileges on the project, which meant the studio pursued its own agenda in postproduction. "For some reason, I thought everything would be OK. . . . And as it turned out, *Dune* wasn't the film I wanted to make, because I didn't have a final say," he told NPR decades later. "Why would anyone work for three years on something that wasn't yours? Why? Why do that? Why? I died a death."

In hindsight, *Dune* is a good example of what the auteur theory can do for movies that were received badly in their time or were otherwise negligible. It's not that critics were necessarily wrong in their dismissals (Roger Ebert called it "a real mess . . . incomprehensible, ugly, unstructured, pointless") but rather that *Dune*'s peculiarity has been made more interesting by what its director has accomplished since. Lynch's film is no longer just an aberration; when speaking of a director who now shows a formal rigor, a capacity for tonal control, and a unique authorial style, one can look at their past foibles as experiments in the service of a larger vision.

The road to this reevaluation began with *Blue Velvet*, which was produced and distributed by De Laurentiis at a fraction of the budget of *Dune*, thus allowing Lynch full creative control. Kyle MacLachlan again stars as an upstanding college student who discovers that his idyllic hometown is teeming with crime and moral decay—personified by a drug-addled gangster (Dennis Hopper) with sadomasochistic sexual fetishes. Is *Blue Velvet* a dark fable? A cautionary tale? A documentary? According to Sheila Benson, the film "takes us behind the working-class American facade, beneath the Technicolor grass, literally underground to the churning turmoil of black, shiny beetles below. It's there. It's always there, Lynch says, if you only look and listen."

At the beginning of the '80s, Canadian director David Cronenberg had a minor hit with his underground sci-fi film *Scanners* (1981) about people with powerful forms of telepathy. It included at least one mind-blowing shot—literally, a head explodes on-screen—and earned the director serious body-horror street cred.

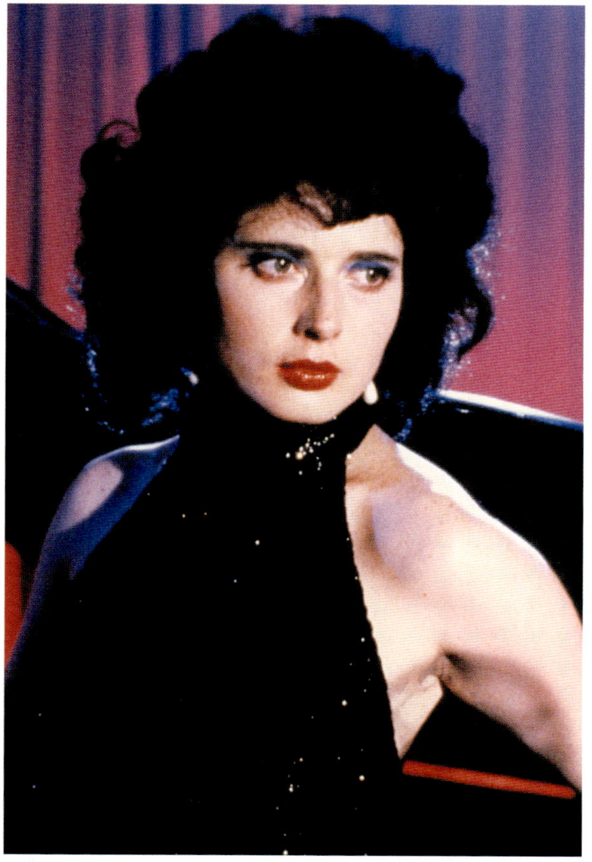

Isabella Rossellini takes the stage in *Blue Velvet*.

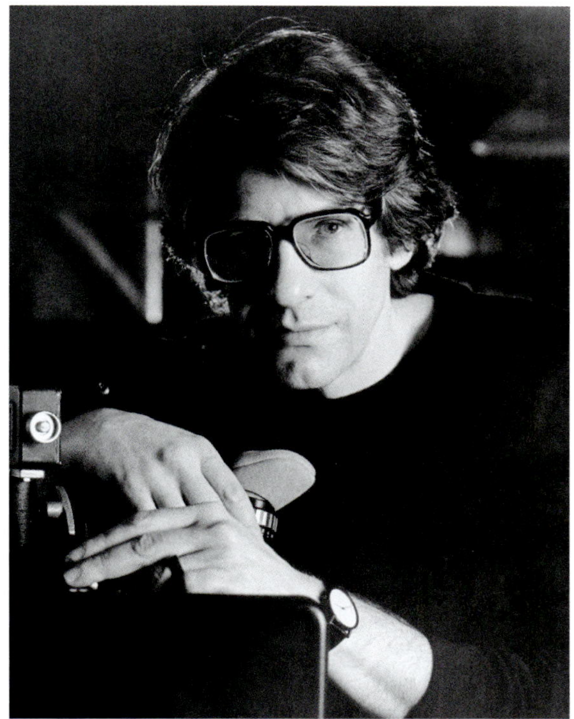

Director David Cronenberg.

He put that reputation to good use with his first studio film, *Videodrome* (1983), which is a landmark not just for its vivid depiction of bodily trauma but also for its exploration of society's relationship to the media. It stars James Woods as the head of a Toronto television station that specializes in "softcore pornography and hardcore violence." Always on the lookout for stimulating programming, he is introduced to a disturbingly graphic show whose broadcast signal causes hallucinations in its viewers. Cue some eye-popping practical effects, designed by the decade's top makeup artist, Rick Baker, including a breathing TV set and a stomach that receives Betamax tapes. "My films tend to be very body conscious," Cronenberg said. "I gradually realized that I was more interested in the things that happen inside you, mentally and physically, than I was in a kind of exterior threat."

He next made films with two of David Lynch's producers. De Laurentiis hired him for the Stephen King adaptation *The Dead Zone* (1983), in which a teacher (Christopher Walken) awakens from a five-year coma with psychic abilities. *The Fly* (1986), about a scientist (Jeff Goldblum) whose experiments with teleportation go awry, was produced by Mel Brooks, who again took his name off the film's credits because of its darker subject matter. Goldblum's costar was his then girlfriend, Geena Davis, playing a woman whose romantic partner is slowly turning into a hideous insect. Though it's presented as a gory sci-fi film, Cronenberg says it's

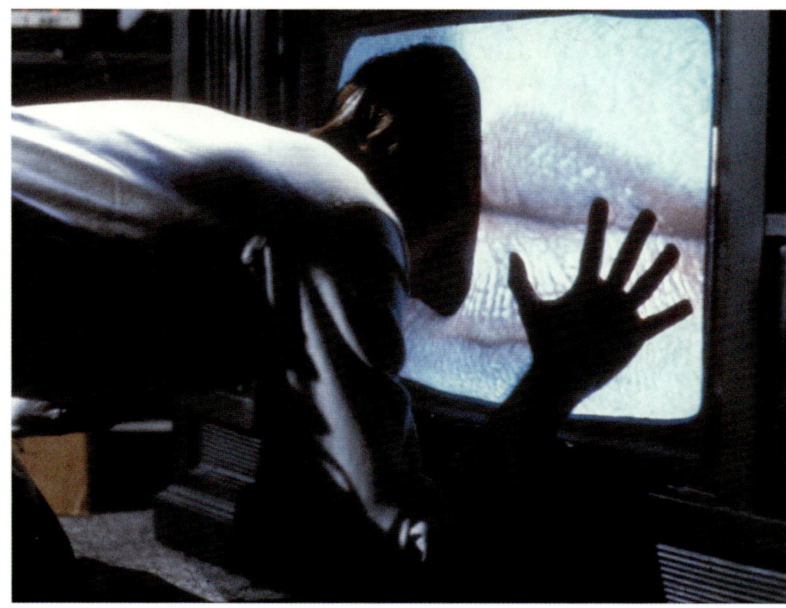

James Woods becomes one with his television in *Videodrome*.

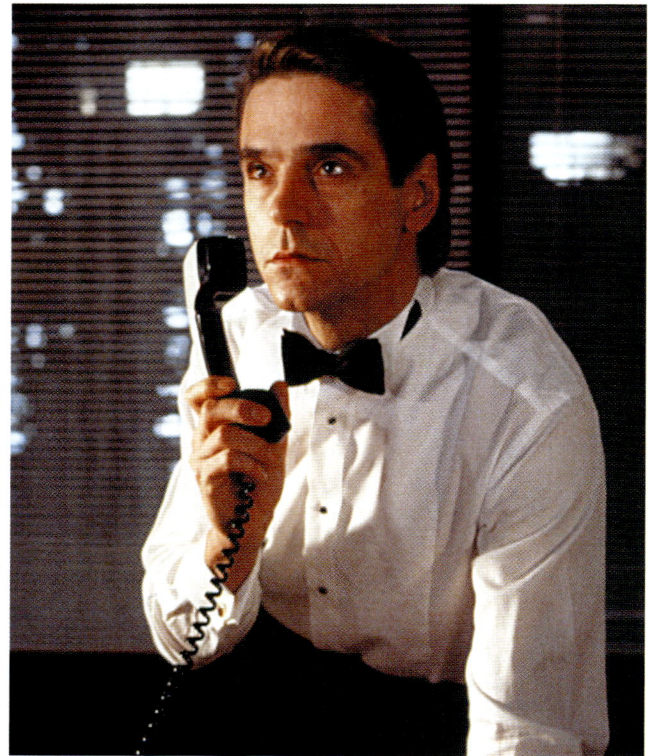

Jeremy Irons in *Dead Ringers*.

really about mortality. "This movie, if it were made as a straight drama, would never have gotten made, because it's really quite depressing," he said. "Try to sell somebody on a movie about two attractive, eccentric people who fall in love and then one of them contracts a hideous wasting disease and the other one watches as he deteriorates . . . this is a tough sell for a movie." It was, in fact, a big hit.

In *Dead Ringers* (1988), Jeremy Irons gives one (or perhaps two) of the most impressive performances of the '80s as identical-twin gynecologists—opposites in personality—who seduce and share their unwitting patients. "Mr. Cronenberg has shaped a startling tale of physical and psychic disintegration, pivoting on the twins' hopeless interdependence and playing havoc with the viewer's grip on reality," wrote Janet Maslin. "It's a mesmerizing achievement, as well as a terrifically unnerving one."

American-born animator Terry Gilliam joined the British comedy troupe Monty Python in the 1960s and made his directorial debut with the cult classic *Monty Python and the Holy Grail* (1975). He followed up with the fanciful *Jabberwocky* (1977) and *Time Bandits* (1981), before making his most celebrated film, *Brazil* (1985)—the first to be completed with studio financing. It presents an absurdist dystopia about a machine-obsessed society in which a clerical error causes the wrong man to be arrested for terrorism. A well-meaning bureaucrat (Jonathan Pryce) tries to remedy the situation but gets drawn into a doom spiral of government repression and ineptitude. The film was hailed by US film critics who were able to screen a rough cut, despite Universal's refusal to release it in its current form. "Films are like flares fired up from a lifeboat to see if anyone else is out there," Gilliam told the *Los Angeles Times*. "*Brazil* was made for America. It's my message in the bottle." It was finally released in December 1985, only after it won the LA Film Critics Circle award for Best Film. He rounded out the decade with another ambitious fantasy, *The Adventures of Baron Munchausen* (1988), completing what has since been called a "Trilogy of Imagination."

Another notable animator turned director was Tim Burton, who worked at Disney in the early '80s on projects like *The Fox and the Hound* (1981) but later admitted that it wasn't a good

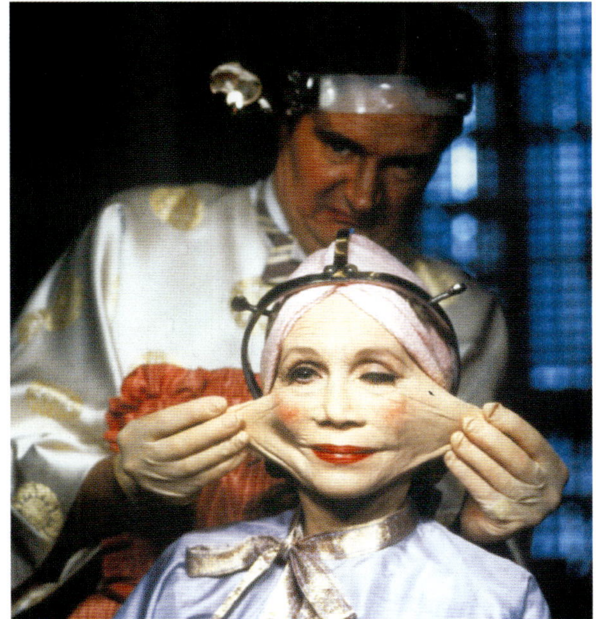

Jim Broadbent and Katherine Helmond in *Brazil*.

fit. "I was just not Disney material," he said. "I could not draw foxes for the life of me." After completing the live-action short *Frankenweenie* (1984), he was fired from Disney because the film's scary subject matter wasn't appropriate for children.

He went on to make three successful films in the '80s, kicking off a long career of whimsical creations. *Pee-wee's Big Adventure* (1985) was a vehicle for comedian Paul Reubens, whose childlike character Pee-wee Herman had debuted onstage years earlier and who would go on to a massively popular TV series in 1986. *Beetlejuice* (1988) was a dark comedy about a recently deceased couple (Geena Davis and Alec Baldwin) who hire a demented "bio-exorcist" (Michael Keaton) to scare off their home's new occupants. In line with Burton's past work, the film made liberal use of practical effects, prosthetic makeup, and stop-motion animation, lending a hand-crafted feel to the netherworld. Because of the box-office success of his first two films, Warner Bros. hired Burton for its 1989 tentpole release, *Batman*—and he delivered. The director's offbeat sense of humor worked well for the caped crusader, as portrayed by Keaton, and he turned Gotham City into a shadowy film-noir purgatory. In addition to being a milestone in mise-en-scène, *Batman* was a massive blockbuster and set the template for superhero films to come.

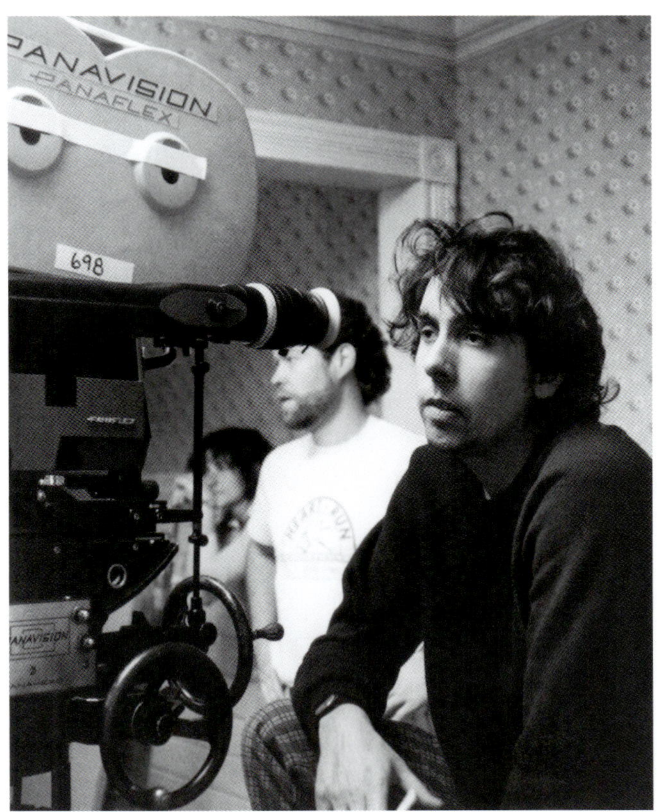

Director Tim Burton on the set of *Beetlejuice*.

Beyond Hollywood: The United Kingdom and Ireland

"The British are coming!" screenwriter Colin Welland cheekily declared when he collected his Oscar for *Chariots of Fire* (1981). The inspirational sports drama soon shocked the audience by winning Best Picture, and the next year's *Gandhi* (1982), an epic biopic about the Indian national hero from actor turned director Richard Attenborough, took home eight more Oscars. In the world of prestige filmmaking, the British were ascendant.

At the same time, production was down in the '80s, due to lower ticket sales and the conservative government's repeal of the Eady Levy, which had helped subsidize filmmaking. As if longing for past greatness, many major films were historical in nature. *Gandhi*, along with James Ivory's *Heat and Dust* (1983), David Lean's *A Passage to India* (1984), and the TV miniseries *The Jewel in the Crown* (1984), was part of a wave of stories about colonial India—a phenomenon novelist Salman Rushdie called "a nostalgic twitch of an amputated limb."

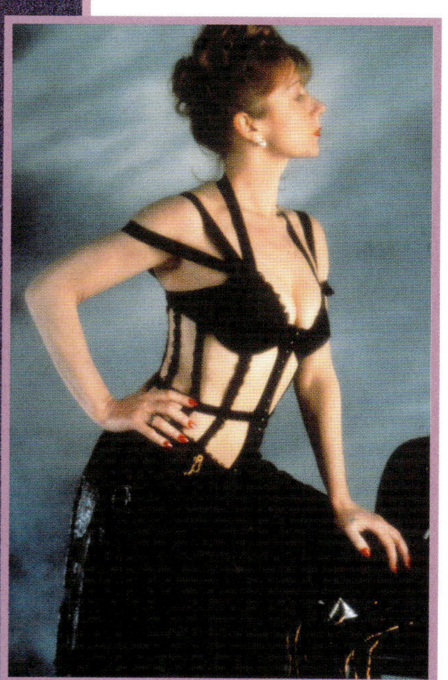

Helen Mirren in *The Cook, the Thief, His Wife & Her Lover*.

Indian producer Ismail Merchant and American director Ivory—partners in business and in life—became famous for literary costume fare like *The Bostonians* (1984), *A Room with a View* (1986), and *Maurice* (1987). John Boorman reached all the way back to mythical Britain with *Excalibur* (1981) and later dramatized his childhood during the London Blitz in the drama *Hope and Glory* (1987). Stephen Frears broke through with a pair of films about queer characters, *My Beautiful Laundrette* (1985) and *Prick Up Your Ears* (1987), but had his biggest hit with *Dangerous Liaisons* (1988), a mordant chamber drama about romance and revenge starring an American cast.

While Ken Russell produced extravagant thrillers like *Altered States* (1980), *Crimes of Passion* (1984),

Gothic (1986), and *The Lair of the White Worm* (1988), Peter Greenaway turned out cerebral and sensual social dramas like *The Draughtsman's Contract* (1982) and the deliciously unappetizing *The Cook, the Thief, His Wife & Her Lover* (1989). Hitting closer to home were "kitchen sink" directors Ken Loach (*Looks and Smiles* [1981]; the documentary *Which Side Are You On?* [1985]) and Mike Leigh (*Meantime* [1983]; *High Hopes* [1988]).

Former Beatle George Harrison and his business manager cofounded HandMade Films in the late '70s to distribute *Monty Python's Life of Brian* (1979). The company went on to produce a number of significant releases, including John Mackenzie's crime thriller *The Long Good Friday* (1980); Terry Gilliam's eccentric fantasy *Time Bandits* (1981); Malcolm Mowbray's satire of postwar rationing, *A Private Function* (1984); and Bruce Robinson's comedy *Withnail and I* (1987), about two unemployed actors on a drunken holiday weekend.

John Cleese and Michael Palin appeared in the irreverent sketch film *Monty Python's The Meaning of Life* (1983) and later reunited—with Jamie Lee Curtis and Kevin Kline—for the crime comedy *A Fish Called Wanda* (1988), the final film from veteran Ealing Studios director Charles Crichton.

Scottish director Bill Forsyth made two beloved comedies: *Gregory's Girl* (1980), about a football player who falls for his female teammate, and *Local Hero* (1983), about an American businessman sent to Scotland to buy a seaside town for his oil company. Irish director Neil Jordan's most celebrated '80s film was the HandMade Films production *Mona Lisa* (1986), with Bob Hoskins as an ex-con who develops feelings for the prostitute he's paid to chauffeur. Jim Sheridan's *My Left Foot* (1989) starred Daniel Day-Lewis in an Oscar-winning turn as disabled Irish painter Christy Brown.

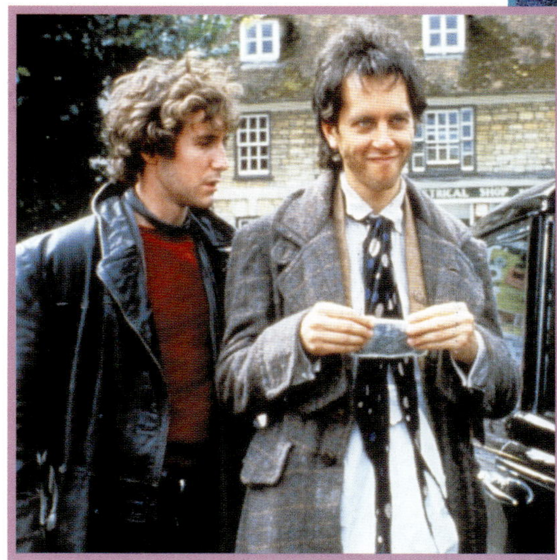

Withnail and I's Paul McGann and Richard E. Grant.

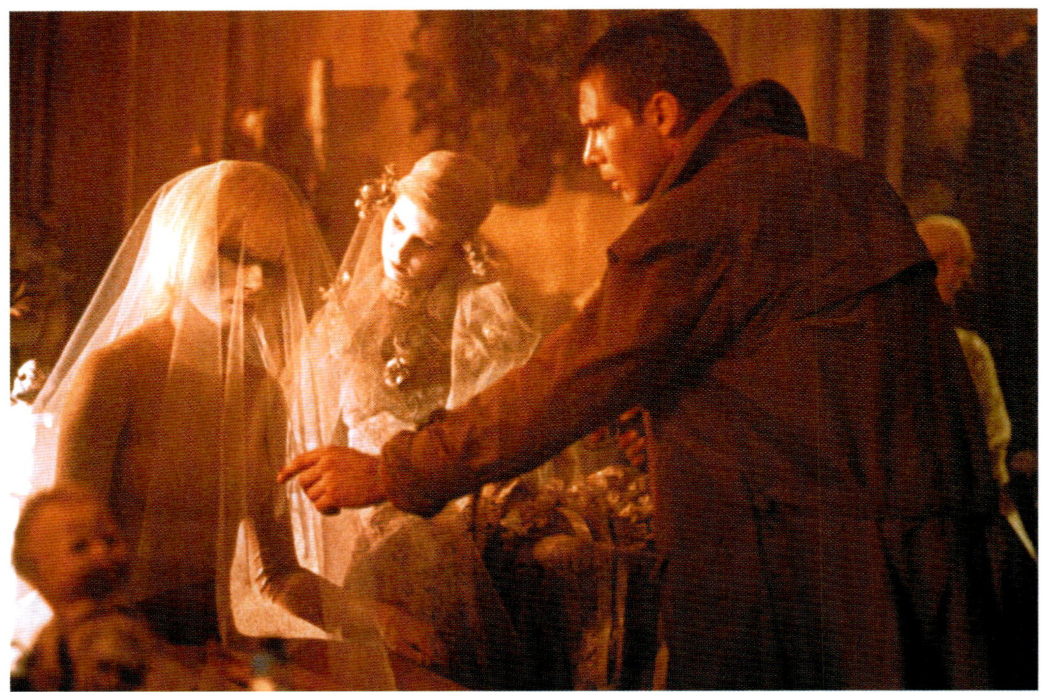

Daryl Hannah and Harrison Ford explore what it means to be alive in *Blade Runner*.

CRIME STORYTELLERS

Several rising filmmakers in the '80s were making landmark movies about criminality and dirty dealings. Writer-director Michael Mann's debut, *Thief* (1981), stars James Caan as an expert safe breaker and ex-con who tries to get his life back together by pulling off one last big score. After launching the hit NBC series *Miami Vice* in 1984, Mann made *Manhunter* (1986), the first adaptation of Thomas Harris's book series about serial killer Dr. Hannibal Lector, with Brian Cox as "Lektor" and William Petersen as an FBI agent who consults with him about another murderer on the loose.

Blade Runner (1982) wowed audiences with its grandiose, futuristic vision of Los Angeles (set in the year 2019) that plays host to the story of a retired cop (Harrison Ford) tasked with hunting down a rogue group of artificial humans known as "replicants." The main character also falls in love with one (Sean Young), leading Ford to joke, "It's a film about whether you can have a meaningful relationship with your toaster." In reality, English director Ridley Scott had crafted a skillful neo-noir and an enveloping visual experience that, while it didn't quite hit on its initial release, has since been recognized as a major moment in science-fiction cinema. His most seen work of the decade may have been his big-budget commercial for Apple's Macintosh computer, which aired during the Super Bowl broadcast of January 1984. In its one-minute running time, a young woman disrupts an Orwellian society of inhuman conformity by taking a sledgehammer to its Big Brother–style overlord.

Box-Office Champs

Forget awards, or even respect. What Hollywood really wants is money, baby. The decade is known for its roster of action and sci-fi spectacles, but they alone don't tell the full story of the domestic box office. Listed below are the number-one moneymakers for each year, along with their initial US grosses.

1980—*The Empire Strikes Back* ($209 million)

1981—*Raiders of the Lost Ark* ($212 million)

1982—*E.T. the Extra-Terrestrial* ($359 million)

1983—*Return of the Jedi* ($252 million)

1984—*Beverly Hills Cop* ($234 million)

1985—*Back to the Future* ($211 million)

1986—*Top Gun* ($176 million)

1987—*Three Men and a Baby* ($167 million)

1988—*Rain Man* ($172 million)

1989—*Batman* ($251 million)

Three Men and a Baby opened on Thanksgiving weekend in 1987 and spent fifteen weeks in the box office top-five.

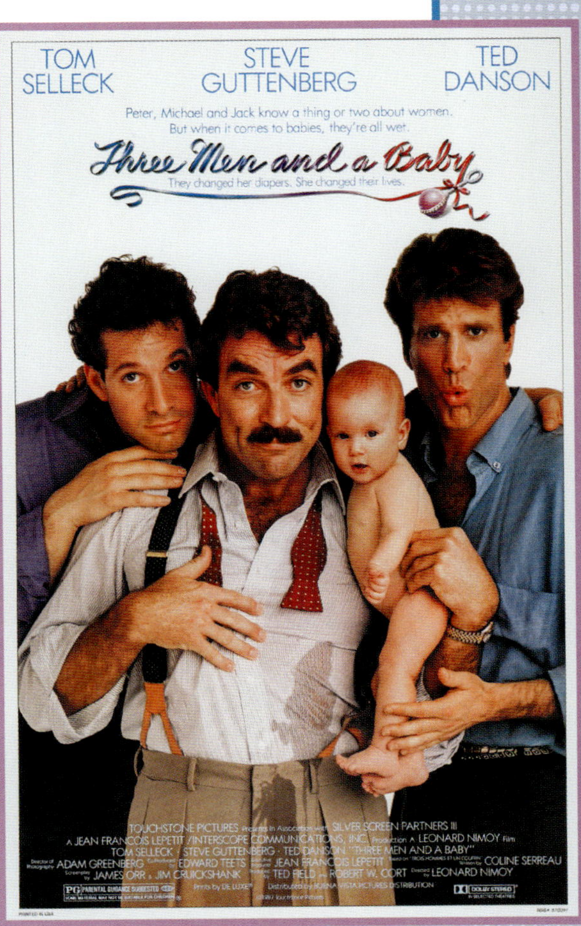

Scott's fellow Englishman Adrian Lyne, director of *Foxes* (1980) and *Flashdance* (1983), is best known for a series of erotic thrillers that began in the 1980s with *9½ Weeks* (1986), in which Mickey Rourke and Kim Basinger embark on an adventurous affair. Next came the box-office sensation *Fatal Attraction* (1987) about a Manhattan lawyer (Michael Douglas) whose weekend fling with a business acquaintance (Glenn Close) leads to a dangerous obsession that threatens to upend his life. The film struck a chord with audiences, with commentators noting societal paranoia about the dangers of sex in the AIDS era. *People* magazine cataloged some additional interpretations: "a put-down of women, perverse proof of women's liberation, trash, a retrograde portrait of sex-loving women as loony sluts, Frankenstein for Freudians, every philanderer's nightmare, and a neo-Biblical injunction against messing around if you value your loved ones." It also became a cultural touchstone, netting Lyne an Oscar nomination.

Jonathan Demme's films are harder to categorize. After the offbeat dramedy *Melvin and Howard* (1980), about the unlikely heir to Howard Hughes's fortune, and the wartime romance *Swing Shift* (1984) with Goldie Hawn and Kurt Russell, he turned his camera to the Talking Heads with the celebrated concert film *Stop Making Sense* (1984) and a pair of crime capers that continued to increase his stature in the industry. In the screwball comedy *Something Wild* (1986), a young tax consultant (Jeff Daniels) is kidnapped by a freewheeling eccentric (Melanie Griffith) with an ex-convict husband (Ray Liotta). *Married to the Mob* (1988) starred Michelle Pfeiffer as a gangster's widow who tries to leave behind his world of crime. Demme's next picture would be the Oscar-winning thriller *The Silence of the Lambs* (1991).

COMEDY AUTEURS

Other filmmakers specialized in comedies, with few as successful—or as notorious—as John Landis, director of *National Lampoon's Animal House* (1978). After that smash hit, his first release was *The Blues Brothers* (1980), a raucous, music-filled extension of the popular *Saturday Night Live* sketch about besuited siblings Jake and Elwood Blues (John Belushi and Dan Aykroyd). His biggest hits of the '80s would feature other *SNL* alumni, most notably Eddie Murphy in *Trading Places* (1983) and *Coming to America* (1988). Chevy Chase joined Aykroyd for *Spies Like Us* (1985) and then costarred with Steve Martin and Martin Short in *Three Amigos!* (1986)—cowritten by *SNL* creator Lorne Michaels. Landis also lent a humorous edge to material that wasn't strictly comedic, like *An American Werewolf in London* (1981). But his achievements were threatened to be overshadowed by criminal charges relating to *Twilight Zone: The Movie*, for which he was ultimately acquitted in 1987.

Controversy would come later for New York comedy icon Woody Allen. The 1980s were a key period of creative and financial prosperity

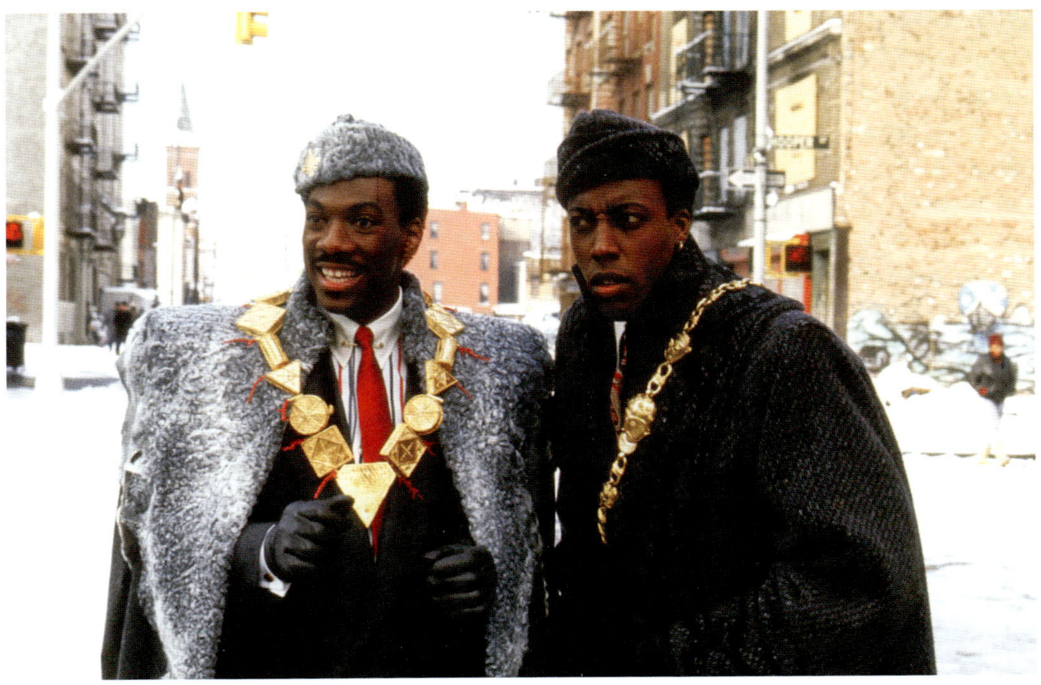

Eddie Murphy and Arsenio Hall arrive in Queens, NY, in *Coming to America*.

for the Oscar-winning writer-director of *Annie Hall* (1977). While his early films had displayed a zanier, absurdist brand of humor, he entered the new decade on an experimental streak, with the Fellini-inspired *Stardust Memories* (1980) about a famous filmmaker with a creative block and the inventive mockumentary *Zelig* (1983) that explores the chameleon-like existence of a mysterious 1920s man—a sly commentary on one's desire to fit in. None of Allen's films were blockbusters, but they were so consistent in their commercial performance that he was able to sign a multipicture deal with Orion that guaranteed him full creative freedom and 15 percent of the gross. He kept budgets low and used techniques like long takes that allowed for quicker shoots, preserved the dialogue as written, and made the editing process more efficient.

Occasionally, the films were not just witty, but also poignant and moving. His Depression-era comedy *The Purple Rose of Cairo* (1985) was about a wistful moviegoer (Mia Farrow) who begins a relationship with a dashing hero (Jeff Daniels) after he magically steps out of the screen. "I just met a wonderful new man," she says. "He's fictional, but you can't have everything." *Radio Days* (1987) was a lavish evocation of his 1940s childhood, and *Crimes and Misdemeanors* (1989) deftly explored the moral implications of one's actions, à la Dostoyevsky. But Allen's most well-received movie of the '80s was the sprawling family drama *Hannah and Her Sisters* (1986), which charts the winds of fortune for three siblings (played by Farrow, Barbara Hershey, and Dianne Wiest) across their various romantic and familial relationships. "With this

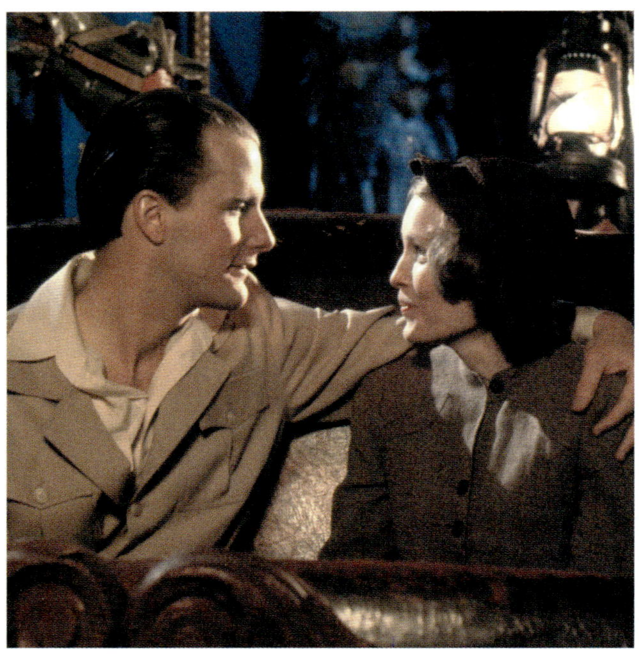

Jeff Daniels and Mia Farrow in *The Purple Rose of Cairo.*

film, it's apparent that Mr. Allen has become the urban poet of our anxious age," wrote Vincent Canby in the *New York Times*, "skeptical, guiltily bourgeois, longing for answers to impossible questions, but not yet willing to chuck a universe that can produce the Marx Brothers."

Another New Yorker who found success as both an actor and a director was *Laverne & Shirley* star Penny Marshall. Her feature film debut came with *Jumpin' Jack Flash* (1986), a Whoopi Goldberg espionage comedy that was already in preproduction when she was hired. Her second film was *Big* (1988), a modern fantasy about a dejected twelve-year-old who wishes to be "big" and wakes up the next day at age thirty. The film was a star vehicle for Tom Hanks who plays the naive kid stuck in a man's body and forced to navigate adult life without any of the wisdom that comes with experience. *Big* was a huge hit, the first movie directed by a woman to hit $100 million at the domestic box office. Penny's brother, Garry Marshall, also began his feature directing career in the '80s with comedies like *Young Doctors in Love* (1982) and *Overboard* (1987).

Television veteran James L. Brooks, creator of *The Mary Tyler Moore Show* and *Taxi*, made a pair of celebrated films in the '80s. First was *Terms of Endearment* (1983), a hilarious and refreshingly authentic mother-daughter drama starring Shirley MacLaine, Debra Winger, and Jack Nicholson, that won moviegoers' hearts and several major Academy Awards. He then tackled the world of live TV with *Broadcast News*

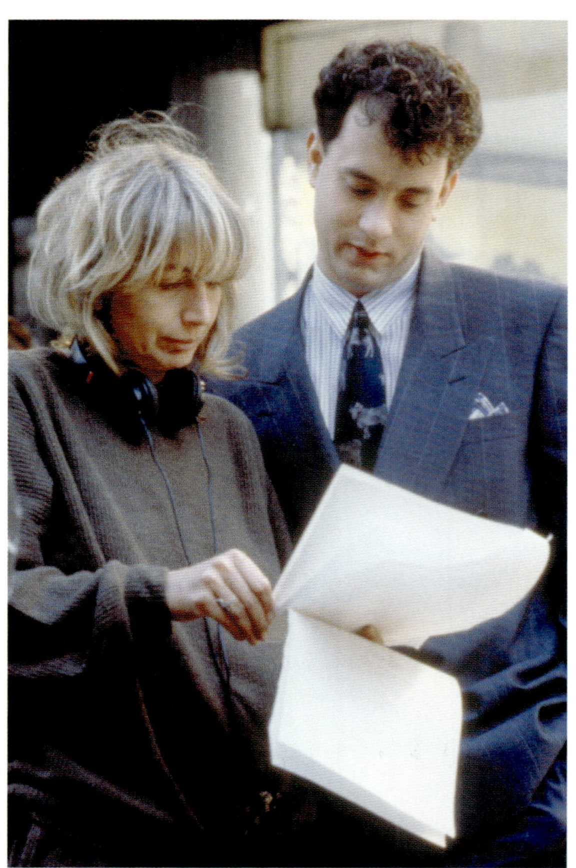

Penny Marshall directs Tom Hanks in *Big*.

(1987), with William Hurt and Albert Brooks (no relation) as competing news reporters and Holly Hunter as their workaholic producer. His long-running animated series *The Simpsons*, developed with creator Matt Groening, launched on Fox in December 1989.

Animal House cowriter Harold Ramis and producer Ivan Reitman collaborated on a series of hit comedies, including *Stripes* (1981), *Ghostbusters* (1984), and *Ghostbusters II* (1989). Reitman directed, while Ramis wrote and starred in all three—and also directed a couple of notable films of his own: *Caddyshack* (1980) and *National Lampoon's Vacation* (1983).

In addition to producing daring work by younger filmmakers, Mel Brooks directed two films in the decade—*History of the World, Part I* (1981) and *Spaceballs* (1987)—which lampooned historical epics and the *Star Wars* trilogy, respectively. His former comedy partner Carl Reiner released several popular films with star Steve Martin following their success with 1979's *The Jerk*, including the inventive film-noir spoof *Dead Men Don't Wear Plaid* (1982), *The Man with Two Brains* (1983), and *All of Me* (1984), in which Martin's character becomes possessed by the soul of a deceased millionaire (Lily Tomlin).

Mike Nichols, who had started out decades earlier in improv theater, had earned a reputation as one of the finest directors of actors in Hollywood. His films were mostly dramas, like the 1983 biopic *Silkwood* about an Oklahoma labor activist and nuclear-plant whistleblower (played by Meryl Streep). But his biggest hit

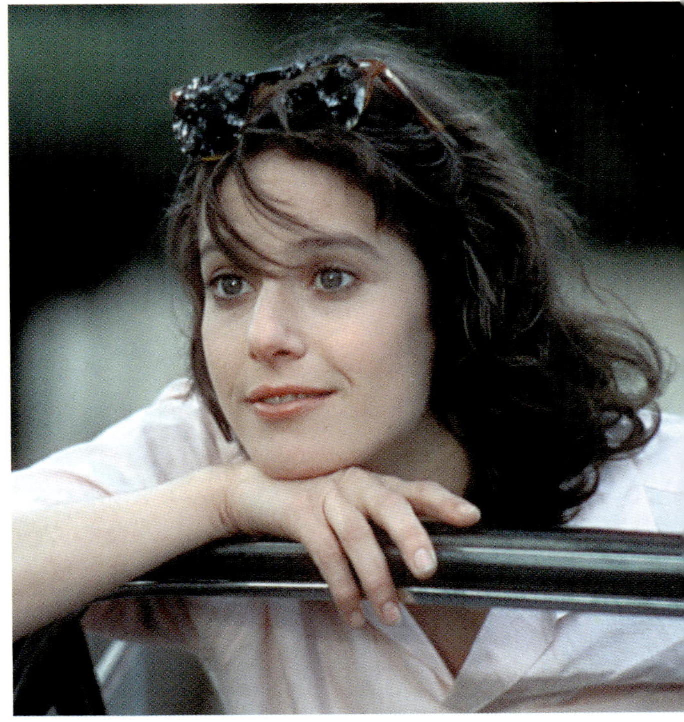

Debra Winger in *Terms of Endearment*.

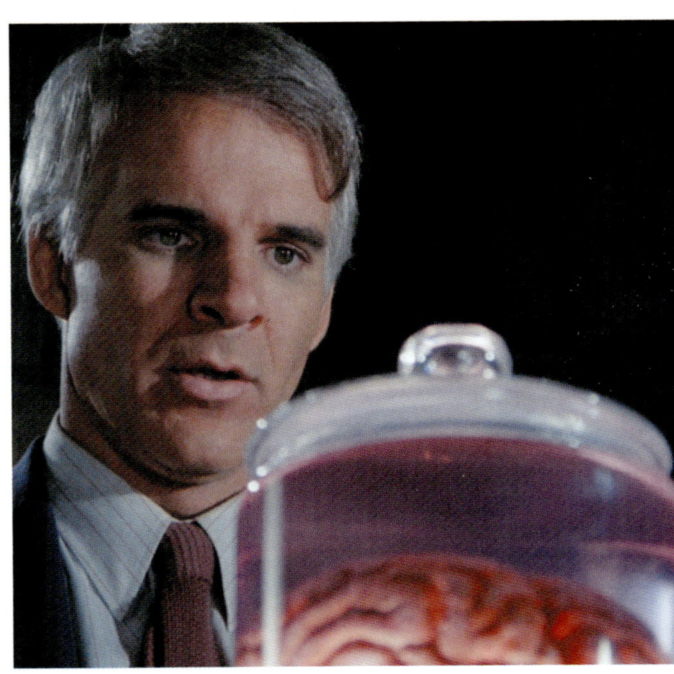

Steve Martin plays a surgeon in love with a telepathic brain in *The Man with Two Brains*.

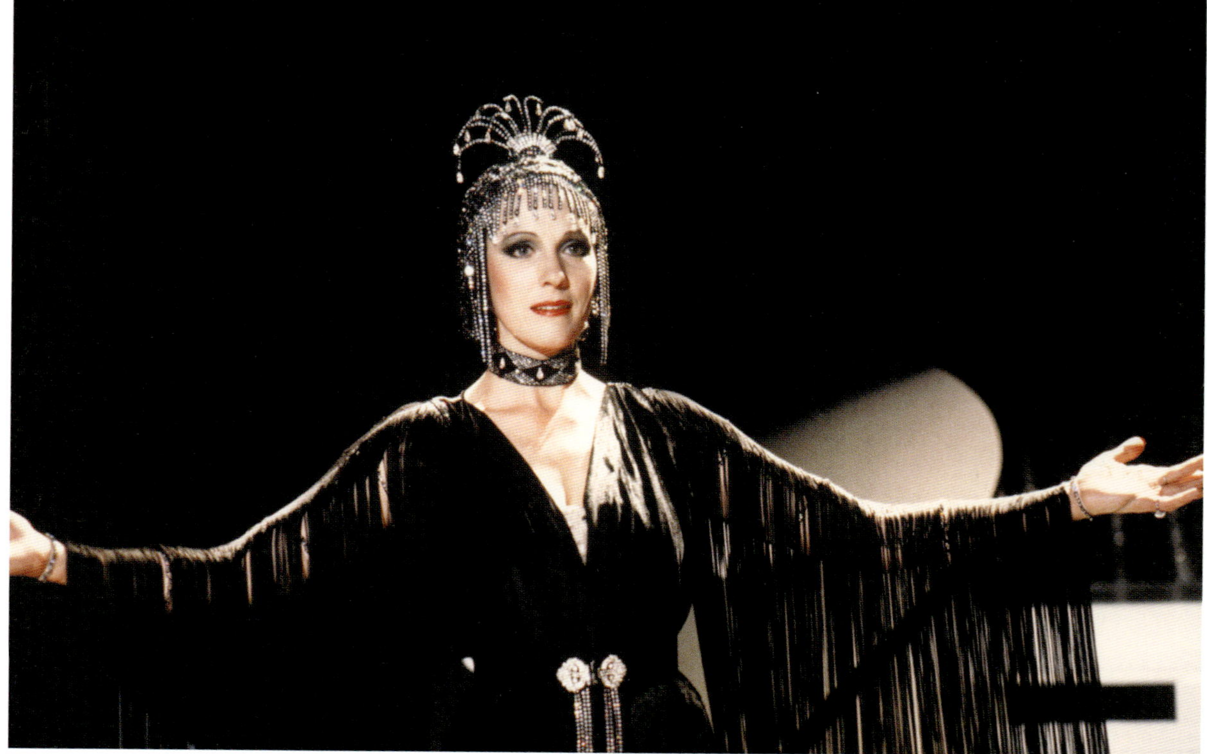

Julie Andrews in double drag in *Victor/Victoria*.

of the decade was the romantic comedy *Working Girl* (1988) about a Manhattan secretary (Melanie Griffith) who impersonates her boss (Sigourney Weaver) in order to climb the corporate ladder. Her beauty is alternately a help and a hindrance in the male-dominated world of finance. "I have a head for business and a bod for sin," she tells costar Harrison Ford. "Is there anything wrong with that?" Blake Edwards's *Victor/Victoria* (1982) also depicted a woman in a man's profession—or, rather, a woman playing a man playing a woman—as performed by his wife, Julie Andrews. The role of a down-on-her-luck cabaret singer in 1930s Paris who finds work as a female impersonator allowed Andrews to shine as both a musician and a comedienne.

WRITER-DIRECTORS

A number of prominent screenwriters wound up directing notable work in the 1980s, like Lawrence Kasdan, whose high-profile scripts for *The Empire Strikes Back* and *Raiders of the Lost Ark* allowed him to make a movie that was completely different but no less engaging—the Miami crime drama *Body Heat*. Across his filmography, intelligent and relatable characters (here played by William Hurt and Kathleen Turner) become anchors for the audience in what otherwise could be disorienting narratives set in unfamiliar worlds. *The Big Chill* (1983) was especially popular for its big cast—William Hurt, Kevin Kline, Glenn Close, Tom Berenger, Jeff Goldblum, Mary Kay Place, and JoBeth Williams—who portray a group of college friends who reunite for a funeral. Essentially a poignant "hangout" movie for disaffected boomers, it came with a classic '60s soundtrack.

Philip Kaufman had already directed several films by the time he assisted George Lucas with the story for *Raiders*. His films *The Right Stuff* (1983) and *The Unbearable Lightness of Being* (1988) likewise deal with historical material—the first with the space race and its roster of personalities that broke the sound barrier and manned NASA's Project Mercury, the second with the "Prague Spring" of 1968. An adaptation of Czech author Milan Kundera's novel starring Daniel Day-Lewis, Juliette Binoche, and Lena Olin, *The Unbearable Lightness of Being* is a literate and frequently sensual depiction of marriage behind the Iron Curtain, challenged by passion and politics.

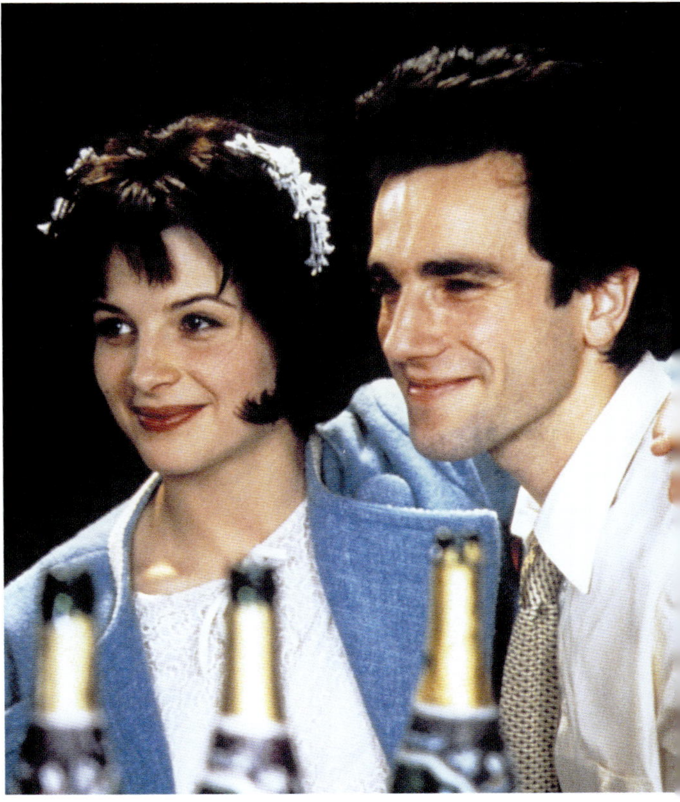

Juliette Binoche and Daniel Day-Lewis in *The Unbearable Lightness of Being*.

Robert Zemeckis and fellow USC graduate Bob Gale had the great fortune to be taken under the wing of Steven Spielberg, who helped produce their early work, *I Wanna Hold Your Hand* (1978) and *Used Cars* (1980), and for whom they wrote *1941*. It wasn't until Michael Douglas hired Zemeckis to direct the adventure film *Romancing the Stone* (1984) that his career really took off, at which point their script for *Back to the Future* (1985) was green-lit by Universal and became a blockbuster, spawning two sequels, an animated series, and a theme-park attraction. Often working at the forefront of film technology, Zemeckis took a bold leap with his Amblin-produced, live-action/animation hybrid feature *Who Framed Roger Rabbit* (1988), which envisioned a 1940s Hollywood populated by both mobsters and cartoons.

Baltimore native Barry Levinson began as a writer for TV variety shows and Mel Brooks films—*Silent Movie* (1976) and *High Anxiety* (1977)—before directing his own work with the breakout hit *Diner* (1982). In it, a group of former high school buddies reunite for a wedding, and much of their time together is spent at the local greasy spoon, where they compare notes on life and relationships. Levinson's career quickly took off—from the Robert Redford baseball film *The Natural* (1984), to the kids' mystery *Young Sherlock Holmes* (1985), to the Robin Williams war comedy *Good Morning, Vietnam* (1987). His

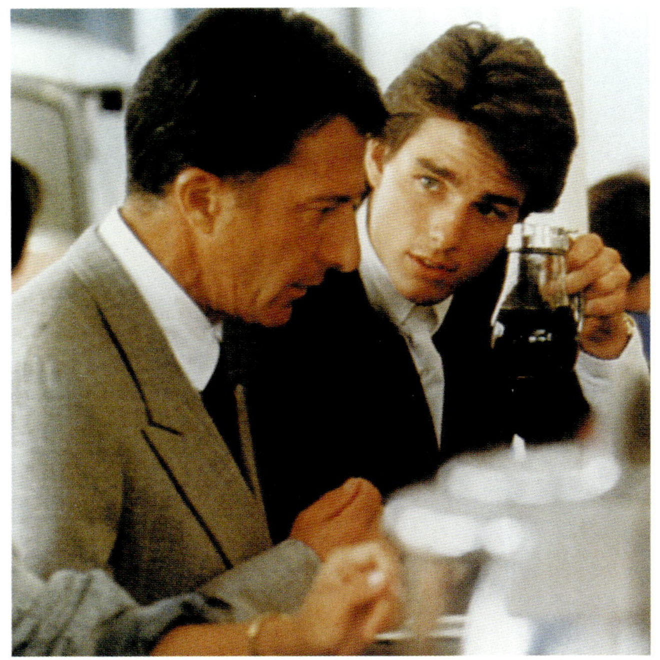

Dustin Hoffman and Tom Cruise bond in *Rain Man*.

biggest success, however, was *Rain Man* (1988), the story of two estranged brothers, one with autism (Dustin Hoffman) and the other filled with resentment (Tom Cruise), who bond during a cross-country road trip. It was the year's biggest box-office hit and its Best Picture winner.

Oliver Stone also won a pair of Oscars in the '80s, for his Vietnam War films *Platoon* (1986) and *Born on the Fourth of July* (1989). Having started out as a writer (his first Oscar was for the screenplay to the 1978 prison film *Midnight Express*), he worked on scripts as diverse as *Conan the Barbarian* (1982), De Palma's *Scarface*, and Michael Cimino's *Year of the Dragon* (1985). Before *Platoon*, he wrote and directed the horror film *The Hand* (1981) and *Salvador* (1986), about a freelance journalist (James Woods) who travels to Central America to cover the Salvadoran civil war. His later films *Wall Street* (1987), with Michael Douglas and Charlie Sheen as high-rolling traders, and *Talk Radio* (1988), with Eric

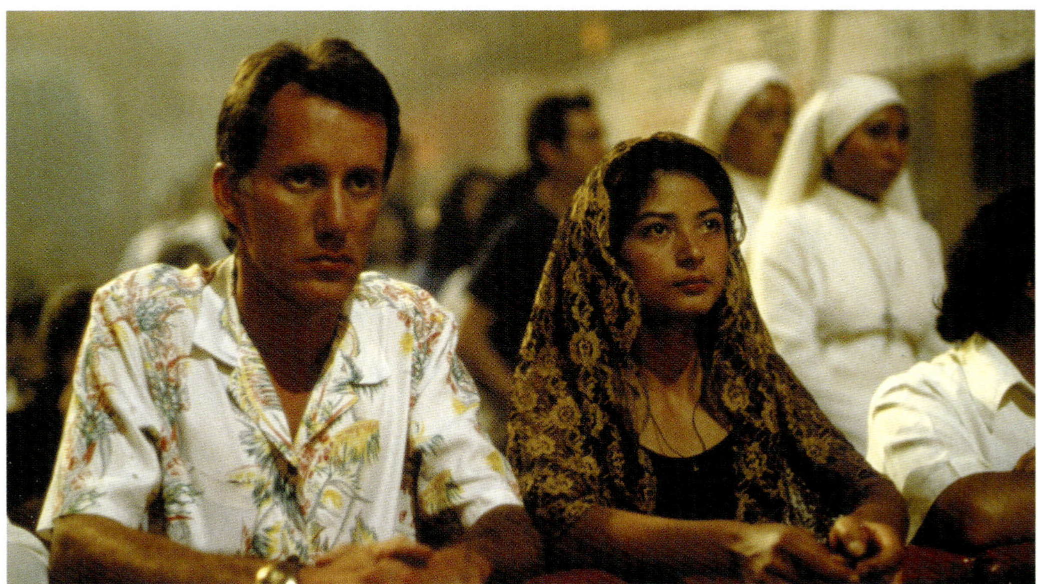

James Woods and Elpidia Carrillo in *Salvador*.

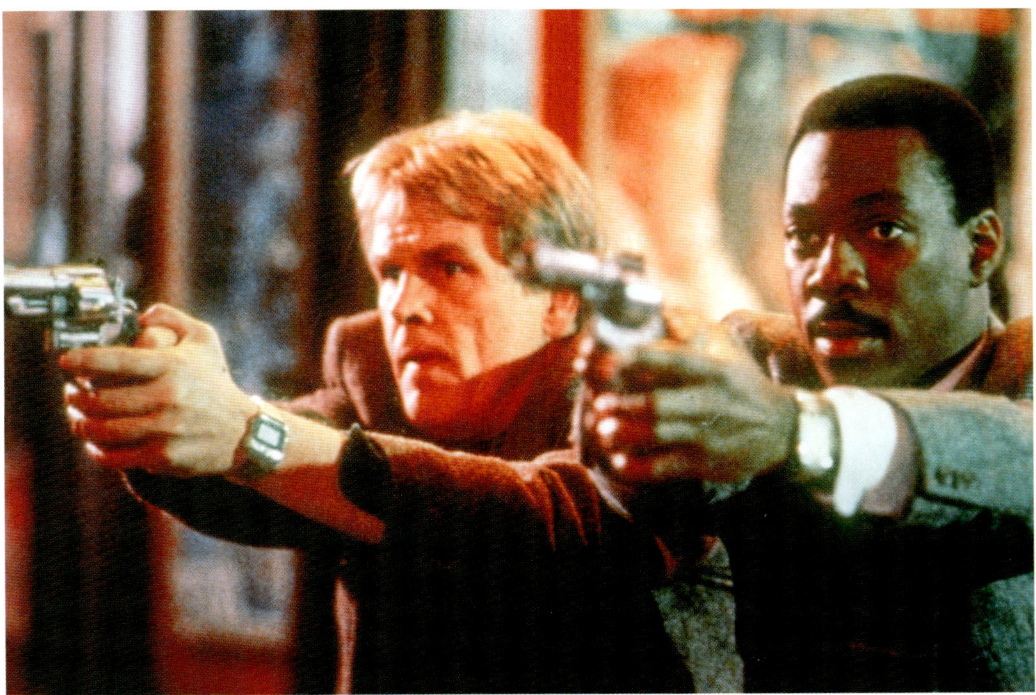

Nick Nolte and Eddie Murphy partner up in *48 Hrs.*

Bogosian as a self-destructive talk-show host, examined the darker aspects of American culture.

John Milius, part of what George Lucas dubbed the "USC Mafia," had been credited for the screenplay of *Apocalypse Now* (1979) and went uncredited on several scripts in the '80s, including treatments of *Indiana Jones and the Temple of Doom* and *Sudden Impact* (1983), which gave "Dirty" Harry Callahan (Clint Eastwood) the immortal line, "Go ahead, make my day." Milius told the *Chicago Tribune* in 1988, "I call myself romantic. I believe in a lot of 19th-century ideals: chivalry, honor, loyalty, romantic love." That sentiment might explain his sense of brute heroism in the films he directed—*Conan the Barbarian*, *Red Dawn* (1984), and *Farewell to the King* (1989).

Though *The Warriors* (1979), a story about teenage gangs in New York, is arguably the film writer-director Walter Hill is most associated with, his work in the 1980s—while eclectic—is no less interesting. His follow-up was another gang story of sorts, *The Long Riders* (1980), about Jesse James and his band of Old West robbers. *Southern Comfort* (1981) was a Vietnam allegory set in the swamps of Louisiana. "No Walter Hill film—not even the good ones—is ever about what it seems to be," wrote Vincent Canby. "And he never lets you forget it." The buddy-cop movie *48 Hrs.* paired Nick Nolte and Eddie Murphy (in his debut), while *Streets of Fire* (1984) was a vibrant mix of *Blade Runner* and *Grease* (1978). Next was a remake of *Brewster's Millions* (1985), in which a Minor League ballplayer (Richard Pryor) is challenged to spend $30 million in thirty days in order to inherit a much larger fortune.

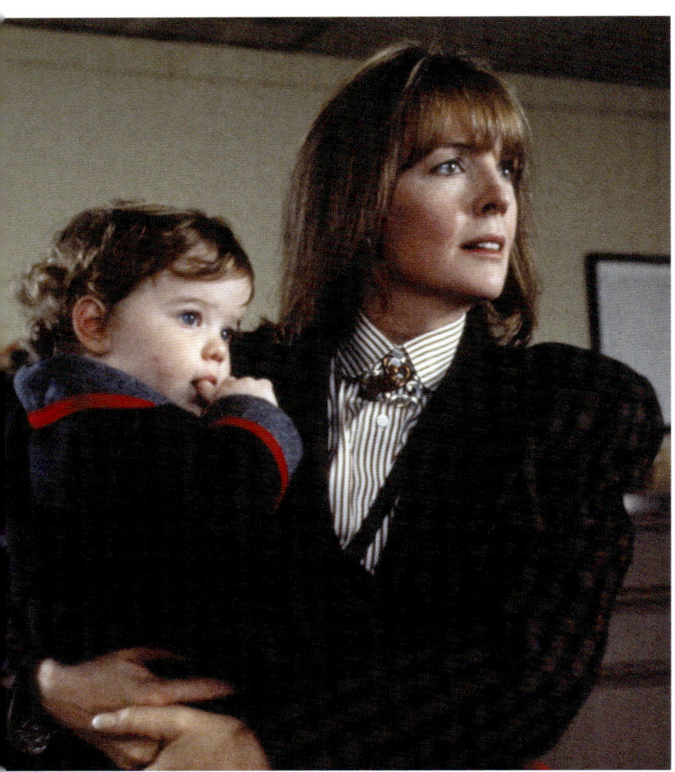

Diane Keaton juggled a career and a child in *Baby Boom*.

Paul Schrader, writer of *Taxi Driver* and *Raging Bull* (1980), also directed several feature films like the erotic dramas *American Gigolo* (1980) and *Cat People* (1982) and stories about artists and their creations, *Mishima: A Life in Four Chapters* (1985) and *Light of Day* (1987). His protagonists often are roiled with internal crises that spill over into their relationships and careers—which is evident even in the movies he merely wrote, like *The Last Temptation of Christ* (1988).

Untouchables writer David Mamet delivered other high-profile screenplays—*The Postman Always Rings Twice* (1981) and *The Verdict* (1982)—while continuing to work onstage. (His play *Glengarry Glen Ross* won the Pulitzer Prize for Drama in 1984.) His directorial film debut was the gambling mystery *House of Games* (1987), which led admirer Roger Ebert to write, "Usually the screenwriter is insane to think he can direct a movie. Not this time. . . . The plotting is diabolical and impeccable."

Several women who would go on to directing careers began as celebrated screenwriters in the '80s, including Nancy Meyers, whose comedic scripts—written with her then husband, Charles Shyer—for *Private Benjamin* (1980), *Irreconcilable Differences* (1984), *Jumpin' Jack Flash* (1986, credited as Patricia Irving), and *Baby Boom* (1987) were centered around women in states of transition and emancipation. Journalist and author Nora Ephron earned Academy Award nominations for Mike Nichols's drama *Silkwood* and Rob Reiner's romantic comedy *When Harry Met Sally* . . . . (1989).

ACTOR-DIRECTORS

If it seems natural to transition from writing to directing, it was definitely less common for actors to step behind the camera. Several actors turned filmmakers had incredibly fruitful careers in the '80s, like young TV star Ron Howard, whose directorial debut at age twenty-three—from a script he threw together in a month with his father, Rance—was the Roger Corman–produced *Grand Theft Auto* (1977). Warner Bros. made his next film, *Night Shift* (1982), which gave Michael Keaton his first major role as a morgue employee who starts a prostitution ring, alongside Howard's *Happy Days* costar Henry Winkler. A moderate success, it led to a major hit with *Splash* (1984), the first release from Disney's new adult Touchstone label. With Tom Hanks as a chronically single New Yorker who starts dating a beautiful mermaid (Daryl Hannah), the literal fish-out-of-water story lit up the box office. The cast of *Cocoon* (1985) was an impressive roster of aging Hollywood actors like Don Ameche, Jessica Tandy, Hume Cronyn, and Gwen Verdon, playing residents of a Florida retirement home who find rejuvenation from a group of extraterrestrial visitors.

Howard consciously tried to make movies with wide, mainstream appeal. "A lot of directors start out making wonderful, interesting and also very entertaining and accessible movies," he told an interviewer in 1985. "Then they become a little more ambitious or more uneasy, and . . . they also become less entertaining and crowd-pleasing. I want to guard against that happening to me." After reteaming with Keaton for *Gung Ho* (1986), about a Japanese company's takeover of a Pennsylvania auto plant, he shifted gears to tackle the sword-and-sorcery epic *Willow*—a project of his friend and *American Graffiti* director, George Lucas—and the Steve Martin family comedy *Parenthood* (1989). Both were huge hits.

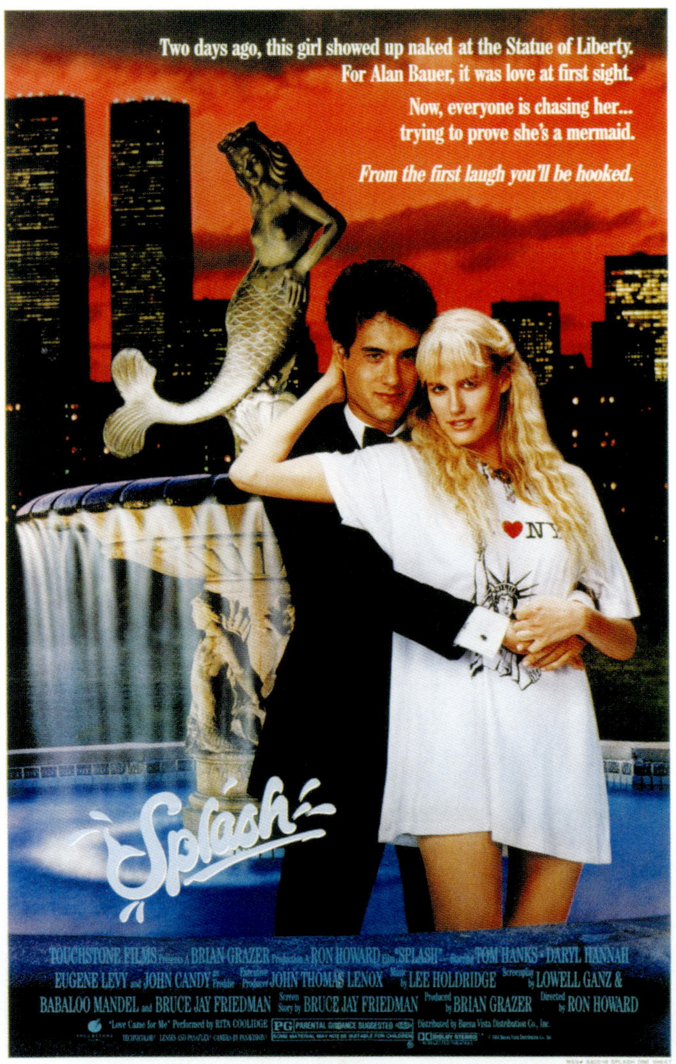

Disney (via its new Touchstone label) had its first mermaid hit of the '80s with *Splash*.

All in the Family star Rob Reiner, son of Carl Reiner, had written for the Smothers Brothers in the late '60s but only made his directing debut in 1984 with the mockumentary *This Is Spinal Tap*. The film about a hapless English metal band whose amplifiers "go to 11" has become a comedy classic and the first of a string of satires by its writer and actor Christopher Guest. After the

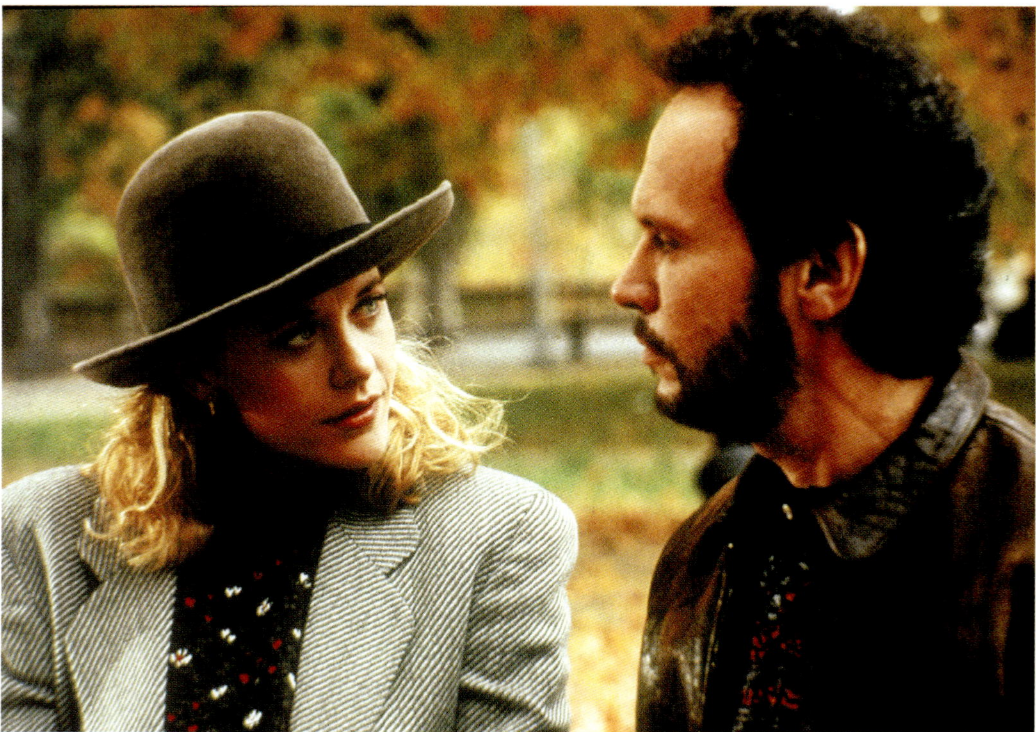

Meg Ryan and Billy Crystal in *When Harry Met Sally. . . .*

success of *The Sure Thing* (1985) and *Stand by Me* (1986), Reiner learned to trust his instincts. "The studio had said 'We'll do whatever you want,'" he recalled years later. "I said, 'I want to make a movie out of *The Princess Bride*.' They said, 'Well, not that.'" But he did, and it too proved popular. With the framing device of a grandfather (Peter Falk) reading a tale of romance and adventure to his young grandson (Fred Savage), its charm lies in its self-awareness, offbeat humor, and emotional sincerity. He ended the decade with the landmark romantic comedy *When Harry Met Sally . . .*, starring Billy Crystal and Meg Ryan as longtime friends turned lovers. Shot around Manhattan in all four seasons, the landmark romantic comedy has since become one of the iconic New York films.

Sydney Pollack had been directing feature films and television since the '60s but had two of his greatest popular successes with a pair of Oscar-nominated '80s films. *Tootsie* (1982) starred Dustin Hoffman as an out-of-work actor who dresses as a woman in order to win a television role. (Pollack played the actor's agent, at Hoffman's insistence.) Best Picture winner *Out of Africa* (1985) was a sweeping historical romance based on the memoirs of Danish writer Isak Dinesen, starring Meryl Streep as the author and Robert Redford as an English hunter.

Clint Eastwood directed and acted in major films throughout the decade—often at the same time. *Sudden Impact* was the fourth and most financially successful of the Dirty Harry franchise. *Pale Rider* (1985) was a classic cowboy picture and "the first decent Western in a very long time," wrote Vincent Canby, approvingly. "Though Mr. Eastwood may have been improving over the years, it's also taken all these years for most of us to recognize his very consistent grace and wit as a filmmaker." *Bird* (1988) may not have been a hit, but the expansive portrait of jazz saxophonist Charlie Parker (Forest Whitaker) was a pet project for the music-loving director and remains a career highlight.

The 1980s also brought Best Director Oscar wins to actors Robert Redford for the family drama *Ordinary People* (1980), Warren Beatty for his Russian revolution epic *Reds* (1981), and Richard Attenborough for the biopic *Gandhi* (1982). Sidney Poitier directed Richard Pryor and Gene Wilder in the comedy *Stir Crazy* (1980), Danny DeVito made *Throw Momma from the Train* (1987) and *The War of the Roses* (1989), Albert Brooks had a *Modern Romance* (1981) and got *Lost in America* (1985), and even Eddie Murphy tried his hand behind the camera with the period crime film *Harlem Nights* (1989). It was a good time to be a star.

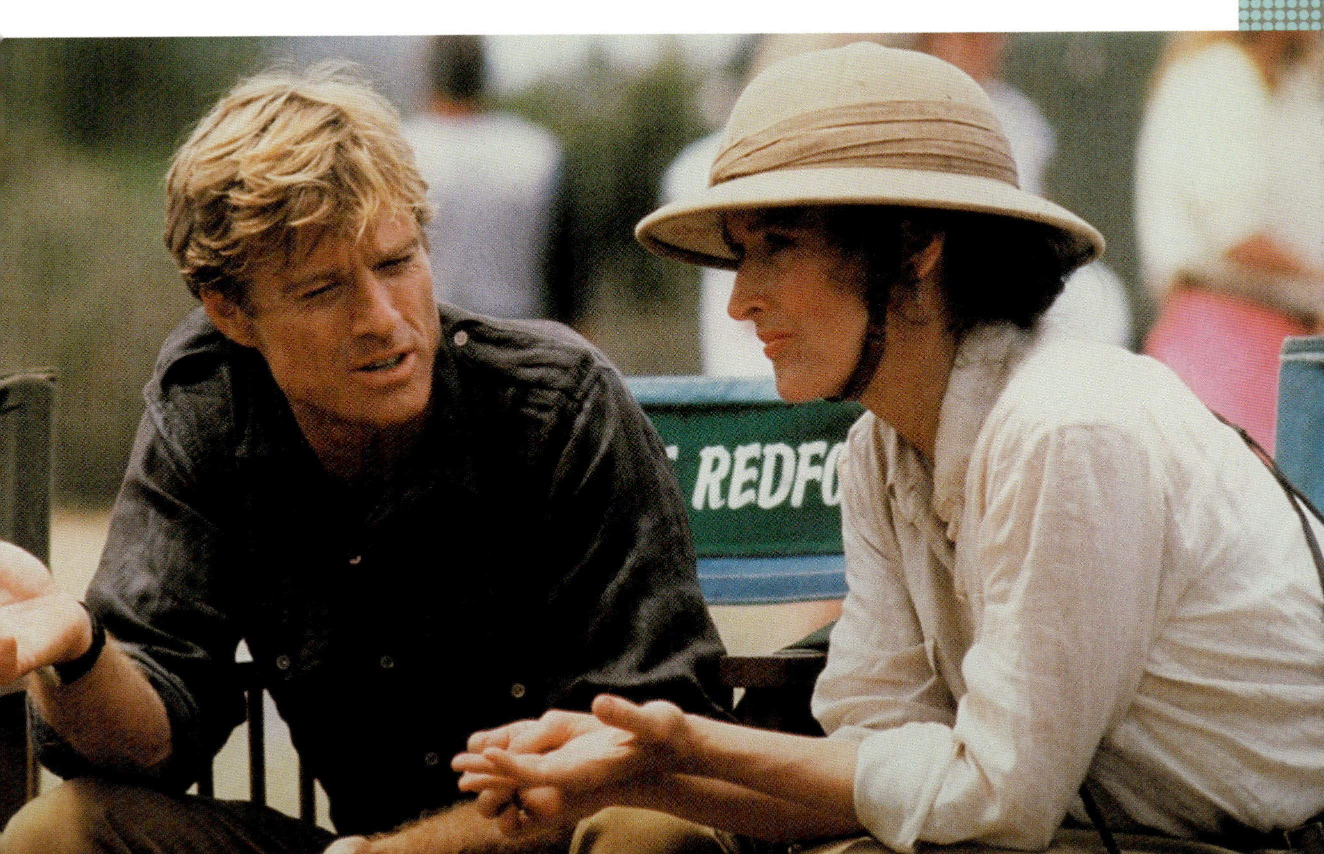

Robert Redford and Meryl Streep on the set of *Out of Africa*.

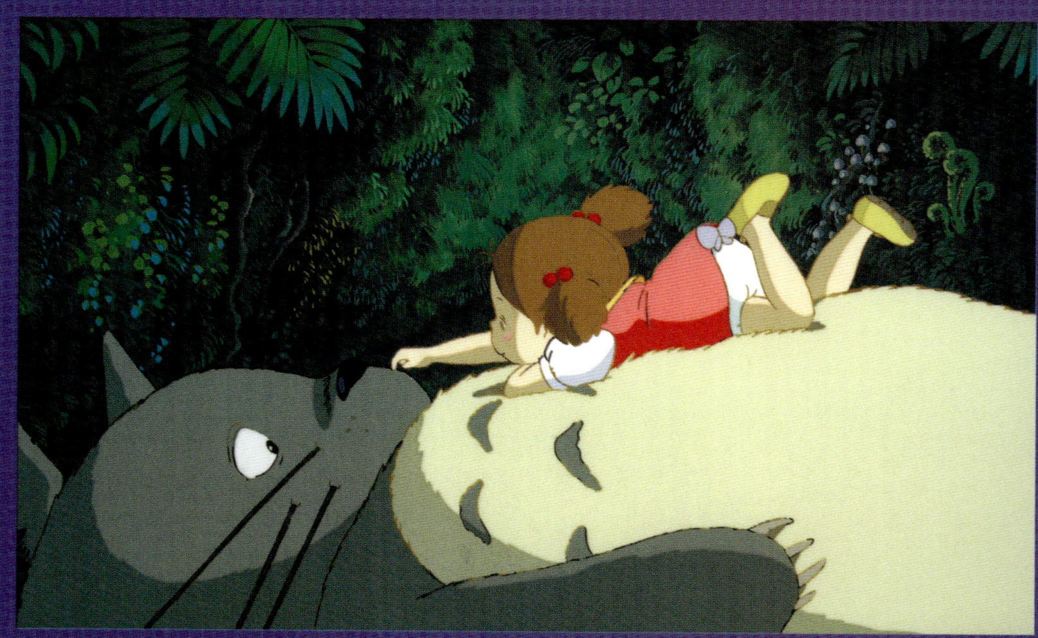

My Neighbor Totoro

The ANIMATION SECTION

Animation was in an exciting state of transition in the 1980s, a decade that witnessed the rise of major new filmmakers and technologies. While corporate-owned studios used animation to promote toy brands and associated television series—Transformers, Care Bears, and He-Man among them—breakout animators like Don Bluth and Hayao Miyazaki established themselves as masters of the craft, and computer graphics company Pixar took its first steps toward what would become a revolution.

For most of the decade, Disney was having as much success reissuing classics as it was with new films. In 1980 alone, *Lady and the Tramp* (1955), *Song of the South* (1946), *The Aristocats* (1970), and *Mary Poppins* (1964) were all given theatrical revivals. *Cinderella* (1950) and *Bambi* (1942) each earned more than $60 million across multiple releases. *Snow White and the Seven Dwarfs* (1937) earned more than $75 million, got a star on the Hollywood Walk of Fame, and opened at number one at the box office in July 1987. "It is heartening because it proves to any sensible reader of trends that there is a hugely lucrative market for quality family movies," wrote Jack Mathews in the *Los Angeles Times*. "It's depressing because Hollywood had to dig 50 years into its past to find one."

More than 150 animated features were given theatrical releases in the United States in the '80s, and many more made overseas have since become cultural landmarks. Meanwhile, a variety of animated shorts were produced, which—along with the cartoons that dominated children's television—confirmed a continuing interest in the form. Along with *Mickey's Christmas Carol* (1983), the first theatrical appearance

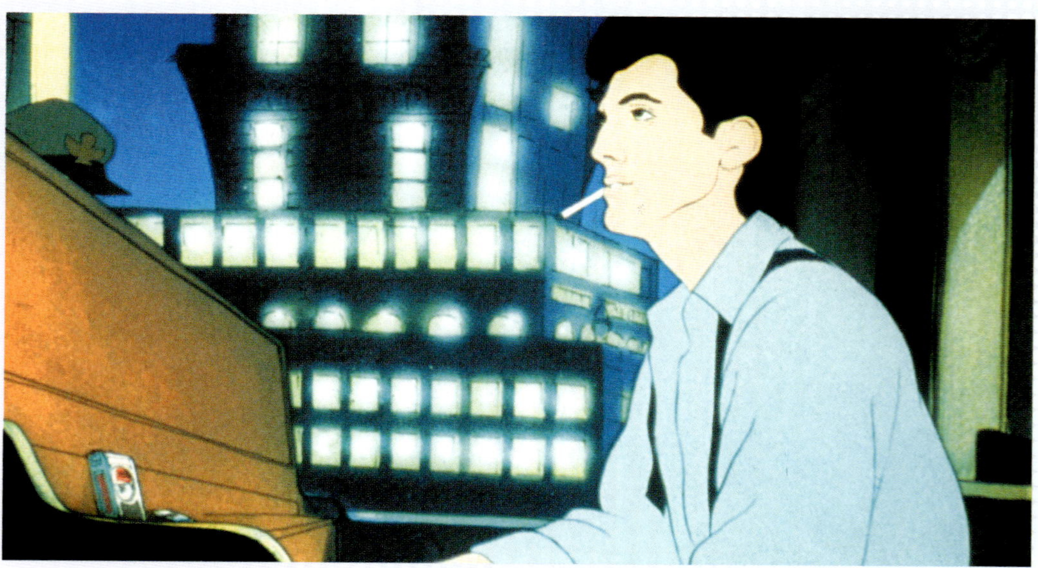

Benny (Richard Singer) performs in *American Pop*.

of Disney's iconic character in more than thirty years, Pixar's trademark desk lamp made its debut in *Luxo Jr.* (1986), and Wallace and Gromit arrived with Aardman's *A Grand Day Out* (1989). Canadian animator Richard Condie won the Academy Award for his nuclear-war allegory *The Big Snit* (1985), but his fellow countryman Frédéric Back won twice—for his rocking-chair short, *Crac* (1981), and the environmental tale *The Man Who Planted Trees* (1987). In America, cartoonist Bill Plympton broke out with acclaimed shorts like *Your Face* (1988) and subsequent work in commercials and music videos.

American Pop (1981)

Ralph Bakshi had made headlines with the first X-rated animated feature, *Fritz the Cat*, in 1972. While subsequent films like *Wizards* (1977) and *The Lord of the Rings* (1978) were toned down, they were still made for a thoughtful, mature audience and were made more realistic by the use of rotoscoping—the technique of animating over live-action footage. Bakshi's *American Pop* is a jukebox musical that covers a century of popular music, told through the story of a family of Jewish immigrants and their descendants. Following the film's success, Warner Bros. decided to release Bakshi's long-shelved project *Hey Good Lookin'* in 1982, but the studio's drastic recut—which removed live-action sequences and rerecorded the voice performances—failed with audiences and was disowned by the director, whose career began to falter.

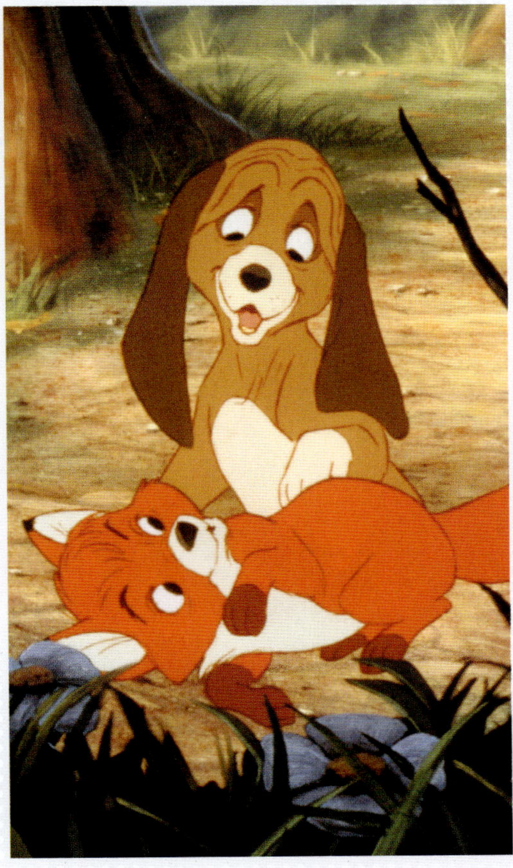

Copper (Corey Feldman) and Tod (Keith Coogan) form an unlikely friendship in *The Fox and the Hound.*

The Fox and the Hound (1981)

Disney's homespun story of friendship turned enmity between the two title creatures, based on the book by Daniel P. Mannix, is enormously affecting and includes voice work by Kurt Russell, Mickey Rooney, and Pearl Bailey. It was the last Disney feature on which Walt's original "nine old men" worked—animators Frank Thomas and Ollie Johnston retired in 1978, having been members of the studio's creative team

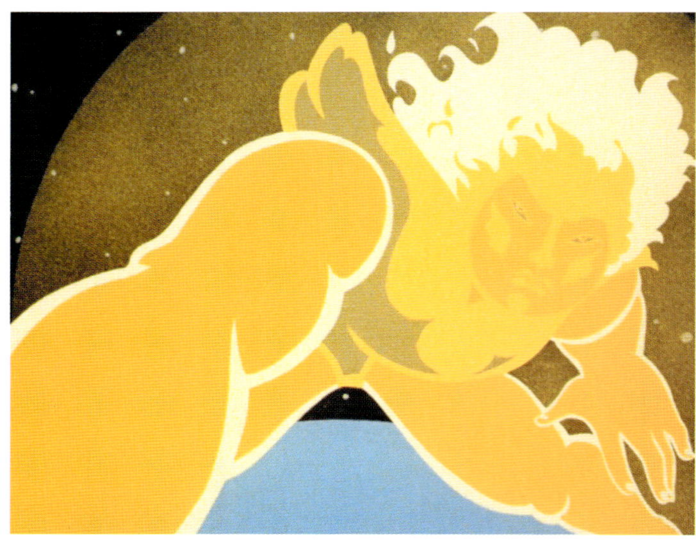

Treeshaker (György Cserhalmi) in *Son of the White Mare.*

since the mid-'30s—and production also endured the walkout of more than a dozen animators who decried the poor state of the once-heralded studio. They were led by animator Don Bluth, who defiantly formed his own company and went toe-to-toe with Disney throughout the '80s. "The atmosphere and the climate here in the last few days have been wonderful," said Disney's then head of production, Ron Miller, after the split. "It's like getting rid of a thorn."

Heavy Metal (1981)

This adult anthology film was based on several serials from *Heavy Metal* magazine, which had been launched by *National Lampoon* in 1977 and had exposed American audiences to European-style comics—complete with violence and nudity. Its various sci-fi segments are backed by a rock-and-roll soundtrack with bands like Black Sabbath, Cheap Trick, and Blue Öyster Cult. *Los Angeles Times* critic Sheila Benson called this now cult classic "the most expensive adolescent fantasy revenge fulfillment wet dream ever to slither onto a screen," before it went on to spend a decade as a mainstay of the midnight-movie circuit.

Son of the White Mare (1981)

Vividly colorful, dreamlike, and deeply Hungarian, director Marcell Jankovics's retelling of a traditional folktale about the human sons of a mythical horse flew under the radar for decades. Produced by the prolific, state-funded studio Pannonia, it wasn't released in the United States until 2020, after years of cheerleading from admirers like animation historian Charles Solomon. Jankovics had made Hungary's first animated feature, *Johnny Corncob*, in 1973, and his decades-in-the-making epic *The Tragedy of Man* was finally released in 2011 and remains one of the longest animated films ever made.

The Time Masters (1982)

French animator René Laloux, famous for his 1973 film *Fantastic Planet*, worked with Hungary's Pannonia studio to produce this sci-fi tale about an orphaned boy who is stranded on Perdide, a hazardous planet overrun by giant hornets, and the space travelers who attempt to rescue him. The lead designer on the film was famed French comics artist Jean Giraud, also known as Mœbius, who created a variety of captivating environments and the fanciful creatures who inhabit them. For Laloux's final feature, *Gandahar* (1987), animation was outsourced to the North Korean studio SEK, which provided inexpensive labor for film and TV projects from all over the world. Sci-fi writer Isaac Asimov translated *Gandahar* to its English version, which was released in the United States as *Light Years*.

The Secret of NIMH (1982)

As soon as Don Bluth and his team of animators left Disney in late 1979, they announced their first full-length project: an adaptation of Robert C. O'Brien's Newbery-winning children's book about a mouse who seeks help for her ailing son from a group of highly intelligent rats, the result of scientific experimentation by humans at the National Institute of Mental Health (NIMH). Bluth had wanted to return to the complex emotional storytelling Disney had excelled at in its classic era. "If Walt had been alive, he would have walked out with us," said animator John Pomeroy. "We weren't doing anything there that he would have liked." The dark fantasy of *NIMH* was, intentionally, unlike anything their former studio had made in decades.

The Plague Dogs (1982)

A similar story of scientific research of lab animals, this adult animated film by director Martin Rosen—who had made the equally mature *Watership Down* in 1973, also from a book by Richard Adams—was even more harrowing than Bluth's film. It follows two dogs who escape

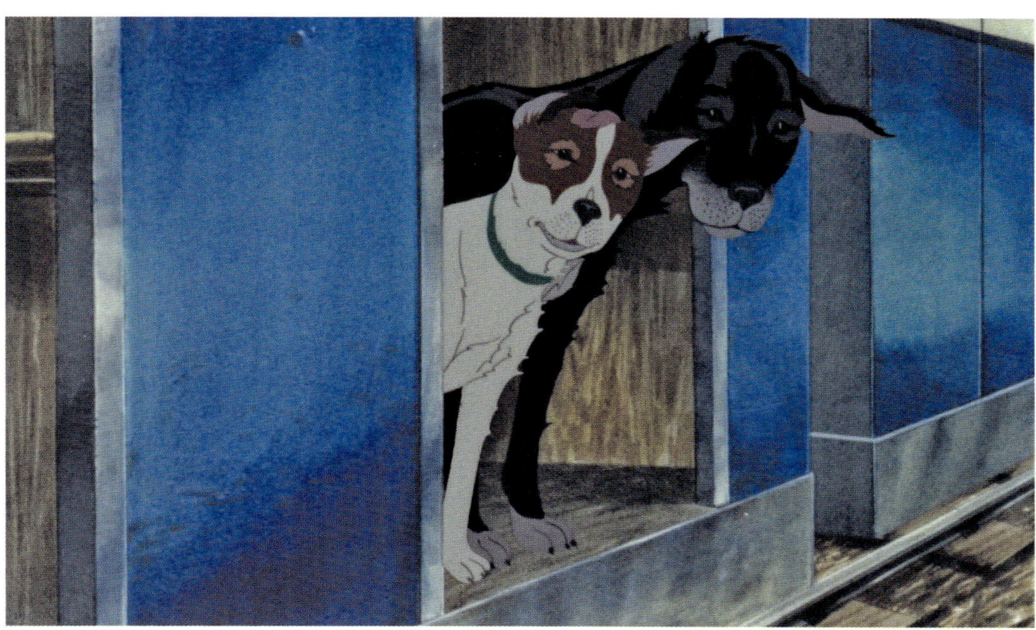

Snitter (John Hurt) and Rowf (Christopher Benjamin) in *The Plague Dogs*.

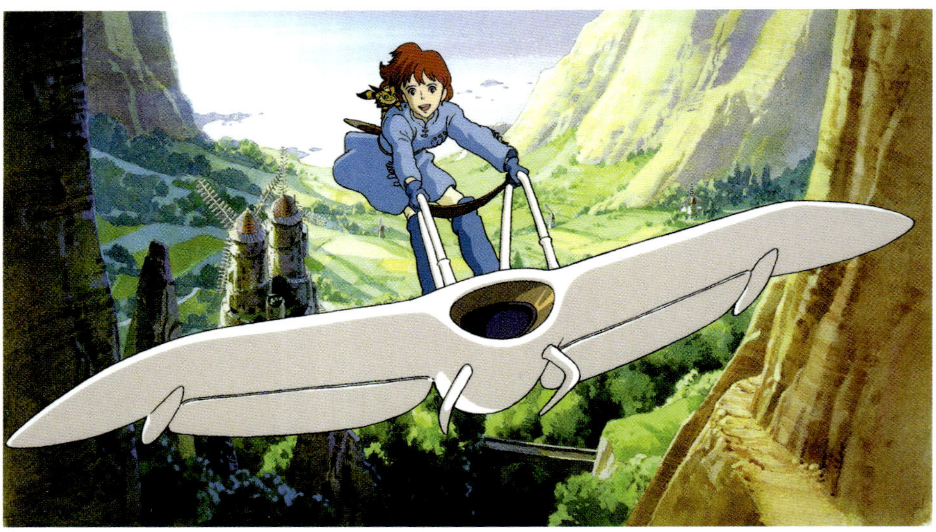

Initially, only a heavily edited version of *Nausicaä of the Valley of the Wind* was released in the United States, titled *Warriors of the Wind*.

from a lab in rural England run by tormenting "whitecoats" who claim the dogs are carrying disease, sparking a chase by authorities, media attention, and public scrutiny of the lab's controversial animal experiments. Rosen didn't shy away from the darker aspects of the story, which may have turned off audiences. "I delivered this very difficult film that was in opposition to all our conceptions about dogs," he later said, ruefully. "Never let it be said that I went the easy way."

The Last Unicorn (1982)

In the early 1980s, Arthur Rankin Jr. and Jules Bass were primarily known for television specials, especially their Christmas shorts about Santa, Rudolph, and Frosty the Snowman. They had also produced two Middle Earth–themed TV specials, including *The Return of the King* (broadcast in May 1980 on ABC), which prepared them for this rare theatrical release: a fantasy film about a unicorn (Mia Farrow) who journeys to the castle of a diminished king (Christopher Lee) who holds the fate of her kind. One of the most celebrated aspects of the film is the song score written by Jimmy Webb and performed by the band America.

Twice Upon a Time (1983)

This trippy and irreverent fable, told through a variety of inventive animation styles, was made courtesy of executive producer George Lucas and the Ladd Company. Director John Korty used a process of illuminated cutout animation dubbed "Lumage" to tell the story of Frivoli (the origin of dreams) and the Murkworks (creators of nightmares), whose villainous leader Synonamess Botch hopes to make bad dreams a permanent reality. Working on the crew were Henry Selick (who later directed *The Nightmare Before Christmas* [1993]) and a young special-effects photographer named David Fincher. Despite the film's pedigree, it was a failure at the box office and, after an attempted reedit for HBO, quickly fell into obscurity.

Nausicaä of the Valley of the Wind (1984)

Japanese animator Hayao Miyazaki had created the environmentalist fantasy *Nausicaä* as a popular manga for *Animage* magazine in 1981 before directing the beloved film version that paved the way for his celebrated career. Set in a postapocalyptic world ravaged by pollution and dominated by giant insects, it follows a fearless young princess who explores the Toxic Jungle and fights to save her people. Thanks to the success of this film, Miyazaki formed Studio Ghibli in 1985 with his producer (and fellow director) Isao Takahata and *Animage* editor Toshio Suzuki.

The Black Cauldron (1985)

After a corporate shakeup at Disney in 1984, this long-gestating, PG-rated response to the sword-and-sorcery film trend of the early '80s was trimmed for length—and for scenes of action deemed too intense for children—but couldn't make back its reported $44 million budget. Based on Lloyd Alexander's award-winning fantasy saga *The Chronicles of Prydain*, it was the first Disney animated film to incorporate computer-generated imagery (CGI) as well as live-action effects elements and was theatrically released in a special 70mm format. It received some positive reviews—Roger Ebert gave it four stars and called it "a rip-roaring tale

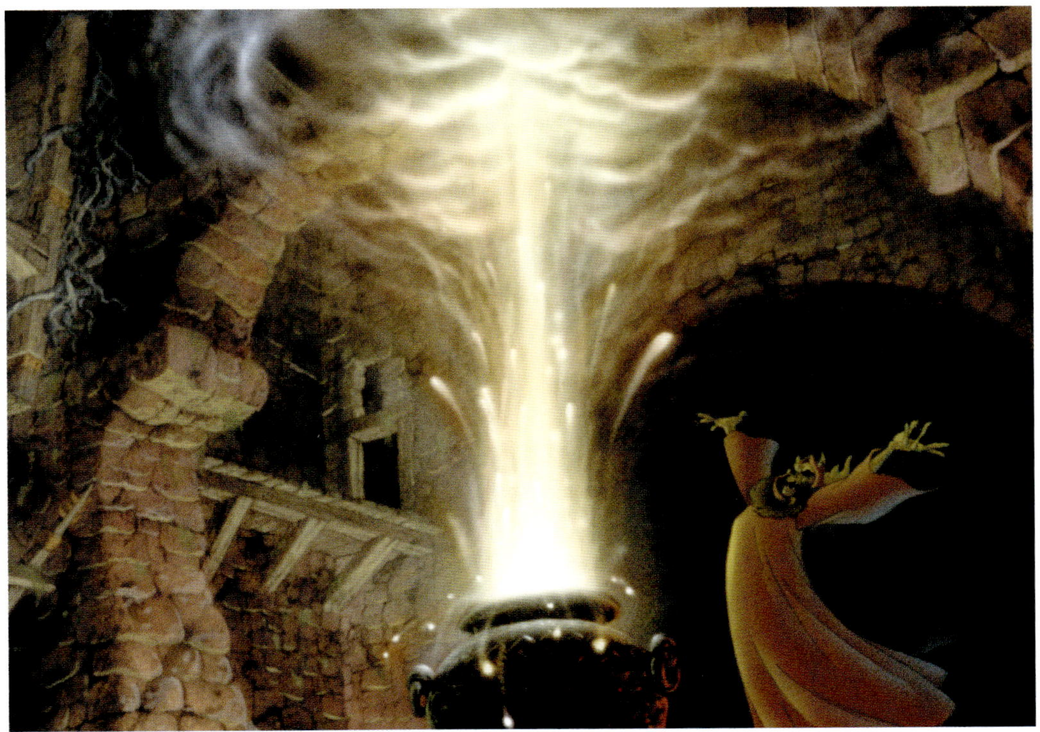

John Hurt continued his voice work as the Horned King in *The Black Cauldron*.

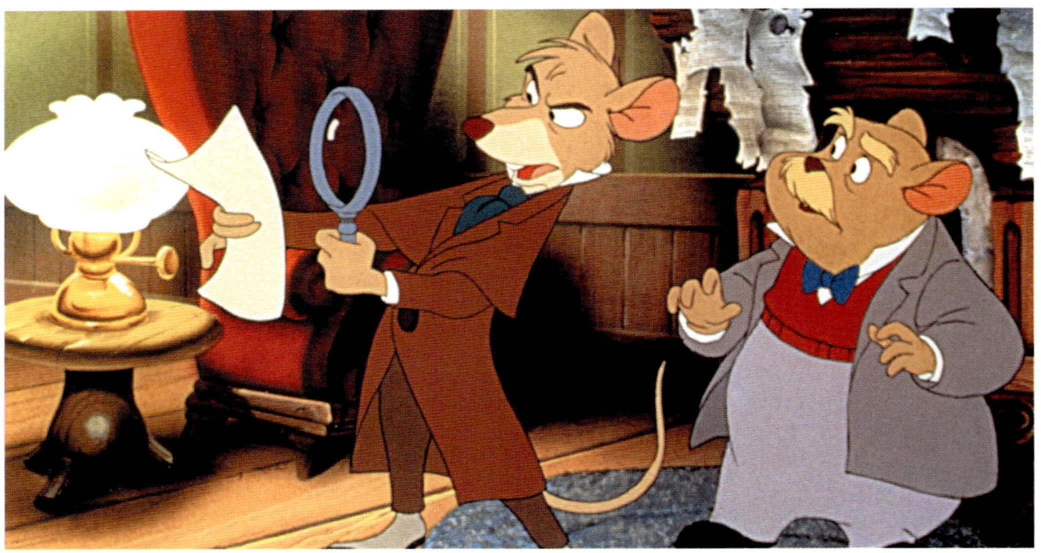

Basil (Barrie Ingham) and Dawson (Val Bettin) on the case in *The Great Mouse Detective*.

of swords and sorcery, evil and revenge, magic and pluck and luck"—but it was a rare financial flop for the studio, which quickly abandoned it. "The lesson to be learned from *The Black Cauldron* was an economic lesson," said new CEO Michael Eisner. "If you're going to fail, don't fail at such a high cost."

The Adventures of Mark Twain (1985)

Claymation artist Will Vinton had been making short films for a decade when he released his first feature, a fantastical portrait of American writer Mark Twain (voiced by James Whitmore), whose birth and death coincide with the appearance of Halley's Comet. In the film, he navigates an airship to meet the comet and is joined by stowaways Tom Sawyer and Huckleberry Finn, who relive some of Twain's famous works along the way. Vinton had already won an Academy Award and performed effects work for major live-action films like *Return to Oz* (1985), but his star would truly rise in 1986 when an ad campaign for California Raisins became an unlikely cultural sensation.

The Great Mouse Detective (1986)

After the fiasco of *The Black Cauldron*, Michael Eisner and Disney studio chief Jeffrey Katzenberg decreed that the company's animated features would need to be made at lower budgets and released on a more regular and faster-paced schedule. First out of the gate was this clever reimagining of the Sherlock Holmes mysteries, starring a shrewd crime-solving mouse named Basil of Baker Street (based on the books by Eve Titus). His nemesis is a deliciously preening rat named Professor Ratigan (Vincent Price) who plans to depose the Mouse Queen on her jubilee. "American animation is overdue for a renaissance," wrote Charles Solomon in the *Los Angeles Times*. "The first hopeful sign is Disney's *The Great Mouse Detective*."

CGI

In the 1980s, Hollywood began to regularly experiment with computer-generated imagery to create virtuosic film sequences and wow audiences. An early landmark was Disney's *Tron* (1982), in which a software developer (Jeff Bridges) enters the cyberspace and attempts to defeat a malevolent artificial-intelligence program. The film contained a dazzling "light cycle" racing sequence that threw down the CGI gauntlet for films to come. In 1984, *The Last Starfighter* included a similar story of a video game coming to life, using complex 3-D renderings for its battle sequences.

Lucasfilm's Graphics Group (which later became Pixar) played a major role in digital effects in the '80s. For *Star Trek II: The Wrath of Khan* (1982), it created an impressive one-minute effects sequence for the demonstration of the powerful Genesis Device, showing how a dead planet can be transformed into a fertile, living world. ("Fascinating," says Spock.) It also created the first CGI-rendered character, a walking stained-glass knight, for *Young Sherlock Holmes* (1985). Meanwhile, the first appearance of a fully CGI animal occurred in the opening credits of *Labyrinth* (1986), in which an owl flies in and out of the frame.

George Lucas's Industrial Light & Magic (ILM) pioneered body-morphing effects, which were famously used in *Willow* (1988) when the lead character seamlessly transforms a goat into an ostrich, a tiger, a turtle, and finally a human being. This same technology was used for the water effects in *The Abyss* (1989), in which shimmering "pseudopods" imitate the film's human characters.

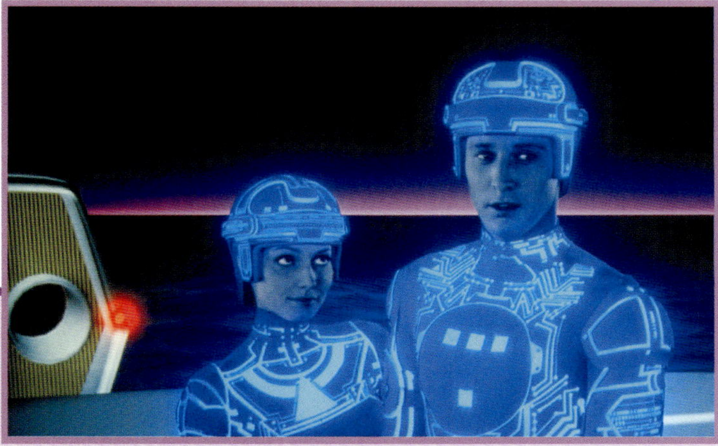

Cindy Morgan and Bruce Boxleitner in *Tron*.

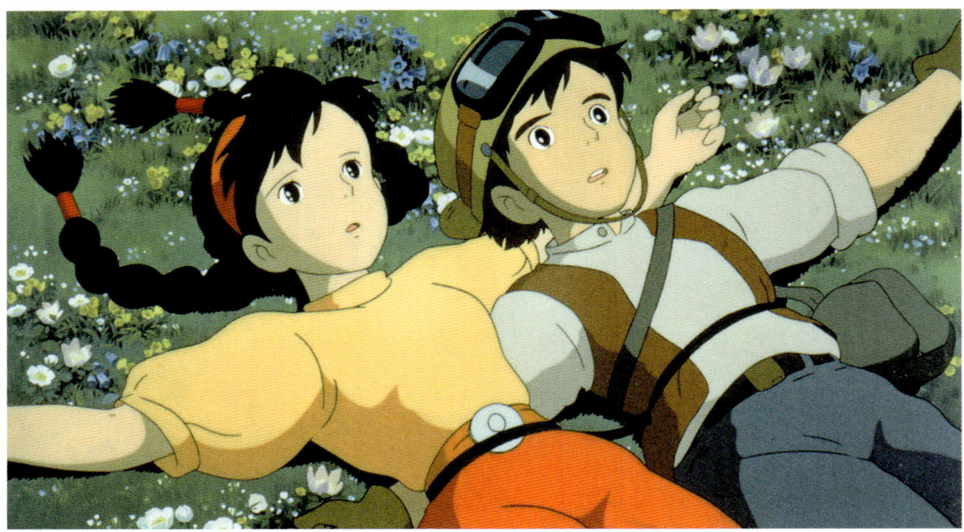

Sheeta (Keiko Yokozawa) and Pazu (Mayumi Tanaka) in *Castle in the Sky*.

Castle in the Sky (1986)

The first film released by Studio Ghibli was this steampunk fantasy about a girl named Sheeta, heir to the throne of the mythical floating city of Laputa, and the working-class boy Pazu who accompanies her. For a story featuring a magic gemstone, a helpful robot, and a band of pirates, director Hayao Miyazaki's influences on the project were numerous. A trip to Wales inspired Pazu's mining town, the city in the sky comes from Jonathan Swift's *Gulliver's Travels*, and French animator Paul Grimault's *The King and the Mockingbird* (1980), with its visionary castle setting, has also been cited as an inspiration. Made specifically for a child audience, *Castle in the Sky* was the first of Miyazaki's films to be distributed in the United States, in 1989.

When the Wind Blows (1986)

This British film about survivors of a nuclear blast was based on a graphic novel by Raymond Briggs, who also wrote the picture book *The Snowman* (made into a beloved animated short in 1982). It follows an older married couple, voiced by John Mills and Peggy Ashcroft, who dutifully prepare for an imminent nuclear explosion near their quaint English cottage. Though they follow government protocols, their decline due to radiation sickness is impossible to avoid. Japanese American director Jimmy Murakami, who had lost a relative in the bombing of Nagasaki, uses a mixture of charming 2-D animation and stark photorealism to suggest the bleak threat posed by nuclear weapons.

An American Tail (1986)

Don Bluth made his second feature film with the powerful backing of Steven Spielberg, whose box-office goliath *E.T. the Extra-Terrestrial* (1982) is often cited as a major reason for the financial failure of *The Secret of NIMH*. Spielberg also provided the story, set in 1885, about how young Fievel Mousekewitz (named for Spielberg's grandfather) becomes separated from his parents on their journey to America and must survive on the streets of New York with a group of other immigrant mice. The film was a huge hit, and it came with an equally popular soundtrack that featured the song "Somewhere Out There," a duet that Fievel and his sister sing to the moon, one hopeful night.

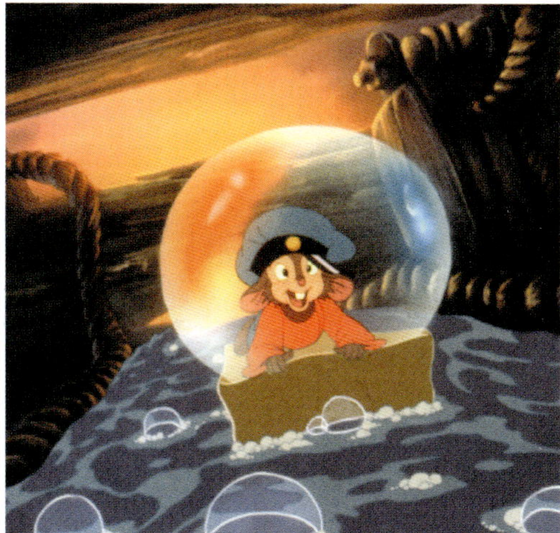

Fievel (Phillip Glasser) sails to a better life in *An American Tail*.

The Brave Little Toaster (1987)

Disney animator John Lasseter envisioned this story of a group of plucky household appliances as the company's first fully CGI film. When executives passed on it, the project was picked up by independent studio Hyperion Pictures, who turned out a whimsical 2-D musical fable about friendship and belonging. Some compared its conceit of talking inanimate objects to *Pee-wee's Playhouse*; its story of loyal consumer products is also a clear forerunner to Pixar's *Toy Story* (1995). After limited theatrical appearances —including the Sundance Film Festival— it aired on the Disney Channel in 1988 and gained a following on home video.

Grave of the Fireflies (1988)

Studio Ghibli cofounder Isao Takahata directed this devastating wartime story about a teenage boy and his little sister, orphaned during the bombing of Kobe, who attempt to navigate a new and unforgiving world. After running away from their cruel aunt, they live alone in a nearby cave, and the boy resorts to stealing food for their survival. Takahata's magnum opus tapped into lingering national trauma and has been proclaimed one of the most powerful antiwar films ever made, animated or otherwise. *Grave of the Fireflies* was released in Japan on April 16, 1988, on a double bill with Miyazaki's *My Neighbor Totoro*—another tale of young siblings, albeit a much more hopeful one.

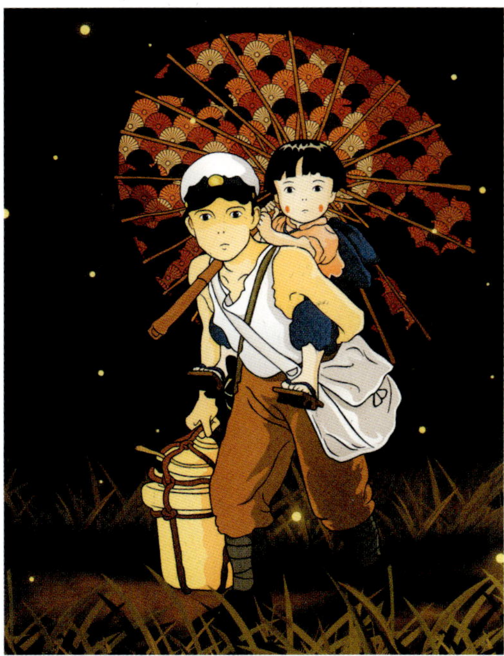

Seita (Tsutomu Tatsumi) and Setsuko (Ayano Shiraishi) in *Grave of the Fireflies*.

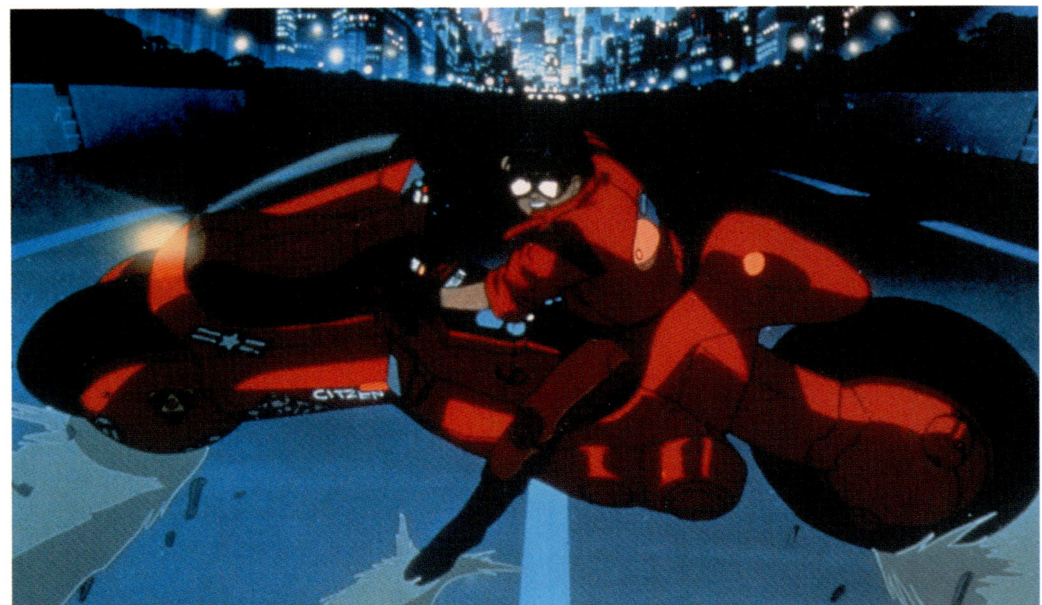

Kaneda's (Mitsuo Iwata) iconic motorcycle slide in *Akira* has been emulated in numerous films over the years.

My Neighbor Totoro (1988)

One of Miyazaki's many charms is his absorbing depiction of the natural world: drops of rain, curious snails, rustling leaves. The simple wonder of nature is foregrounded in this film about two sisters (Satsuki and little Mei) who move with their father to a rustic country house to be near their ailing mother—a premise drawn from the director's own childhood. There they meet the many spirits that inhabit the forest, ride a "catbus," grow a magical tree, and live out other childhood imaginings. Simple, poetic, and delightful, *Totoro*'s characters have come to define the art and ethos of Studio Ghibli.

Who Framed Roger Rabbit (1988)

This 1940s-set neo-noir, a live-action/animation hybrid depicting a fantastical Hollywood in which cartoons live and work alongside humans, was a watershed film for the Walt Disney Company. Directed by Roger Zemeckis and produced in partnership with Spielberg's Amblin Entertainment, the story of a detective (Bob Hoskins) who helps a cartoon rabbit framed for murder became a huge box-office hit and signaled a revival of the studio's ingenuity and commercial viability. It also brought together animated icons from other studios, including Betty Boop, Woody Woodpecker, and Bugs Bunny. "Is it for kids, or adults, or both?" asked Roger Ebert in a four-star review. "I have a sneaky hunch that adults will appreciate it even more than kids, because they'll have a better appreciation of how difficult it was to make, and how effortlessly it succeeds."

Akira (1988)

This "cyberpunk" landmark from director Katsuhiro Otomo, set in a dystopian Neo-Tokyo plagued by biker gangs and the military police who oppose them, gained a cult following in the United States and was a breakthrough for anime in the West. Among the film's vigilantes is the psychic teenager Tetsuo, whose newfound powers are similar to the mythical Akira, the destroyer of Tokyo thirty years earlier. Otomo had created the original *Akira* manga in 1982, which ran biweekly in Japan's *Young Magazine* until 1990. "I wanted to draw this story set in a Japan similar to how it was after the end of World War II," he later explained. "Rebelling governmental factions, a rebuilding world, foreign political influence, an uncertain future, a bored and reckless younger generation racing each other on bikes. *Akira* is the story of my own teenage years, rewritten to take place in the future."

Alice (1988)

Czech stop-motion animator Jan Švankmajer creates surreal compositions of everyday objects and materials that dazzle in their expressiveness. His 1983 short *Dimensions of Dialogue* showed a series of exchanges between couples using a scrambled, swirling collection of organic items and inanimate objects. His first full-length feature was made in Switzerland, due to a lack of support in his home country. Based on Lewis Carroll's beloved *Alice's Adventures in Wonderland*, it combines live-action footage of a young actress (occasionally played by a doll) interacting with a variety of creatures and magical objects.

The Land Before Time (1988)

"I was never hoping to become the next Walt Disney," said Don Bluth. "All we wanted to do was make the kind of animated movies that got us when we were kids." Fittingly, his next film combined the dramatic structure of *Bambi* (1942) with the prehistoric tableaux of the "Rite of Spring" segment in *Fantasia* (1940) to create an emotionally rich dinosaur epic about family, friendship, and destiny. Partnering again with Amblin and Universal, the story of the young sauropod Littlefoot's journey to the fabled Great Valley boldly opened the same day as Disney's newest animated feature, *Oliver & Company*. "I like movies that fill you with hope," said Bluth. "I like things that free you from your ills, your prejudices, and all the other things that hold us in spiritual darkness.... Movies have the power to do that."

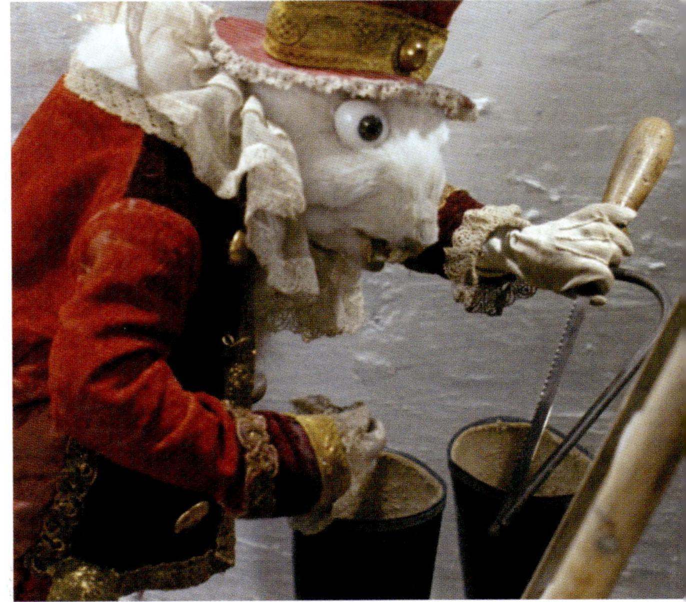

Alice's iteration of the White Rabbit.

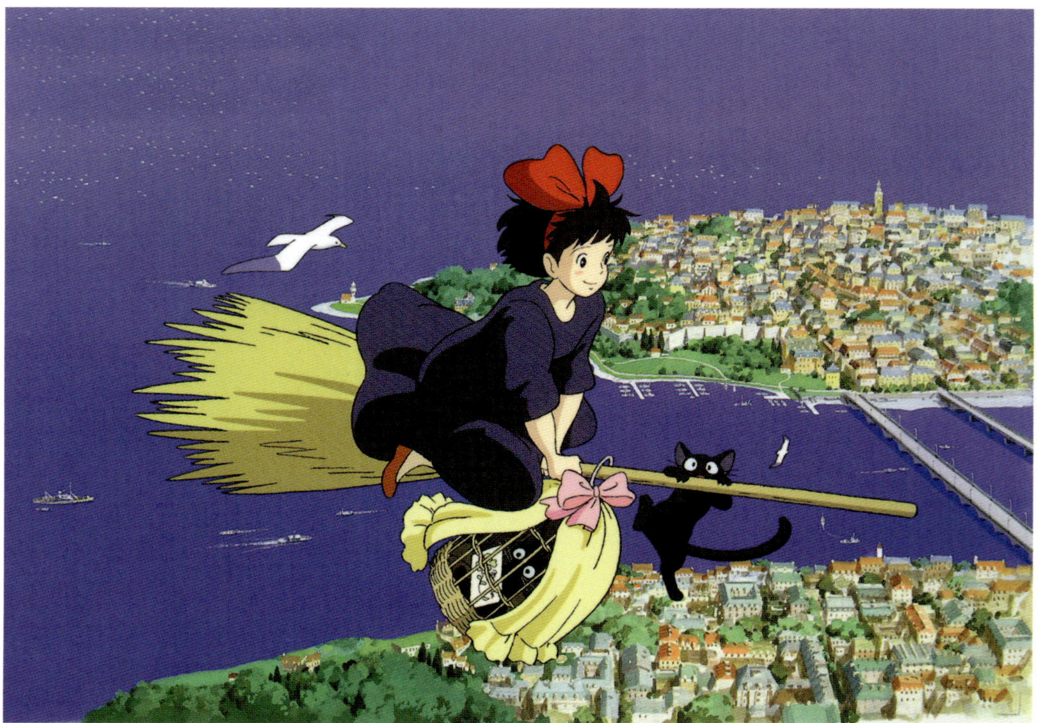

Kiki (Minami Takayama) and her cat Jiji (Rei Sakuma) in *Kiki's Delivery Service*.

Oliver & Company (1988)

Disney had a good reason for choosing a November 18 release date: it was Mickey Mouse's sixtieth birthday. Ironically, their new movie was about a cat. The first animated feature green-lit under the Eisner-Katzenberg regime was an updated and sanitized version of *Oliver Twist*, set in modern-day New York City, in which an orange tabby (Joey Lawrence) is taken in by a pack of stray dogs. Among those providing voice work were a pair of the era's top musical talents—Billy Joel and Bette Midler—who also contributed songs to the film's soundtrack. One motivation for Joel's involvement was his young daughter. "I wanted to be a hero to her more than I wanted to be a star in a movie," he told the *Los Angeles Times*.

Kiki's Delivery Service (1989)

At the tender age of thirteen, a young witch leaves home to begin her training. Off she flies on a broomstick, talking cat in tow, to a new city where she starts an aerial delivery service and ultimately gains the confidence she needs to be a successful witch. The theme of young female empowerment runs throughout Miyazaki's films of the '80s. Rather than battling a traditional villain, Kiki's challenge is to overcome her own self-doubts. "In Kiki's life we see reflected the lives of so many young Japanese girls today," said the director. "The biggest problem . . . is the fight to break through the barrier of independence."

All Dogs Go to Heaven (1989)

Just as they had the year before, Don Bluth and Disney released new animated films on the same day in November 1989. This time, Bluth's hero wasn't a brave mouse or a cute dinosaur, but a very bad dog with a shot at redemption. German shepherd Charlie (Burt Reynolds) is sent to heaven—where all dogs go, by default—but manages to return to earth to confront the villain who did him in, while saving an orphaned girl. The film was made under a multi-picture deal with British production company Goldcrest Films, and while it wasn't a box-office smash like Bluth's previous efforts, it had a very successful afterlife on home video.

The Little Mermaid (1989)

One of the most beloved of all animated movies was elevated to no small degree by the contribution of lyricist Howard Ashman, who helped develop the overall film alongside its writer-directors. He reunited with his *Little Shop of Horrors* composer, Alan Menken, to deliver a slate of songs that remain part of the modern musical songbook thirty years later, including the Oscar-winning "Under the Sea" and the archetypal I-Want song, "Part of Your World." The film's story, derived from Hans Christian Andersen, tells of a young mermaid who longs to be human and is given the chance by one of the decade's juiciest villains: the tentacled sea witch Ursula. The Disney renaissance had officially begun.

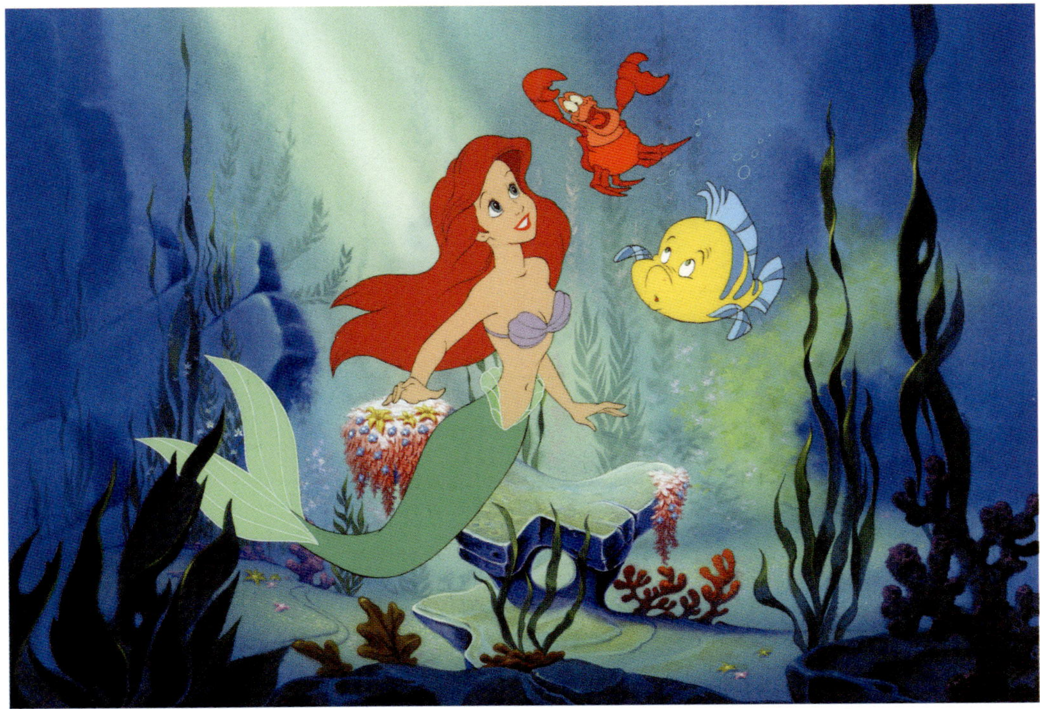

Ariel (Jodi Benson), Sebastian (Samuel E. Wright), and Flounder (Jason Marin) in *The Little Mermaid*.

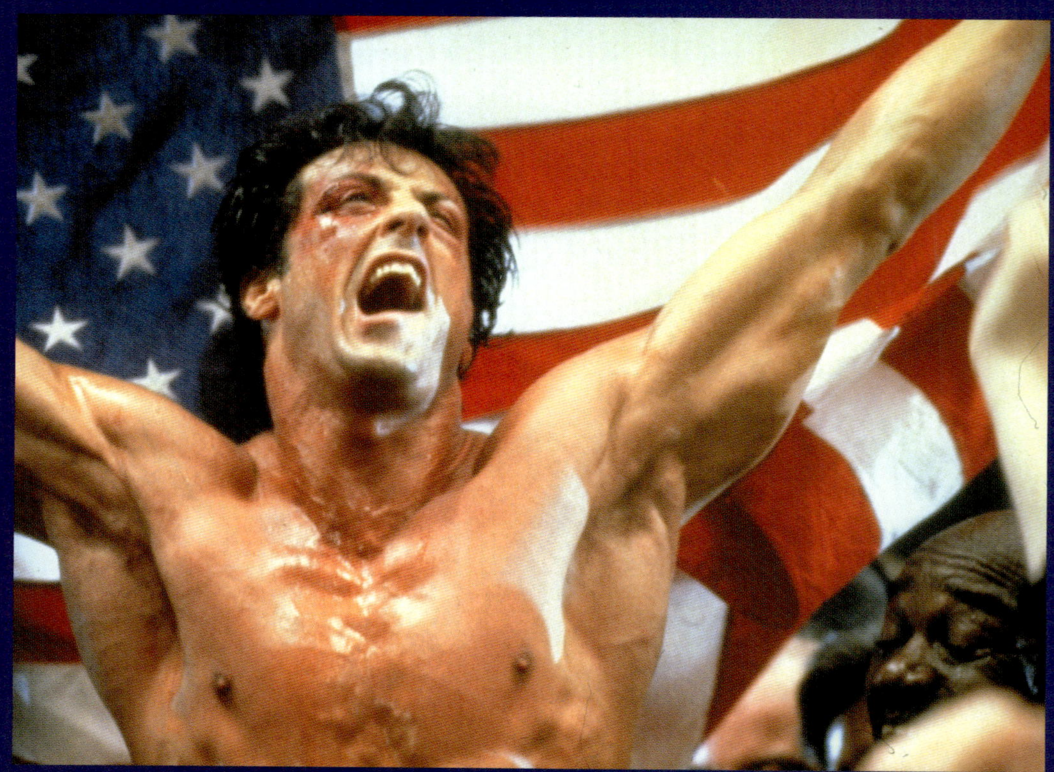

Rocky IV

CHAPTER THREE

The COLD WAR

AFTER WORLD WAR II, THE SOVIET UNION BECAME AMERICA'S MAIN geopolitical adversary—and by extension, Russians became some of the most prominent villains in Hollywood movies. America's "cold" war with Russia impacted the film industry directly through the Red Scare and the House Un-American Activities Committee, which led to an infamous blacklist of supposed communist filmmakers. The nuclear arms race followed, with its potent fear of "mutually assured destruction," as well as the space race—all of which made it onto movie screens, often in the form of science fiction.

Soviet control extended beyond the borders of the USSR to the Eastern-bloc countries of central Europe, and its influence was felt in nations around the world—like Cuba, which by 1959 endured a communist revolution that established Fidel Castro as its leader. The Cuban Missile Crisis of 1962, a standoff between the United States and the Soviet Union over its plans to base a nuclear arsenal in the Caribbean nation, briefly made full-scale war between the two superpowers a real and terrifying possibility. America's ensuing involvement in Vietnam, a drawn-out and ultimately fruitless attempt to prevent a communist takeover of the country, was widely seen as a proxy war with Russia and communist China and served to foment domestic turmoil.

In the 1980s, this decades-long conflict reached a tipping point, as the peace-through-strength posture of popular president (and former Hollywood actor) Ronald Reagan challenged a decaying political and economic situation in the Soviet Union. Filmmakers in both hemispheres explored new ways to address these geopolitical realities and the frustrations and paranoia that affected the average citizen. As American movies dealt with the fallout from Vietnam and rode a wave of cultural ascendancy, Russian and Eastern-bloc films were finally able to take sober and critical new stances.

REDS

Warren Beatty was not, and had never been, a member of the Communist Party. He was just a good old Hollywood Democrat who was interested in telling compelling stories about people in extraordinary circumstances. For years, he had wanted to make a film about John Reed, the American writer and activist who traveled to Russia to report on its 1917 revolution. Beatty waited until after his directing debut—the fantasy rom-com *Heaven Can Wait* (1978)—to tackle the epic historical project, which was heavily invested in politics that were seen as antagonistic to corporate Hollywood. "It was

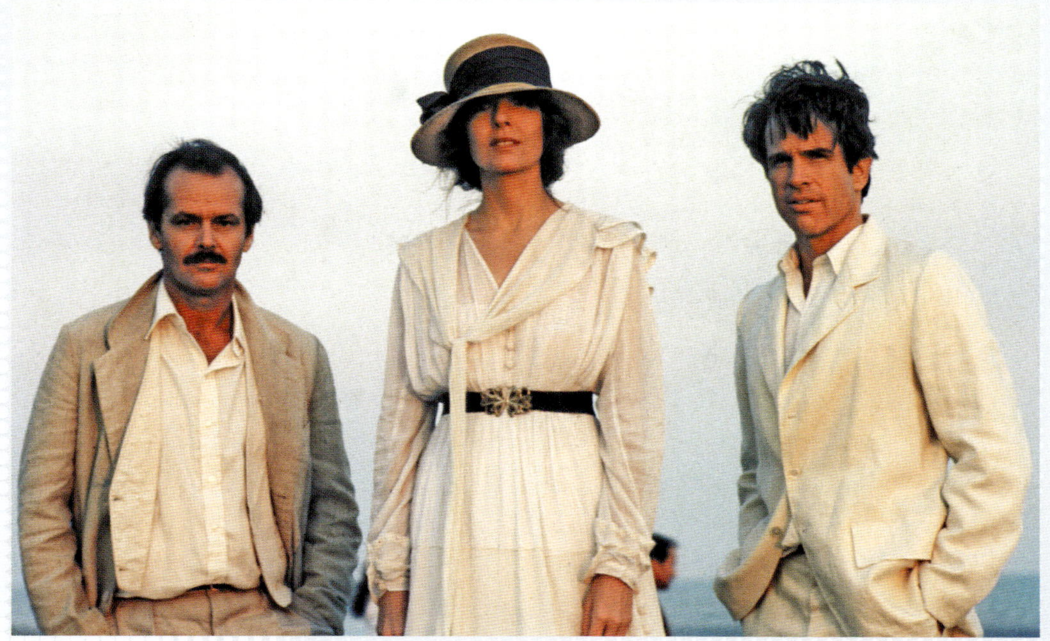

Jack Nicholson, Diane Keaton, and Warren Beatty in the political romance *Reds*.

very much motivated by my own political activism at that time," he said. "It probably had a lot to do with what I thought was a mistaken American paranoia about communism and most particularly in Vietnam." On the other hand, what studio would back a movie like *Reds*?

"It was so much a project not of the mind, but of the heart," said Paramount CEO Barry Diller, whose company took the plunge. The movie not only was a passion project, but also contained a compelling central romance between Reed (Beatty) and writer Louise Bryant (Diane Keaton) and her sometime lover Eugene O'Neill (Jack Nicholson). Lending immediacy to the story is Beatty's inclusion of filmed testimonials with dozens of historical "witnesses"—people who knew and associated with the characters in real life. Their insights and sometimes conflicting points of view help *Reds* come across as less a liberal Hollywood fantasy than a legitimate historical exercise.

When the film opened in December 1981, its reception was positive but not rapturous. *Variety* found it "ultimately too ponderous . . . a Marxist history lesson." The *New York Times* called it "a big romantic adventure movie," with critic Vincent Canby suggesting that "only the very narrow-minded will see the film as communist propaganda." The Academy appreciated the movie, rewarding Beatty's vision with the Best Director prize. He also went to the White House for a screening of *Reds* with the new president, who reportedly wished the film had a happier ending. "I was quite friendly with Ronald Reagan," said Beatty. "I didn't agree with him, but I liked him very much."

VIETNAM

The Cold War wasn't entirely cold, as evidenced by America's military involvement in Vietnam that escalated in the late '60s and ended with the fall of Saigon in 1975. Almost three million US troops had served in the war, and millions of civilians were involved in antiwar demonstrations at home. For the most part, Hollywood dealt with the war indirectly, through films about violence (*The Wild Bunch*), counterculture (*Easy Rider*), and eager small-town boys getting lost in a concrete jungle (*Midnight Cowboy*, all 1969). Aside from documentaries and John Wayne's film *The Green Berets* (1968), there were essentially no depictions of the war until the late '70s, when films like *The Boys in Company C* (1978), *The Deer Hunter* (1978), and *Apocalypse Now* (1979) appeared in succession.

It can be assumed that all war movies in the 1980s are in some ways commenting on Vietnam, even if they're explicitly not about the war. Peter Weir's *Gallipoli* (1981) followed two Australian runners who patriotically enlist in World War I and are quickly disillusioned. Walter Hill's *Southern Comfort* (1981) sees a squad of the National Guardsmen, led by a Vietnam veteran, become embroiled in a fight for their survival in a Louisiana swamp. After a screening

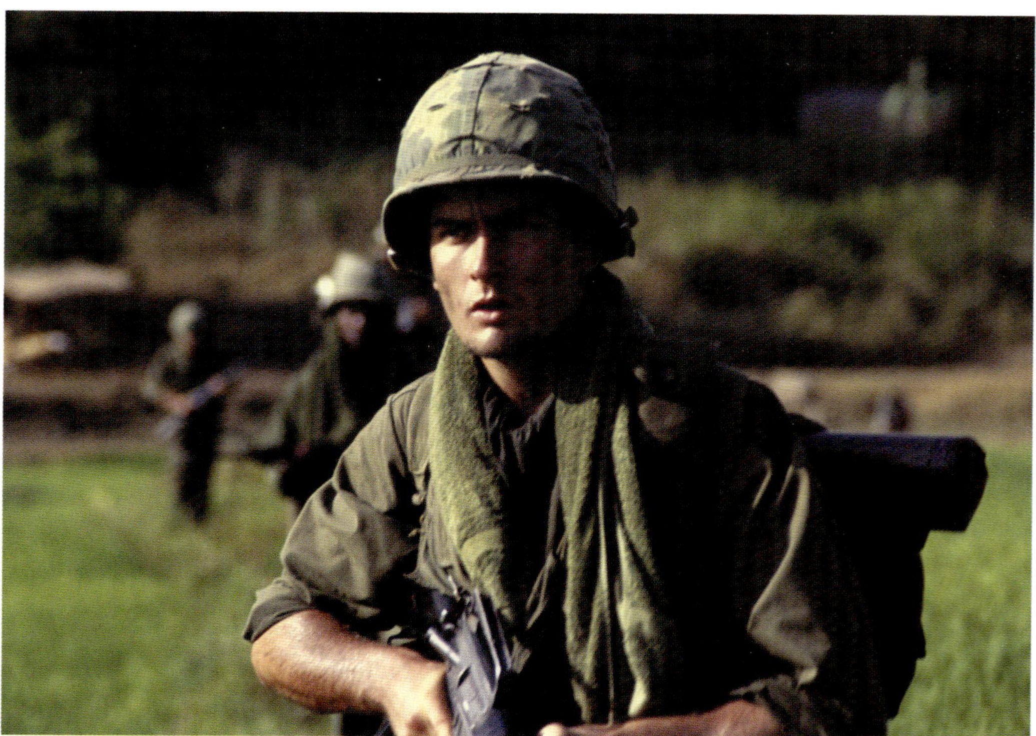

Charlie Sheen as US Army volunteer Chris Taylor in *Platoon*.

of Terence Young's *Inchon* (1981), Ronald Reagan reviewed it in his diary as "a brutal but gripping picture about the Korean War and for once we're the good guys and the Communists are the villains."

By mid-decade the dam had burst, and movies about combat soldiers in Vietnam spilled forth. The most celebrated of these films was *Platoon* (1986), Oliver Stone's personal drama of young soldier Chris Taylor (Charlie Sheen) who volunteers for a tour of duty, as Stone himself had done in April 1967. Taylor finds himself in an infantry unit led by two dominant personalities, representing opposing philosophies of modern warfare: the ruthless Staff Sergeant Barnes (Tom Berenger) and the more tactful, realist Sergeant Elias (Willem Dafoe). "People like Elias get wasted. People like Barnes just go on making up the rules any way they want," says Taylor, in voice-over narration. "So what do we do? Sit in the middle and suck on it."

The film has been described as one of the more accurate cinematic depictions of the combat experience in Vietnam, and it doesn't skirt around thorny moral questions about America's involvement. "There's no great fuss or layering about *Platoon*: it goes to the heart of the matter with unrefined directness," wrote film historian David Thomson, who likened Stone's film to *Billy Budd*, "an epic Manichaean conflict" between impulse and tact. The *New York Times* called it a *Lord of the Flies* for Vietnam, "as powerful a portrait of the mindlessness and absurdity of war as has ever been put on the screen."

The year 1987 brought the combat film *Hamburger Hill*, Stanley Kubrick's often surreal *Full Metal Jacket*, and *Good Morning, Vietnam* with Robin Williams as an armed-services radio deejay. The film *84C MoPic* (1989) is a drama in the form of a vérité-style documentary that follows an army cameraman (coded as "84 Charlie") assigned to make a training film. Bill Couturié's documentary *Dear America: Letters Home from Vietnam* (1987) was praised for its moving use of soldiers' real correspondence with their loved ones, read by actors—many of whom had appeared in major Vietnam-set films to that point, like Robert De Niro, Martin Sheen, Berenger, and Dafoe.

Brian De Palma's *Casualties of War* (1989) tells of a group of US soldiers who rape and murder a Vietnamese girl, from the perspective of the private (Michael J. Fox) who reports them. Veterans' groups criticized the film, but critics appreciated its direct look at the way war can corrupt the morality of those involved. "It showed that we were over there basically fighting ourselves instead of the enemy," said De Palma.

Stone's *Born on the Fourth of July* (1989) was an indictment of the entire system that led young men like him to join up in the first place, told through the true story of veteran (and screenwriter) Ron Kovic, who was wounded and paralyzed in Vietnam and ultimately became an outspoken war critic and demonstrator. "When is President [George H. W.] Bush going to get up before Congress and read an apology to the Vietnamese? Never, is the obvious answer," wrote

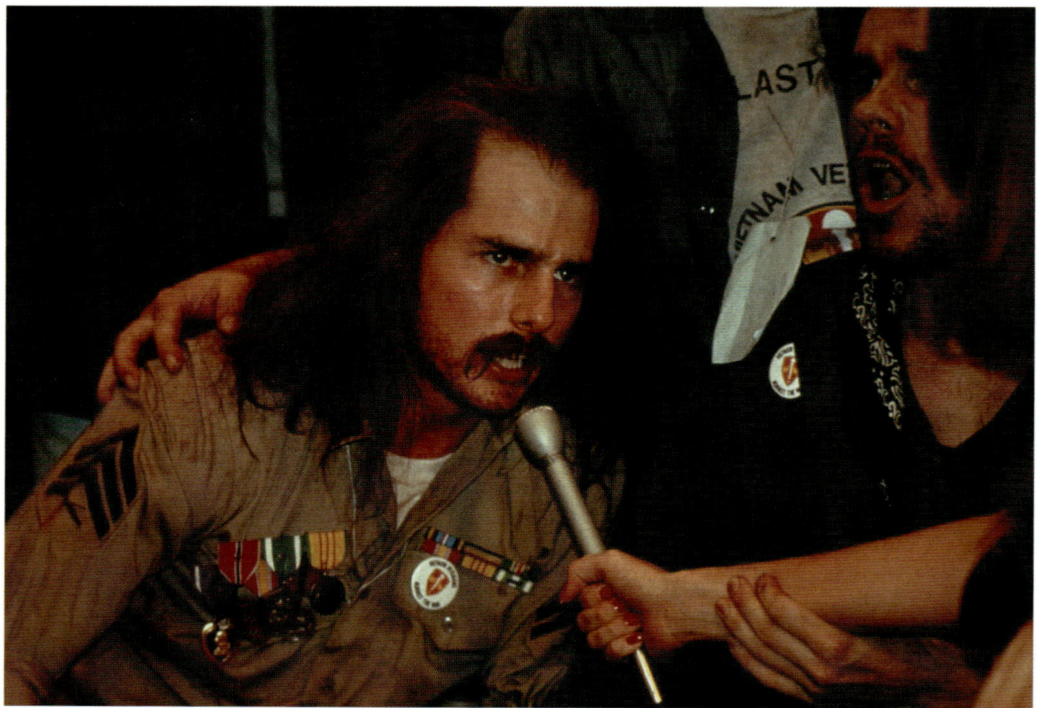

Tom Cruise in *Born on the Fourth of July*.

Roger Ebert in his review. "*Born on the Fourth of July* is an apology for Vietnam, uttered by Stone, who fought there."

In depicting the struggles of returning soldiers, films alternated between emotional realism and graphic violence. *Cutter's Way* (1981), *Blue Thunder* (1983), and *In Country* (1989) dealt with post-traumatic stress disorder (PTSD), while Louis Malle's *Alamo Bay* (1985) showed a veteran struggling with the presence of Vietnamese immigrants in his Texas hometown.

The war seeped into other genres as well. Richard Pryor starred as a returning POW who attempts, but constantly fails, to start a normal life in the comedy *Some Kind of Hero* (1982). *House* (1985) is a horror comedy about a novelist and Vietnam vet who finds himself living in a haunted home.

The most famous Vietnam veteran in Hollywood films is John Rambo (Sylvester Stallone), whose debut in *First Blood* (1982) as a Green Beret who is hunted by law enforcement in the forests of Washington State launched one of the decade's most high-profile franchises. Through its depiction of PTSD, the film encouraged a respect for veterans that was consistent with a growing national movement to honor those who served in the war, culminating in the opening of the Vietnam Veterans Memorial in Washington, DC, that same year. In *Rambo: First Blood Part II* (1985), Stallone's character—more muscular and less traumatized—is sent on a covert mission to investigate the continued existence of POW camps in Vietnam. Whereas *First Blood* shed light on John Rambo's challenged reintegration into society, *Part II* is essentially a jingoistic revenge fantasy in which Rambo asks his superior, "Do we get to win this time?" and dispatches the enemy with poisoned arrows, bowie knives, and a lot of firepower. Though multiple official investigations turned up no evidence of American soldiers being held by the Vietnamese after the war, the provocative theory nonetheless formed the basis for multiple films, including *Uncommon Valor* (1982) and Chuck Norris's *Missing in Action* series (1984–1988).

"Today's Cold War films are something else. They don't worry much about any rottenness within, except for the vaguely leftist, wishy-washy Government types who allowed the Vietnam War to be lost," wrote Canby in 1985, summing up the new wave of post-Vietnam Cold War cinema. "They're action melodramas first, with political subtexts (the value of God, country, family) that aren't boringly spelled out but efficiently represented in the iconography—an American flag, a nondenominational church, a tot-packed school bus, a close-up of Sylvester Stallone's right bicep."

THE RUSSIANS ARE COMING, THE RUSSIANS ARE COMING

For decades after World War II, Nazis had been the go-to screen villains. Things had changed in the era of Vietnam, when the image of Americans at war was suddenly not as pristine as it had been earlier. The late '60s ushered in a wave of more introspective films about government corruption and domestic social concerns. But by the time of *Star Wars* (1977), with its sinister galactic empire, Hollywood began to look outward again for tales of good and evil.

Of course, Soviet villains were nothing new. During the Red Scare, Hollywood tended to either put out virulent anti-Russian movies (*The Red Menace* [1949]) or address communist paranoia through clever genre exercises (*Invasion of the Body Snatchers* [1956]). *Dr. Strangelove* and *Fail*

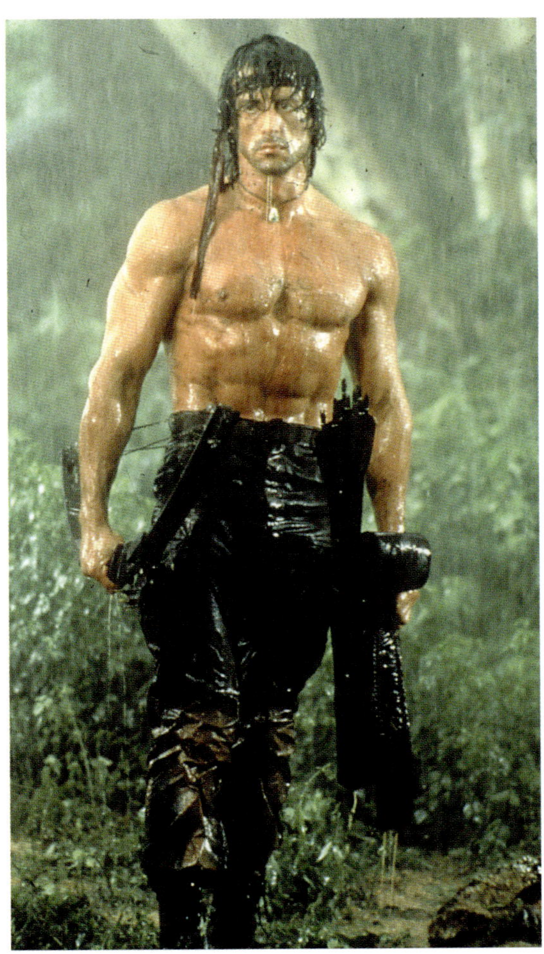

Sylvester Stallone increased the action in *Rambo: First Blood Part II.*

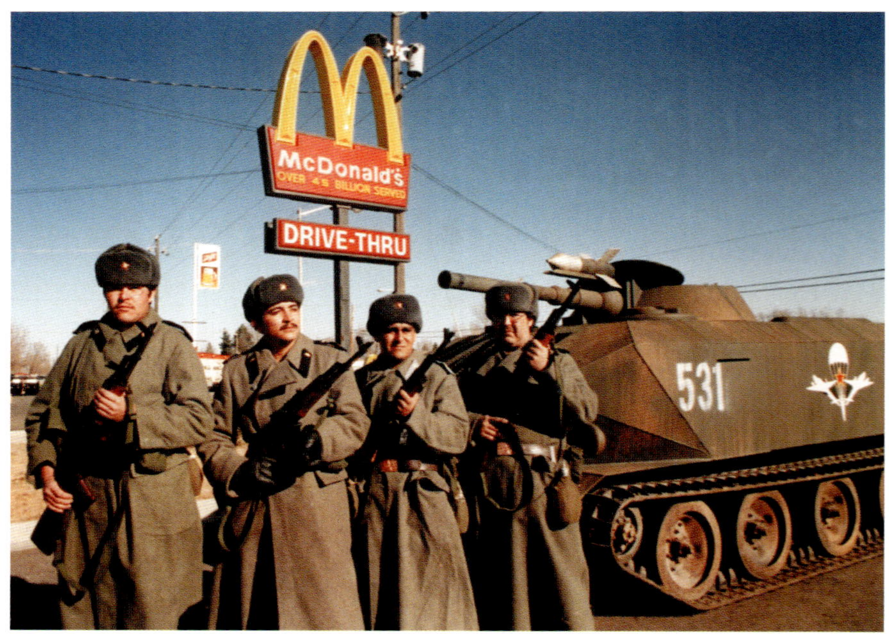

The Soviet military arrives on US soil in *Red Dawn*.

Safe (both 1964) had in their own ways spoken to the precariousness of the nuclear arms race, while *The Russians Are Coming, the Russians Are Coming* (1966) satirized the conflict with its story of a Soviet submarine that runs aground off the coast of New England.

Espionage fiction was popular across the board, from television series like *The Man from U.N.C.L.E.* and *Get Smart* to novels by John le Carré and subsequent film adaptations of his work, like *The Spy Who Came in from the Cold* (1965). Kicking off this craze was the 007 franchise, which began with star Sean Connery as the suave MI6 agent James Bond in *Dr. No* (1962). In the 1970s, the lighthearted but credible Scottish actor had handed the reins to Roger Moore, whose several installments had seen the series further and further into the ridiculous—including the post–*Star Wars* space high jinks of *Moonraker* (1979).

The Soviet government was not usually Bond's main antagonist; that would be too straightforward. The main villain role was typically filled by an evil industrialist or rogue agent out for some form of world domination. In *For Your Eyes Only* (1981), which attempted to return the series to a more serious tone, an international smuggler plans to sell a submarine tracking device to the Russians. In *Octopussy* (1983), a defiant Russian general tries to weaken NATO by causing a nuclear incident at an American base in Germany. In *A View to a Kill* (1985), an ex-KGB operative plots to destroy Silicon Valley in order to dominate the microchip industry.

In an unusual turn of events, Sean Connery returned for one final Bond appearance in *Never Say Never Again* (1983). This second adaptation of Ian Fleming's *Thunderball* was not one of the official 007 films made by Eon Productions, but the return of Connery's Bond—in a film that didn't ignore his advancing age, unlike the Roger Moore cycle—was a welcome respite for audiences and critics.

After the commercial disappointment of *A View to a Kill*, Moore stepped away from the character. Replacing him was Timothy Dalton, whose first entry, *The Living Daylights* (1987), saw Bond assigned to assassinate the new head of the KGB while helping his predecessor defect to the West. After *Licence to Kill* (1989), in which Bond resigns from MI6 and pursues a drug lord in a fit of vengeance, Dalton too threw in the towel. At decade's end, with the collapse of the Soviet Union on the horizon, the 007 series went dark for its longest period.

If spy movies were big business in Cold War Hollywood, so were films about Soviet infiltration of US institutions. Arthur Penn's *Target* (1985) is a father-son thriller in which Gene Hackman is revealed to be an ex-CIA agent whose wife has been kidnapped by an old nemesis, while *Daniel* (1983) and *Little Nikita* (1988) both deal with the concept of parents as Soviet agents. The two young protagonists of *The Falcon and the Snowman* (1985) sell US government secrets to the Soviet Union. Rutger Hauer's journalist character in *The Osterman Weekend* (1983) stages a get-together with his three closest friends, who turn out to be Russian spies. In *No Way Out* (1987), a naval intelligence officer (Kevin Costner) is tasked with investigating the murder of the defense secretary's mistress, complicated by rumors of a Russian mole. The genre was given a dose of comedy in *Spies Like Us* (1985), with Chevy Chase and Dan Aykroyd as two rookie agents sent as decoys on a mission to Central Asia. The teen action film *Red Dawn* (1984) depicted a group of Colorado high schoolers—played by Patrick Swayze, Charlie Sheen, C. Thomas Howell, and more—who defend their small town against a communist invasion. Writer-director John Milius was chided by many critics for the film's celebration of guerrilla warfare, overt nationalism, and brute machismo. (Howell's character is at one point made to drink the blood of a slaughtered deer. "When you drink it, you'll be a real hunter," Sheen tells him.) "How to explain the robust $8.2 million in ticket sales on its first weekend of release, when most

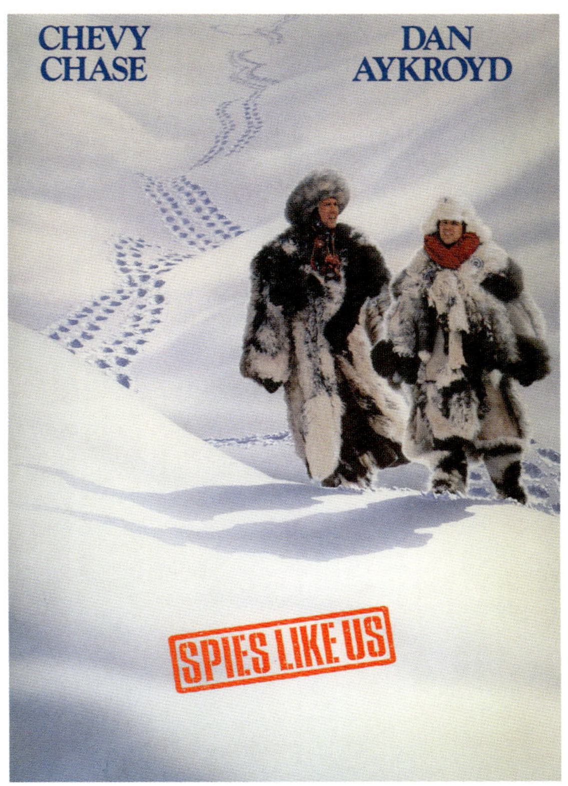

Spies Like Us spoofed Cold War–era espionage with a nod to the classic "Road to . . ." movies.

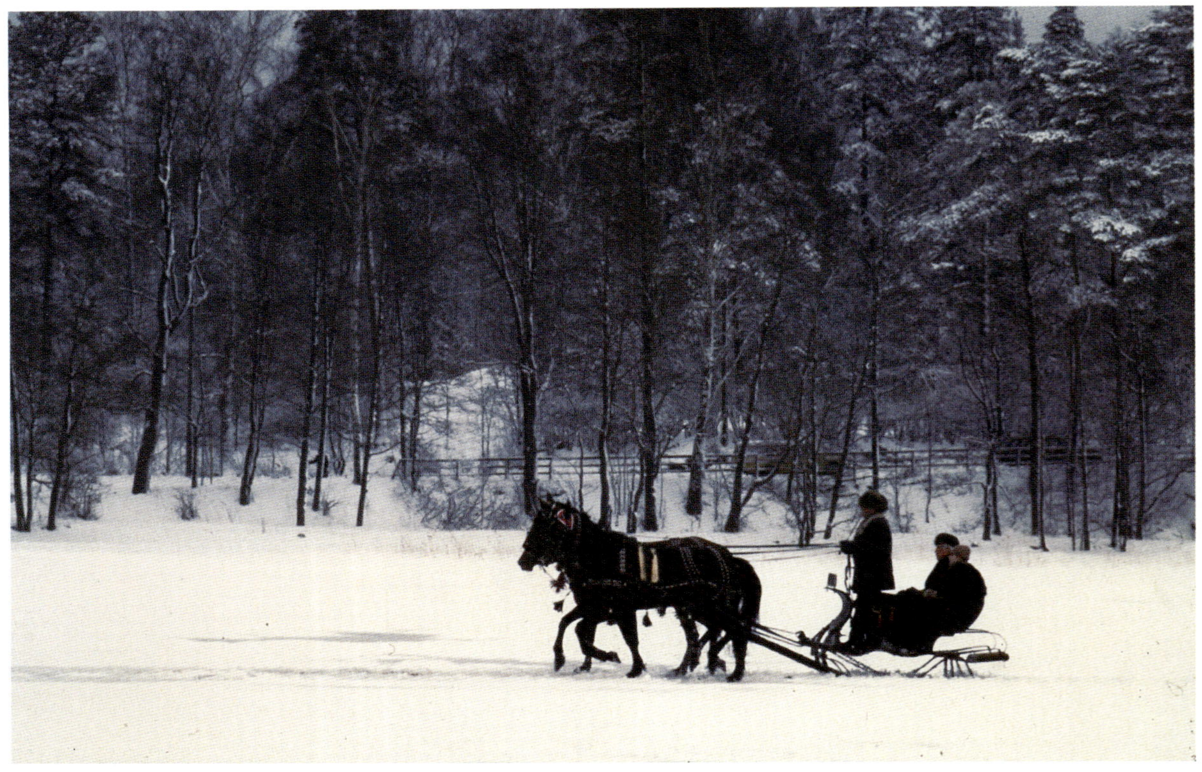

Lee Marvin and Joanna Pacuła ride through a snowy landscape in *Gorky Park*.

Americans were engaged in the sissy activity of watching the Olympics?" asked Richard Corliss in *Time*, sarcastically. "Perhaps the film's audience loves guerrilla theater, no matter who the bad guys are. You can, after all, key a crowd up by shooting at anything that moves. It doesn't even have to be red."

In several high-profile cases, A-list actors went up against Soviet villains on-screen. In *Firefox* (1982), Clint Eastwood plays a Vietnam veteran and fluent Russian speaker who enters the Soviet Union undercover to steal a highly advanced new fighter jet. *Top Gun* (1986) intentionally kept quiet on which nation Tom Cruise and crew were opposing in the film's climactic sequence; director Tony Scott suggested it was originally North Korea, but the enemy's use of MiG fighter planes is characteristic of Russian forces. Sylvester Stallone's two hugely popular franchises took on the USSR in the '80s, beginning with *Rocky IV* (1985), in which the southpaw successfully fights against the powerful Russian fighter Ivan Drago (Dolph Lundgren) and earns the adoration of his Soviet audience. For *Rambo III* (1988), Stallone's character—no longer the shell-shocked veteran from *First Blood*—undertakes a covert rescue mission in Soviet-occupied Afghanistan to aid local rebel groups in their fight against Russia.

Meanwhile, some big stars actually portrayed Russians in American films. William Hurt plays a Moscow police officer investigating a triple homicide while battling institutional corruption in *Gorky Park* (1983). Arnold Schwarzenegger plays a stoic Russian policeman who teams up with American cop Jim Belushi to nab an escaped Georgian drug lord in Walter Hill's action comedy *Red Heat* (1988). Belgian martial artist Jean-Claude Van Damme used steely expressions and a vaguely European accent to play Russian villains in *No Retreat, No Surrender* (1986) and *Black Eagle* (1988). In Paul Mazursky's *Moscow on the Hudson* (1984), Robin Williams stars as a Soviet saxophonist in a traveling circus troupe who defects to the West.

Soviet defections anchored the plots of a variety of other films—including the Disney comedy *Condorman* (1981), about a comic-book artist who becomes a winged superhero to help extract a rogue KGB agent. More famously, *White Nights* (1985) showed two sides to the equation with an American dancer (Gregory Hines) who left America for Russia in protest over the Vietnam War and a defected Russian ballet star (Mikhail Baryshnikov, who actually had defected to the West in 1974) who finds himself accidentally back in his home country. They both ultimately return to America through a combination of music, love, and crafty politics.

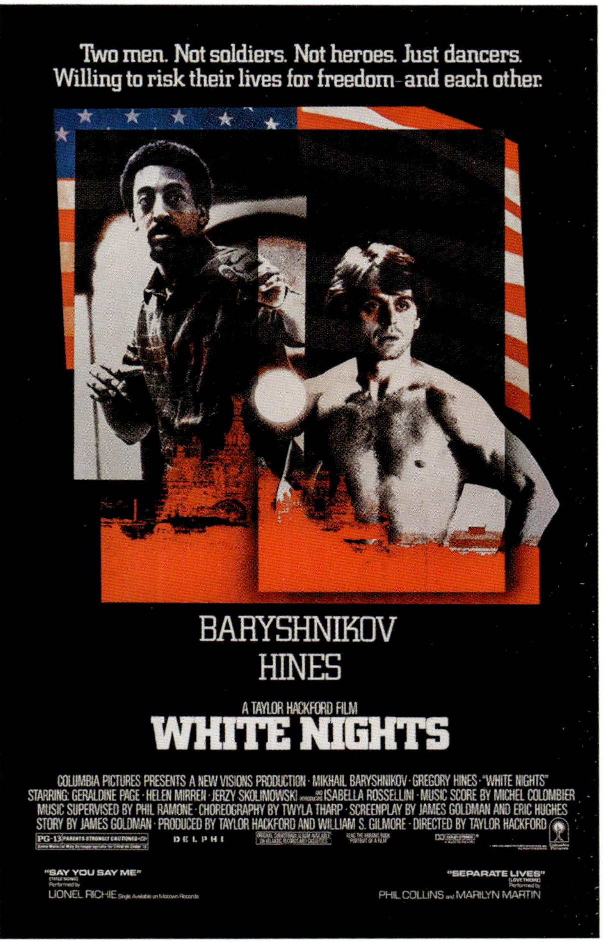

Director Taylor Hackford's dance-infused *White Nights* is notable for its Oscar-winning music.

BACK IN THE USSR

In the Soviet Union, filmmaking took place under a system of government censorship that was centrally controlled through Goskino, the State Committee for Motion Pictures. Each of the country's fifteen republics (including Russia) had at least one studio that was allowed to choose the films it made and the liberty to make them in its local language—though they would ultimately be dubbed in Russian for distribution throughout the Soviet Union and the Eastern bloc. The most prominent of these studios was Mosfilm (founded in Moscow in 1924), which used as its logo the image of a man and woman holding aloft a hammer and sickle—a reminder that social realism was the directive for all Soviet filmmakers. Film historian

David Cook described this unwritten policy as "a noose around filmmakers' necks" that could be tightened or loosened depending on who was in charge.

For the first half of the 1980s, things were more or less status quo in Soviet filmmaking. One early success was the romantic comedy *Moscow Does Not Believe in Tears* (1980), which had been a big hit with moviegoers in Russia and shocked many observers by winning the Oscar for Best Foreign Language Film in 1981. "What made the movie so immensely popular was probably the simple fact that it showed Soviet people a bit of themselves in a sympathetic, even romantic light . . . instead of idealized socialist heroes," wrote Serge Schmemann in the *New York Times*, in a 1983 report on developments in Russian cinema.

Detective films and television series, often written by current or former KGB officials and police officers, were especially popular with Soviet audiences. These included adaptations of the work of writer Yulian Semyonov, whose 007-esque spy Stierlitz is a Russian agent who infiltrates the German Gestapo. For *Teheran 43* (1981), Mosfilm partnered with studios in France and Switzerland to produce a hit World War II–era political thriller. The satirical films of Eldar Ryazanov also performed well, such as *The Garage* (1980), about a set of bourgeois city dwellers who fight over a prized parking space.

Director Andrei Tarkovsky is one of the most celebrated Russian auteurs of this period (and in all of Soviet history) among film connoisseurs in the West. He had produced a handful of films by the '80s, like the historical epic *Andrei Rublev* (1966) and the science-fiction drama *Solaris* (1972), both of which won critical acclaim and prizes at international film festivals. But he was an exception to the rule in Soviet filmmaking. "Tarkovsky did not hew to the party line but expressed his own interpretation of events," said Soviet film journalist Val Golovskoy in 1982. "Now the Party and government close their eyes and allow Tarkovsky to direct films 'for export.'"

Nostalghia (1983), a film made in Italy about the melancholy of a Russian man working abroad, was crafted to feel "as if it were the window in a train traveling through your life," said the director. An art film through and through, it was funded by Italian public broadcaster Rai and the French studio Gaumont after Mosfilm pulled out of production. At the 1983 Cannes Film Festival, Soviet authorities—via jury member Sergei Bondarchuk—lobbied for it not to be awarded the Palme d'Or, which led to Tarkovsky's decision to stay permanently in the West. "I am not a Soviet dissident," he said, though he knew he could no longer work freely in Russia. He made *The Sacrifice* (1986) in Sweden with many of Ingmar Bergman's regular crew, including cinematographer Sven Nykvist and actor Erland Josephson. It would be his last film, as the self-exiled director died in Paris in December 1986.

The year of Tarkovsky's passing also marked the first utterances of the terms *perestroika* (restructuring) and *glasnost* (transparency) by

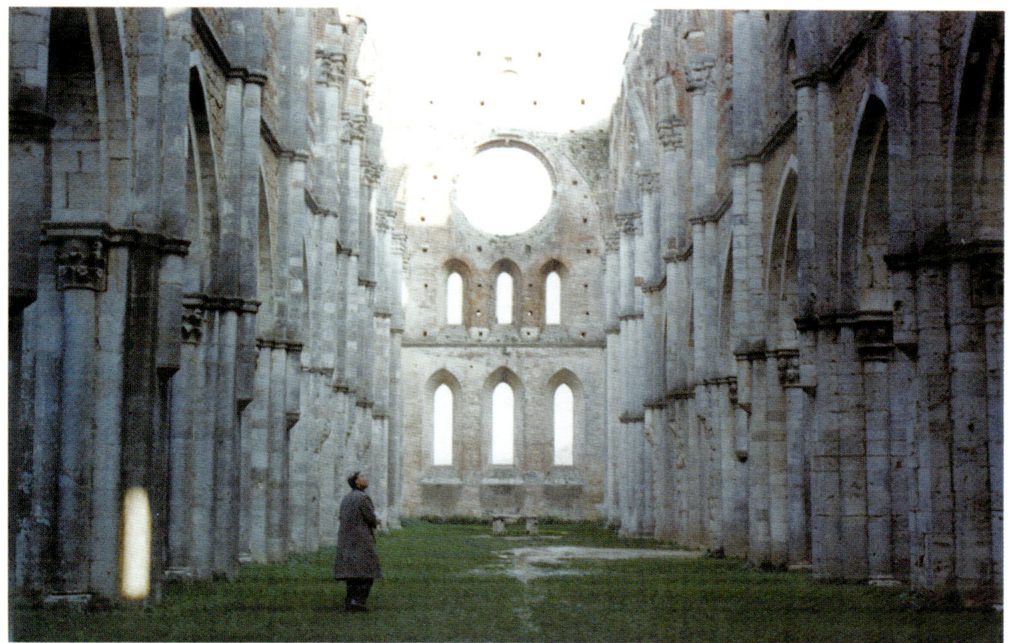

Oleg Yankovsky in the Abbey of San Galgano in *Nostalghia*.

new Soviet premier Mikhail Gorbachev. Faced with a stagnant economy and a growing inability to compete with the West, liberal reforms were introduced across many areas of society, including the film industry. Studios were given greater control over the films they produced, and postproduction censorship was largely dropped. Gorbachev's entreaties to the media to report on political corruption and bureaucratic inefficiencies led to a film trend called *chernukha* ("black stuff," akin to "noir") that acted like investigative journalism. *The Cold Summer of 1953* (1988) explored the rise in crime after the death of Joseph Stalin and the subsequent release of prisoners from Soviet gulags. Films like *Little Vera* (1988) and *The Asthenic Syndrome* (1989), while deeply critical of society, were also formally inventive and sexually provocative. Science-fiction films like *Kin-dza-dza!* (1986), a black comedy about two Moscow men who are teleported to a desert planet, began to openly satirize life in the USSR.

One of the key figures in the loosening of film restrictions after glasnost was director Elim Klimov, who was elected to be the head of the Filmmakers' Union in 1986 in a revolt against old leadership. Under his guidance, many films that had previously been censored were reconsidered and approved. For instance, the Georgian film *Repentance* (1984), which had sat on the shelf for three years for criticizing Stalinism, was finally released in 1987 to great international acclaim.

Klimov had been selected for the position in part because of the success of his epic war drama *Come and See* (1985), which depicted the wartime devastation of a Belorussian village by Nazi occupiers, told through the eyes of a teenage boy (Aleksei Kravchenko) who joins the resistance.

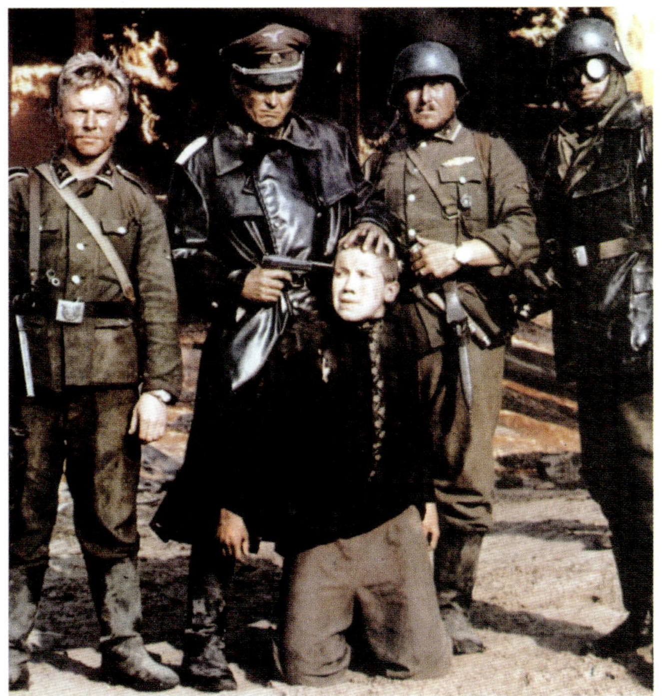

Aleksei Kravchenko, held at gunpoint, in *Come and See*.

An award winner at the 1985 Moscow International Film Festival, it was first shown in the United States at the Museum of Modern Art's 1986 series "A Salute to the Soviet Republics" and has since been acclaimed as one of the greatest films ever made.

GERMANY: EAST AND WEST

One of the most potent symbols of the Cold War was not in Russia but in Germany, where since 1961 the Berlin Wall encircled the western (and Western-aligned) half of the city. Throughout the '80s, the Federal Republic of Germany (West Germany) and the German Democratic Republic (communist East Germany) were separate countries with distinct film industries.

The East, having inherited most of the country's filmmaking infrastructure after the war, centralized production through the state-owned studio DEFA. Films faced similar regulations and censorship as the Soviet industry, though East German films were often distributed in West Germany as well. *Solo Sunny* (1980), about an aspiring pop singer, was a huge hit among audiences on both sides of the wall and the last film made by major East German director Konrad Wolf. *Apprehension* (1982) follows a thirtysomething woman in an anxiety-filled twenty-four hours before her cancer operation, while Frank Beyer's *The Turning Point* (1983) follows a German soldier in a Polish POW camp who is falsely accused of war crimes.

Later in the decade, DEFA's films became more open to diverse viewpoints and personal expression. In the revealing documentary *Winter Adé* (1988), director Helke Misselwitz interviewed women throughout the country about their lives, careers, and aspirations. Heiner Carow's landmark queer film *Coming Out* (1989), a moving and honest portrayal of gay life in the East, was evidence of the liberalization of laws affecting LGBTQ+ people and, by extension, society at large. It premiered in East Berlin on November 9, 1989—the night the wall was finally opened.

Meanwhile, the West German film industry had experienced a significant artistic development in the mid-1960s, similar to the New Hollywood. The "New German Cinema" saw a group of young filmmakers reject the commercial dictates of the established studio system and start to make smaller, more personal films. The

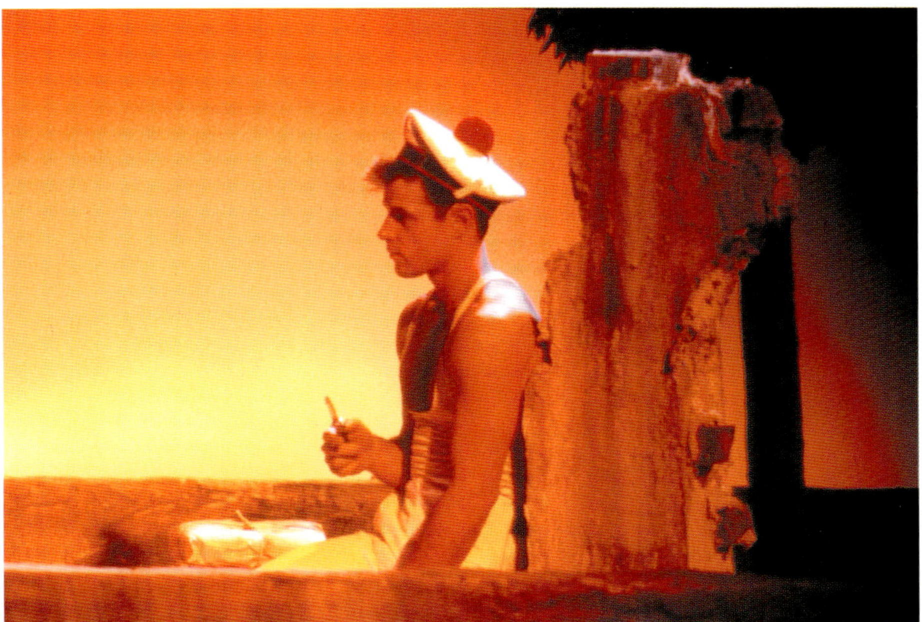

Brad Davis in *Querelle*.

new wave arguably reached its zenith in 1982 with major wins at the Berlin, Cannes, and Venice Film Festivals.

Unburdened by censorship, few topics were off the table. Whereas *Coming Out* had appeared at the very end of the decade, the sexually audacious *Taxi zum Klo* (*Taxi to the Toilet* [1981]) was made years before in the West. Its story of a schoolteacher who is active in the Berlin gay scene illustrates the cultural gap between the two sides. Queer icon Rainer Werner Fassbinder's final film, *Querelle* (1982), was brazenly homoerotic, with its melodramatic crime story about horny sailors in port shot against expressionistic set designs that include enormous phallic imagery. Rosa von Praunheim continued to push the limits with his punk musical *City of Lost Souls* (1983) that featured drag queens and trans performers and directly addressed the AIDS crisis with *A Virus Knows No Morals* (1986).

Werner Herzog made an infamous action-adventure film in the Amazon basin about an obsessive rubber baron who hires a team of native Peruvians to pull a steamboat over a mountain. *Fitzcarraldo* (1982), starring mercurial actor Klaus Kinski, has been called one of the most difficult (and foolhardy) productions in film history—due in part to Herzog's insistence that a real ship be dragged over an actual mountain.

Wim Wenders began the decade working in Hollywood on *Hammett* (1982), a neo-noir about acclaimed mystery writer Dashiell Hammett that was largely reshot by his dissatisfied producer, Francis Ford Coppola. His most enduring work was a pair of visually striking fiction films that explore alienation and longing. American road movie *Paris, Texas* (1984), written by playwright and actor Sam Shepard, stars Harry Dean Stanton as a mysterious drifter who reunites with his family after years away and won the Palme d'Or at the Cannes Film Festival. The year 1987's *Wings of Desire*, shot in West Berlin, focused on a disillusioned angel (Bruno Ganz) who longs to become human and live among the people of the city. The film's exploration of the divided city was beautifully encapsulated in the gap between the mortal and the immortal and enhanced by the alternating use of black-and-white and color cinematography.

The most internationally successful German filmmaker in the '80s was Wolfgang Petersen, whose World War II submarine thriller *Das Boot* (1981) earned him an Oscar nomination and, after the hit fantasy film *The NeverEnding Story* (1984), a lengthy career in Hollywood.

RAISING THE IRON CURTAIN

Many Eastern European nations that were under the thumb of the Soviet Union, and equally as repressive of speech and the media, nevertheless had robust film industries. One such country was Poland, whose best films were routinely screened and celebrated at international festivals and found distribution in the West. Veteran filmmaker Andrzej Wajda's *Man of Iron* (1981) was a drama about Solidarity, the early-'80s trade union turned social movement led by future Polish president Lech Wałęsa, who has a cameo in the film. It was banned in Poland for its criticism of the government, which imposed martial law in 1981 to quell dissent. So were two dramas—*Fever* and *A Lonely*

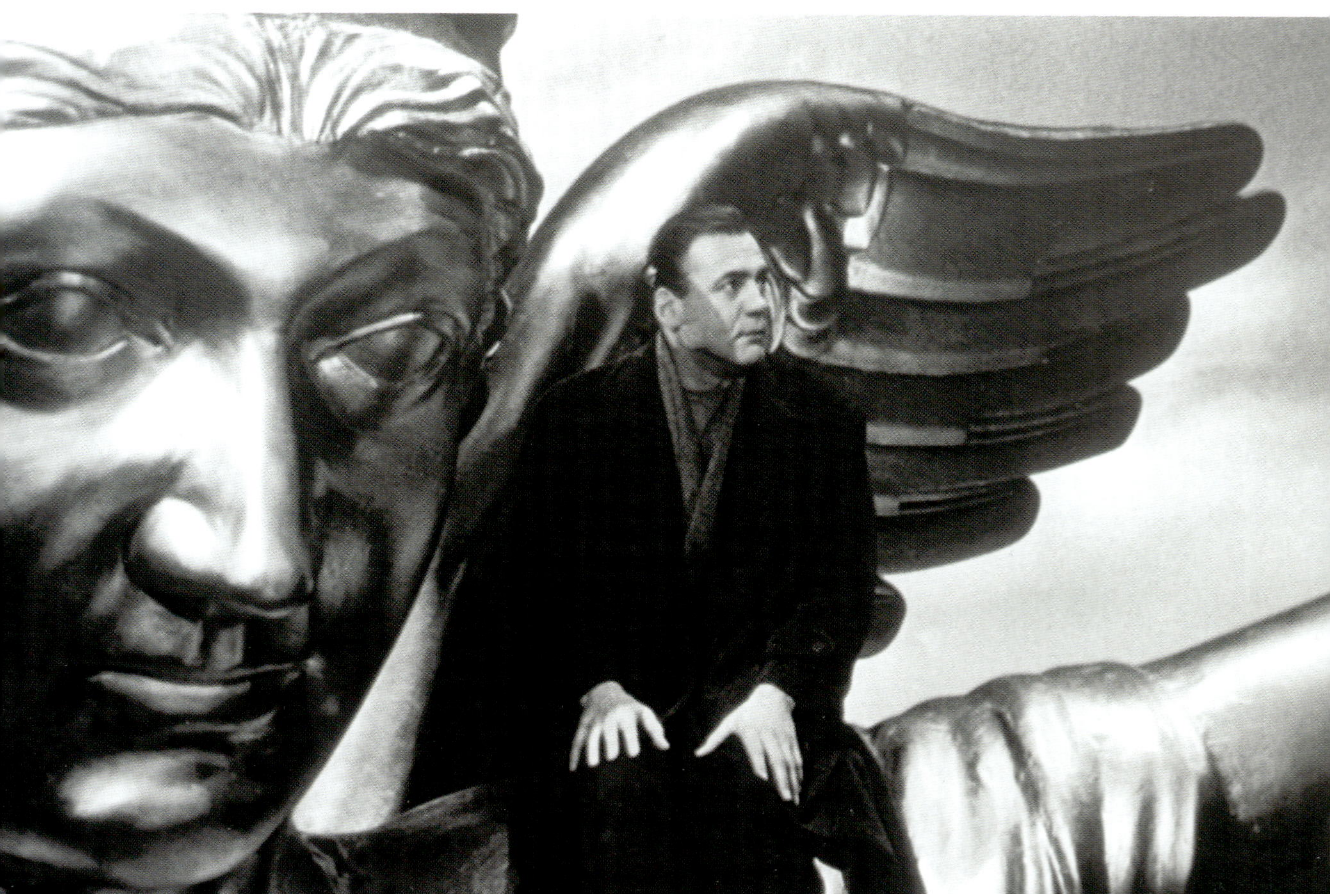

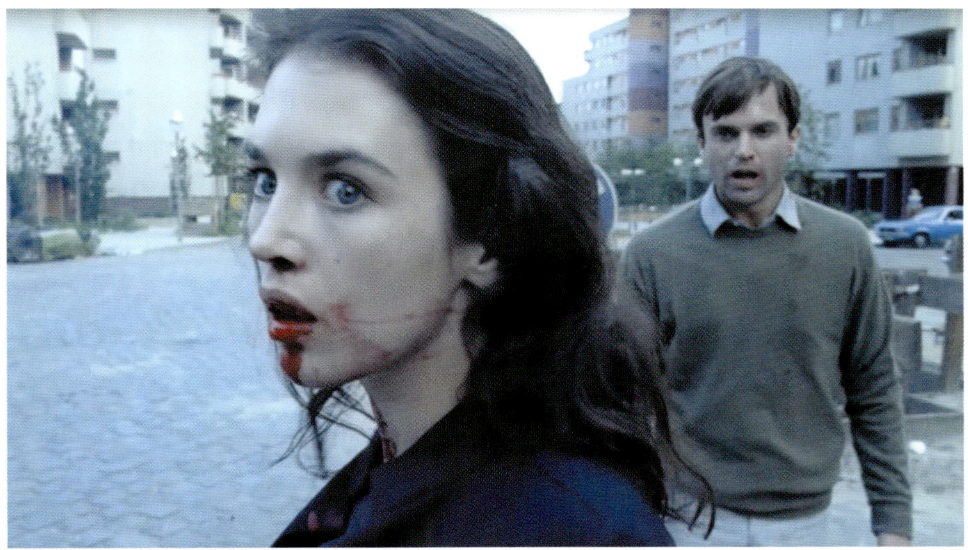

Isabel Adjani and Sam Neill in Andrzej Żuławski's harrowing *Possession*.

Woman (both 1981)—by Agnieszka Holland, who had begun as a writer and assistant director to Wajda. Like those two, director Jerzy Skolimowski began to work outside the country in the 1980s. His film *Moonlighting* (1982), made in England, recounts the Solidarity protests and subsequent crackdown from the perspective of a Polish foreman (Jeremy Irons) working in London.

Andrzej Żuławski's *Possession* (1981) was made in West Berlin in the aftermath of his messy divorce and his ban from filmmaking in Poland. It depicts the disintegration of a marriage through scenes of horror that veer into the supernatural. Sam Neill plays a Western spy whose unhappy wife (Isabel Adjani) has taken up her own secret life that rips their family apart—a clear allegory for the Iron Curtain that divided Europe and the German capital. The film's shocks are vividly physical, including a repulsively violent scene of Adjani alone in a subway station. The film uses the Berlin Wall conspicuously in many scenes to add to the threat of violence and to suggest that the film's characters are surrounded by a creeping evil.

One of the most celebrated Polish filmmakers in the 1980s was Krzysztof Kieślowski, whose films *Blind Chance* (1981) and *No End* (1985) were subject to censorship. His boldest feat was the ten-part television series *Dekalog* (1989), of which two episodes were expanded into the 1988 theatrical releases *A Short Film About Killing* and *A Short Film About Love*. Each hourlong episode takes one of the Ten Commandments as a jumping-off point to explore an aspect of contemporary Polish society. "Chaos and disorder ruled Poland in the mid-1980s—everywhere, everything, practically everybody's life," said Kieślowski, who avoided using overt political messages in the series. "Politics aren't really important. In a way, of course, they define where we are and what we're allowed or aren't allowed to do, but they don't solve the really important human questions."

Bruno Ganz as the angel Damiel in *Wings of Desire*.

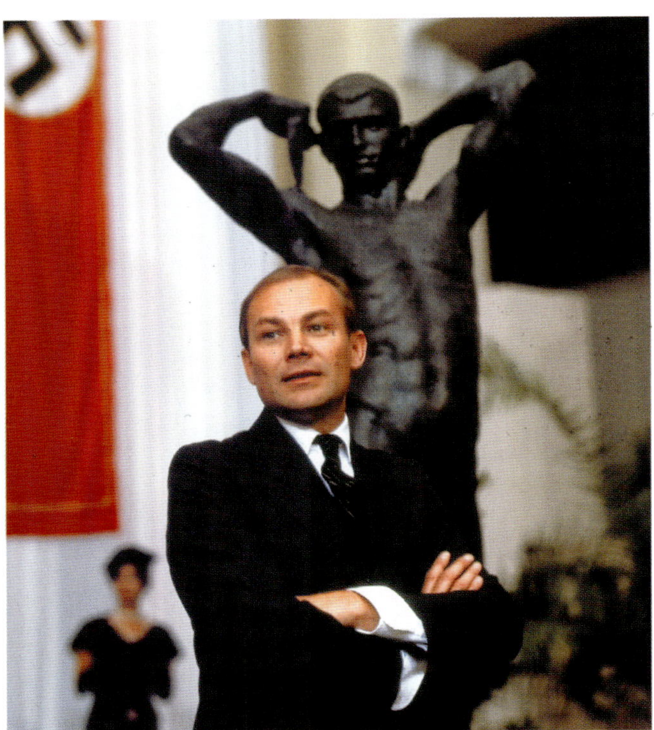

Klaus Maria Brandauer in *Mephisto*.

Political topics were safer when clouded by genre. Director Piotr Szulkin created a series of fantastical science-fiction films that corresponded to contemporary society, including *The War of the Worlds: Next Century* (1981) and *O-Bi, O-Ba: The End of Civilization* (1985). Meanwhile, the absurdity of life under Soviet control was cleverly mocked in comedies from directors like Stanisław Bareja (*Teddy Bear* [1981]), Juliusz Machulski (*Vabank* [1981]; *Sexmission* [1984]), and Janusz Majewski (*H.M. Deserters* [1986]).

In Czechoslovakia, director Věra Chytilová—famous for her anarchic 1968 comedy *Daisies*—continued to satirize the government in *Panelstory; or, Birth of a Community* (1981), an absurdist take on a housing unit under construction, and *Calamity* (1982), a romantic comedy about a college dropout who becomes a train engineer. She later made the teen horror film *Wolf's Hole* (1987), a thinly veiled critique of authoritarianism. Jiří Menzel's charming comedy *My Sweet Little Village* (1985) remains a more popular film about a hapless truck driver's assistant whose country cottage becomes the envy of a city bureaucrat. Hungary's István Szabó made an international splash with *Mephisto* (1981), the story of a rising actor in Nazi Germany who trades his soul for fame on the stage, while Márta Mészáros had a hit with her semiautobiographical drama *Diary for My Children* (1984), about a teenager in postwar Budapest.

Yugoslavia—not aligned with the Soviet Union, but nonetheless a socialist state—saw the release of Serbian director Emir Kusturica's debut feature (*Do You Remember Dolly Bell?*) in 1981. He followed up with a second coming-of-age drama and Palme d'Or winner, *When Father Was Away on Business* (1985), set in the volatile political climate of the 1950s.

THE ROCKETS' RED GLARE

Move over, Godzilla. American movies during the Cold War were rife with allusions to nuclear war, a trend that experienced a small uptick in the early '80s. The 007 franchise dealt consistently (though not seriously) with the apocalyptic plans of its villains, like the Russian general who attempts to detonate a nuclear warhead and destabilize NATO in *Octopussy*. But 1983 saw the release of several alarming films that spoke of the country's vulnerability to a nuclear strike and the devastating consequences that would follow.

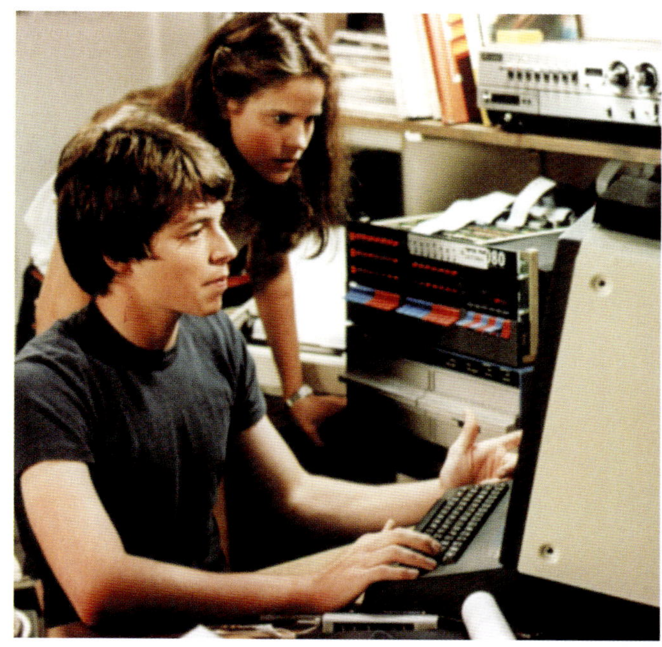
Matthew Broderick and Ally Sheedy in *WarGames*.

Film critic Leonard Maltin memorably described *WarGames* (1983) as "*Fail Safe* for the Pac-Man generation." In it, a teenager computer whiz played by Matthew Broderick manages to accidentally hack into NORAD (North American Aerospace Defense Command), whose automated simulator responds with an escalating series of exercises, nearly triggering World War III. The entertaining film was warmly received by critics and was a hit at the box office.

"As to the credibility of the story," wrote critic Stanley Kauffmann in the *New Republic*, "it's at least sufficiently plausible to make the U.S. Air Force deny its possibility." On the other hand, when Ronald Reagan viewed *WarGames* shortly after its release, the security threat dreamed up by the film's writers led the president to issue National Security Decision Directive 145, the "National Policy on Telecommunications and Automated Information Systems Security," in September 1984.

Testament (1983) offered a much more sobering experience. Starring Oscar nominee Jane Alexander, it was based on a short story published in *Ms.* magazine about a California woman and her family as they live through the fallout of a nuclear blast. The movie is a stark warning and, wrote Roger Ebert, "a tragedy about manners. It asks how we might act toward one another, how our values might stand up, in the face of an overwhelming catastrophe." Two weeks after its release, ABC aired *The Day After*, an ensemble film with Jason Robards, JoBeth Williams, Steve Guttenberg, and John Lithgow that depicted the devastating results of a nuclear strike in middle America. The film garnered much media attention and was viewed by a record one hundred million people in its initial broadcast. It was even shown on Soviet television in 1987, the year that Reagan and Gorbachev signed a landmark nuclear-arms-control treaty.

The documentary *The Atomic Café* (1982) is constructed entirely of midcentury government propaganda films that advise citizens on how to live happily in the age of nuclear weapons. Between scenes of soldiers being taught about radiation sickness and elementary school children practicing "duck and cover," the film could be seen as just a collection of kitschy Americana if it weren't so pathetically terrifying. "The humor isn't injected into the movie," said producer Kevin Rafferty. "The humor *is* the movie. The whole concept of living with World War III comes out funny."

Hollywood's Latin America

As in Vietnam and Cuba, the Cold War ultimately took on global dimensions as American political leaders attempted to quash socialist movements on virtually every continent. Stories of military coups, government corruption, and US interventions were seemingly all that Hollywood knew about Latin America in the '80s, from Arnold Schwarzenegger taking on a deposed dictator who kidnaps his daughter in *Commando* (1985) to . . . Arnold Schwarzenegger taking on an invisible alien creature in a Central American jungle in *Predator* (1987).

Clint Eastwood dramatized the American invasion of Grenada in *Heartbreak Ridge* (1986), while Chuck Norris's *Invasion U.S.A.* (1985) played into paranoia about mass immigration as an avenue for a communist takeover. The gangster epic *Scarface* (1983) showed enterprising Cuban refugees as violent drug smugglers—while also functioning as a capitalist critique. A more humane portrait of immigration came from American director Gregory Nava, whose *El Norte* (1983) follows two Guatemalan teenagers who journey to the United States.

There were movies on civil wars in El Salvador (*Salvador* [1986] and *Romero* [1989]) and Nicaragua (*Under Fire* [1983] and *Latino* [1985]) as well as America's role in the 1973 military coup in Chile (*Mission* [1982]). On a lighter note, *Romancing the Stone* (1984) paired Kathleen Turner with Michael Douglas on a trek through the Colombian rainforest, and *Moon over Parador* (1988) saw Richard Dreyfuss impersonate a deceased South American dictator.

For a small taste of the work of actual Latin American filmmakers, see Héctor Babenco's gripping story of young Brazilian criminals, *Pixote* (1982), or Luis Puenzo's Argentinian Oscar winner, *The Official Story* (1985), about the personal toll wrought by the country's military dictatorship.

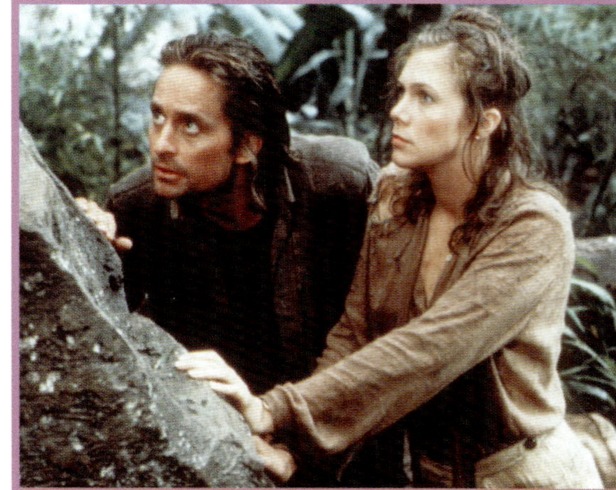

Michael Douglas and Kathleen Turner in *Romancing the Stone*.

Absurdity gave way to fantasy in *Repo Man* (1984), a science-fiction parable about nuclear war "and the demented society that contemplated the possibility thereof," according to director Alex Cox. Also set in Los Angeles was *Miracle Mile* (1988), Steve De Jarnatt's apocalyptic romance with Anthony Edwards and Mare Winningham as star-crossed lovers. *Superman IV: The Quest for Peace* (1987) saw the man of steel (Christopher Reeve) attempt to rid the world of atomic weapons and fight a radioactive "Nuclear Man." In *Gymkata* (1985), an American martial artist (Olympic gymnast Kurt Thomas) competes against a devious military commander for the rights to place a satellite monitoring station in Central Asia. And Godzilla? He made a return in the Japanese reboot *The Return of Godzilla* (1984), which foregrounded the arms race between America and the Soviet Union. It was recut and released in the United States as *Godzilla 1985*, with a special role for actor Raymond Burr, who had appeared in the American version of the original 1954 film.

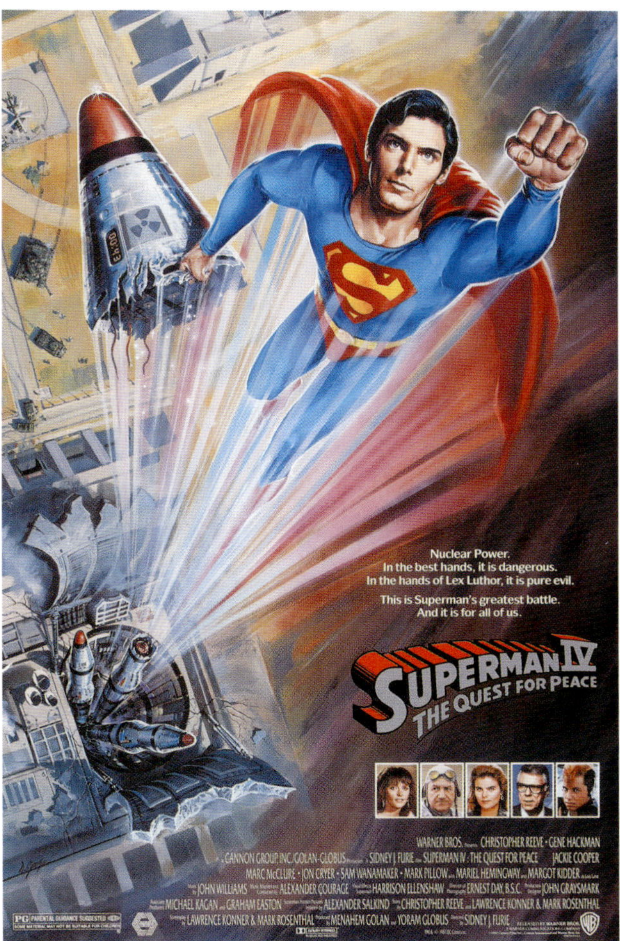

The nuclear-arms focus of *Superman IV* originated with star Christopher Reeve.

THE SPACE RACE

The 1980s saw a minor renaissance in the portrayal of American astronauts on-screen, thanks to the popularity of *Star Wars* and the launch of NASA's first space-shuttle orbiter, *Columbia*, in April 1981. Cameras captured the events of that initial flight, STS-1, for the IMAX documentary *Hail Columbia* (1982), made in coordination with NASA. Another large-format documentary about the shuttle program, *The Dream Is Alive* (1985), proved popular by eventually earning more than $70 million.

Philip Kaufman's *The Right Stuff* (1983) was an epic adaptation of Tom Wolfe's nonfiction book about the space race. It opens with intrepid pilot Chuck Yeager (Sam Shepard) who broke the sound barrier in 1947, continues through the 1957 launch of Soviet satellite Sputnik, and follows the training and flights of the Mercury Seven astronauts. Though the film lost money during its theatrical run, it won four Oscars (for

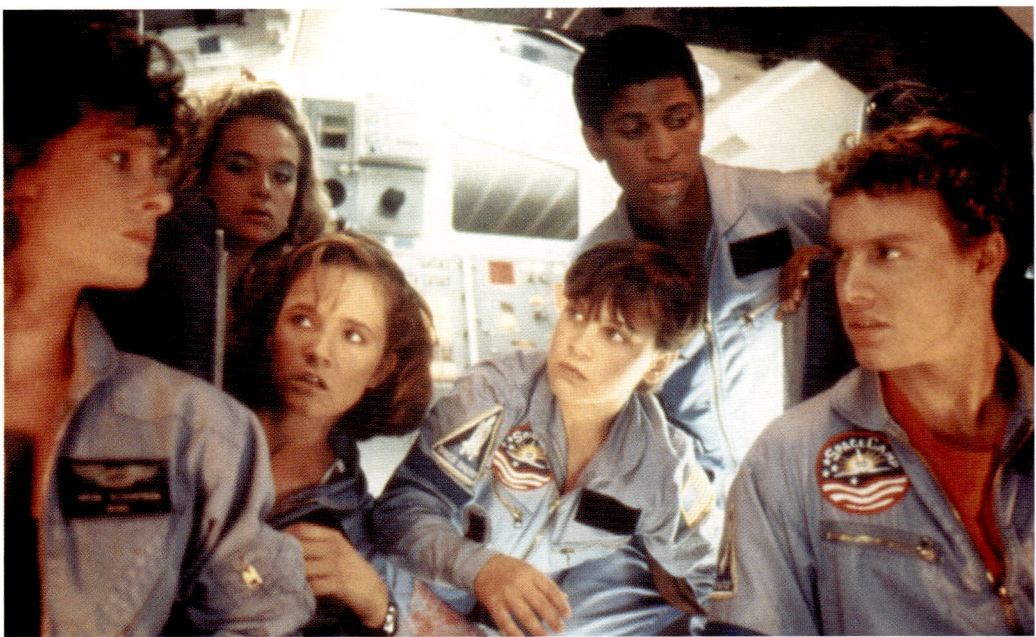

(from left) Kate Capshaw, Kelly Preston, Lea Thompson, Joaquin Phoenix, Larry B. Scott, and Tate Donovan in *SpaceCamp*.

its editing, score, sound, and sound editing) and grew in popularity when released on home video. Critics' reviews were glowing. Sheila Benson of the *Los Angeles Times* called it "a brash, beautiful, deeply American film . . . a generous, high-spirited look at the bravery and lunacy that was that era."

NASA programs crept into many of the decade's science-fiction films. The alien presence in John Carpenter's *Starman* (1984) appears in response to the Voyager 2 probe, which had launched in 1977. The space shuttle is key to the plot of several films—often involving UFOs—like *Hangar 18* (1980), *Lifeforce* (1985), and *Moontrap* (1989). *Airplane II: The Sequel* (1982) jumps into the future for its zany satire about a malfunctioning lunar passenger shuttle.

Kids take to space in several films, including *Explorers* (1985) and *Flight of the Navigator* (1986). Set at the US Space & Rocket Center in Huntsville, Alabama, *SpaceCamp* (1986) told of a group of teenage wannabe astronauts who accidentally get blasted into orbit during a space-shuttle engine test. The film was released a few months after the tragic explosion of the space shuttle *Challenger* and had a difficult time at the box office—though attendance at the actual Space Camp program doubled in its wake.

MAGIC TIME

"The world is changing," said Academy Awards producer Gil Cates, ahead of the 1990 broadcast. "And hopefully the awards show is changing, matching the changes in the world." Throughout the show, various presenters beamed in live from locations around the world like London, Sydney, and Buenos Aires. The most notable

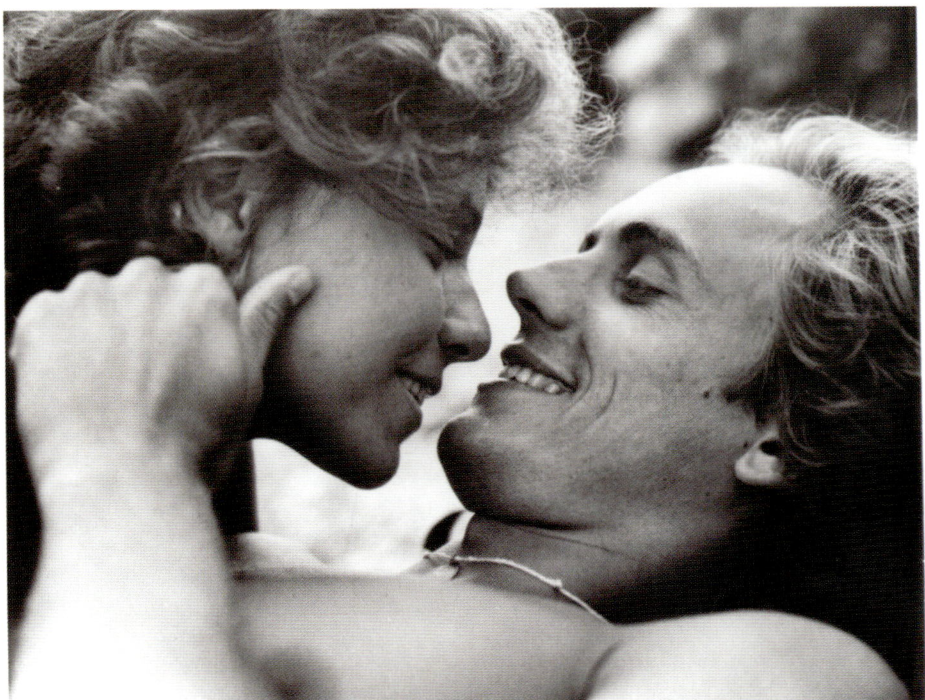

Natalya Negoda and Andrey Sokolov in *Little Vera*.

of these segments—in a show that aired four months after the fall of the Berlin Wall—was for the announcement of the Best Foreign Language Film.

"Right here, right now, in Moscow, it is magic time," said Jack Lemmon. His copresenter was Soviet film actress Natalya Negoda, who recently had been seen on American screens in *Little Vera*—even appearing on the cover of *Playboy* in May 1989 to promote the sexually frank film. After decades of treating Russians as villainous, godless, and corrupt—a threat to world order and American values—the tide had turned in favor of cooperation and understanding. Before giving an award to that year's winner, Italian nominee *Cinema Paradiso*, Lemmon and Negoda shared some friendly banter.

"How many of your films show a profit?" he asked her.

"Profit? In Russia we never hear this word 'profit.'"

Lemmon chuckled. "Welcome to the club."

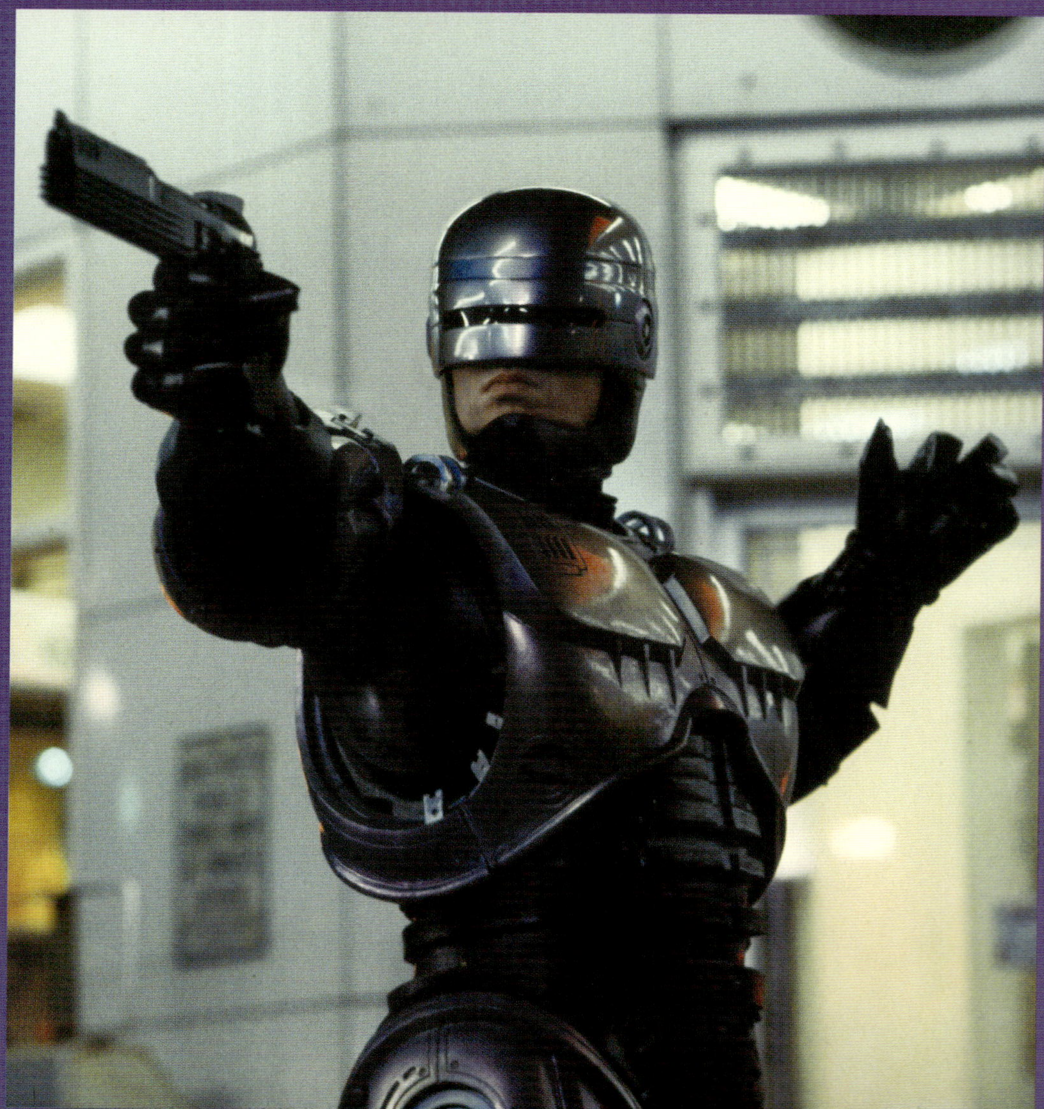

Robocop

The ACTION SECTION

Eighties cinema is often defined by its deep bench of iconic action movies. The genre was arguably at its creative peak, with muscle-bound heroes storming multiplexes each summer with guns blazing, engines roaring, and explosions aplenty. This bold, loud, and exceedingly cinematic trend spoke to the industry's target demographic—young men—in a way that few others did, and in many cases their box-office success led to bigger and more expensive sequels. This was the era of the action movie star: Arnold Schwarzenegger, Sylvester Stallone, Bruce Willis, Jean-Claude Van Damme, Chuck Norris, Carl Weathers, and other tough guys whose characters were more brawny than brainy. It was nurtured by production companies like Cannon and Carolco that specialized in thrilling screen violence.

Politics tends to infiltrate a lot of action cinema, and many of these films represent a forceful response to post-Vietnam America and its wounded sense of pride. At the same time, filmmakers like John Carpenter and Paul Verhoeven were able to make clever social critiques of '80s society, wrapped in attractive action packages for a wide audience.

The lines of the genre are blurry. Some films immediately spring to mind—the *Mad Max* series, for instance—but there were many

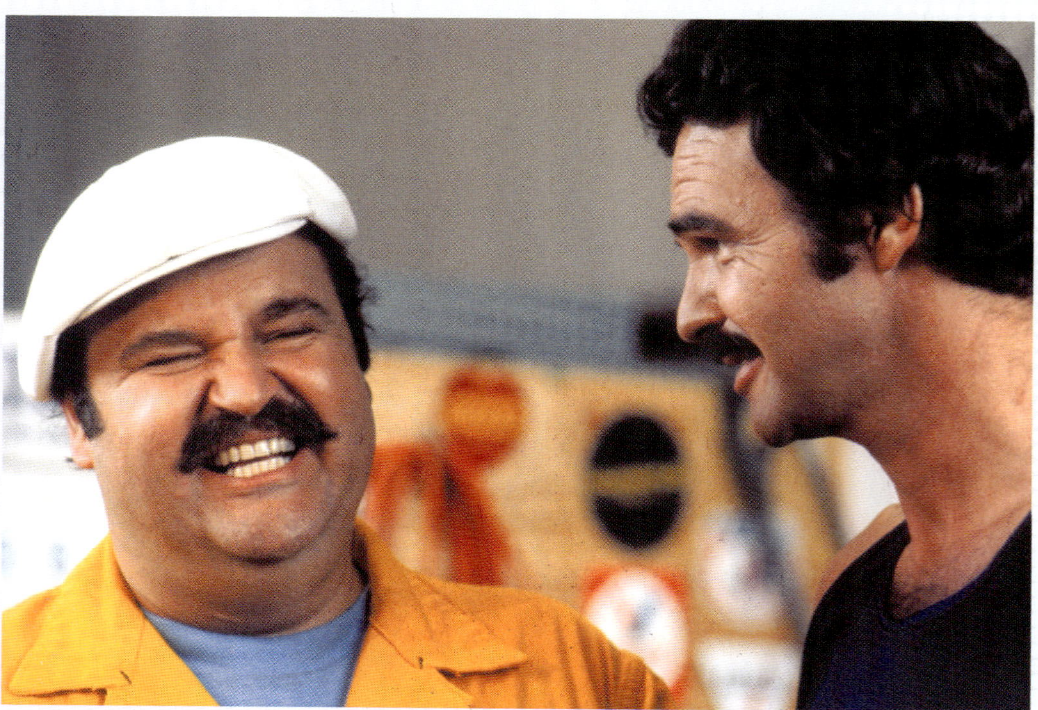

Dom DeLuise and Burt Reynolds partner up for *The Cannonball Run's* race.

movies across the decade that used physicality, kinetic movement, and brute force as key plot elements. The list of notable action films below is chock-full of car chases, stunt work, machine guns, martial arts, and fiery explosions. It includes espionage, science fiction, and historical adventure, but fantasy action is addressed separately, as are sports dramas and conventional war movies. (For the *Rambo* films, see the preceding chapter.)

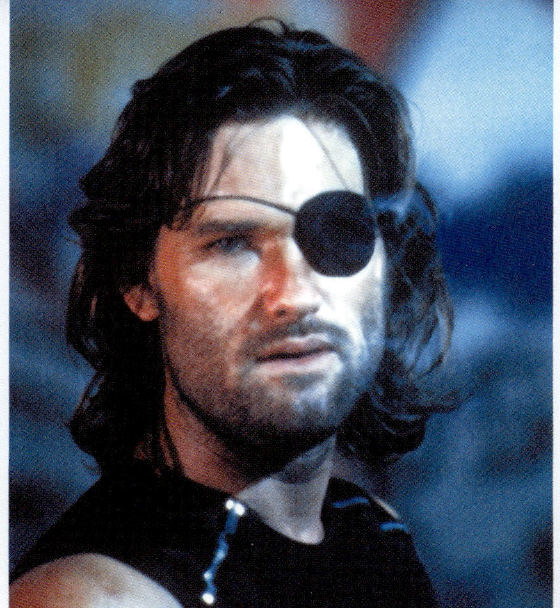

Kurt Russell as Snake Plissken in *Escape from New York.*

The Cannonball Run (1981)

This raucous star vehicle from stuntman turned director Hal Needham was based on the actual Cannonball Run car race that began in the '70s—the brainchild of automotive journalist Brock Yates, who wrote the film's script. Hollywood's then top box-office star Burt Reynolds is surrounded by an odd collection of characters, including Farrah Fawcett as an environmentalist photographer, 007 Roger Moore as himself, Dean Martin and Sammy Davis Jr. as con artists, and a mop-topped Jackie Chan (whose home studio Golden Harvest financed the film). This silly comedy got terrible reviews but incredible box office and might be the ultimate "dad movie."

Das Boot (1981)

This German World War II submarine film is a gripping suspense drama from director Wolfgang Petersen about a war correspondent (Herbert Grönemeyer) who deploys with a cynical captain (Jürgen Prochnow) and his young crew in a months-long battle against British forces in the Atlantic. Essentially an undersea disaster movie, it is set apart from other war films by its constant state of tension as the U-boat hunts down and attacks enemy destroyers. Though the film is punctuated by harrowing action sequences, more often the real battle is in the sailors' minds as they wait in dread, defenseless against the structural integrity of the claustrophobic submarine.

Escape from New York (1981)

A dystopian Manhattan (set in 1997) becomes a maximum-security prison in this John Carpenter film about a war hero turned criminal (Kurt Russell) who is offered a pardon if he can rescue the captive US president (Donald Pleasence), whose hijacked plane has crashed there. The film literalizes the caricature of New York at the time as a city overrun by crime, complete with lawless gangs, fights to the death, and a hair-raising cab ride through trash-strewn streets.

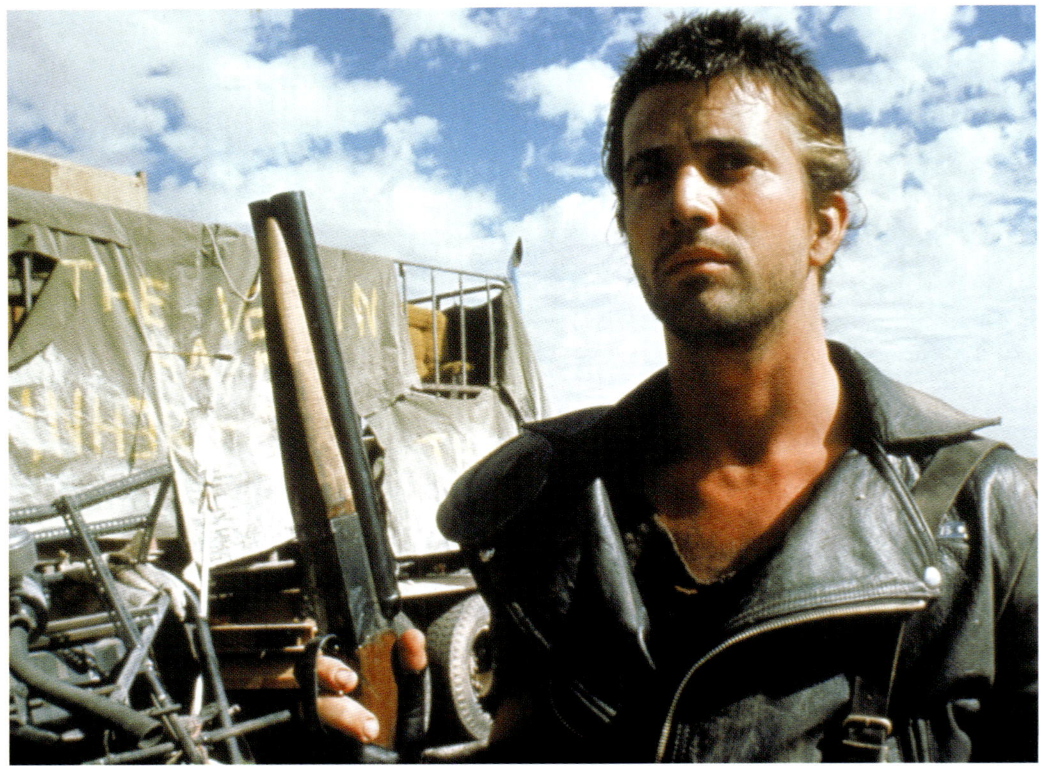

Mel Gibson in *Mad Max 2*.

For Your Eyes Only (1981)

The best of the Roger Moore 007 films of the '80s sees Bond attempt to retrieve a nuclear submarine tracking device before it falls into the hands of the Soviets. After the outer space antics of *Moonraker* (1979), this Aegean Sea– and Alps-set twelfth entry in the series brought Bond back to earth, even reviving his old nemesis Blofeld (an uncredited John Hollis) for the opening sequence. Moore returned as Bond in two more films: *Octopussy* (1983) and *A View to a Kill* (1985).

Mad Max 2 (1981)

Because the first *Mad Max* (1979) fared poorly with American audiences, this sequel was renamed *The Road Warrior* for its US release. Set years after the events of the original, George Miller's bigger, badder, and wildly stylized sequel about a postapocalyptic Australia where oil is currency contains some of the best action choreography of the decade. Mel Gibson's wandering title character helps defend a refinery besieged by a menacing horde of motorists, becoming a vigilante hero in a society where fanciful big rigs function more dependably than law and order.

Raiders of the Lost Ark (1981)

From its opening escape from a Peruvian temple to the shoot-out in a Nepalese pub and a turbulent car chase in the desert, this Lucas-Spielberg wartime adventure is one of the most iconic action movies of all time and what the director called "a James Bond film without the hardware." Instead, it's given a heavy dose of the supernatural, as Indy (Harrison Ford) races the Nazis to find the legendary Ark of the Covenant. It spawned many successors, from the 3-D *Treasure of the Four Crowns* (1983) to the rom-com adventure *Romancing the Stone* (1984).

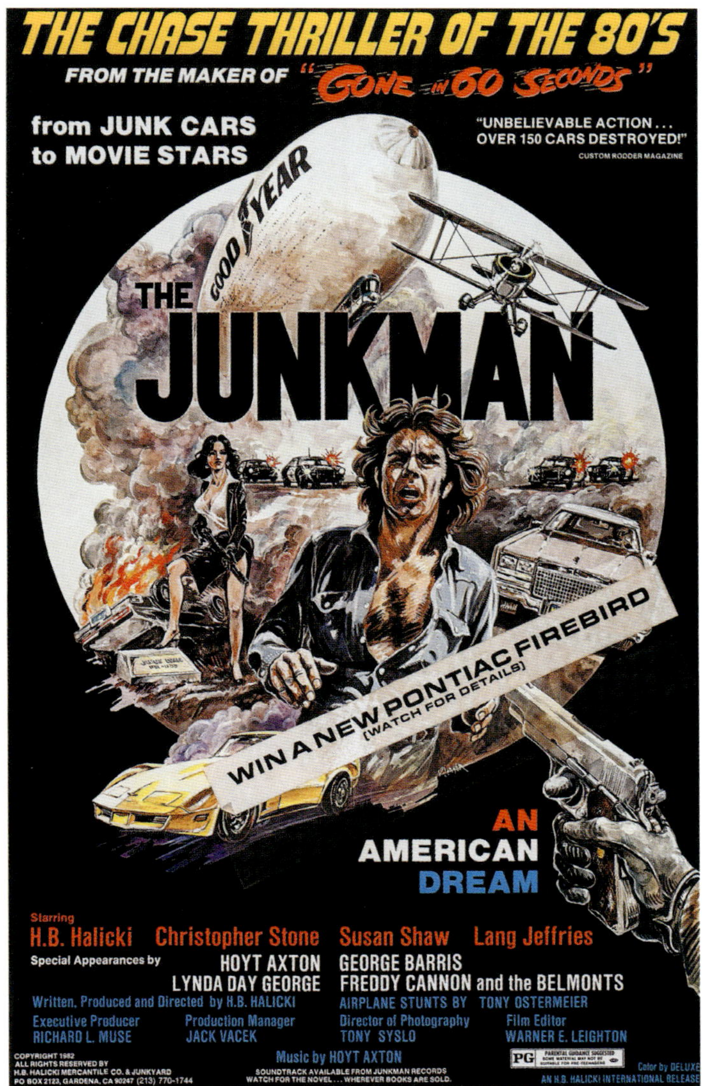

H. B. Halicki wrote, directed, produced, and starred in *The Junkman*.

The Junkman (1982)

A fun example of an independently produced action movie is this carsploitation flick from H. B. "Toby" Halicki, the filmmaker behind the cult classic *Gone in Sixty Seconds* (1974) who self-referentially uses the Hollywood premiere of his earlier film as a major plot point in this car-crash extravaganza. Its thin story tells of a film producer who is being chased through Southern California by assassins hired by his jealous brother-in-law, but the real appeal is its gonzo vehicular violence. *The Junkman* set a record for the most cars destroyed in a movie—150—that stood for almost thirty years.

Lone Wolf McQuade (1983)

Though he had notably appeared opposite Bruce Lee in *The Way of the Dragon* (1972), martial artist Chuck Norris found his groove playing the title Texas lawman—with a literal pet wolf—who is assigned a partner (Robert Beltran) to tame his renegade ways. Together, they take on an arms dealer (David Carradine) who hijacked a US Army convoy. Norris soon made other hit films like *Missing in Action* (1984) and *Code of Silence* (1985), but the Texas Ranger persona would follow him throughout his career.

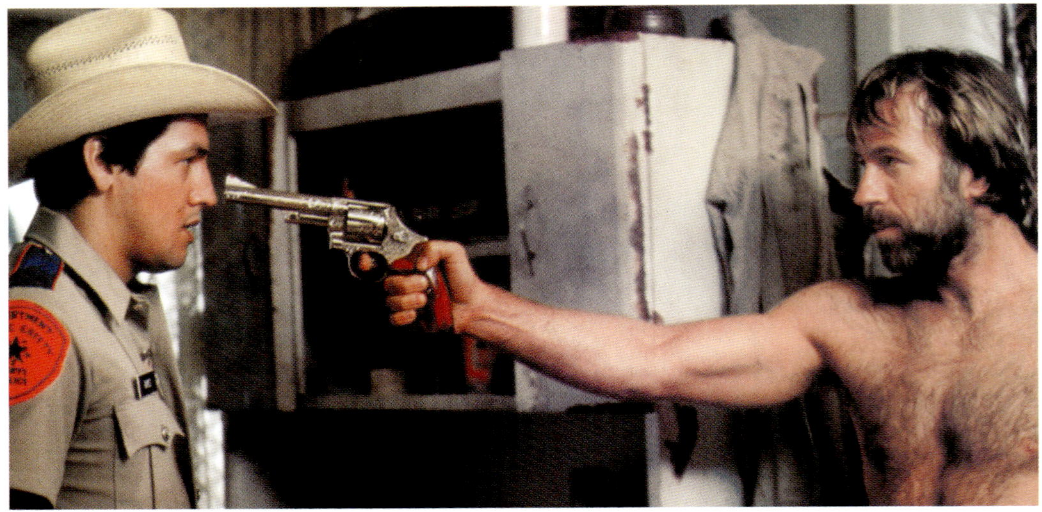

Robert Beltran and Chuck Norris in *Lone Wolf McQuade*.

Project A (1983)

In his return to Hong Kong cinema after testing the waters in Hollywood, Jackie Chan starred as a nineteenth-century coast guardsman turned cop who fights against marauding pirates and corruption in the police force. Chan maintained creative control by writing and directing many of his own films, and his unique appeal with audiences was due to his combination of slapstick humor, impressive fight scenes, and daredevil stunts. In *Project A*, he choreographs a madcap bicycle chase through city streets and executes a dizzying fall from a clock tower, à la Harold Lloyd.

Sudden Impact (1983)

This fourth entry in the *Dirty Harry* series was the most financially successful and the only one directed by its star, Clint Eastwood. After the hero's reckless law-enforcement methods run him afoul of his superiors, he is given a forced vacation where he crosses paths with a woman (Sondra Locke) on her own quest for vengeance. They enjoy each other's company, but surly Harry really needs only two friends: Smith and Wesson. "Go ahead," he tells a man robbing a diner. "Make my day."

The Terminator (1984)

Writer-director James Cameron warned audiences about nefarious AI with this time-traveling thriller about a powerful android (Arnold Schwarzenegger) who is sent from the future to kill Sarah Connor (Linda Hamilton), the mother of the machines' human nemesis. At $6.4 million, the film was a lower-budget indie production. Few expected it to kick off a powerhouse franchise or propel its star onto the A-list, but when Arnold said, "I'll be back," he meant it.

Commando (1985)

Schwarzenegger added comedic quips to his arsenal as John Matrix, a retired army colonel whose daughter (Alyssa Milano) is kidnapped

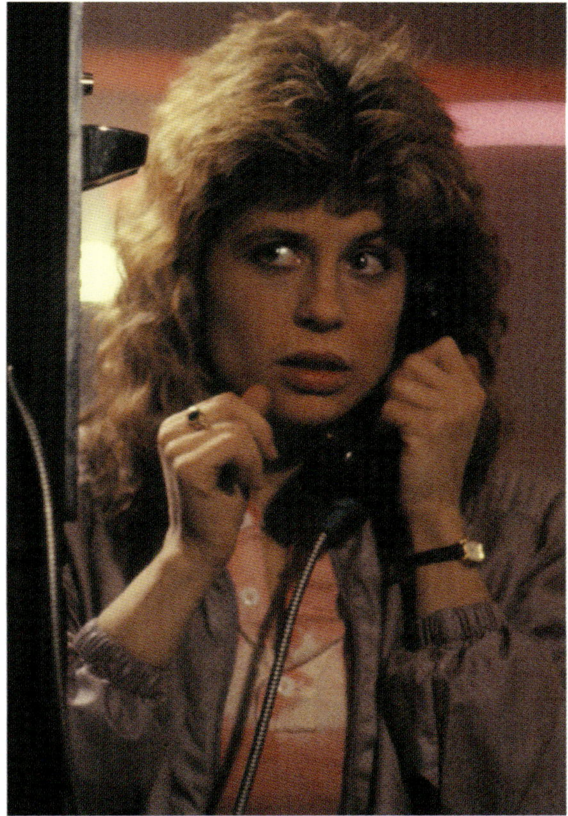

Linda Hamilton on the run from *The Terminator.*

by Latin American mercenaries as revenge for his special-forces team having deposed a dictator. But two can play at that game, and Matrix sets out in pursuit, armed with heavy weaponry and ample wisecracks. After dropping one bad guy off a cliff, he explains to his flight attendant sidekick (Rae Dawn Chong), "I let him go." The over-the-top role—part Terminator, part John Wayne—fit the Austrian actor like a glove and opened up a new comedic career path.

Police Story (1985)

This Jackie Chan landmark was designed as a series of action set pieces threaded together by a basic plot: a cop pursues a drug lord, gets framed for murder, and must clear his name. But what amazing set pieces! The film opens with a chaotic sequence in a Hong Kong slum, followed by Chan's climb onto a speeding bus with an umbrella. The iconic shopping-mall finale is a frenzy of broken glass and incredible physical feats, including a slide down a multistory pole covered in Christmas lights, a stunt so good that the movie shows it three times. Moments like that inspired critic J. Hoberman to call Chan "the Fred Astaire of outrageous mayhem."

Runaway Train (1985)

Russian filmmaker Andrei Konchalovsky directs a demented Jon Voight and a dopey Eric Roberts (both of whom received Oscar nominations) as a pair of violent criminals who break

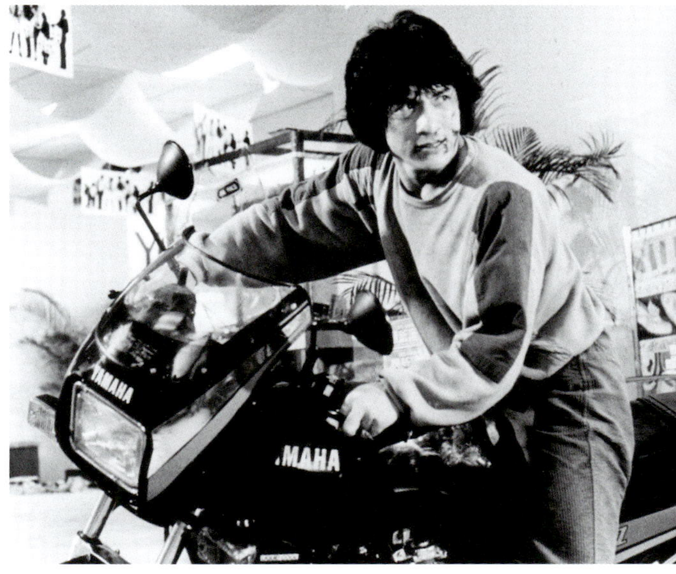

Jackie Chan in *Police Story.*

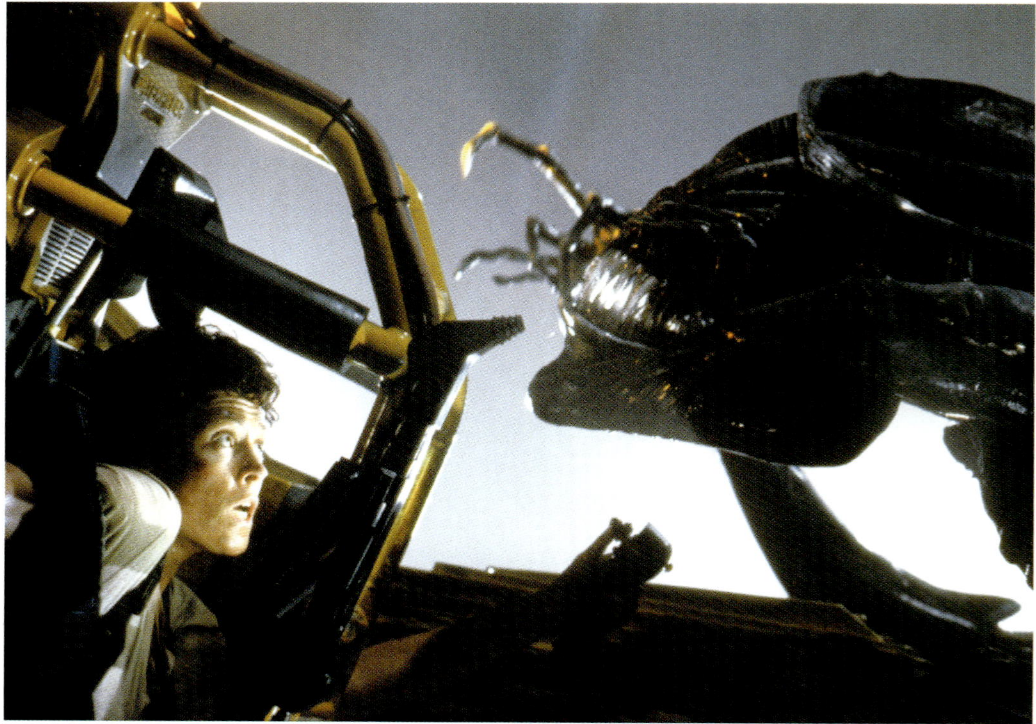

Ripley (Sigourney Weaver) comes face-to-face with the queen xenomorph in *Aliens*.

out of a maximum-security prison in Alaska. They stow away on a train that turns out to be unmanned, forcing them to find a way to stop it before it crashes. This nail-biting suspense film, which started as an Akira Kurosawa project, later became the inspiration for *Speed* (1994).

To Live and Die in L.A. (1985)

Director William Friedkin's gripping crime movie follows crooked cop Richard Chance (William Petersen) who seeks revenge on his late partner's murder by the head of a counterfeiting operation (Willem Dafoe). The film's bravura action sequence, reminiscent of the New York car chase in Friedkin's *The French Connection* (1971), sees Chance and his partner evade a team of pursuers through Los Angeles streets, viaducts, and freeways—sometimes driving in the wrong direction—shot with panache by Dutch cinematographer Robby Müller.

Aliens (1986)

The lone survivor of a devastating extraterrestrial encounter, Ellen Ripley (Sigourney Weaver) agrees to return to the desolate moon where the sinister life forms were first discovered. Whereas Ridley Scott's original 1979 film was a slow-burn horror film, this sequel is a weaponized creature feature on steroids, courtesy of action auteur James Cameron, that builds up to a climactic showdown between the monstrous alien queen and Weaver's badass heroine.

Merchandising

"Merchandising! Merchandising! Where the real money from the movie is made!" Mel Brooks's *Spaceballs* (1987) included a surreal scene in which the wise character Yogurt (played by Brooks) shows off various *Spaceballs* tie-in products for sale, including a VHS copy of the movie itself.

In addition to the major revenue streams of home video (JVC's VHS and Sony's Betamax engaged in a format war, while LaserDisc technology appeared from MCA and Philips) and soundtrack albums (which had been around for decades but achieved new prominence in the '80s), studios were finding new and interesting ways of licensing their intellectual property for extra cash. *Star Wars* (1977) no doubt led the way, and the releases of its sequels *The Empire Strikes Back* (1980) and *Return of the Jedi* (1983) saw everything from Kenner action figures and playsets to Thermos-brand lunch boxes, a Yoda-themed Magic 8 Ball, and even a C-3PO ceramic tape dispenser.

R-rated films were also fair game. The '80s saw properties like *Alien*, *Rambo*, and even *The Toxic Avenger* turned into animated series and toy lines for kids.

Whether for the Atari 2600, the Commodore 64, or the Nintendo Entertainment System, video games based on hit movies (and sometimes the flops as well) were big business for studios in the '80s, offering everything from *The Karate Kid* to *Howard the Duck*.

Fans could also pick up a *Ghostbusters* (1984) Play-Doh Playset (based on the spin-off animated series *The Real Ghostbusters*) and *Batman* (1989) breakfast cereal. Readers could engage in the world beyond the movie with books like *E.T.: The Book of the Green Planet*, while novels like *The Han Solo Adventures* helped keep franchises alive between film installments.

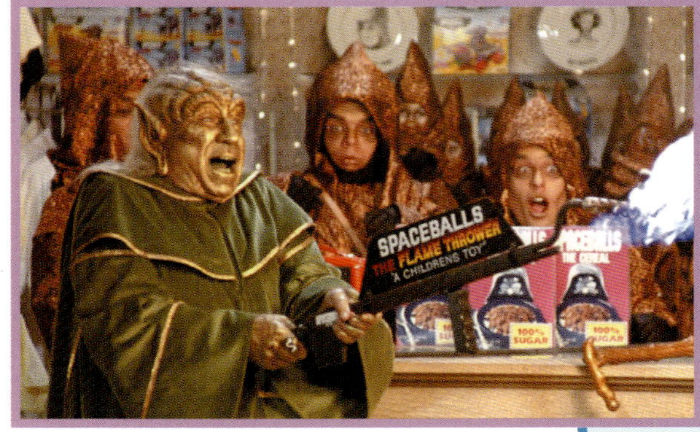

Mel Brooks's Yogurt with an officially licensed *Spaceballs* flame thrower.

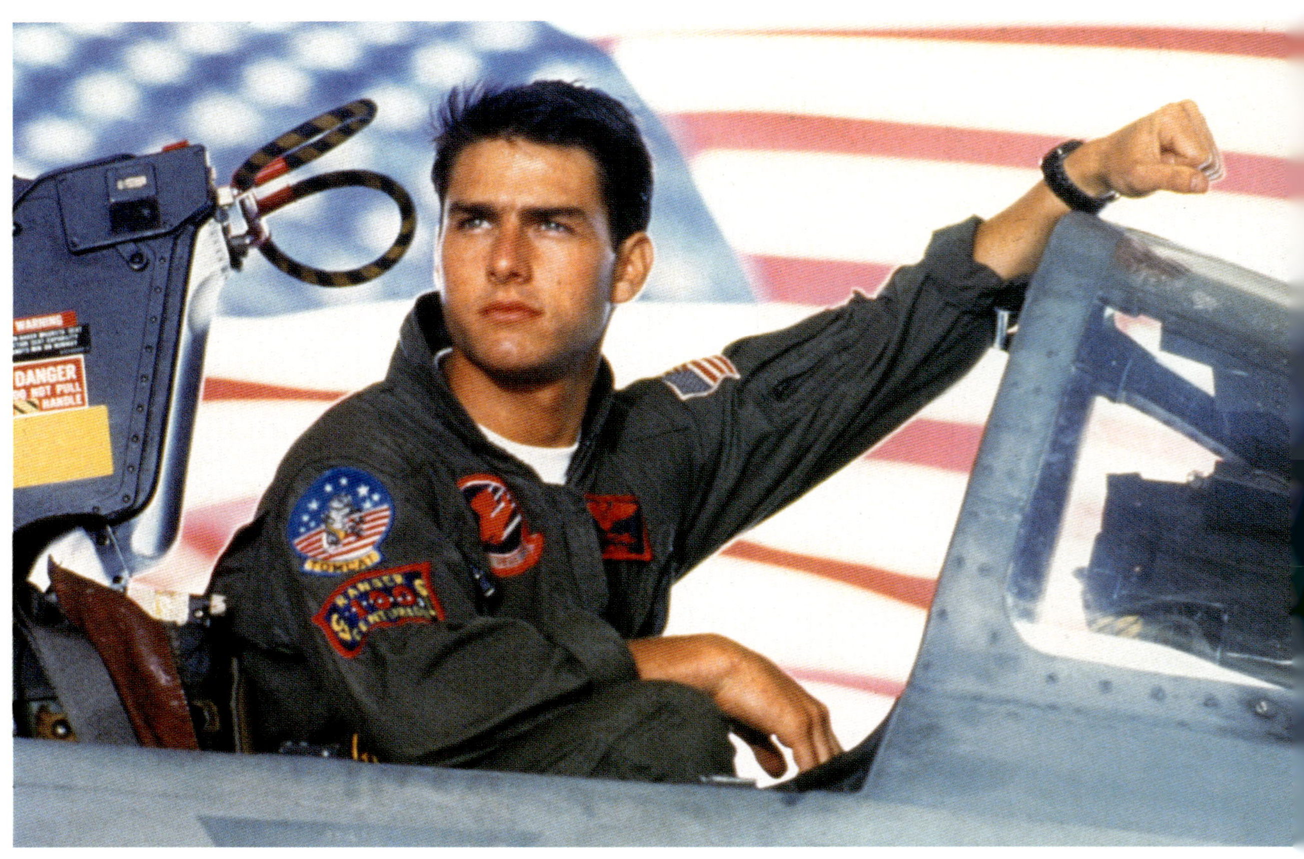

Tom Cruise as naval aviator Pete "Maverick" Mitchell in *Top Gun*.

F/X (1986)

Justice Department agents hire movie special-effects artist Rollie Tyler (Bryan Brown) to stage a phony assassination so they can scurry away a Mafia turncoat (Jerry Orbach) into witness protection. When Tyler discovers he has been set up, it kicks off a twisty chase plot in which he must outsmart the nefarious agents with gimmicks and misdirection honed from his work in the movies, with the assistance of a friendly NYPD detective (Brian Dennehy) who's also after the Mob boss.

Top Gun (1986)

Tony Scott's sky-high blockbuster is full of thrilling aerial acrobatics, but it became a classic thanks to the cocky chemistry of Maverick (Tom Cruise) and his friend Goose (Anthony Edwards), two pilots in training at the navy's elite Fighter Weapons School. Though it squeezes in a romance with a female instructor (Kelly McGillis), Roger Ebert suggested that "its real love affair was with airplanes"—like when Maverick tangos with an enemy MiG before snapping a victorious Polaroid. *Top Gun* was so inspiring that it was later cited as a successful military recruiting tool.

Lethal Weapon (1987)

A cop on the verge of retirement (Danny Glover) and his fearless—and possibly suicidal—new partner (Mel Gibson) discover a rogue drug-trafficking element within the CIA while investigating the suspicious death of a friend's daughter. Of all the buddy-cop movies of the '80s—*48 Hrs.* (1982), *Beverly Hills Cop* (1984), *Red Heat* (1988), *Tango & Cash* (1989)—this hard-boiled affair by director Richard Donner and writer Shane Black is the most high-octane, with a strong central pair worth caring about in between the explosions, car chases, and flying bullets.

Predator (1987)

Arnold Schwarzenegger turns Rambo in this tropical sci-fi thriller. He stars as Dutch, a Vietnam veteran and special-forces operative who leads a team of mercenaries to Central America to rescue a diplomat held hostage by a guerrilla army. They raid a Soviet military camp and are warned about a mysterious threat: "The jungle . . . it just came alive." Soon it becomes clear they are being hunted by an invisible extraterrestrial foe that all their firepower can't match, forcing Dutch to go off the grid.

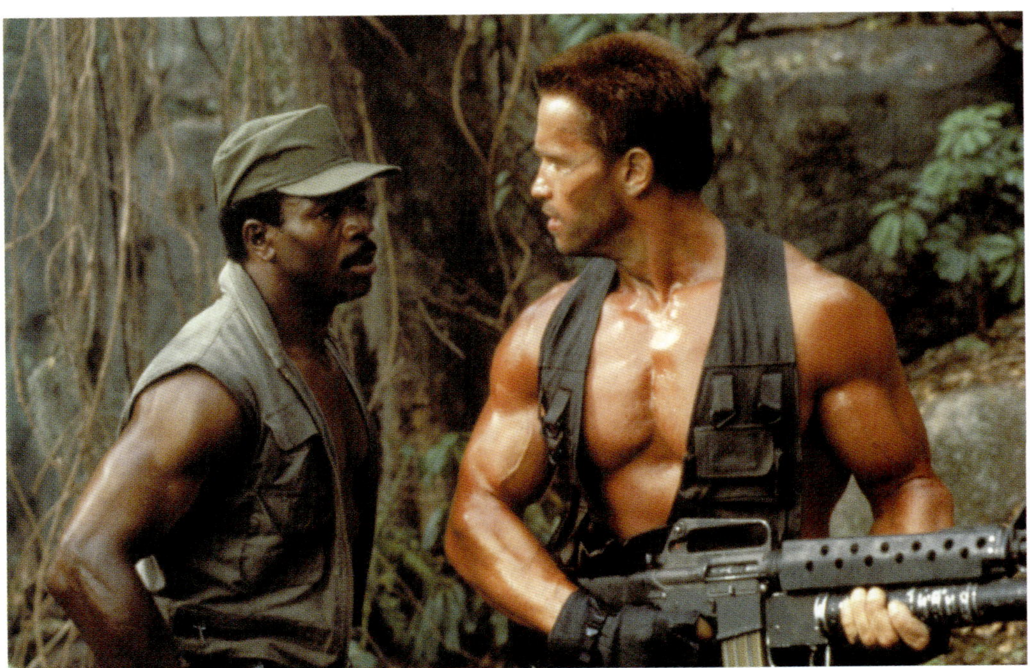

Carl Weathers and Arnold Schwarzenegger on the hunt for *Predator*.

RoboCop (1987)

"I like violence in movies," said director Paul Verhoeven, and he proves it early in this satire of Reagan-era law-and-order policies as a mechanized robot goes haywire and brutally kills an executive during a test demonstration. But the corporate suits that control crime-ridden Detroit's police force won't be deterred and quickly authorize the use of the city's first cyborg officer (Peter Weller). In between scenes of urban strife, the film shows news reports about armed satellites that misfire and commercials for products like "Nukem," a family board game about preemptive strikes.

Bloodsport (1988)

A prime example of martial-arts action cinema in the '80s is Cannon Films' explosive exposé of the high-stakes Hong Kong tournament known as the Kumite, which gave the world its first good look at Belgian fighter Jean-Claude Van Damme. The "Muscles from Brussels" plays an American army captain whose extensive ninjutsu training earns him an invitation to compete in the twice-a-decade event, the interest of a reporter (Leah Ayres), and a chase from two military investigators (Forest Whitaker and Norman Burton).

Die Hard (1988)

After *Predator*, director John McTiernan made this story of a New York cop (Bruce Willis) whose holiday plans are disrupted by terrorists, without a doubt the finest Christmas-set action movie of all time. What starts as a swanky party at his estranged wife's LA office

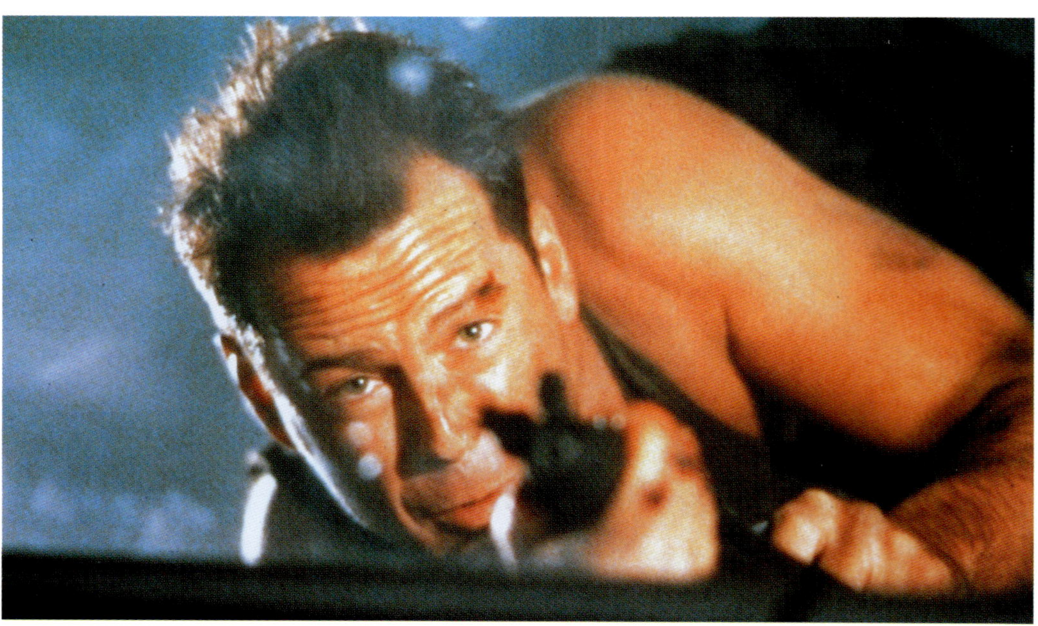

Bruce Willis seamlessly transitioned from television drama to big screen action with *Die Hard.*

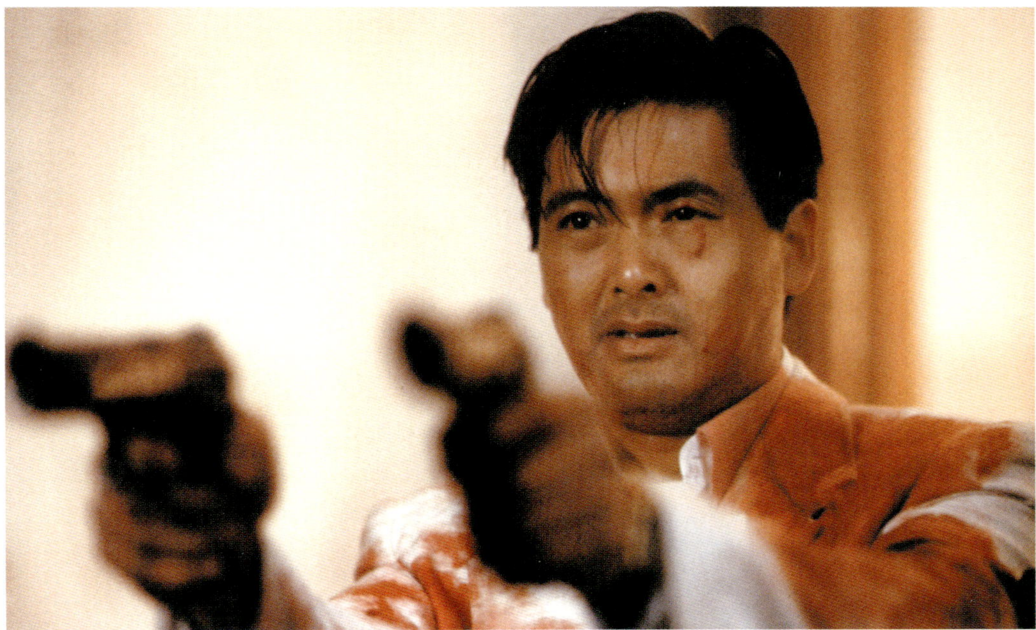

Chow Yun-fat in *The Killer*.

turns into a desperate situation—hostages inside, law enforcement outside—with only Willis's stealthy John McClane able to fix things. The film's one-man-army conceit led to a number of action spectacles like *Under Siege* (1992) and *Con Air* (1997), as well as several direct sequels.

Batman (1989)

The decision to hire offbeat director Tim Burton to helm this big-budget comic book reboot seems like a no-brainer in hindsight. Its immersive noir atmosphere, gothic-deco set design, and carefully controlled wackiness could only have been conceived by an outlandish talent. It sets the stage for a demented battle between Michael Keaton's caped crusader and Jack Nicholson's sly, devious Joker, who threatens Gotham City's residents with poisoned toiletries. It's no laughing matter.

The Killer (1989)

"When I shoot action sequences I think of great dancers, Gene Kelly, Astaire," said John Woo. "I feel like I'm creating a ballet." *The Killer* is the first of the Hong Kong director's action spectacles to include all of his trademarks: *wuxia*-inspired gun battles, slow-motion carnage, noir heroes, and flocks of symbolic doves. Lead actor Chow Yun-fat, who had appeared in Woo's hit *A Better Tomorrow* (1986) and its 1987 sequel, plays an assassin for hire who accidentally blinds a nightclub singer (Sally Yeh) in his latest gunfight and becomes her protector.

Fantasy Action

Among the many trends that *Star Wars* (1977) kicked off was a renewed interest in fantasy action, not just in a galaxy far, far away but in the magical past (or future, or present). While *The Empire Strikes Back* (1980) and *Return of the Jedi* (1983) continued the space opera's domination at the box office, the popularity of role-playing games like *Dungeons & Dragons*—as shown at the beginning of *E.T. the Extra-Terrestrial* (1982)—and fantasy literature like *The Lord of the Rings* convinced producers to invest in a new wave of sword-and-sorcery films.

Two early highlights based on classic tales were the Greek mythology film *Clash of the Titans* (1981), with stop-motion animation by Ray Harryhausen, and director John Boorman's *Excalibur* (1981), an earnest and lushly detailed rendering of the Arthurian legend. More space fantasies were released, with mixed commercial success, like *Flash Gordon* (1980), *Superman II* (1980), *Star Trek II: The Wrath of Khan* (1982), and *Krull* (1983).

The sword-and-sandal subgenre was epitomized by *Conan the Barbarian* (1982), featuring Arnold Schwarzenegger as the title warrior on a quest for vengeance against the cult leader Thulsa Doom (James Earl Jones). Critics were incredulous—*Time* called it "stupid and stupefying"—but audiences ate it up. Other films played a similar tune. *Dragonslayer* (1981), roughly *Star Wars* with fire-breathing dragons, starred Peter MacNicol as a sorcerer's apprentice. *The Beastmaster* (1982) tells the story of a prince who was magically transferred in utero from his mother's womb to a bull and can now communicate with animals, which is helpful in his fight against an evil wizard. "It looks both big and cheap," said the *New York Times* of the now cult classic.

Major celebrities participated: Tom Cruise followed his breakout role in *Risky Business* (1983) with Ridley Scott's dark adventure *Legend* (1985), David Bowie memorably appeared as the Goblin King Jareth in Jim Henson's *Labyrinth* (1986), and Sean Connery had a supporting role in *Highlander* (1986), the story of an immortal Scottish swordsman who battles his longtime nemesis in present-day New York. Even kids movies got in on the action, with cherished films like *The NeverEnding Story* (1984), *Return to Oz* (1985), *The Princess Bride* (1987), and *Willow* (1988).

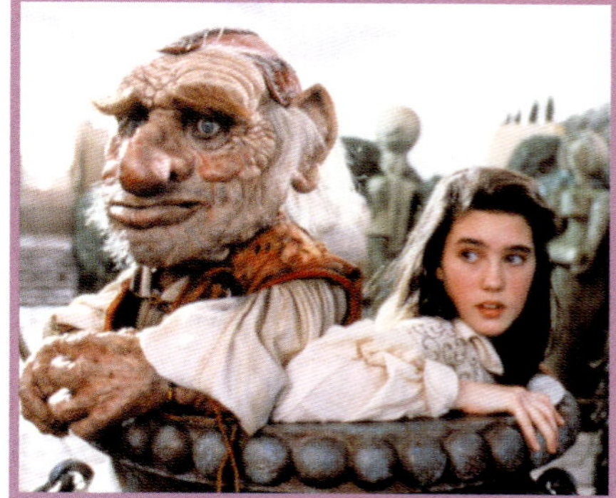

Hoggle (voiced by Brian Henson) and Sarah (Jennifer Connelly) in *Labyrinth*.

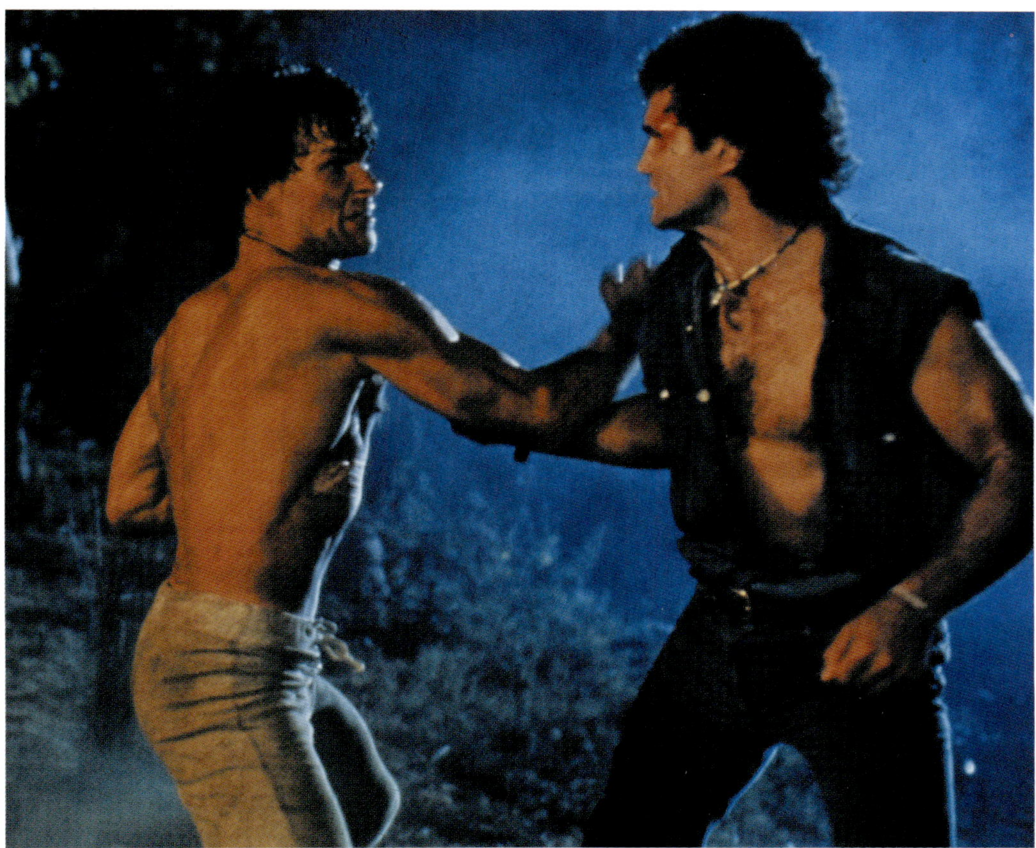

Patrick Swayze fights Marshall R. Teague in *Road House*.

Licence to Kill (1989)

Timothy Dalton's brief run as James Bond ended with this island-set thriller in which the secret agent leaves MI6 in order to enact revenge on the Caribbean drug lord who murdered his friend's wife. After the tongue-in-cheek Roger Moore era, the Bond films became more explosive and action heavy, like this film's breathless chase sequence involving multiple eighteen-wheeler tanker trucks, various cars, and an airplane. *Licence to Kill* was the last 007 film of the Cold War, and the series went dark for an unprecedented six years until the release of *GoldenEye* (1995).

Road House (1989)

Patrick Swayze, fresh off his star-making turn in *Dirty Dancing* (1987), plays a bouncer at the "Double Deuce," a rough-and-tumble Missouri bar where the clientele seems to always be fighting (the band stage is protected from the mayhem by chicken wire), but his attempts to clean up the joint run afoul of a powerful local crime boss (Ben Gazzara). The film, directed by the appropriately named Rowdy Herrington, delivers one over-the-top brawl after another, an orgy of broken beer bottles and fractured limbs.

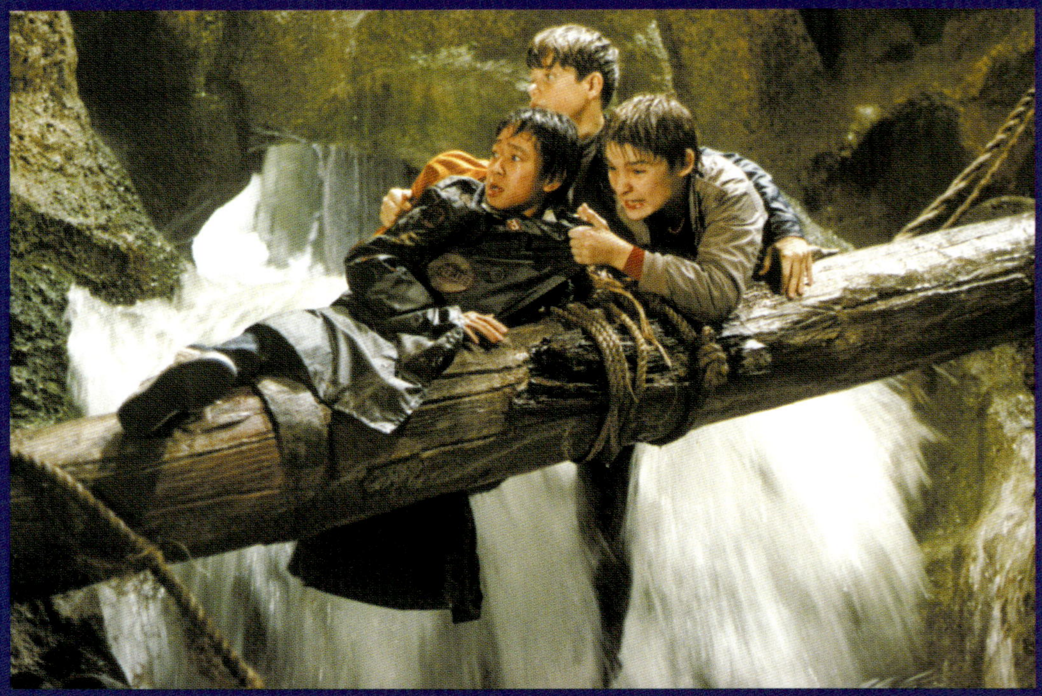

The Goonies

CHAPTER FOUR

TEEN MOVIES

AFTER THE BOX-OFFICE BEHEMOTHS *JAWS* (1975) AND *STAR WARS* (1977) showed Hollywood the way forward, the studios began to aggressively chase the youthful audience that made those summer blockbusters so successful. At the beginning of the 1980s, younger boomers were navigating high school and college, while the first wave of Generation X was turning fifteen, hormones ablaze. As the thinking went, few things moved young people to go to the multiplex more than seeing themselves on-screen.

Teen movies were nothing new. The *Andy Hardy* series of the 1930s—arguably the genre's urtext—made Mickey Rooney the biggest box-office draw of his day, while costar Judy Garland and Universal's Deanna Durbin became America's musical sweethearts. James Dean's performance as a red-jacketed misanthrope in *Rebel Without a Cause* (1955) and his tragic death that same year marked a cultural inflection point, while Disney appealed to more genteel middle-American audiences with wholesome stars like Hayley Mills and Tommy Kirk. Indie studio American International Pictures had been formed in the '50s to make films specifically for teenagers—films full of action, sex, and rebellious attitudes. Twenty-year-old Annette Funicello successfully moved from the *Mickey Mouse Club* to a prominent role in AIP's *Beach Party* series of the early 1960s, which featured a group of fun-loving California kids who seemingly made the rules up as they went along.

AIP was sold off in 1979, marking the end of an era. But a new wave of high school- and college-set movies was having a huge impact at the box office, the effects of which would be felt for years to come. *Grease* (1978) became the biggest movie musical to date with its infectious songs set against the story of a hot rod–obsessed "greaser" gang and the Pink Ladies clique of Rydell High. Its star John Travolta had played nineteen-year-old Tony Manero in *Saturday Night Fever* the year before and would struggle to shake off the persona forged by these two hits (a rebel whose cause was music). The summer of 1978 also saw the release of *National Lampoon's Animal House*. Set at a small college fraternity in the early '60s, and juvenile in almost every way, John Landis's zany comedy foregrounded sophomoric high jinks, crass humor, and sex—and was exceedingly popular.

Studios were catching on. In the ensuing years, Hollywood would experiment with a combination of high school comedy, teen sex, slasher gore, and pop-heavy soundtracks to lure young people to the movies. Never before had the industry catered so strongly to this demographic, making the 1980s a golden age of teen cinema.

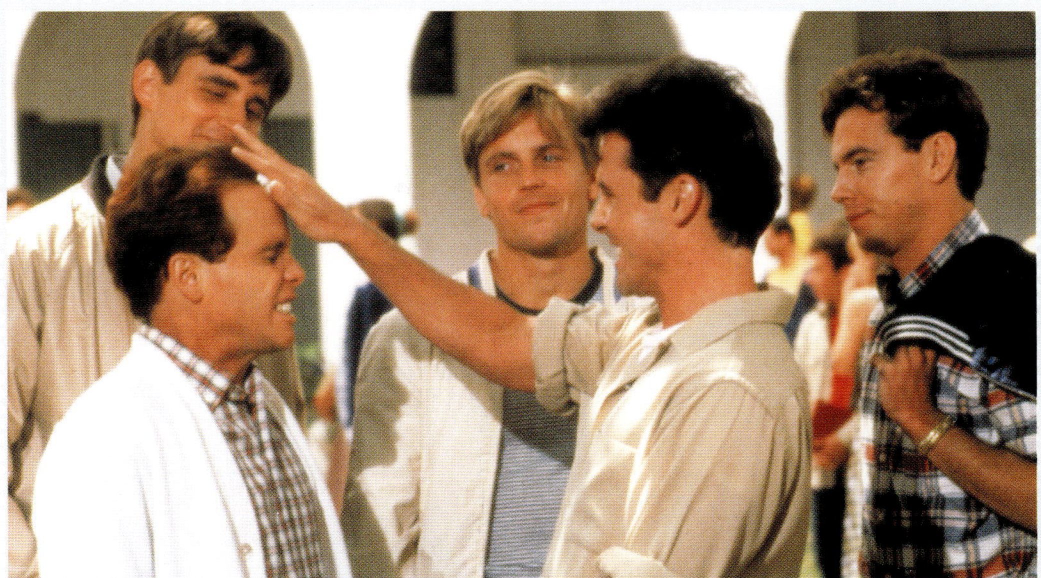

The hormonal cast of *Porky's*.

SCHLOCK FEST

Animal House had several lewd successors in the early '80s. Chief among them is *Porky's*, released in March 1982. Like *Animal House*, it is set in the past (1950s Florida) and takes on a tinge of nostalgia, though everything about the movie is secondary to its obsession with sex, played out through its cast of mostly shameless dudes who want to lose their virginity. Their ludicrous antics in pursuit of girls—be it fellow students or local prostitutes at Porky's roadhouse—drive the plot forward, leading many viewers to knock the film as wholesale misogyny. "The male characters are neurotic about the usual three subjects: the size, experience, and health of their reproductive organs," wrote Roger Ebert. "The female characters, on the other hand, are seen almost entirely as an undiscovered species from a lost continent." The film's infamous shower sequence, in which the boys spy on the girls after gym class, could be Exhibit A for the Male Gaze.

Director Bob Clark, a southerner who found work in the Canadian film industry in the 1970s, countered the accusations of sexism by suggesting that the boys in the film are actually the butt of all its jokes, while the girls were able to express their sexuality—like Kim Cattrall's Miss Honeywell, who howls loudly during sex. He also tried to inject a dose of progressive politics into the film, set in the era of segregation. "People were railing about how racist the characters are, but this was 1954 we're talking about, and we made it clear that they were contemptuous of the racism around them." This nuanced take tends to get lost in the larger discourse surrounding the movie, but it can be argued that while the movie is about dumb stuff, it is not dumb itself. As *Newsday* wrote, "*Porky's* is a softcore sexploitation movie that knows exactly what it is doing."

Soon after, Cannon Films released *The Last American Virgin* (1982), a remake of the Israeli hit

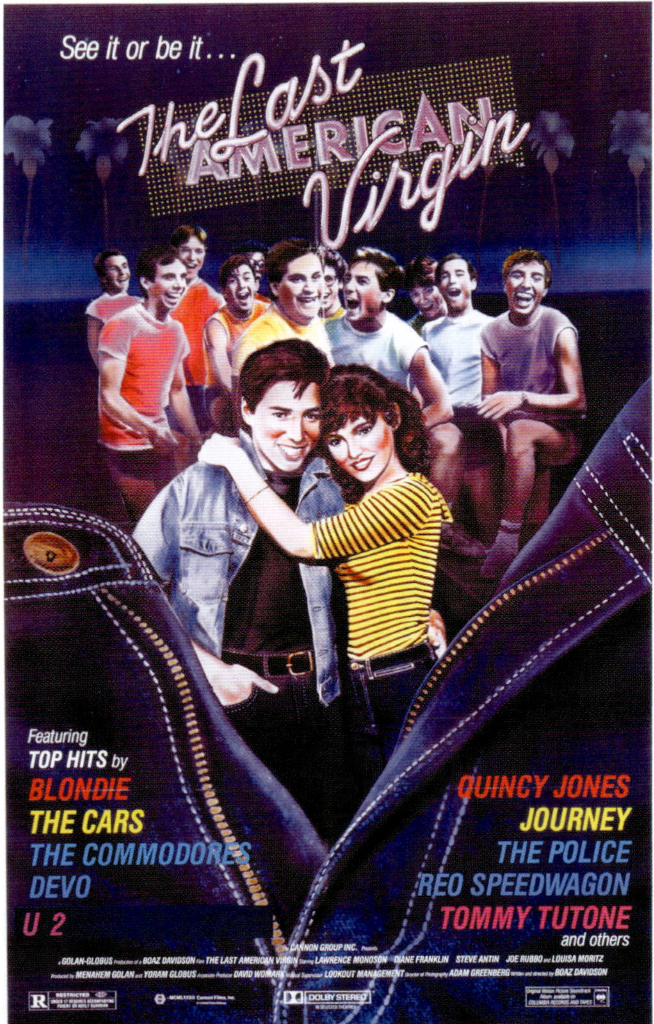

The Last American Virgin's soundtrack played a major role in the film's marketing campaign.

Lemon Popsicle (1978) that tells of a high school love triangle and an unwanted pregnancy—a fairly compelling story, wrapped in an otherwise shallow teen-sex comedy. The director of both versions was Boaz Davidson, but unlike the original, which was a nostalgia trip set in the 1950s, *Virgin* takes place in contemporary Los Angeles and features a modern pop soundtrack (a major fixture in the film's marketing campaign) with Blondie, the Police, Devo, and more. The film wasn't a huge hit like *Porky's*, but it became a mainstay on cable, thanks in part to its famous twist ending.

Regardless of the merits of these two sordid landmarks, movie theaters in the early '80s soon became overrun with formulaic sex comedies, most with interchangeable plotlines of shallow boys trying to seduce shallow girls with varying degrees of success, and loaded with dumb antics and silly set pieces.

Roger Corman's New World Pictures delivered *Screwballs* (1983), about five 1960s high school boys who ogle a girl named "Purity Bush." In *Homework* (1982), a high school virgin gets seduced by Joan Collins. ("A miserable excuse for a movie," according to critic Gene Siskel.) The poster for *Spring Break* (1983) features four boys planting a flag like the marines on Iwo Jima, but this time on a woman's bikini-clad thigh. The horny guys in *Hot Chili* (1985) work at a beach resort in Mexico, while *Hot Dog . . . The Movie* (1984) is set at a skiing competition in Squaw Valley. Bob Clark returned to direct *Porky's II: The Next Day* (1983), with a plot involving a Shakespeare festival and the Ku Klux Klan. (A third installment, *Porky's Revenge*, followed in 1985.)

Joy of Sex (1984) was based on the popular sex manual in title only. In actuality it was just another high school farce that even *National Lampoon* removed its branding from after

John Hughes's original screenplay was rewritten. (Director Martha Coolidge, who was fired during postproduction, called the shoot "miserable.") There were plenty more, with evocative titles like *Goin' All the Way!* (1981), *The First Turn-On!* (1983), *Losin' It* (1983), *Hardbodies* (1984), and *Hot Moves* (1984). Had filmmakers learned the right lessons from the success of *Animal House*?

SERIOUSLY, THOUGH

As it turns out, teenagers could occasionally also be treated like real people. A key moment for earnest portrayals of high schoolers in the early '80s was Timothy Hutton's Oscar win for *Ordinary People* (1980), a moving family drama that was also Robert Redford's directorial debut. Despite his win as a "supporting" actor, Hutton plays the main character, Conrad Jarrett, living through the fallout from the tragic death of his older brother. The film follows Conrad's deteriorating relationship with his parents (Mary Tyler Moore and Donald Sutherland) and the fracturing of their marriage, as he interacts with classmates and a psychologist (Judd Hirsch). *Ordinary People*, based on a popular novel by Judith Guest, was one of the most celebrated movies of 1980, winning additional Oscars for Best Picture, Director, and Adapted Screenplay.

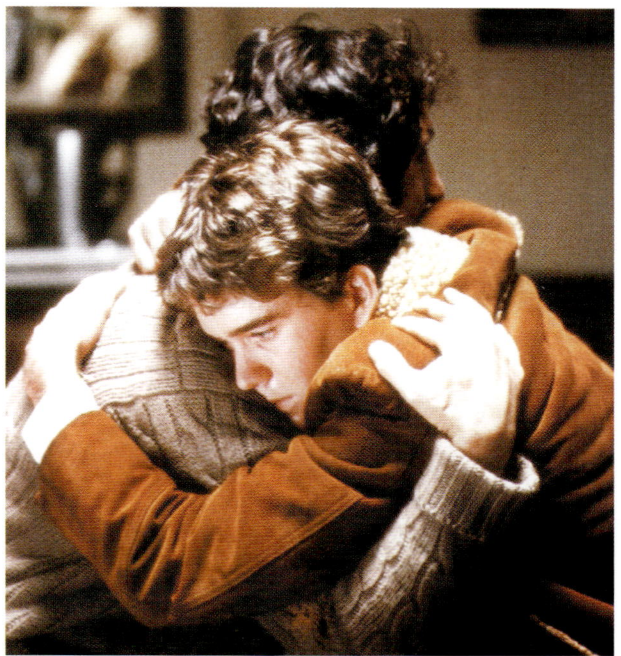

Judd Hirsch and Timothy Hutton embrace in *Ordinary People*.

Just as there were teen-sex comedies, there were also teen-sex dramas. Fifteen-year-old actress and Calvin Klein model Brooke Shields had already made headlines for her controversial role as a prostitute in *Pretty Baby* (1978) when she appeared in the coming-of-age dramas *The Blue Lagoon* (1980) and *Endless Love* (1981), both of which again called for nudity. Her star was rising, but she was becoming unfortunately typecast as a sexualized beauty. "It was about these males needing me to be in a certain category to serve their story, and it never was about me," Shields later said. "It was fun and loving at times, but I was just there, I was a pawn, I was a piece, I was a commodity." Around the same time, *Foxes* (1980) with Jodie Foster and *Little Darlings* (1980) with Tatum O'Neal and Kristy McNichol both presented adolescent girls with real sensitivity, treating their sexuality as a legitimate and serious topic rather than a series of cheap thrills or a sleazy box-office play.

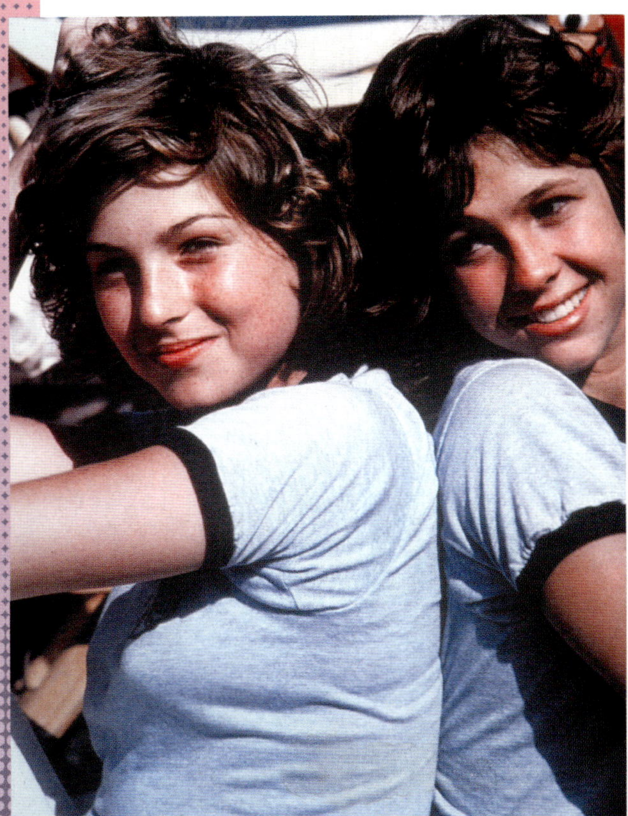

Tatum O'Neal and Kristy McNichol in *Little Darlings*.

One male love interest in *Little Darlings*, sixteen-year-old Matt Dillon, went on to star in a series of dramas in the early '80s that were all based on books by Oklahoma author S. E. Hinton. *Tex* (1982), *The Outsiders*, and *Rumble Fish* (both 1983) were realistic takes on teenage life that explored the concerns of their young characters—often dealing with broken families or absent parents—with emotional honesty. In a special 1984 episode of *At the Movies* about rising male stars, Dillon was singled out as a promising young talent, "a natural screen actor, sort of in the same tradition as Cary Grant, believe it or not. . . . He has the same kind of easiness on the screen," said Roger Ebert. Despite the occasional comedy, like 1984's *The Flamingo Kid*, Dillon's career would primarily consist of weightier projects. He ended the decade with acclaimed work in Gus Van Sant's gritty independent drama *Drugstore Cowboy* (1989).

Another major actor who got his start in the early '80s was Tom Cruise—one of Dillon's costars in *The Outsiders*—whose fame rose with the release of his atmospheric high school film *Risky Business* (1983). While it may not be realistic (Cruise plays senior Joel Goodsen, who runs a brothel at his home when his parents leave town), the film used its over-the-top premise to speak to genuine pressures placed on suburban kids in the '80s. Its biting social commentary about the extremes of capitalism is presented in a strange void; Joel's parents are out of the picture and have no agency. *Risky Business* is about what teenagers would do if suddenly plunked down into the adult world. (They'd promptly make a mess of it.)

Thanks in large part to this film, Cruise's persona became that of a good-hearted boy with bad instincts. Joel Goodsen is a moral disaster, but the young actor is terrific in the part: cool and collected (unless he's dancing in his underwear), swaggering (until he's brought low), believable as a high schooler in over his head. Crucially—in *Risky Business*, as in most of his movies—he is unafraid of looking foolish. "Cruise is one of the first young actors who seems unaffected by the impact of Brando or Clift, and much more inspired by the example of a Gable or a Grant. He wants to work," said film historian David Thomson.

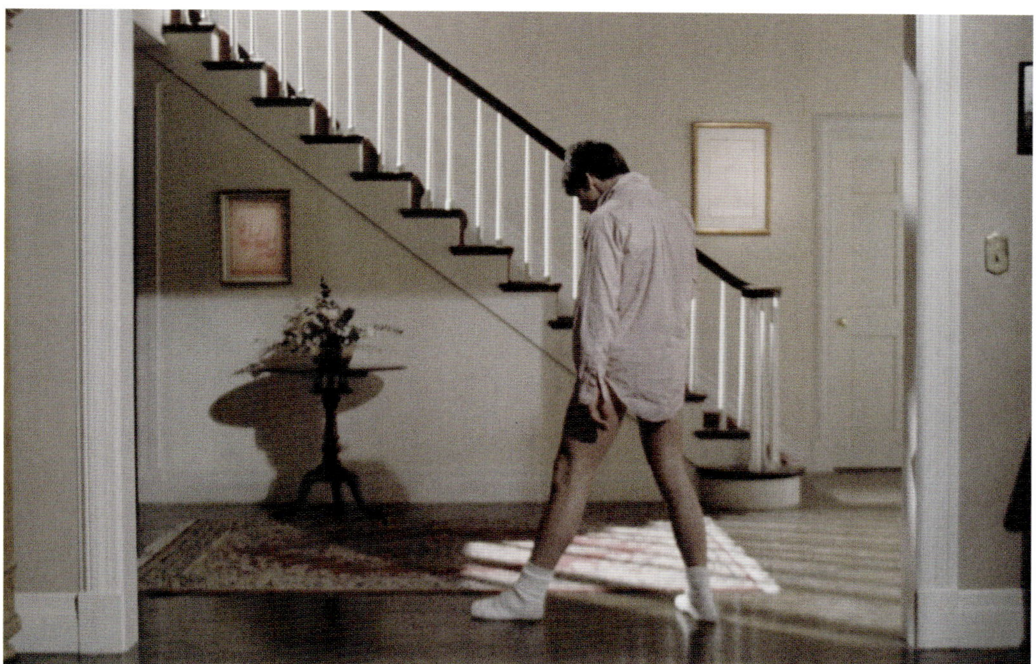

Tom Cruise slides into *Risky Business.*

Where the plot of Cruise's movie stretched the limits of believability, the story in *Fast Times at Ridgemont High* (1982) was well grounded. The film is based on the experiences of music journalist (and later film director) Cameron Crowe, who went undercover in a California high school in 1978–1979 and reported his findings in a book-length exposé. Crowe also wrote the screenplay, which paints teenage life in a more relaxed, prosaic way. As in *Risky Business*, parents are mostly absent. Director Amy Heckerling explained, "Parents open a whole box of stuff I didn't want to get into. I just wanted to say 'Here's the world of kids in their own universe. This is real. This is this particular time and place. These are real characters and what they were going through.'"

The film's teenagers seem to flow back and forth between the twin poles of school and the mall—their prime social spaces—with the occasional detour home. Refreshingly, the humor and conflict aren't derived from outlandish plot devices, but rather from what the kids make of their everyday life. "I was surprised at how not-bad it is," wrote Pauline Kael in the *New Yorker*. "*Fast Times* is like the *Beach Party* movies at a later stage—as if they'd evolved and gained a higher form of consciousness."

Authenticity was the standard for Heckerling. An NYU and AFI Conservatory grad, she had made a short film about losing one's virginity (*Getting It Over With* [1978]) that led Universal to hire her for *Fast Times*. In an era when studios were requiring directors to include female nudity in comedies, believing that's what young audiences wanted, Heckerling's film is noteworthy for her attempts to level the playing field. "How come you can see naked girls

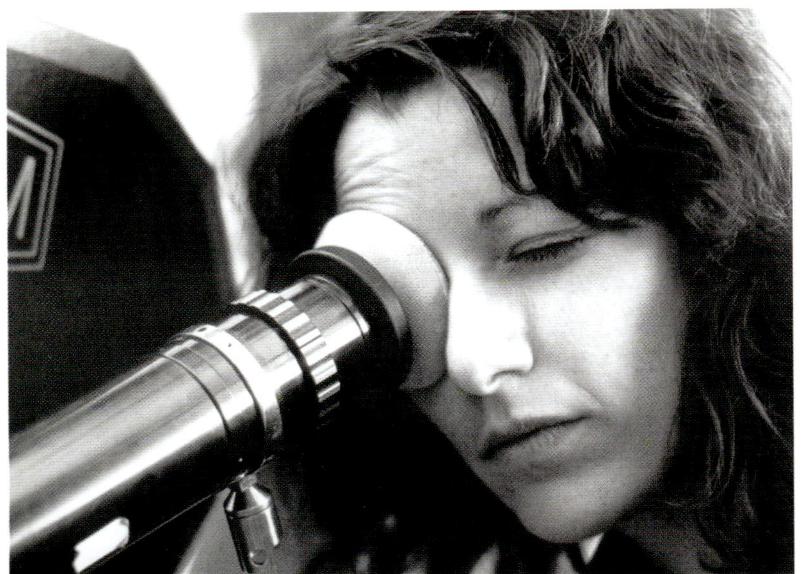

Director Amy Heckerling on the set of *Fast Times at Ridgemont High.*

and you can never see naked guys?" she asked. The ratings board answered, "Because the male organ is aggressive." In the end, the film does show nudity of both sexes and exposes guys in other revealing ways—like an infamous scene of a character caught masturbating.

The film's ensemble includes names like Jennifer Jason Leigh, Judge Reinhold, and Phoebe Cates and an assortment of smaller parts played by Forest Whitaker, Eric Stoltz, and Anthony Edwards (blink and you'll miss Nicolas Cage). But the most famous cast member is undoubtedly Sean Penn as stoned surfer dude Jeff Spicoli. Penn's practice of "method" acting meant that he remained in character during the duration of the shoot, which paid off with the film's most charismatic and authentic performance. When Penn is on-screen—sunbaked, Valley accented, and perfumed with pot—it's impossible to look away.

Penn had an unusual career for a young actor in the '80s. He rarely played comedic characters (one could argue that the key to Spicoli is that Penn doesn't try to make him funny). Instead, he leaned into serious dramatic roles: a military school recruit in *Taps* (1981), a drug addict in the Cold War film *The Falcon and the Snowman* (1985)—both opposite Timothy Hutton—and a Vietnam soldier in Brian De Palma's *Casualties of War* (1989). A curve ball was the adventure comedy *Shanghai Surprise* (1986), which was a poorly received pairing with his then wife, Madonna.

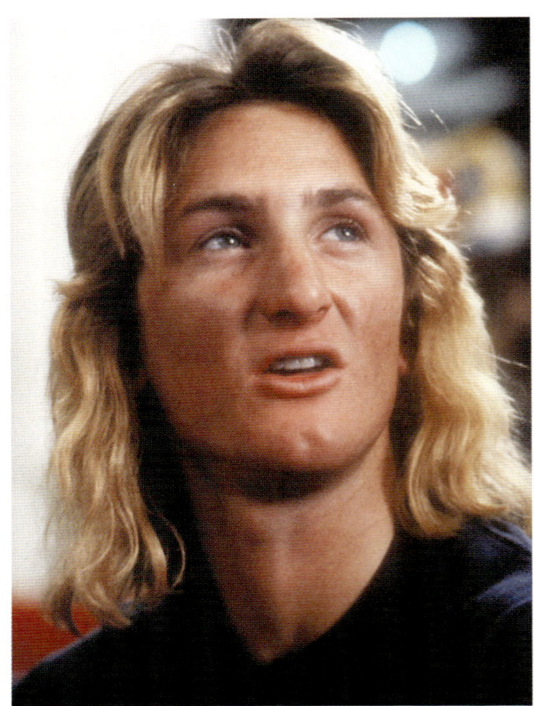

Sean Penn as Jeff Spicoli in *Fast Times at Ridgemont High.*

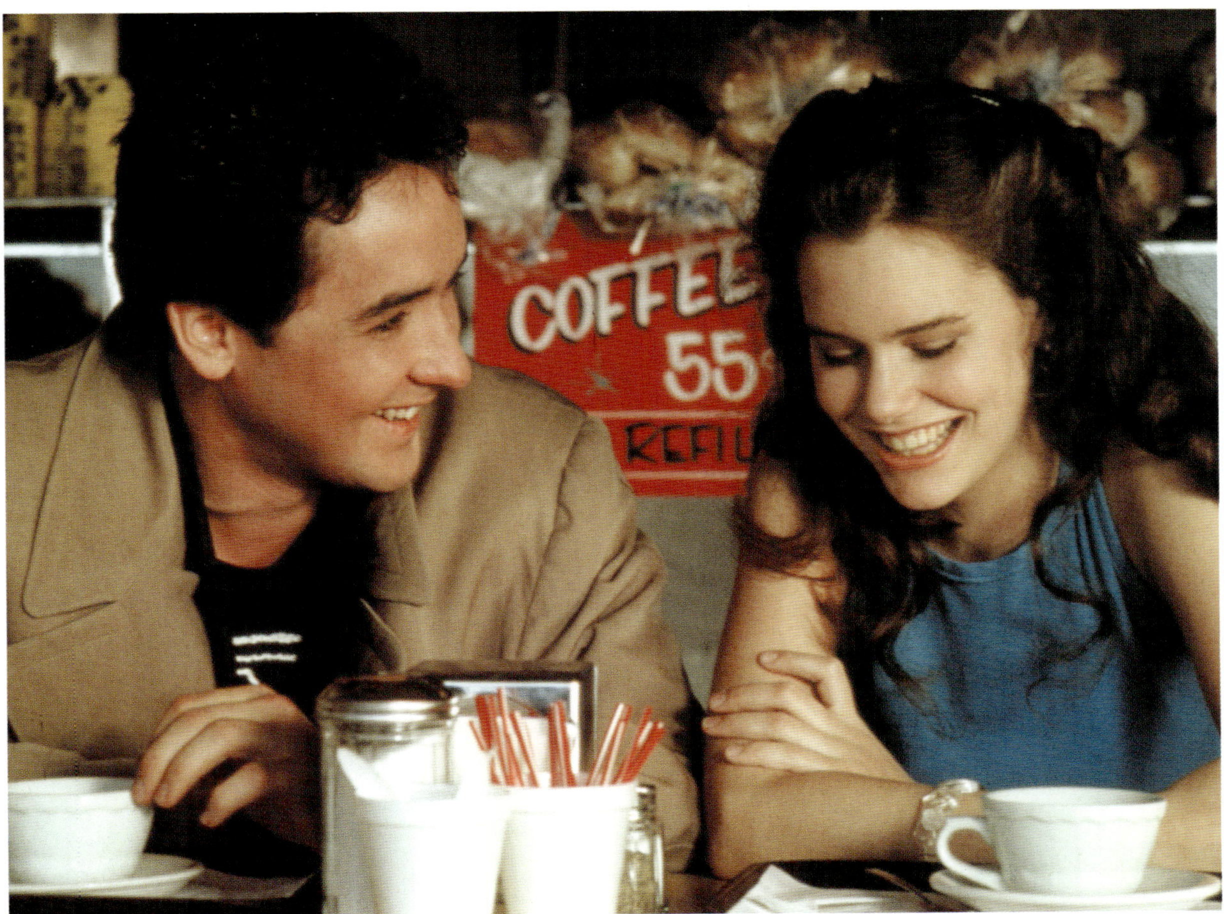

John Cusack and Ione Skye in *Say Anything. . . .*

Fast Times was significant for all the careers it launched, from Penn and his fellow young actors to its creative team. Heckerling went on to direct the gangster movie spoof *Johnny Dangerously* (1984), *National Lampoon's European Vacation* (1985), and *Look Who's Talking* (1989), a big hit that grossed more than $140 million. Cameron Crowe wrote a second movie, *The Wild Life* (1984), that was marketed as a spiritual successor to *Fast Times* (Crowe disputes this), before directing his debut feature, *Say Anything . . .*, in 1989. One of the best teen movies of the era, it provided John Cusack with a star-making role as an aimless high school senior who dates a girl outside of his social group. Sheila Benson praised it in the *Los Angeles Times* as "a film of warmth, insight, humor, and surprising originality. . . . When it's good, which is every moment John Cusack is on-screen, it's a living joy."

Unfortunately, *Fast Times* wasn't treated very seriously by Universal, which underestimated the appeal of such a project. When the movie later took off on home video, it was clear that America's teenagers were hungry for movies about their real lives and experiences.

Sports Movies

You've got to hand it to Hollywood—they'll try anything, once. In addition to *Hoosiers* (1986), *Raging Bull* (1980), and iconic baseball movies like *The Natural* (1984), *Bull Durham* (1988), and *Field of Dreams* (1989), every conceivable sport seemed to crop up in the '80s. Here's a sampling of the more creative offerings:

Cycling: *American Flyers* (1985)

Tennis: *Spring Fever* (1982), *Jocks* (1987)

Gymnastics: *American Anthem* (1986), *Flying* (1986)

Soccer: *Gregory's Girl* (1981), *Victory* (1981)

Motocross: *RAD* (1986)

Track and Field: *Chariots of Fire* (1981), *Personal Best* (1982), *Running Brave* (1983)

Hockey: *Touch and Go* (1986), *Youngblood* (1986)

Martial Arts: *The Karate Kid* (1984)

Wrestling, High School: *Vision Quest* (1985)

Wrestling, Professional: *No Holds Barred* (1989)

Wrestling, Arm: *Over the Top* (1987)

Golf: *Caddyshack* (1980)

Skiing: *Hot Dog . . . The Movie* (1984)

Sports movies occasionally require some suspension of disbelief. "We're asked to believe that Anthony Michael Hall is the country's leading high school football prospect, and that Robert Downey Jr. is his back-up man," wrote the *Los Angeles Times* in its review of *Johnny Be Good* (1988). "Now, Hall is an amusing actor at times, but here, even packing 30 extra pounds, he looks no more like a star high school quarterback than Eric Dickerson looks like Spike Lee. You could name hundreds of better choices: Huntz Hall. Annie Hall. Maybe even the Albert Hall."

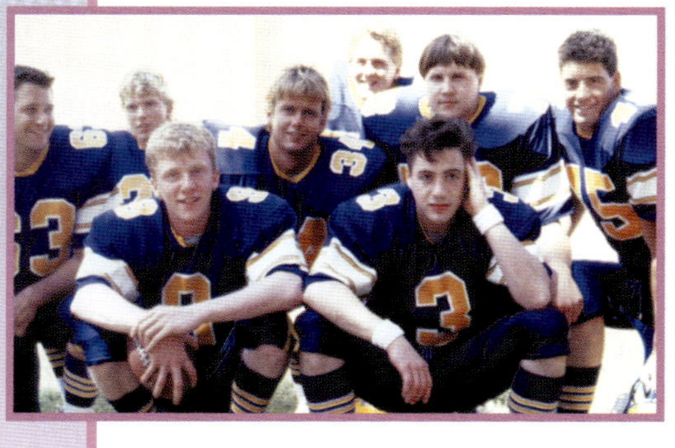

Anthony Michael Hall and Robert Downey Jr. (in front) star in *Johnny Be Good*.

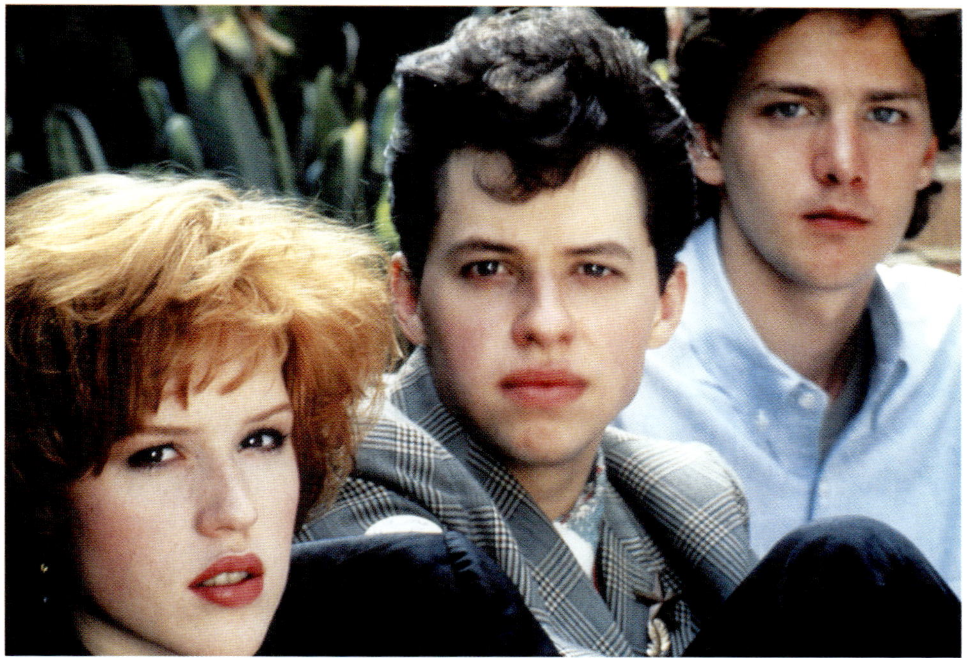

Molly Ringwald, Jon Cryer, and Andrew McCarthy in *Pretty in Pink*.

PAYING HUGHES HIS DUES

When it comes to taking teenagers seriously in the movies, the work of *National Lampoon* writer John Hughes consistently rises to the top. He got his start in film writing scripts in the early '80s like *National Lampoon's Class Reunion* (1982), a failed attempt to follow up on the brand's success with *Animal House*, and the New Zealand adventure film *Savage Islands* (1983). He then wrote a pair of hits: *Mr. Mom* (1983), a Michael Keaton comedy about the modern-day swapping of gender roles, and *National Lampoon's Vacation* (1983), which introduced Clark Griswold (Chevy Chase), America's most overzealous father who takes his family across the country in a station wagon. He would pen the sequels *European Vacation* and *Christmas Vacation* (1989), the latter becoming a perennial holiday classic.

But if there's such a thing as the John Hughes cinematic universe, it clearly began with his directorial debut, *Sixteen Candles* (1984). With this film and the ones that came after, Hughes rebelled against the use of teens as simply immature, horny, or melodramatic, portraying them instead as relatable people with mostly relatable problems. Hughes's films are set in the middle-American world in which he grew up—often in suburbs of Chicago—and speak to young adults in their own language.

Sixteen Candles is about a high schooler (fifteen-year-old Molly Ringwald) who feels unappreciated by her family, who forget her birthday amid the hubbub of her older and more beautiful sister's wedding. Viewed in hindsight, the film's tone seems like a stepping-stone between raunchy teen flicks of the early '80s and the wiser slice-of-life comedies that Hughes

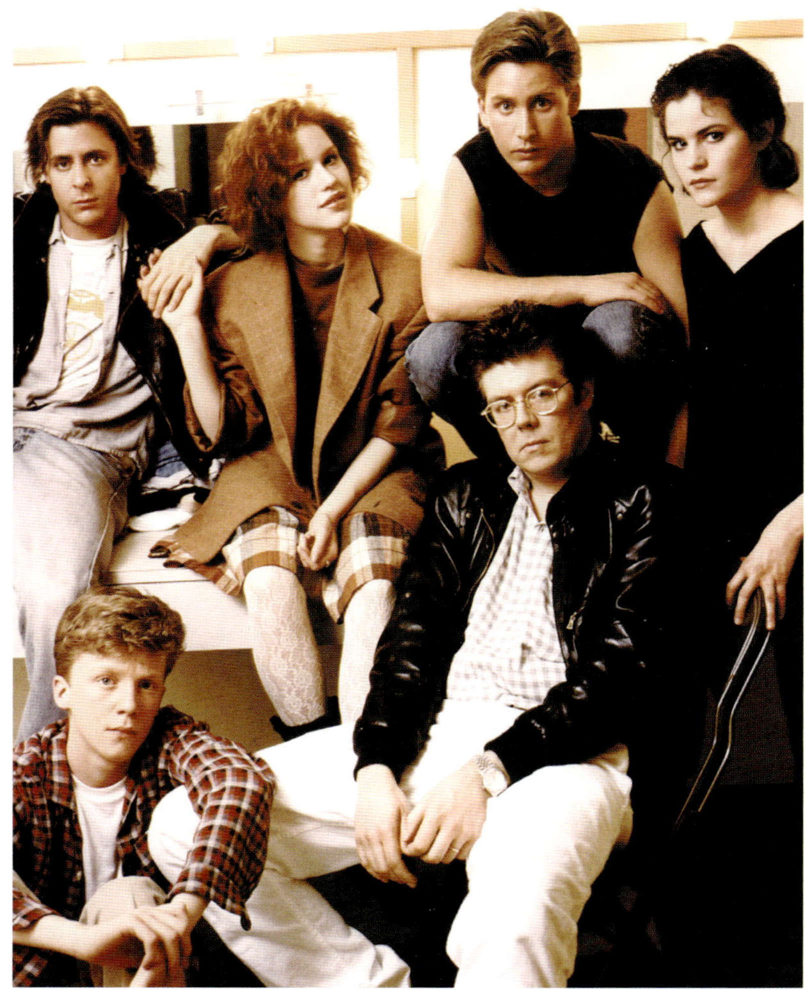

Writer-director-producer John Hughes (foreground, right) with the cast of *The Breakfast Club*.

would soon do better than anyone. Sometimes the humor veers into the offensive: an Asian exchange student is made the butt of jokes, and there is a lighthearted treatment of what amounts to date rape. In these ways, *Sixteen Candles* feels like a rough draft of more mature work to come.

On the positive side, it features a realistic female protagonist who isn't longing for sex—that alone distinguishes *Sixteen Candles* from most of its peers. Ringwald's character is given real agency, and while sex is present, it's not a driving force in the movie. The actress formed a close working relationship with Hughes. "I feel like there was a big part of him that was still a teenager," she later said. "High school was not easy for him, and he just held onto every hurt and personal injury from that period of his life. He was a real grudge keeper, and I feel like a lot of that mentality fueled him creatively later in life."

The Breakfast Club was released in February 1985 and became an instant classic. In its observances of the complexity of being a teenager, it marked a turning point: there are pre–*Breakfast Club* teen movies and post–*Breakfast Club* teen movies. Unique in its genre, and most of American cinema, it's a studio film that is completely character driven. As with an ensemble film like its predecessor *The Big Chill* (1983), it gathers a group of disparate kids, made to serve detention on a Saturday morning, and draws its meaning and momentum from their clashing personalities.

With no silly plot contrivances or gratuitous sex scenes to be found, the film allows the kids to be honest representatives of their generation without the plot mechanics of the typical teen film. It pits character types against each other—from jock to outsider to nerd—in a sort of cinematic social experiment. Emilio Estevez is the "athlete," a wrestler who longs for approval. Molly Ringwald is the "princess" who skipped school to go shopping. Judd Nelson is the "criminal," a tough outsider from a broken home. Ally Sheedy is the "basket case," a quiet loner who shows up at detention because she had nothing better to do. Anthony Michael Hall is the "brain," the nerd who can't tolerate getting a bad grade. If the film has a fault, it's how easily the characters change toward the end—the only contrived aspect of *The Breakfast Club*, but an emotionally satisfying one.

Anthony Michael Hall starred in Hughes's next movie, the techno-fantasy *Weird Science*, which opened just a few months later in August 1985. It was Hughes's only partnership with young producer Joel Silver, who owned the rights to the material and would soon go on to make major action films like *Lethal Weapon* and *Die Hard*. In this case, rather than feeling like a typical character-driven Hughes comedy, *Weird Science* has more of the high-concept rowdiness that would become Silver's trademark. The story is about two high school computer geeks (Hall and Ilan Mitchell-Smith) who use a computer to build the perfect woman (Kelly LeBrock). "Should we give her a brain?" Hall asks. "Yeah, we can play chess with her," Mitchell-Smith replies. With its horndog misogyny and smattering of gay jabs, the film's gender politics are a problematic mess. "Mr. Hughes shows that he can share the kind of dumb joke that only a fourteen-year-old boy could love," wrote the *New York Times*. All criticism aside, *Weird Science* is a showcase for Anthony Michael Hall: an unlikely hero with great comic timing who, though often typecast as the scrawny and intimidated nerd, commands the screen.

One of Hughes's most compelling teen films is one he didn't direct, instead handing the reins

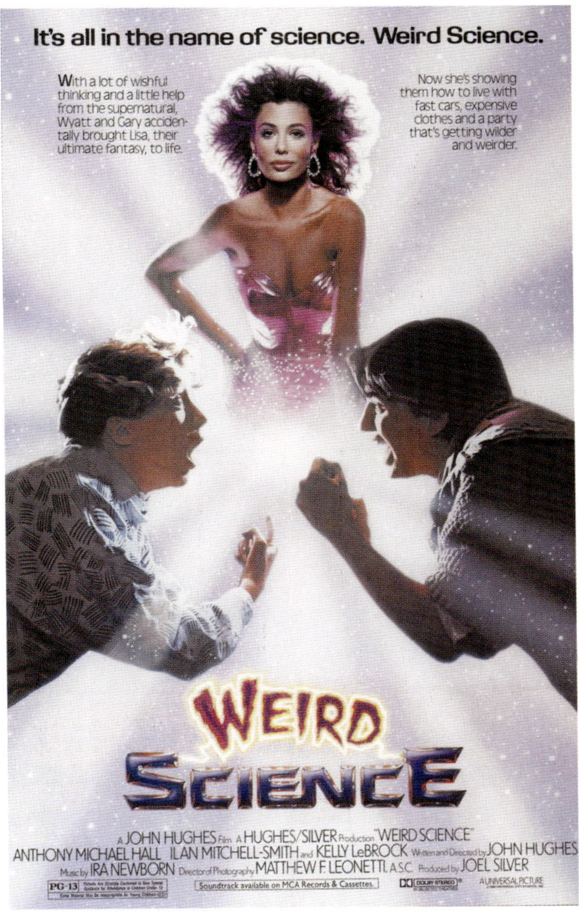

Weird Science combined "inflamed male teenage fantasies and Frankenstein's monster," wrote Roger Ebert.

to his protégé Howard Deutch. *Pretty in Pink*, which opened in January 1986, was written for Ringwald and reflects her personal tastes—in friends, in clothes, and in boys. Given that the film was about her character's chronic indecision—she's torn between her geeky friend "Duckie" and handsome rich boy Blane—Ringwald made it clear that her character's love interest should be someone she'd actually be attracted to. Enter Andrew McCarthy, who had first appeared in 1983's *Class* and was fresh off *St. Elmo's Fire* (1985), in both of which he played sensitive, thoughtful friends opposite Rob Lowe's alpha male. Anthony Michael Hall reportedly turned down the role of Duckie, so as not to be typecast, and the part went to Jon Cryer. The result is that Ringwald's character, Andie, with no gregarious boys chasing after her (save for James Spader's jealous Steff), shines even brighter and has full control over her decisions. The film also offers some socioeconomic commentary: Andie lives with her down-on-his-luck father (Harry Dean Stanton), while Steff and the other rich kids flaunt their privilege.

Andie is so on the fence about her love life that the boy she chooses at the climactic prom scene was actually changed, and the sequence reshot, after test audiences found the original ending unsatisfying. Spoiler alert: Andie now winds up with Blane, turning the film into a Cinderella story. (Ringwald had hoped the prom dress she found hideous would also be changed in reshoots, but no such luck.) "Jon was fantastic in that role, but to me, in my mind, Duckie was clearly a gay boy with a fierce crush on his friend," Ringwald told *Vogue* magazine in 2021. "The character was based on my best friend Matt Freeman, who ended up coming out later in life. . . . Some of our friends suspected he might be gay, but he and I always had an extremely nonromantic relationship, and I felt the same way about Andie and Duckie. The studio agreed."

While Deutch was directing *Pretty in Pink*, Hughes was starting production on *Ferris Bueller's Day Off* (1986), which starred Matthew Broderick as a high schooler who skips school one spring day to hang out with his friends. "Life moves pretty fast," explains Ferris, Gen X philosopher. "If you don't stop and look around once in a while, you could miss it." The film was written in a weeklong burst of energy just before an ensuing writer's strike was due to start. "I know how the movie begins, I know how it ends. I don't ever know the rest, but that doesn't seem to matter," Hughes told the *Chicago Tribune*. "It's not the events that are important, it's the characters going through the event. Therefore, I make them as full and real as I can. This time around, I wanted to create a character who could handle everyone and everything."

In a less risqué take on the absent-parents conceit of *Risky Business*, Ferris spends the day cavorting in downtown Chicago—even singing "Twist and Shout" on a parade float—with his girlfriend, Sloane (Mia Sara), and depressed best friend, Cameron (Alan Ruck), whose conflict with his father provides the deepest emotional

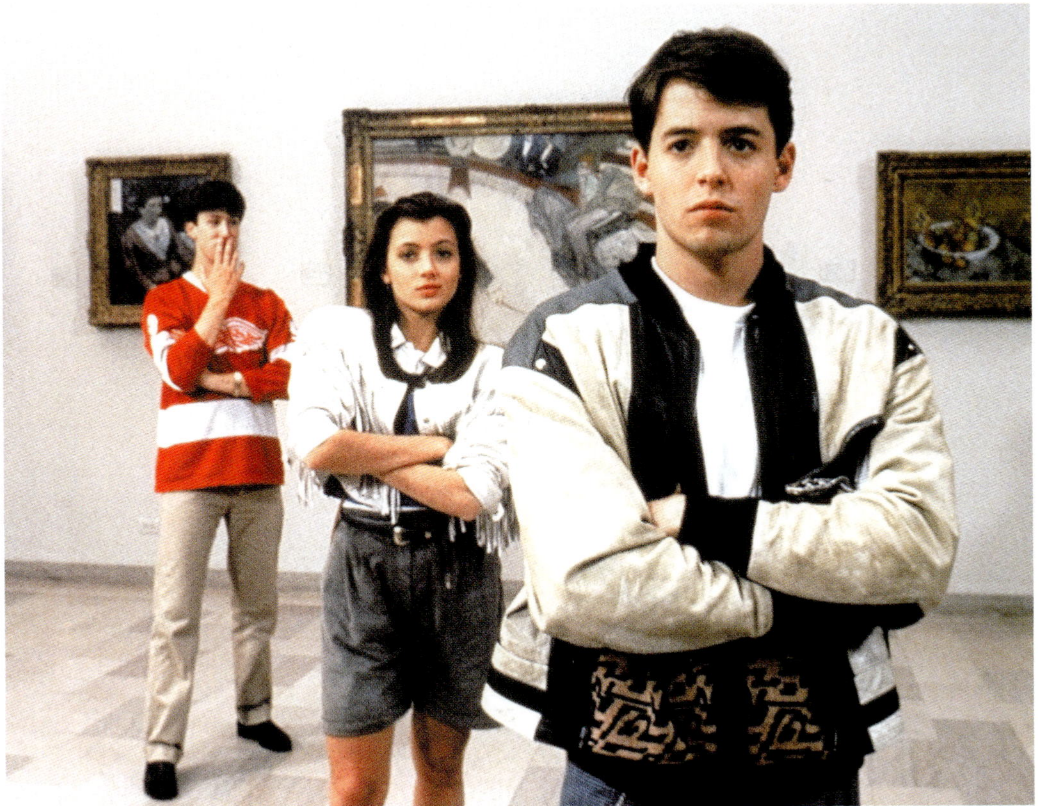

Alan Ruck, Mia Sara, and Matthew Broderick in *Ferris Bueller's Day Off.*

pull of the movie. At odds with Ferris is his meddling sister (Jennifer Grey) and the school's dean (Jeffrey Jones) who makes it his goal to prove that Ferris has been skipping class. But Ferris is too smart for them, and too well liked, to boot. "The sportos, the motorheads, geeks, sluts, bloods, wastoids, dweebies, dickheads—they all adore him. They think he's a righteous dude," explains the school secretary, played by iconic '80s character actress Edie McClurg.

Broderick got his start as an actor on Broadway, winning a Tony Award in 1983 for Neil Simon's *Brighton Beach Memoirs*, before starring in the film *WarGames* (1983) as a teenage computer hacker who nearly starts a nuclear conflict with the Soviet Union. He and Ruck were appearing together in *Biloxi Blues* in 1985 when Hughes attended the show; because of their obvious chemistry, the director asked them to audition as a pair for *Ferris Bueller*. Terrific in the lead role, Broderick has been associated with the artful high school dodger ever since. "What's my legacy?" he mused in a 2023 interview with the *Guardian*. "Well, I'm Ferris Bueller, I suppose. I have to accept it. And I like it. I've made my peace with it."

It's tempting to cite *Ferris Bueller* as the pinnacle of the '80s teen movie (admittedly a high bar). It's a film in which the hero—unencumbered by peer pressure or sexual angst or anxiety about

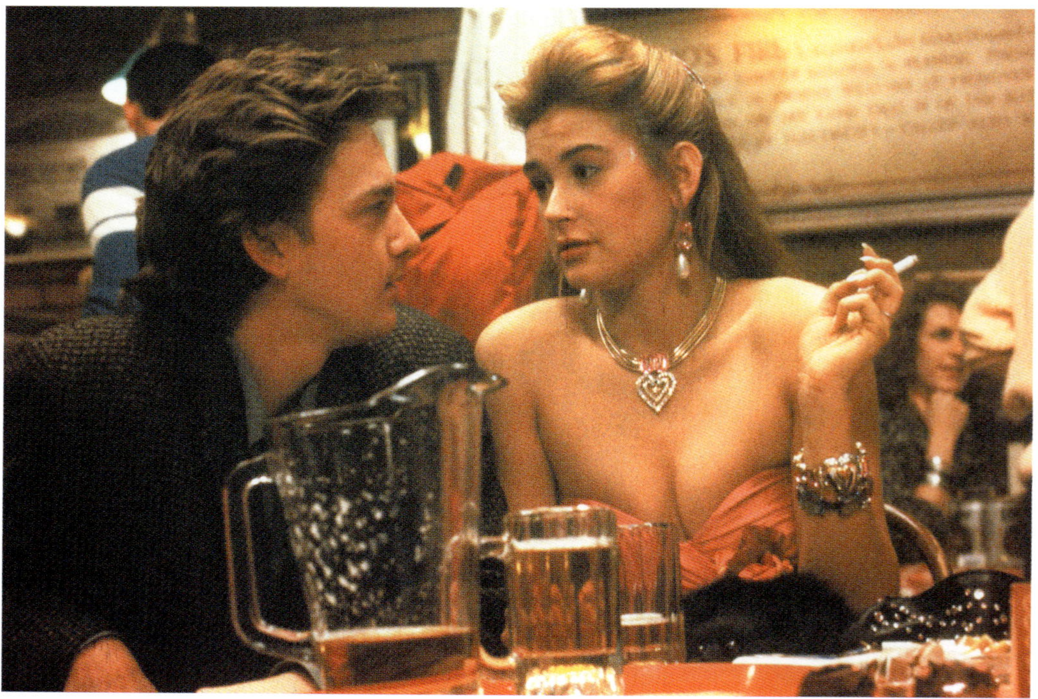

Andrew McCarthy and Demi Moore in *St. Elmo's Fire*.

his future or Saturday detention—wins the day in an audacious display of self-confidence. The spiritual opposite of Benjamin Braddock in the boomer lodestar *The Graduate* (1967), Ferris embraces life with cunning, optimism, and nonchalance. For mid-'80s suburban America, it's not a middle finger, but an exclamation point.

John Hughes would struggle to match the success of *Ferris Bueller* without departing from the teen-movie genre. His scripts for *Christmas Vacation* and two *Home Alone* films (1990, 1992) would lead to bigger box-office returns, but teen rom-com *Some Kind of Wonderful* (1987) with Eric Stoltz, Lea Thompson, and Mary Stuart Masterson, directed again by Deutch, was hampered by a rocky preproduction period and received somewhat dismissively as a *Pretty in Pink* retread. He directed three more movies in the 1980s: *Planes, Trains and Automobiles* (1987), *She's Having a Baby* (1988), and *Uncle Buck* (1989), each of which shows his ability to write complex, often hilarious adult characters in addition to the teenagers with whom he is so closely associated.

BRATS

In the fall of 1984, *Breakfast Club* cast members Emilio Estevez, Judd Nelson, and Ally Sheedy reunited on the Georgetown set of *St. Elmo's Fire* to tell the story of a group of new college graduates navigating adult relationships and careers. The film, released in 1985 a few months after *The Breakfast Club*, is technically not about teenagers. But then again, the three actors weren't technically teenagers, either. The one-two punch of these iconic ensemble films would

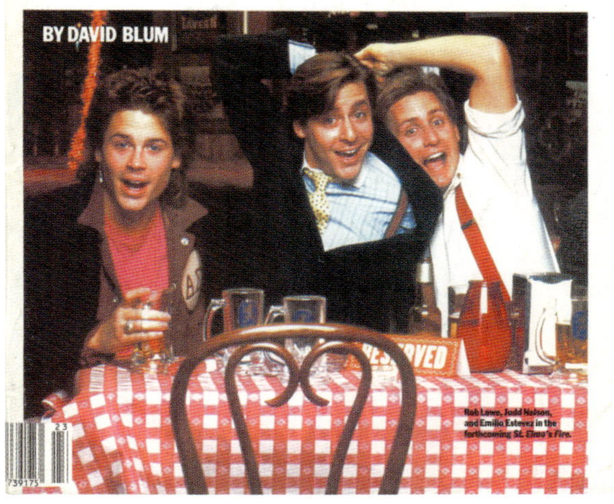

David Blum's coinage of the term "brat pack" in a June 1985 *New York* cover story continues to haunt a generation of actors.

cast a shadow over their careers, as well as those of many of their young peers.

Joining the *Breakfast Club* trio were Rob Lowe, who takes center stage as an ex-frat boy with an alcohol problem; his *Class* costar Andrew McCarthy as the sensitive writer; Demi Moore as the reckless, fun-loving banker; and Mare Winningham as the more responsible social worker. The movie did well with audiences but was not a critical hit. "Sex and money and love occupy most of their thoughts," complained Gene Siskel of the film's emotionally immature characters. "Now that, of course, makes these kids fairly normal. But this movie treats them as if they were the only creatures on earth experiencing such traumas." That sensibility alone is enough to link the film to teenage cinema. The line between self-absorbed high schoolers and the "Greed Decade" social climbers of *St. Elmo's Fire* is hazier than the arguments for trickle-down economics.

However, the film is most noteworthy for an article that was published just weeks before its premiere. The cover of the June 10, 1985, issue of *New York* magazine featured a photo of Lowe, Nelson, and Estevez—a cropped publicity shot for the movie—under the headline "Hollywood's Brat Pack." Journalist David Blum had gone out with the three actors one evening and reported on what he observed. "There were many boys in the bar that Thursday night, many of them as handsome as those at this one round table, but these boys—these young studs, all under 25 years old, decked out in *Risky Business* sunglasses and trendish sport jackets and designer T-shirts—they were the Main Event."

Blum surmised that these kids had achieved fame not by their talent but through their box-office success. "You can be 'hot' and be a shamelessly poor actor," admitted Nelson. Whereas Marlon Brando and James Dean and Al Pacino had engaged in "years of acting study," many of the new generation skipped that step. Several, like Estevez, already had family members in the business, which gave them an undeniable leg up. Compared to the Rat Pack of the 1950s—the essence of cool—these entitled boys seemed to be playing at fame. The article described them throwing their weight around: picking up girls in the Hard Rock Café, cutting lines at popular clubs, and getting comp tickets to sold-out shows.

Who was in the Brat Pack? A few names are mentioned by Blum. Emilio Estevez is the "unofficial president"; his *Outsiders* costar Tom Cruise is "the hottest of them all," while Rob Lowe has "the most beautiful face." Judd Nelson is "the overrated one" (ouch), Timothy Hutton is "the only one with an Oscar" (at that point), Matt Dillon is "the one least likely to replace Marlon Brando" (huh?), and Nicolas Cage fills "the ethnic chair," whose looks relegate him to "the part of brother or best friend." Sean Penn is "the most gifted of them all . . . the natural heir to Robert De Niro's throne."

Blum cast a wide net, seemingly entrapping every successful young actor of the '80s—especially if they had appeared in ensemble films like *Taps*, *The Outsiders*, and *The Breakfast Club*—and no one was happy about it. "We're members of a club we never asked to join," griped Andrew McCarthy. The group that composed the Brat Pack wasn't some insular clique or tight-knit friend group, and the artificial label roped them together in a deeply condescending way. For McCarthy, the role of Kevin in *St. Elmo's Fire* played to his strengths as a contemplative outsider, which was more or less his real-life persona and part of the reason he was so turned off by being lumped in with others in the Brat Pack.

The group did its best to disperse. "Immediately after the article appeared, actors began to actively avoid making any movie that might be considered a Brat Pack endeavor and helped to kill off the current cycle of youth ensemble movies," explained McCarthy in his 2021 autobiography, *Brat*. "An every-man-for-himself attitude pervaded as actors ran for whatever cover they could find or invent."

Pretty in Pink was already in production by that point, and his wealthy teen character who wins the girl may be the most enduring of all his performances, even if it wasn't a lead role. That would come with his next film, the department store fantasy *Mannequin* (1987), which he affectionately called "a silly movie." It performed well with audiences and led to McCarthy's casting in later '80s films like *Less than Zero* (1987), based on the Bret Easton Ellis novel about drug addiction. The dark Christmas-set story paired him

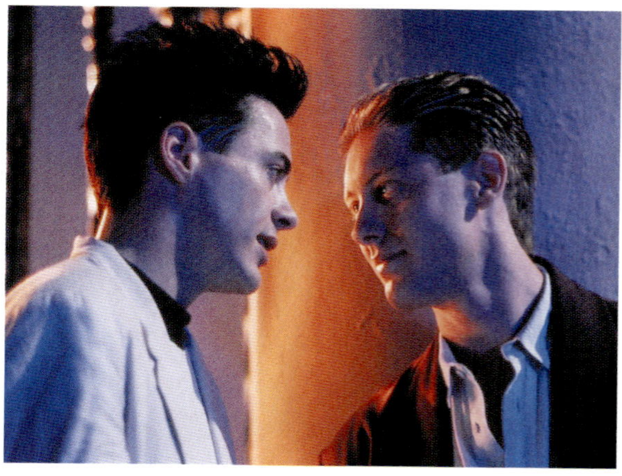

Robert Downey Jr. and James Spader in *Less than Zero*.

with Robert Downey Jr. and, for a third time, James Spader as the main antagonist. *Weekend at Bernie's* (1989) was also dark, but comedic. McCarthy and costar Jonathan Silverman play two New York coworkers who discover their boss has died but keep up the illusion that he is alive so they can enjoy his Hamptons beach house over Labor Day weekend.

Rob Lowe's first starring role was in *Oxford Blues* (1984) as an American kid who improbably enrolls in Oxford University and joins the rowing team in order to be with an English girl. His roguish pretty-boy persona would follow him for years to come, from the hockey drama *Youngblood* (1986) to the sexual thriller *Masquerade* (1988). In *About Last Night . . .* (1986), based on David Mamet's play *Sexual Perversity in Chicago*, he and Demi Moore play more grounded characters than their shallow *St. Elmo's Fire* yuppies. They meet in a bar, fall in love, and attempt to set up a life together before arguments and angst lead to a breakup. "It is my best work of this period of my life," said Lowe. "I'd put it up against any 'date night' movie ever made."

Moore had been a model and *General Hospital* actress before landing parts in *Blame It on Rio* (1984) and *St. Elmo's Fire*. She quickly transitioned to more adult fare—one of which was made by her fellow Brat Packer and then fiancé, Emilio Estevez. Buzzed about in the press as a new Orson Welles due to his youth and multi-hyphenate screen credit (writer-director-star), Estevez cast Moore as his leading lady and partner in crime in *Wisdom* (1986). The film was an altruistic spin on Bonnie and Clyde in which the two bank robbers cancel mortgage loans rather than stealing cash, but it failed with critics and audiences. To quote Moore's character in *About Last Night . . .*, "See what happens when you take life too seriously?"

One of Estevez's most beloved films was much less serious and actually was released before the Brat Pack commotion. *Repo Man* (1984) was British director Alex Cox's feature debut, in which Estevez plays a punk rocker who helps repossess a mysterious 1964 Chevy Malibu. It was also a sci-fi parable about the

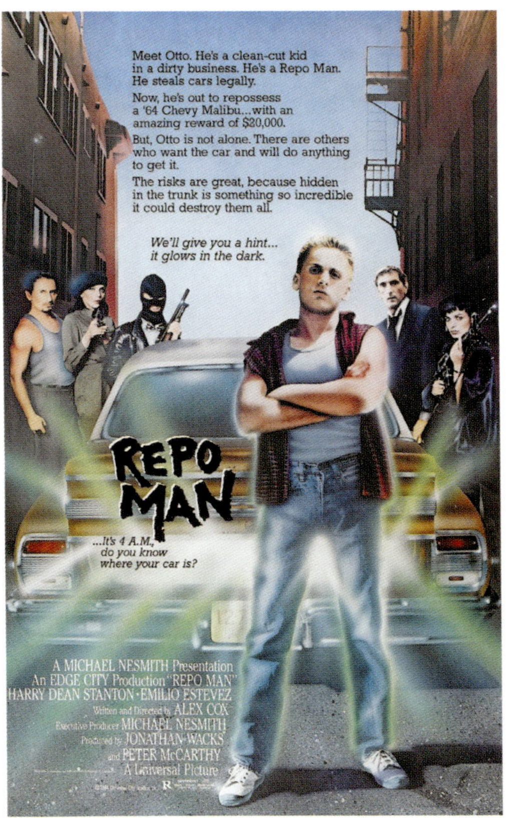

Since its release in 1984, *Repo Man* has become an iconic LA-set cult film.

dangers of nuclear war. Though it wasn't a huge success upon its release, it has since become a cult classic.

His younger brother, Charlie Sheen, also broke out in the '80s, appearing in five films in 1986 alone, including a cameo in *Wisdom* and a small scene in *Ferris Bueller's Day Off*. He played a caring high school football player opposite Corey Haim in *Lucas* and an avenging drag racer in *The Wraith*, but his most high-profile role was as a disillusioned new recruit in Oliver Stone's Vietnam War drama *Platoon*. The movie struck a chord with its realistic depiction of a soldier's experience, and Sheen's compelling performance led to more top-tier films like *Wall Street* (1987) and *Major League* (1989). The two brothers also reunited for *Young Guns* (1988), a youthful western about Billy the Kid (Estevez) and the "Regulators" gang.

Though the members of the Brat Pack dismissed the term as pejorative in 1985, time has been kind to their legacy. Fans today view these actors and their work together through the warm lens of nostalgia. "It always pains me when I see some of the other folks who don't realize how much love is infused into the Brat Pack," said Lowe. "It's nothing but good will now."

TEENSEMBLES

Like *The Outsiders*, *The Breakfast Club*, and *St. Elmo's Fire*, many teen movies of the '80s didn't have just one main character but grouped together a diverse team of (often quirky) individuals who navigate their adolescence as a group. They ranged in age and could also span a variety

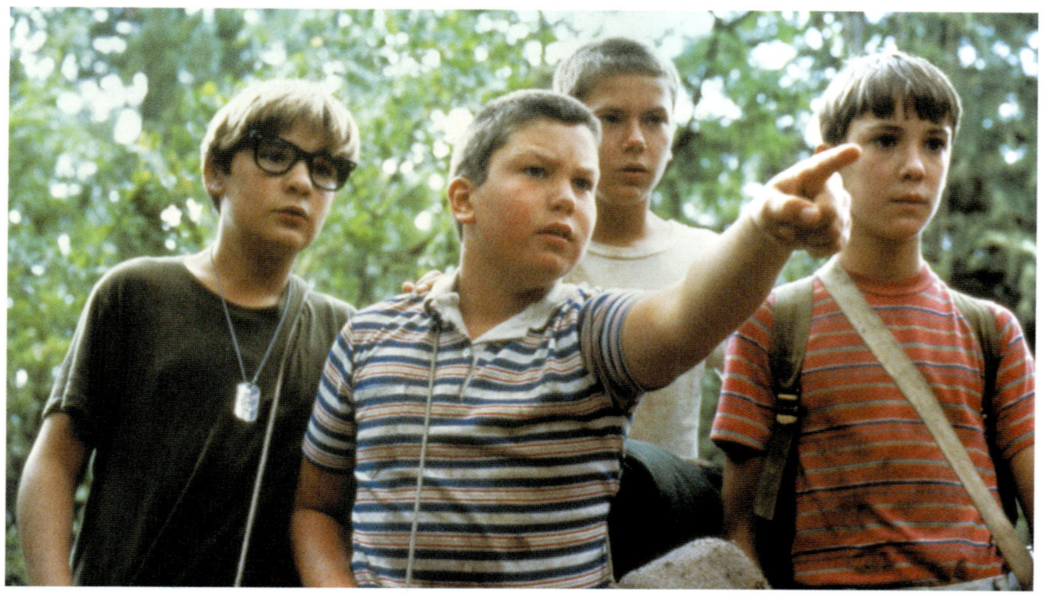

Corey Feldman, Jerry O'Connell, River Phoenix, and Wil Wheaton in *Stand by Me*.

PG-13

On July 1, 1984, the Motion Picture Association of America rolled out its new "PG-13" rating, situated between the milder content of PG and the more mature R. The new rating was created in response to a series of movies that sat "awkwardly beyond PG," according to MPAA president Jack Valenti—in particular, *Indiana Jones and the Temple of Doom* and *Gremlins*, which were both released earlier that summer. Understandably, the image of a heart being ripped out of a man's chest or a little monster exploding in a microwave might tend to induce nightmares in a preteen crowd.

The first PG-13 rated release was the teen vigilante film *Red Dawn* (1984), which included intense action sequences and depicted a potential World War III, a terrifying geopolitical prospect that, if nothing else, likely would have flown over younger kids' heads. (The first film to actually receive the rating was *The Flamingo Kid* with Matt Dillon, though it wasn't released until that December.)

Parents, you've been strongly cautioned.

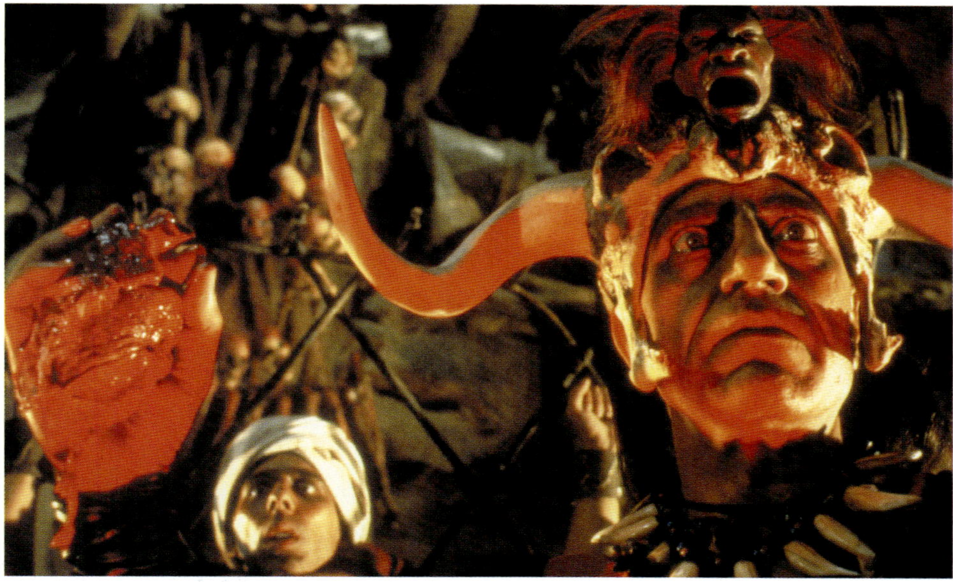

Amrish Puri ritualistically removed a still-beating heart in *Indiana Jones and the Temple of Doom*.

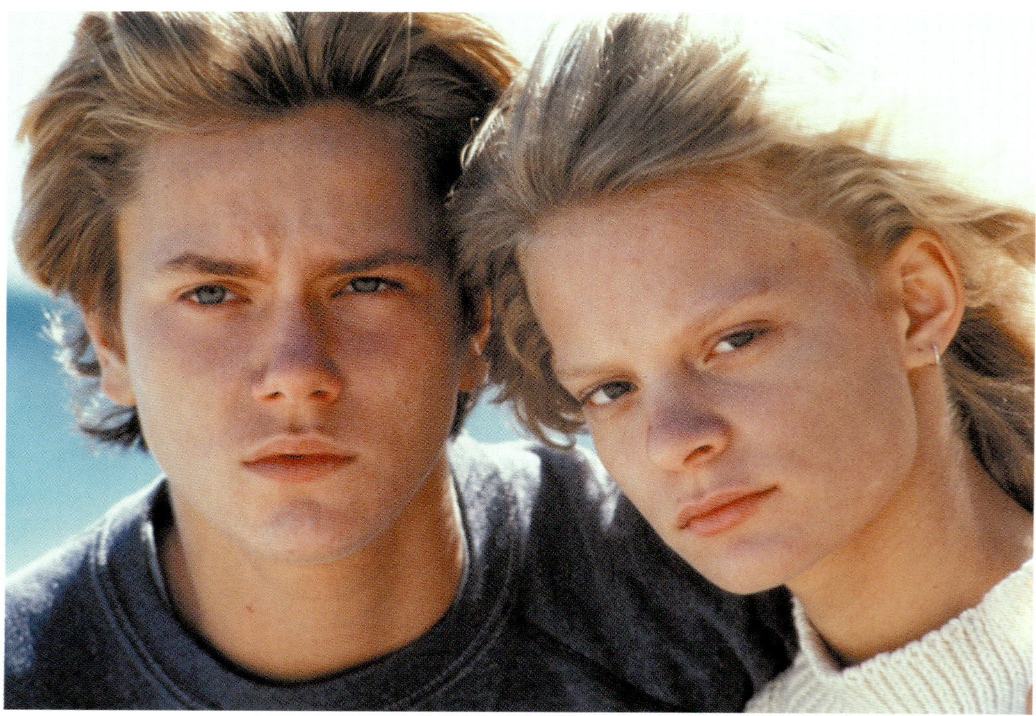

River Phoenix and Martha Plimpton in *Running on Empty*.

of genres, as seen with *Young Guns*. At the younger end of the scale were two adventure movies with mostly male casts: *The Goonies* (1985), from Steven Spielberg and director Richard Donner, which follows a group of middle schoolers who go on a treasure hunt and cross paths with a family of gangsters, and *Stand by Me* (1986), a Rob Reiner film based on a Stephen King short story about the search for the body of a missing boy.

Typical for the time, there was crossover in the casting, with Corey Feldman playing a major part in both films. However, the most famous face in *The Goonies* was arguably young Ke Huy Quan as "Data," who was fresh off a major role in *Indiana Jones and the Temple of Doom* (1984). Feldman's fellow *Stand by Me* actors included Jerry O'Connell, Wil Wheaton, and Kiefer Sutherland—the last of whom he would soon appear with again in the small-town vampire film *The Lost Boys* (1987). (To go a step further, *The Lost Boys* was also the first of nine films that paired him with Corey Haim.)

Stand by Me featured another of the era's breakout stars, River Phoenix, who was seen opposite Harrison Ford and Helen Mirren a few months later in Peter Weir's *The Mosquito Coast* (1986). The story of a man so disillusioned with American life that he moves his family to the Honduran jungle was not a box-office hit, but it suggested that Phoenix was a teen actor capable of more complex dramatic roles. It also paired him with *The Goonies*' Martha Plimpton, who became both his girlfriend and his costar in *Running on Empty* (1988), director Sidney Lumet's film about a couple (Judd Hirsch and Christine Lahti) on the run from the FBI, whose seventeen-year-old son wants to pursue his own dreams. "He's never studied formally, but boy, does he know how to reach inside himself," praised Lumet. "So long as River follows his instincts, takes stuff he believes in, there'll be no stopping him." Phoenix's sensitive performance earned an Oscar nomination for Best Supporting Actor. His highest-profile role came next, as the young version of the title character in *Indiana Jones and the Last Crusade* (1989)—another movie with Harrison Ford, although the two Indys obviously do not share screen time.

Ethan Hawke had appeared with Phoenix in their 1985 debut, *Explorers*, a sci-fi adventure directed by Joe Dante about kids who build a spaceship in their backyard. But its failure with audiences—having been released the same month as *Back to the Future*—led Hawke to forgo acting for several years. "I would never recommend that a kid act," he later cautioned. But his interest remained, and he performed onstage in high school and (briefly) at Carnegie Mellon. In 1989, a bit older and wiser, he starred alongside Robert Sean Leonard and Josh Charles as pupils of a nonconformist poetry teacher played by Robin Williams in *Dead Poets Society*. This time the film was a huge hit. "It was kind of hard working with Robin," he told the *New York Times*. "I like being the center of attention, and you could never be the center of attention with him."

Back to the Future was the big-screen breakout of its lead actor, twenty-four-year-old *Family Ties* star Michael J. Fox. Playing his mother in the film was Lea Thompson, who—just nine days older than Fox—had already appeared in a number of major teen films, including *All the Right Moves* (1983) and *Red Dawn* (1984). Though she was one of the most consistent young screen actors of the day, she found the industry challenging as a woman. "It's easier to be a man and a movie star," she said. One of the few lead roles she landed was in *Howard the Duck* (1986), a George Lucas–produced comic-book adaptation that famously flopped. The next year she appeared in the John Hughes–scripted *Some Kind of Wonderful*, later marrying her director, Howard Deutch.

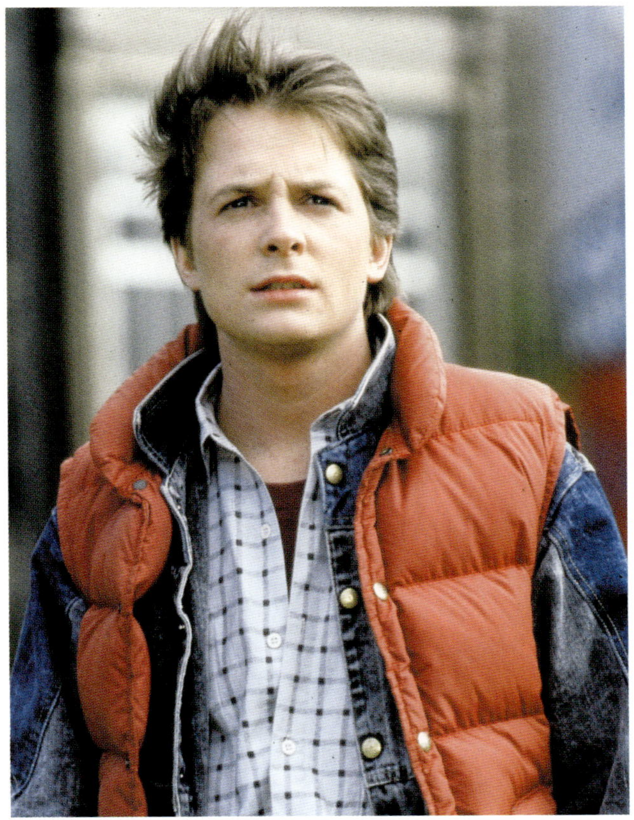

Michael J. Fox in *Back to the Future*.

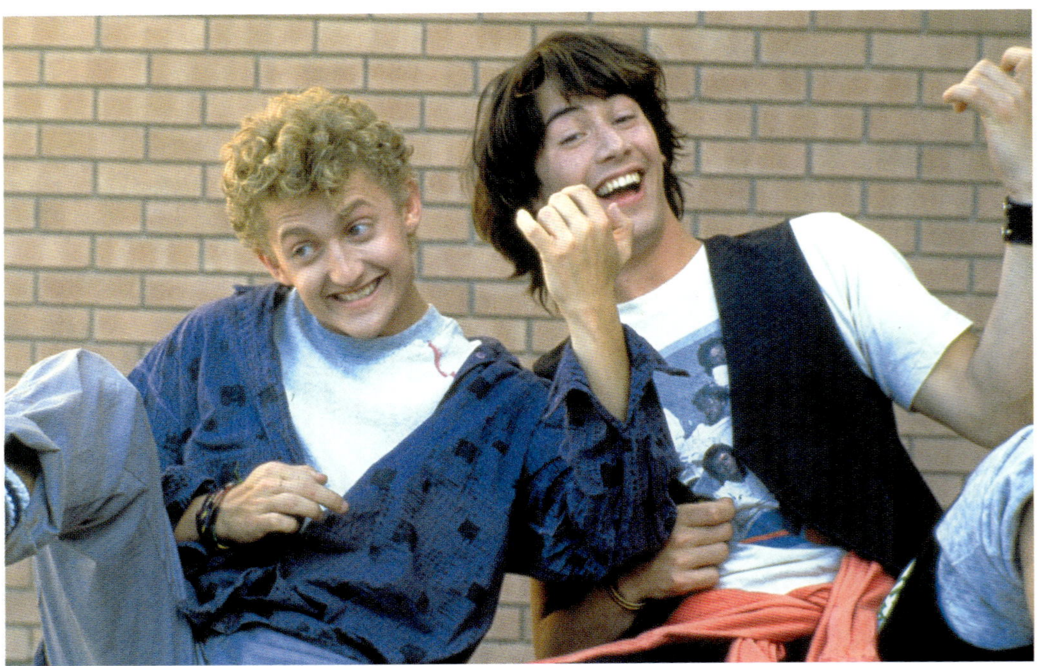

Alex Winter and Keanu Reeves might change the world if only they can pass their history final in *Bill & Ted's Excellent Adventure*.

Keanu Reeves grew up in Toronto, where he got his start on Canadian television. He appeared with Crispin Glover (Lea Thompson's husband in *Back to the Future*) in the independent crime film *River's Edge* (1986) and had a supporting role in Stephen Frears's Oscar-winning period drama *Dangerous Liaisons* (1988) in which his naive nobleman is used to seduce a young Uma Thurman. He would act in a diverse array of films throughout his career, appearing opposite River Phoenix for Gus Van Sant's story of queer drifters, *My Own Private Idaho* (1991), for example. But it was the 1989 comedy *Bill & Ted's Excellent Adventure* that put him on the map. Reeves and costar Alex Winter play two high school dopes who complete their end-of-year history project with the help of a time traveler (George Carlin) who introduces them to Socrates, Napoleon, Genghis Khan, Joan of Arc, and Abraham Lincoln. "Be excellent to each other," advises the sixteenth president. "And party on, dudes!"

Stage actor Patrick Dempsey broke into film in 1987 with the comedy *Can't Buy Me Love*, in which his geeky character pays a cheerleader (Amanda Peterson) to pose as his girlfriend—a movie famous today for its romantic final scene on a lawnmower. One month later, he appeared in Phil Alden Robinson's *In the Mood* (1987), the true story of a teenager in the 1940s who had affairs with older women, including a soldier's wife played by Beverly D'Angelo. He does something similar in Joan Micklin Silver's *Loverboy* (1989), where his college-age pizza-delivery man becomes an unlikely call boy for unsatisfied wives. "Why am I getting these kind of roles?" he asked rhetorically in an interview with the *Los Angeles Times*. "What is my problem with women?"

Toxic relationships may have reached a peak with *Heathers* (1989), a black comedy with Christian Slater and Winona Ryder, the breakout star of *Beetlejuice* (1988). Slater, who had played mostly dramatic roles to that point, takes on the role of troubled teen J. D., who kills off several cruel members of their school's elite clique and stages them as victims of suicide. "Are we going to prom or to hell?" Ryder's character asks in her diary. Screenwriter Daniel Waters knew he was pushing buttons with the film's dark satire. "What's the *Full Metal Jacket* of high school films? What's the *Dr. Strangelove* of high school films?" he had asked himself. "I thought, 'I guess I've gotta stop waiting around for it, hoping somebody else makes it. I'm just gonna write it and see what happens.'" The indie film did not perform well with audiences but has since become a classic—even spawning a stage musical in 2013.

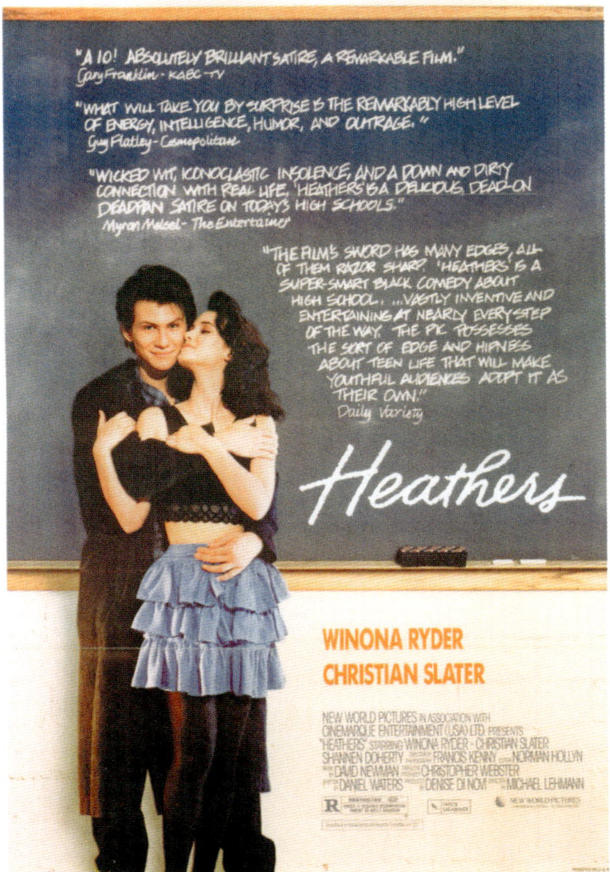

Heathers was conceived as a rebellious alternative to lighter teen movies of the era.

Heathers wasn't the first darker-themed movie that Slater had been a part of. In Matthew Robbins's road-trip comedy *The Legend of Billie Jean* (1985), he plays the younger brother of a Texas girl (Helen Slater, no relation) who seeks justice from the town bullies. After some gunplay, the two go on the run from police. Billie Jean wins the PR battle by restyling herself as a modern-day Joan of Arc with a chopped blonde haircut, inspiring young people everywhere to celebrate her teenage outlaw hero—and making the film an '80s cult classic.

C. Thomas Howell, who had played the central role of Ponyboy in *The Outsiders*, starred in the controversial comedy *Soul Man* (1986). The story about a white California kid who poses as African American to get a diversity scholarship to Harvard Law School—darkening his skin with experimental tanning pills—goes out of its way to excuse its blackface conceit. The hero personally experiences racial slurs and police prejudice, and his professor (James Earl Jones) ultimately deems it an important learning experience. The film makes a play for the humor and

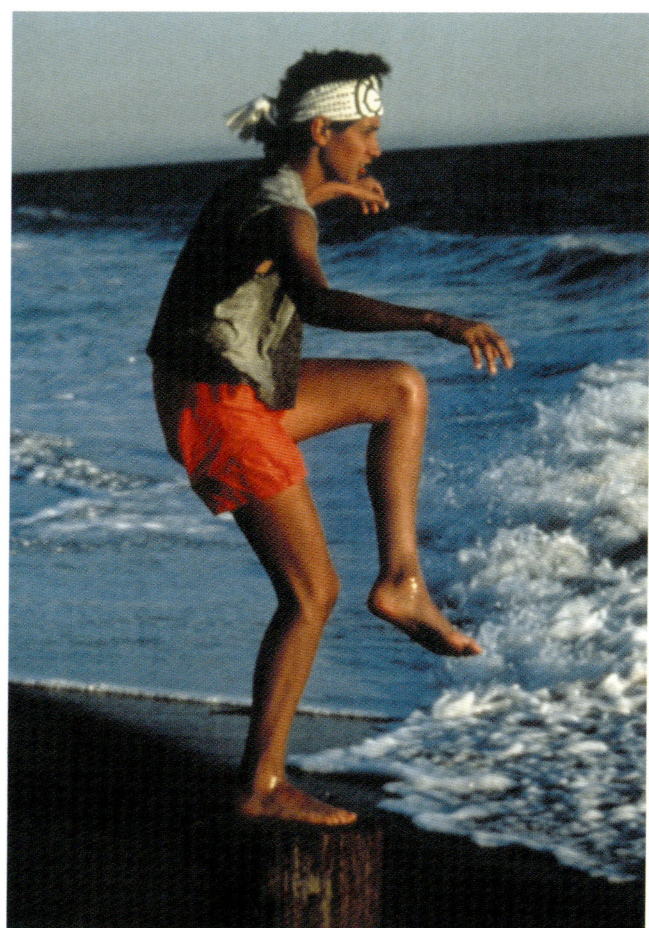

Ralph Macchio in *The Karate Kid.*

poignancy of *Tootsie* (1982), which had examined gender inequality, but *Soul Man*'s awkward racial politics prevented it from being received like the beloved Dustin Hoffman film.

Howell's *Soul Man* costar (and later wife), Rae Dawn Chong—daughter of Cheech & Chong comedian Tommy Chong—had broken out in the Canadian prehistoric drama *Quest for Fire* (1981) and had prominent roles in films as varied as the hip-hop classic *Beat Street* (1984) and the Arnold Schwarzenegger action film *Commando* (1985). As a mixed-race actress, Chong found navigating Hollywood to be a complicated affair. "I never get the role that's racially specific. They will go with Whoopi Goldberg or Alfre Woodard. You look at them and you know what's going on," she later told an interviewer. "With me being mixed, I never had a chance to get into what they call 'blackting.' I went for the parts that were non-specific and did not depend on me pulling in this other baggage."

Ralph Macchio—also an *Outsiders* alumnus—hit it big with *The Karate Kid* (1984), the story of a New Jersey teen transplanted to Southern California who is instructed in the martial arts by a kindly Japanese repairman (Pat Morita). The slight-of-build Macchio identified with the main character who learns to defend himself against the town bullies, eventually taking them on at a local tournament. The film was such a success that two sequels were released within the decade, and the franchise continues to this day. Harvard student Elisabeth Shue, who played Macchio's on-screen love interest, followed up her work here with Chris Columbus's directorial debut, *Adventures in Babysitting* (1987), the Tom Cruise vehicle *Cocktail* (1988), and *Back to the Future Part II* (1989).

LIFE MOVES PRETTY FAST

If the biggest teen success story from the '80s was megastar Tom Cruise, his career development from age eighteen to twenty-eight, by decade's end, is both extraordinary in its success and typical of the way roles for the era's young actors naturally matured. After *The Outsiders*

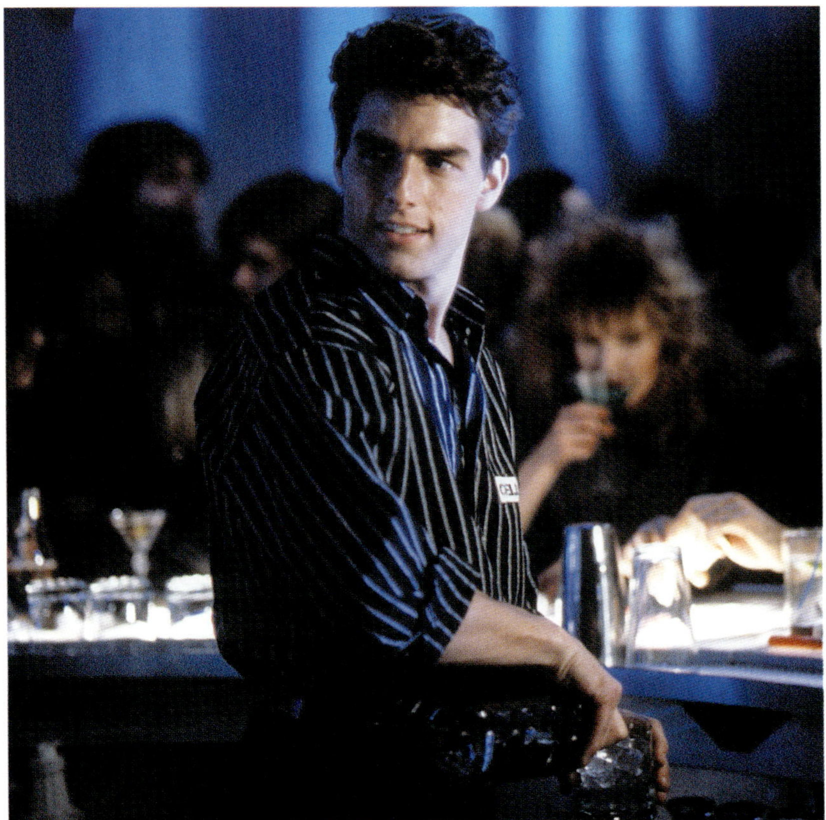

Tom Cruise mixes things up in *Cocktail*.

and *Risky Business*, he starred in the landmark action blockbuster *Top Gun* (1986) and then appeared opposite Paul Newman in *The Color of Money* (1986) and Dustin Hoffman in *Rain Man* (1988), which won the Oscar for Best Picture. He ended the '80s on another high note. "Nothing Cruise has done will prepare you for what he does in *Born on the Fourth of July*," wrote Roger Ebert. "His performance is so good that the movie lives through it." The role of paraplegic Vietnam veteran Ron Kovic in Oliver Stone's 1989 true story about an all-American kid who becomes a disillusioned protester of the nation's military adventurism is a fitting summation of Cruise's career journey. His persona may have remained that of a cocky, headstrong young man, but his parts ceased to be juvenile.

He wasn't alone. Suddenly, Matt Dillon, Sean Penn, Diane Lane, Emilio Estevez, Demi Moore, Lea Thompson, and others were playing full-fledged adults on-screen, with some careers transcending their famous teenage roles more successfully than others. But at the end of the day, teen movies aren't about the teens *in the movies*; they're about the teens who watch them—in darkened theaters, late at night on VHS, or through clips on TikTok. Decades on, '80s teen cinema shows no signs of slowing down.

Beyond Hollywood: Australia and New Zealand

The Australian New Wave—a burst of creative energy in the early 1970s, with new talent who were supported by government funding and the opening of the Australian Film, Television and Radio School (AFTRS)—was still going strong in its second decade. Peter Weir was one of several of the industry's leading lights who were scooped up by Hollywood in the '80s. His World War I film *Gallipoli* (1981) followed two young friends (Mel Gibson and Mark Lee) who serve together in the Australian Army, and Gibson appeared as a foreign correspondent in 1960s Indonesia in *The Year of Living Dangerously* (1982). Weir then made two of his most successful films for major studios: Paramount's *Witness* (1985) with Harrison Ford and Touchstone's *Dead Poets Society* (1989) with Robin Williams.

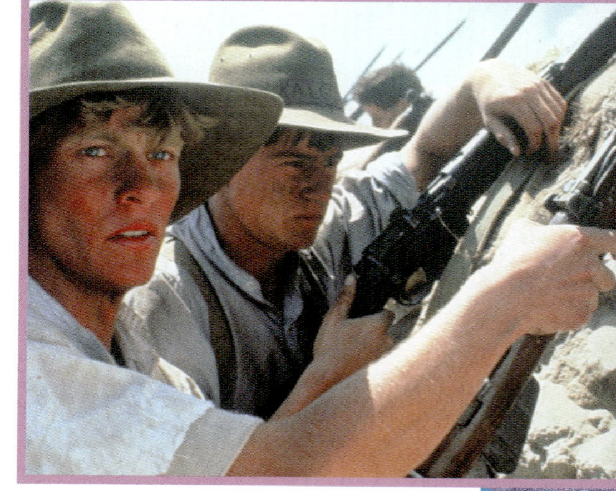

Mark Lee (left) in *Gallipoli*.

Bruce Beresford similarly went from the celebrated *Breaker Morant* (1980), about the Boer War in turn-of-the-century South Africa, to the Hollywood films *Tender Mercies* (1983), *Crimes of the Heart* (1986), and *Driving Miss Daisy* (1989), which won the Best Picture Oscar. George Miller, whose apocalyptic thriller *Mad Max* (1979) had been a wild financial success everywhere except America, was vindicated by the popularity of its two sequels, *Mad Max 2* (1981) and *Mad Max Beyond Thunderdome* (1985), which again starred Mel Gibson as the legendary road warrior. Meanwhile, Miller contributed to the anthology film *Twilight Zone: The Movie* (1983) and directed Jack Nicholson, Cher, Michelle Pfeiffer, and Susan Sarandon in *The Witches of Eastwick* (1987).

After scoring a hit with *My Brilliant Career* (1979)—the breakout film for its star, Judy Davis—Gillian Armstrong made the teenage pop musical *Starstruck* (1982) and the period romance *Mrs. Soffel* (1984) with Mel Gibson and Diane Keaton. She reunited with Davis for *High Tide* (1987), about a backup singer who unexpectedly reunites with her estranged daughter. Armstrong had been a member of the first class at AFTRS, along with director Philip Noyce, who broke out with his Great Barrier Reef–set thriller *Dead Calm* (1989), starring Nicole Kidman, Sam Neill, and Billy Zane. After a couple of homegrown hits, Fred Schepisi worked primarily in America, directing films like *Roxanne* (1987) with Steve Martin and *Evil Angels* (*A Cry in the Dark* [1988]) with Meryl Streep.

Brian Trenchard-Smith specialized in low-budget "Ozploitation" movies like *Turkey Shoot* (*Escape 2000* [1982]), about a dystopian prison colony where inmates are hunted for sport; *BMX Bandits* (1983), featuring Kidman's debut performance; and *Dead-End Drive In* (1986), about a movie theater that entraps its teenage audience. The biggest and most unexpected hit from Australia in the '80s was *Crocodile Dundee* (1986), a comedy about a fearless and down-to-earth Outback explorer (screenwriter Paul Hogan) who is visited by an American journalist (Linda Kozlowski). In a plot reminiscent of *King Kong* (1933), she brings him back to New York City where the fish-out-of-water bushman is forced to navigate the modern world.

New Zealand also produced several notable directors in the '80s. Geoff Murphy made the hit road comedy *Goodbye Pork Pie* (1981) and the war film *Utu* (1983). His wife, Merata Mita, was a key figure in Maori cinema and the director of the love story *Mauri* (1988), the first feature by an indigenous New Zealand woman.

AFTRS graduate Jane Campion shot several notable short films in the '80s, including *Peel* (1982)—winner of the Short Film Palme d'Or at Cannes—before making her first feature, *Sweetie* (1989), about two wildly different sisters growing up in suburban Sydney. Meanwhile, future *Lord of the Rings* filmmaker Peter Jackson showed an early predilection for the weird and grotesque with his low-budget gross-out film *Bad Taste* (1987) and the adult puppet musical *Meet the Feebles* (1989).

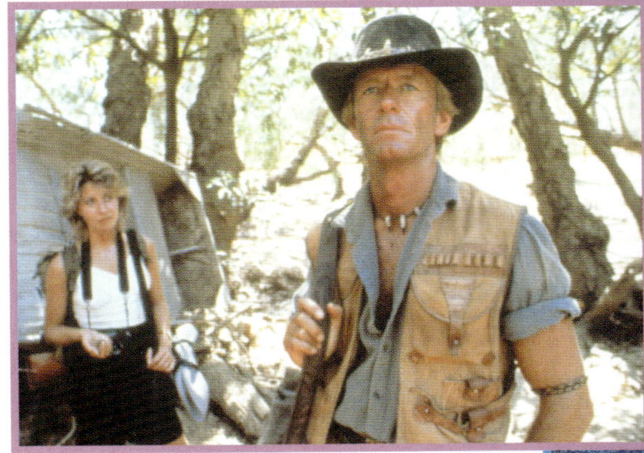

Linda Kozlowski and Paul Hogan in *Crocodile Dundee*.

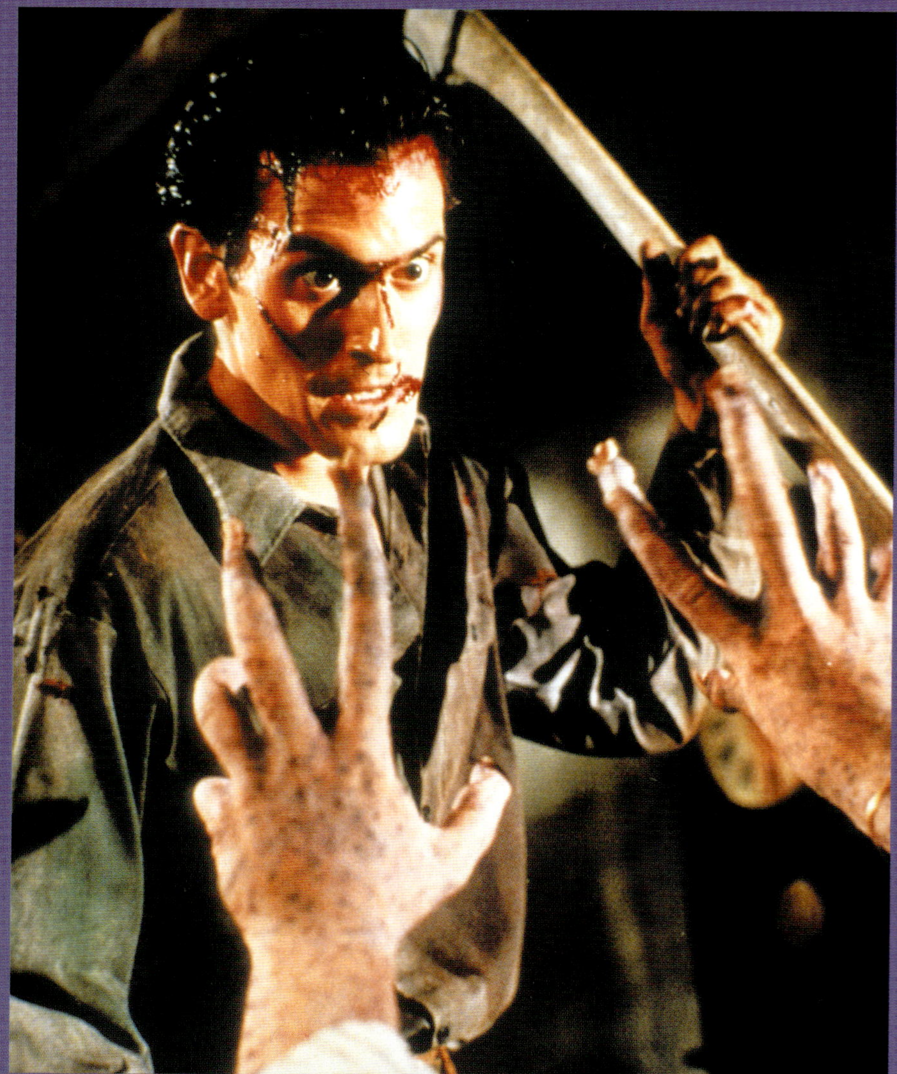

Evil Dead II

The HORROR SECTION

Horror cinema, with all its attendant subgenres—splatter, slasher, monster, supernatural—was big business in the 1980s. The appeal of these films was not in their stars or production values, but in the spine-tingling stories and salacious thrills that younger viewers hungered for. With the rise of new distribution platforms like home video and cable, horror flicks were made quickly and cheaply without having to worry about drawing an audience to the theater, which allowed smaller independent studios to get in on the action.

"The ideal low-budget movie is set in the present, with few sets, lots of interiors, only a couple speaking actors (none of them known), no major optical effects, no horses to feed," said indie filmmaker and sometime horror screenwriter John Sayles. "It's no wonder so many beginning moviemakers set a bunch of not-yet-in-the-Guild teenagers loose in an old house and have some guy in a hockey mask go around and skewer them."

Horror films had experienced mainstream success in the 1970s, with major releases like *The Exorcist* (1973), *Jaws* (1975), and *The Omen* (1976) garnering big box-office success and critical acclaim, while Italian *giallo* directors like Dario Argento and Mario Bava lent an art-house credibility to the genre. At the same time, Roger Corman and other exploitation filmmakers continued to produce edgy, daring films on the margins of the industry. The hits kept coming: *The Texas Chainsaw Massacre* (1975), *Carrie* (1976), *Dawn of the Dead* (1978), *Halloween* (1978).

The next ten years would deliver more iconic moments of gore, fright, and suspense, with countless sequels and imitators continuing into the '90s and beyond. The list below is a curated sampling of the wide variety of horror movies made throughout the decade, arranged by their level of intensity. Though it's not a substitute for parental guidelines or MPAA ratings, the chapter starts with family-friendly fare and ends with content strictly for the more mature.

Something Wicked This Way Comes (1983)

Fantasy-mystery writer Ray Bradbury adapted his own novel for this Disney-produced film about two young friends—both born on Halloween—who discover the secrets behind a mysterious traveling carnival headed by Mr. Dark (Jonathan Pryce). The film's rich autumnal colors (shot in Vermont) and blustery fall weather set a spooky tone for a clever story about deepest desires and lost youth.

The Monster Squad (1987)

A group of young Universal Monsters fans find themselves battling Dracula, the Wolf-Man, the Mummy, and more during a once-in-a-century fight between the forces of good and evil. The movie has been described as a mashup of *Our Gang* and *Abbott and Costello Meet Frankenstein* (1948) and has become an audience favorite since its disappointing run in theaters.

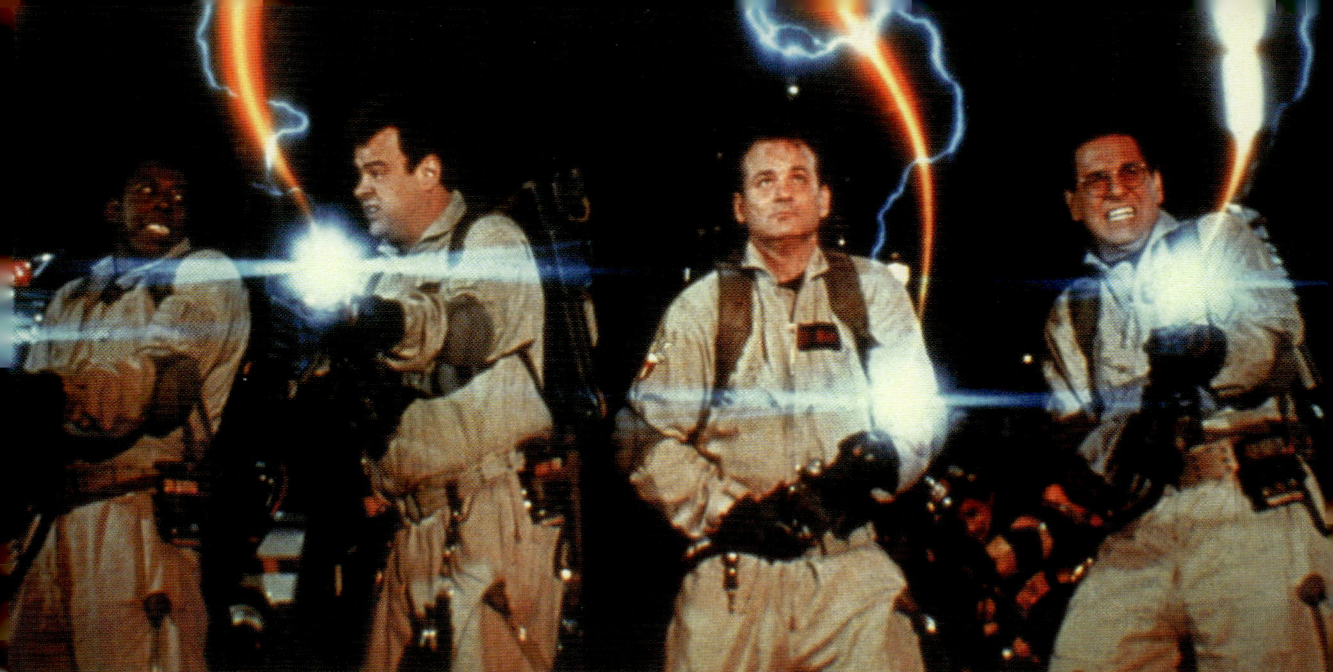

Ernie Hudson, Dan Aykroyd, Bill Murray, and Harold Ramis battle an ancient god in *Ghostbusters*.

Little Shop of Horrors (1986)

Songwriters Howard Ashman and Alan Menken adapted Roger Corman's B-movie horror comedy about a man-eating alien plant into a 1982 rock musical, which was then made into this big-budget film directed by Muppets veteran Frank Oz. Starring opposite the "mean green mother from outer space" are Rick Moranis as a naive florist, Ellen Greene as his coworker and love interest, and a roster of comic actors like Steve Martin, Bill Murray, and John Candy.

Ghostbusters (1984)

The story of a group of Columbia University researchers who decide to market their services as exterminators of the supernatural came from Dan Aykroyd, who—inspired by a family history of spiritualism—turned out this witty action-horror script with costar Harold Ramis. The film is full of creative, oddball choices, from the ghostly green "Slimer," to a refrigerator that becomes a portal to hell, to the iconic Stay Puft Marshmallow Man.

They Live (1988)

An itinerant construction worker (Roddy Piper) puts on an unusual pair of sunglasses and discovers that American society is run by a race of aliens that control humans through subliminal messages in advertising ("Submit," "Obey," "Stay Asleep"). Writer-director John Carpenter was inspired by '50s-era sci-fi parables like *Invasion of the Body Snatchers* (1956) when he crafted this cautionary tale about consumerism and Reaganomics. "They're still here," Carpenter warned, decades later. "They're making more money than ever and they're still among us."

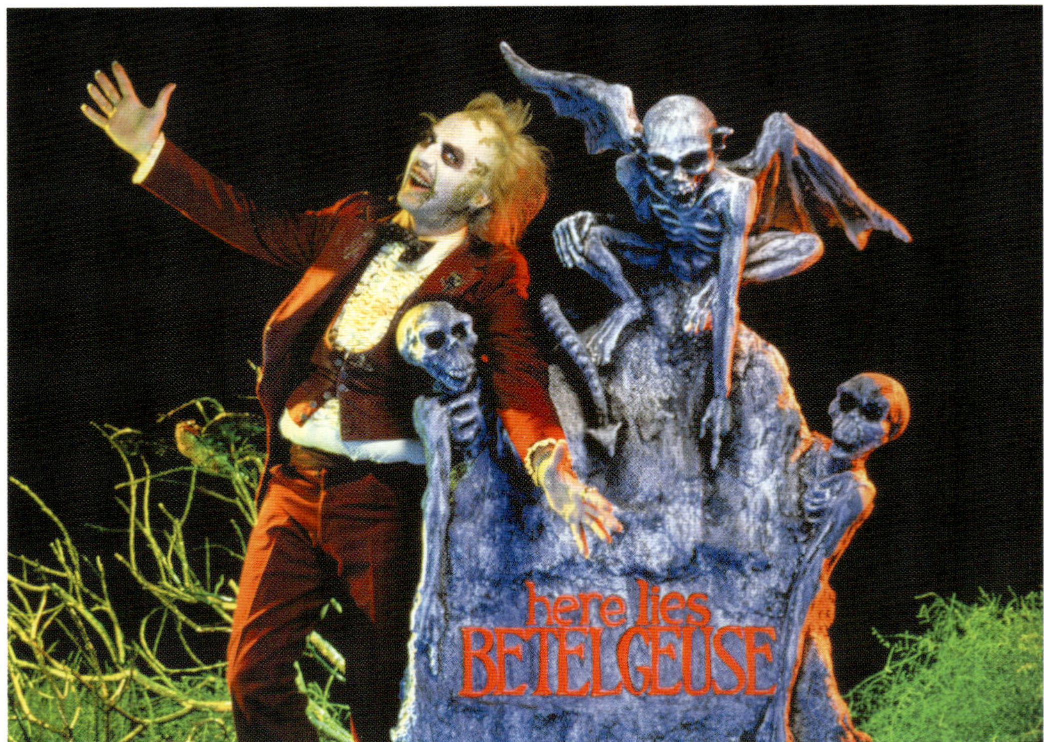

It's showtime for Michael Keaton in *Beetlejuice*.

Beetlejuice (1988)

Director Tim Burton's visual imagination ran wild in this tale of a recently deceased couple who hire a "bio-exorcist" (Michael Keaton) to rid their home of its new human inhabitants. Comedic, offbeat, and morbid, the film's presentation of the afterlife as an inefficient bureaucracy is almost as disturbing as the scene in which the central couple rapidly decompose on the dining room table.

An American Werewolf in London (1981)

Practical effects artist Rick Baker won the first Academy Award for Makeup for this creature feature about a pair of American backpackers who are attacked by a werewolf on the moors of northern England. The movie's lighter tone, courtesy of *Animal House* (1978) director John Landis, sets it apart from other werewolf films of the era like *The Howling* (1981) or *Silver Bullet* (1985)—though it's definitely more serious than *Teen Wolf* (1985).

Fright Night (1985)

Screenwriter Tom Holland (*Psycho II* [1983]) made his directorial debut with this story of young horror-movie fan Charley Brewster (William Ragsdale) who discovers that his charming next-door neighbor is a vampire. After being rebuffed by the police and failing to convince the adults around him, Charley enlists the help of a late-night horror TV host (Roddy McDowall) to clean up the neighborhood before it's too late.

The Lost Boys (1987)

Teenagers Michael (Jason Patric) and Sam (Corey Haim) move to a town on the California coast that is overrun with vampires posing as a young motorcycle gang. As Michael becomes part of their ranks, Sam joins up with two vampire hunters to take them down. The film's scares aren't as memorable as its cast of young '80s stars (including Kiefer Sutherland, Jami Gertz, and Corey Feldman), its hit soundtrack, or its shirtless cameo by saxophonist Tim Cappello.

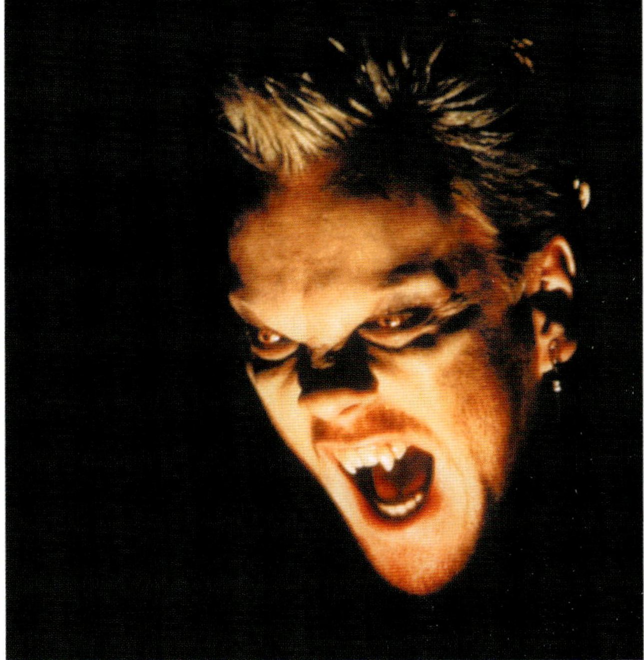

Kiefer Sutherland in *The Lost Boys*.

The Changeling (1980)

George C. Scott stars as a composer who moves into a historic Seattle mansion after the tragic deaths of his wife and daughter. There he learns of the secret murder of a young boy in the house decades earlier and the involvement of a wealthy US senator (Melvyn Douglas). The strength of this creepy Canadian-produced drama lies in the simmering grief of fathers and sons.

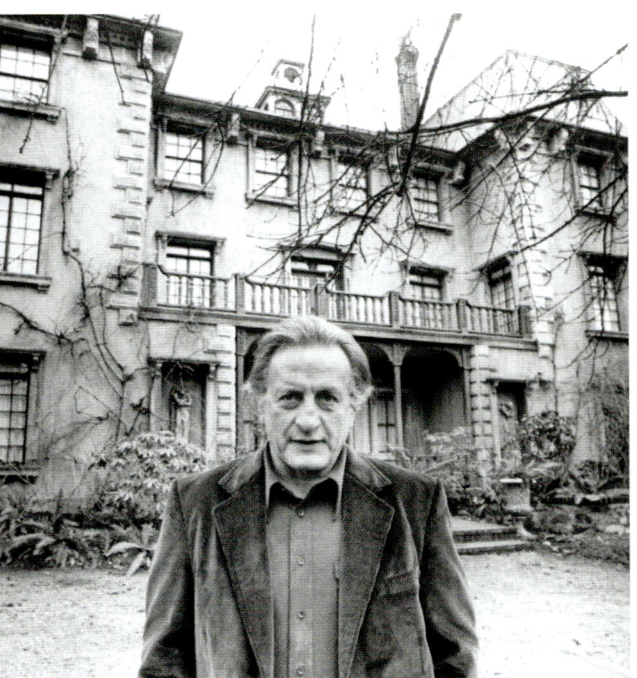

George C. Scott in *The Changeling*.

Alligator (1980)

This tongue-in-cheek monster movie is like *Jaws* on land, with an intriguing premise: a baby alligator is flushed into the Chicago sewage system where it survives for a decade off of the carcasses of chemically altered lab animals and grows to abnormally large proportions. The humongous reptile then unleashes terror on its unsuspecting victims—including, in a signature scene, the guests at a hoity-toity wedding reception.

Creature Features

Following the success of *The Muppet Movie* (1979), TV puppeteer Jim Henson began working more often in feature films, not just to extend the Muppet brand—he directed *The Great Muppet Caper* (1981) and produced *The Muppets Take Manhattan* (1984)—but to push the limits on creature features. With his friend and fellow puppeteer Frank Oz, who had performed the role of Yoda in *The Empire Strikes Back* (1980), he made the fantasy film *The Dark Crystal* (1982), which contained no human characters. He later directed David Bowie, Jennifer Connelly, and a cast of goblins and other magical beings in *Labyrinth* (1986).

In the wake of *Empire* and *E.T. the Extra-Terrestrial* (1982), other live-action films began to use practical effects to create nonhuman characters. Special-effects designer Chris Walas created the cute (and, later, terrifying) little monsters in *Gremlins* (1984), a commercial hit that led to several ridiculous knockoffs like *Critters* (1986), *Munchies* (1987), and *The Garbage Pail Kids Movie* (1987). Horror films of the '80s were rife with gruesome figures, from *An American Werewolf in London* (1981) to *The Fly* (1986), to the otherworldly life forms of *The Thing* (1982) and *Aliens* (1986).

The master of stop-motion creature effects, Ray Harryhausen, delivered his final work in the Greek mythology epic *Clash of the Titans* (1981), including the flying Pegasus, the slithering villain Medusa, the giant Kraken, and a mechanical owl.

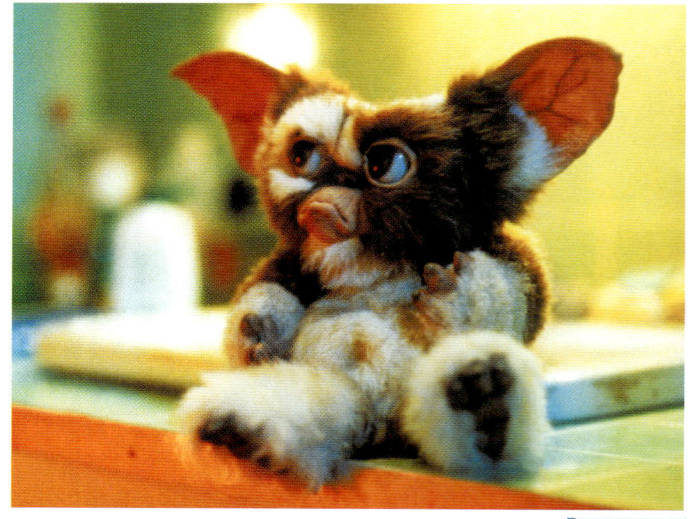

Gizmo stole hearts in *Gremlins*.

Gremlins (1984)

This Christmastime nightmare, released in June (the same day as *Ghostbusters*), is scary fun all year long. Steven Spielberg had appreciated director Joe Dante's work on *The Howling* and sent him the script for this not-so-subtle critique on consumer culture, a warped tale of a cute little fuzzball that multiplies when it gets wet. Whatever you do, don't feed it after midnight.

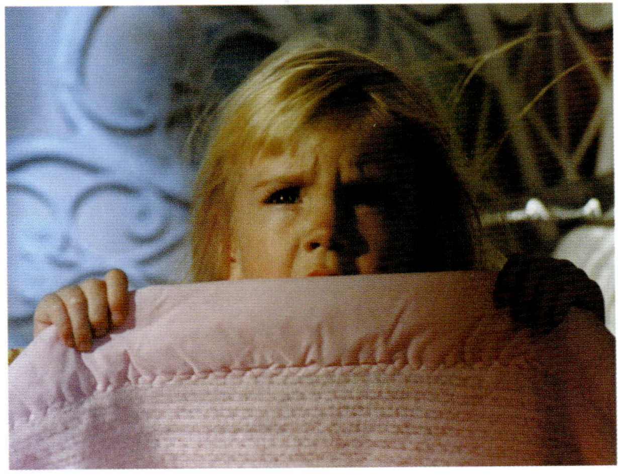

Heather O'Rourke takes cover in *Poltergeist*.

Killer Klowns from Outer Space (1988)

From practical-effects artists the Chiodo Brothers comes this loony tale of hostile extraterrestrial circus clowns—one of several films, like *Night of the Comet* (1984) and *Lifeforce* (1985), that rode a wave of enthusiasm around the 1986 appearance of Halley's Comet. The clowns are pretty creepy, but the intensity peaks with some bloody human faces trapped in cotton-candy cocoons and a man getting pelted (and melted) by cream pies.

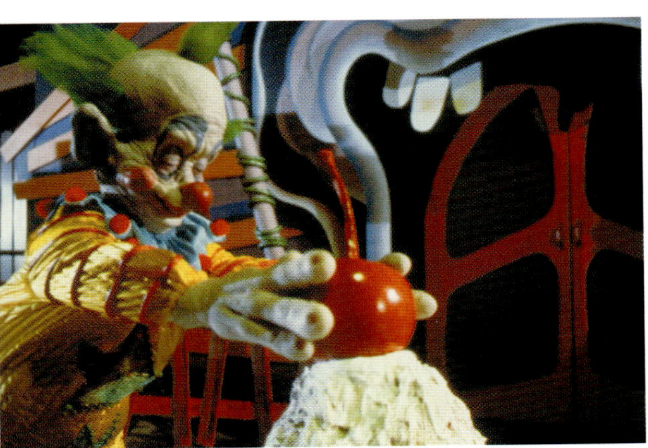

Shorty, one of the titular *Killer Klowns from Outer Space*.

Poltergeist (1982)

"They're here," intones five-year-old Carol Anne (Heather O'Rourke) after a ghost reaches out to her from a television set in director Tobe Hooper's haunted-house classic. With Steven Spielberg writing and producing, *Poltergeist* retains the family dynamic and expert story structure of his best films and adds an abandoned cemetery, a portal to "the other side," and one of cinema's most iconic mediums (Zelda Rubinstein).

The Shining (1980)

Director Stanley Kubrick took Stephen King's paranormal parable of alcoholism and made it the ultimate cinematic statement on cabin fever. Jack Nicholson is downright terrifying as a writer and winter caretaker of the secluded Overlook Hotel who devolves from loving father to axe-wielding psychopath. John Alcott's stalking Steadicam turns the hotel into a labyrinth of endless hallways and eerie lobbies, with dread lurking around every corner.

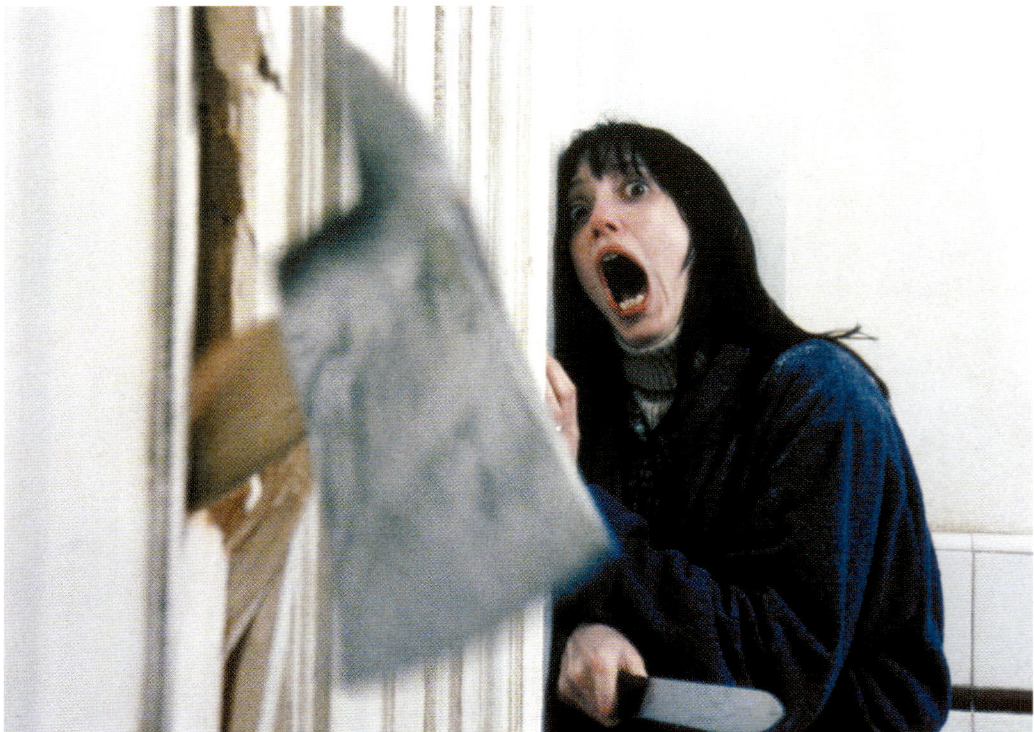

Shelley Duvall in *The Shining*.

The Fog (1980)

After making *Halloween*, John Carpenter wanted to make "an old-fashioned ghost story." The film opens fittingly with a spooky campfire tale about a local shipwreck a hundred years earlier, and soon the seaside town is overtaken by a mysterious fog that brings with it the vengeful spirits of the drowned crew. Populating the atmospheric film are Hal Holbrook, Adrien Barbeau, and mother-daughter scream queens Janet Leigh and Jamie Lee Curtis.

Creepshow (1982)

George A. Romero directed this spine-chilling anthology film inspired by 1950s EC Comics (publisher of *Tales from the Crypt*). The first screenplay from horror novelist Stephen King—who also stars in one segment—is made up of five unconnected stories, including "Something to Tide You Over," in which Ted Danson is buried up to his neck on a sandy beach, and "The Crate," about the terrifying contents of a box found in a university basement.

The Fly (1986)

"Be afraid. Be very afraid." Canadian body horror auteur David Cronenberg had one of his biggest successes with this update of the 1958 film about a scientist (Jeff Goldblum) whose experiments with teleportation lead to some nasty results. His inexorable transformation into a giant housefly was cast by some '80s

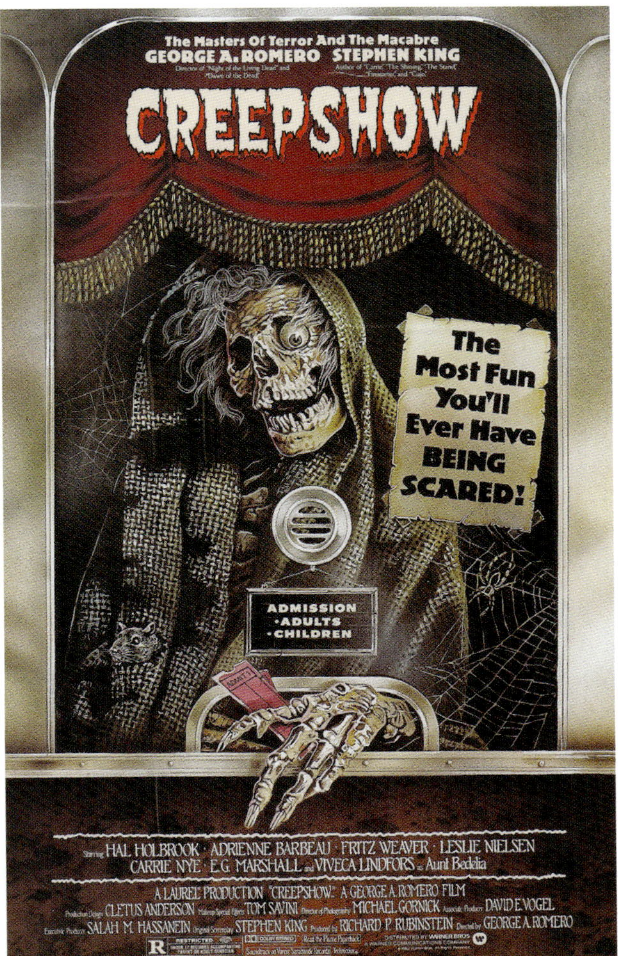

Stephen King wrote *Creepshow* and stars in the film's second segment.

reviewers as an AIDS allegory, but Cronenberg took a broader stance. "For me, the movie was just about the normal process of aging," he explained. "The inevitability of deterioration and death . . . anyone can relate to it."

The Return of the Living Dead (1985)

This punk-rock zombie comedy was the first in an alternate franchise stemming from *Night of the Living Dead* (1968) by that earlier film's cowriter John Russo (separate from director George A. Romero's *Dead* series). After a negligent foreman (James Karen) at a Kentucky medical warehouse accidentally exposes human cadavers to toxic gas—two things that should probably not be mixed—it leads to the important cinematic discovery that zombies are hungry for "Brains!"

Dressed to Kill (1980)

Never one to let a good Hitchcock film go unreferenced, Brian De Palma made this twisted and graphic salute to *Psycho* (1960) about a woman (Nancy Allen) who witnesses a murder, becomes a prime suspect, and sets out to find the killer herself. The director is known for violent images, but here—aside from a disturbing early scene in an elevator—he sticks to psychological trauma. "The genre is one of the few forms that hasn't been invaded by television," he said about horror. "It's the closest thing we have today to pure cinema."

Near Dark (1987)

Director Kathryn Bigelow's first solo movie was this modern vampire western about a group of undead roughnecks, including their reckless leader, Severen (Bill Paxton), and the beautiful Mae (Jenny Wright), who attack and then take in a young Oklahoman (Adrian Pasdar). Notably, the film turns typical gender roles on their heads—as when a female vampire bites a man and later feeds him blood from her wrist.

The 3-D Craze

The early 1980s saw a brief revival of a moviegoing fad that had last popped up with cheesy 1950s sci-fi films: 3-D technology. What had essentially started as a gimmick to get audiences out of their living rooms and back into theaters became a delivery system for otherwise mediocre offerings—the real attraction wasn't the stirring plots or memorable characters—that led to its demise. The '80s reboot began with producer Tony Anthony's low-budget spaghetti western *Comin' at Ya!* (1981), "a 3-D movie that wouldn't be worth the time of day in 2-D," according to the *New York Times*.

Three-D soon became the domain of horror cinema, with releases like *Parasite* (1982), a William Castle–esque creature feature whose ads promised, "You will be part of the terror." Slasher films like *Silent Madness* (1984) and *Friday the 13th Part III* (1982)—"a new dimension in terror"—sent sharp objects and body parts flying toward the audience, while *Amityville 3-D* (1983) put the format to better use in its title card than in the actual movie.

The best way to appreciate this moment in stereographic film history may be to regard the resulting movies as popcorn-munching camp. How else to explain the plot of *Jaws 3-D* (1983), in which the giant man-eating predator breaks into SeaWorld and has his toothsome way with the park staff? Try not to shriek in panic as the dead-eyed fish glides ever so slowly toward the camera and smashes into an underwater observation deck, signaled by a (very fake-looking) explosion of shattering glass.

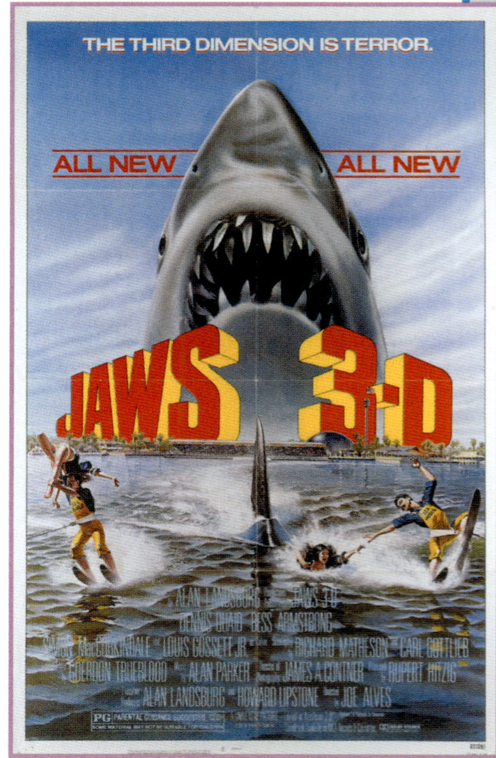

Until the rise of 3-D technology for home viewing, VHS and DVD copies of the film were reduced to 2-D and retitled *Jaws 3*.

Sleepaway Camp (1983)

"Camp" is right. This cult favorite follows a pair of cousins to a lakeside summer getaway beset by creepy staff and troublesome fellow campers, not to mention a serial killer. The film features several creatively lethal weapons—like a curling iron and a beehive—plus plenty of jean shorts and crop tops, a needlessly extended softball sequence, and one of horror cinema's most infamous final shots.

Evil Dead II (1987)

Since he didn't have the rights to his 1982 original, director Sam Raimi spent the opening moments of this sequel reworking the plot of the first film: a young couple (Bruce Campbell and Denise Bixler) visit a cabin in the woods where a strange recording causes the woman to become possessed by a demon. From there, the movie surges ahead as a schlocky horror comedy with a physical performance by Campbell that must be seen to be believed.

Basket Case (1982)

"What's in the basket?" is a popular question in Frank Henenlotter's low-budget splatter film, which in addition to its human bifurcations and bloody scalpel humor also contains a touching story of brotherly devotion. "I never felt that I made 'horror films,'" said Henenlotter. "I always felt that I made exploitation films. . . . They're a little ruder, a little raunchier, they deal with material people don't usually touch on." No kidding.

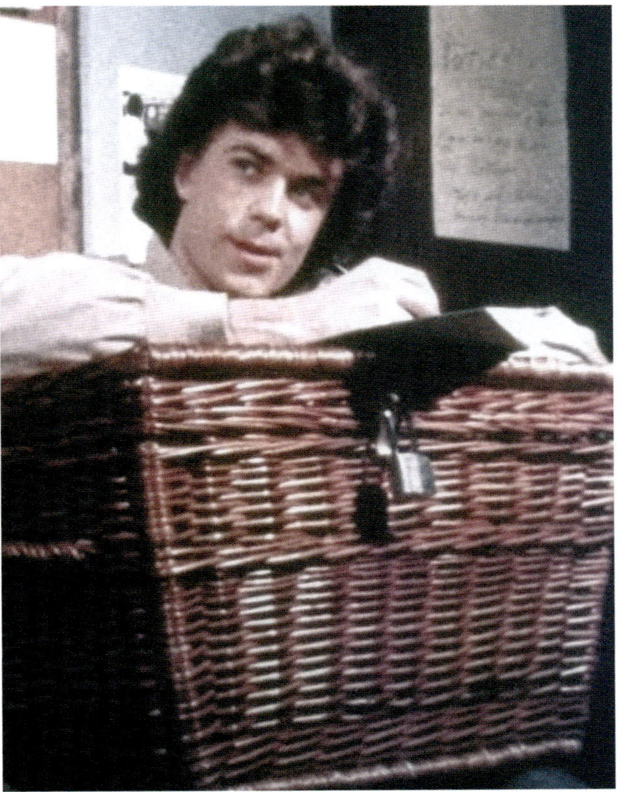

Kevin Van Hentenryck in *Basket Case*.

The Toxic Avenger (1984)

The most famous release from B-movie studio Troma Entertainment is this gory comedy about a bullied health-club janitor who falls into a vat of chemical waste and transforms into a disfigured crime-fighting hulk. The trashy superhero spoof took no prisoners with its gleefully offensive humor and shocking acts of violence, things that made it a midnight-movie hit.

Halloween III: Season of the Witch (1982)

This story about an evil toymaker who plots to kill America's kids with weaponized Halloween masks is an outlier in the iconic horror franchise;

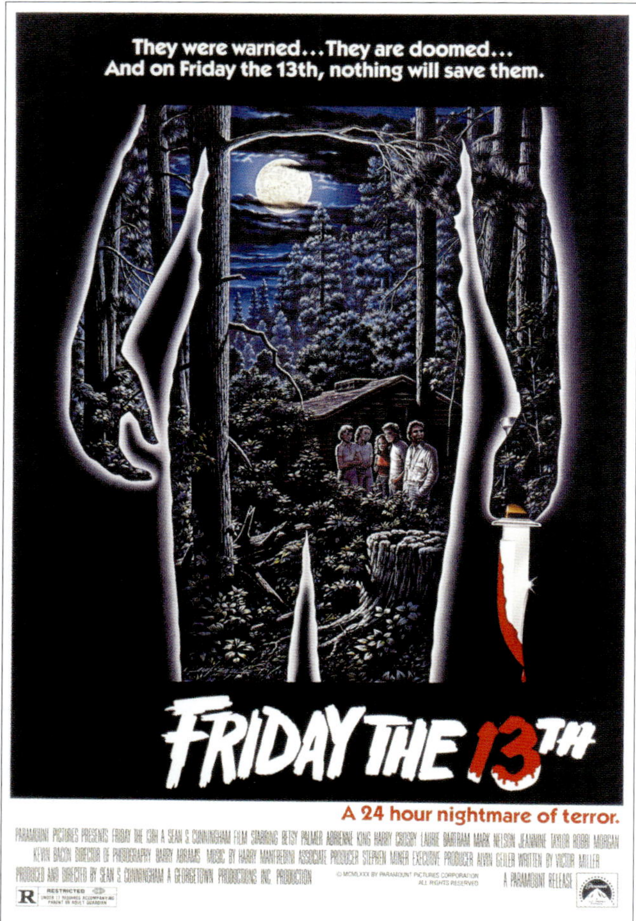

Friday the 13th kicked off a long-running horror franchise that saw the release of seven sequels in the '80s alone.

neighborhood killer Michael Myers is nowhere to be found. (If he's what you want, jump ahead to 1988's *Halloween 4*.) Creator John Carpenter originally planned the series as an anthology, with films connected only by the spooky holiday. When this now cult favorite underperformed at the box office, Myers returned for good.

Friday the 13th (1980)

One of the signature slasher films of the '80s, this murder mystery set at a long-dormant summer camp kicked off a series of movies about Jason Voorhees, a boy who (supposedly) drowned there twenty years earlier. Producer-director Sean S. Cunningham borrowed freely from earlier films like *Halloween* and *Black Christmas* (1974) and brought in George A. Romero's makeup effects artist Tom Savini to provide the gore. The movie hit at just the right time for audiences hungry for easy frights.

The Slumber Party Massacre (1982)

Screenwriter Rita Mae Brown and director Amy Holden Jones (a rare female creative team on a horror film) devised this feminist twist on the slasher craze for Roger Corman's New World Pictures. It's the simple story of a group of high school girls who are menaced by a power drill–wielding killer on the loose. Though Brown's parodic tone was mostly lost in favor of genre conventions (including some female nudity), it's still self-aware. Jones explained, "The central metaphor is about a virgin's fear of sex: 'Oh no! He's coming at me with that big thing! What's he gonna do to me?'"

The Thing (1982)

John Carpenter's chilling alien movie was largely dismissed during its original release but is now considered one of the great '80s films. An Antarctic research team discovers a long-buried extraterrestrial spacecraft and a strange life form that takes over the bodies of other living things—including their fellow humans. As the team is picked off one by one, the remaining

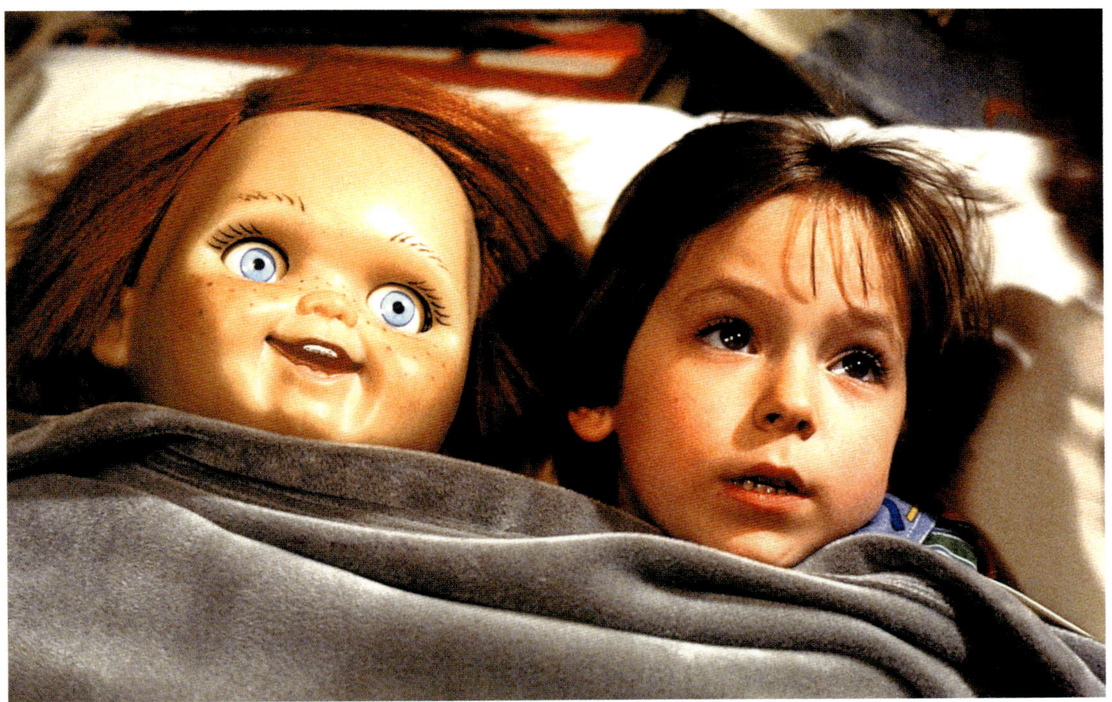

Chucky (voiced by Brad Dourif) and Alex Vincent in *Child's Play*.

members (including Kurt Russell's R. J. MacReady) fall prey to a deep paranoia. Rob Bottin's disturbing creature effects led Roger Ebert to call *The Thing* "the barfbag movie of July . . . the most nauseating thing I've ever seen on a movie screen."

Child's Play (1988)

The brainchild of writer Don Mancini, Chucky is a three-foot doll possessed by the spirit of a serial killer (Brad Dourif) who enacts vengeance on his enemies and attempts to use voodoo ritual to transfer his soul into a human body—in this case, that of the doll's six-year-old owner, Andy (Alex Vincent). In the tradition of *Gremlins* and inspired by the Cabbage Patch Kids craze of the mid-'80s, *Child's Play* is a wry commentary on consumerism and the marketing of products to children.

A Nightmare on Elm Street (1984)

Writer-director Wes Craven's greatest contribution to horror cinema is arguably Freddy Krueger (Robert England), the blade-handed, burn-scarred killer who attacks teenagers in their sleep. This first installment in a long series of films follows Nancy Thompson (Heather Langenkamp) and her friends who all dream of Freddy, a serial child murderer who was burned alive twenty years earlier and is seeking vengeance. With its iconic villain, alarming premise, and series of clever attacks (Johnny Depp's character is sucked into his own bed), *Nightmare* is one of the premier slasher films.

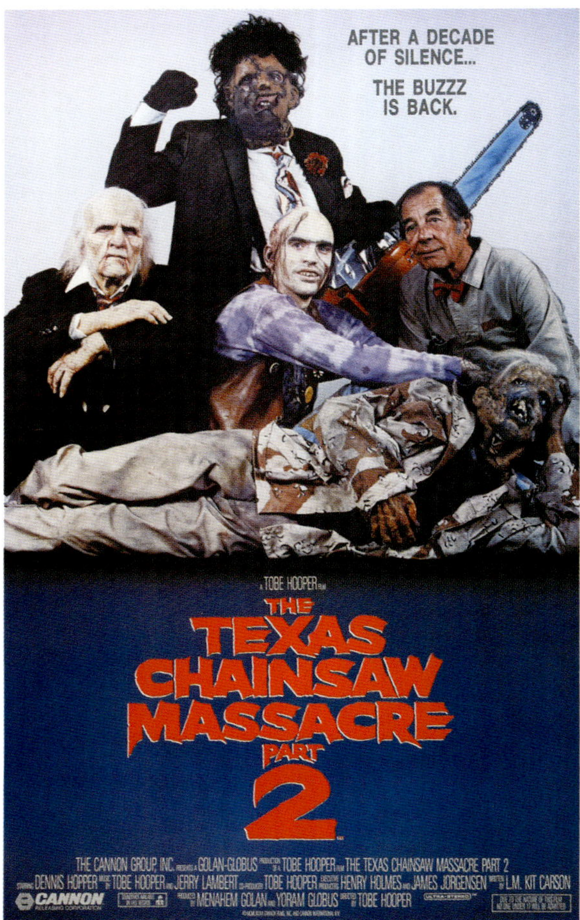

The poster for *The Texas Chainsaw Massacre 2* parodied *The Breakfast Club*.

The Texas Chainsaw Massacre 2 (1986)

Where director Tobe Hooper's 1974 original was a bloody nightmare, his long-awaited sequel was the bloodiest of comedies. The story of a radio deejay (Caroline Williams) who records a pair of grisly murders and a Texas lawman (Dennis Hopper) on a mission to find Leatherface takes gore to new and absurd levels (and got the film banned in several countries). Even the poster was having fun; it featured the cannibalistic Sawyer family posed in the style of *The Breakfast Club* (1985).

Videodrome (1983)

"None of my films are monster movies," said director David Cronenberg. "In fact, to a certain extent it's your own body that's the monster, your own existence." This unsettling story of a TV programmer (James Woods) who plumbs the depths of depraved content and winds up the unwitting victim of a mind-altering political conspiracy is a shrewd commentary on society's relationship to media. When asked about the ethics of airing torture and murder on television, the main character responds, "Better on TV than on the streets."

Re-Animator (1985)

This gruesome, Lovecraftian movie about a mad scientist (Jeffrey Combs) who develops a glowing serum capable of reviving dead bodies was so gory that the filmmakers at first didn't bother submitting it to the ratings board. Sure enough, a heavily diced-up version was later given an R for mainstream release—but *New Yorker* critic Pauline Kael was a fan of the original cut. "The bloodier it gets, the funnier it is," she wrote. "This is the same blood that flows through the Hammer horror movies."

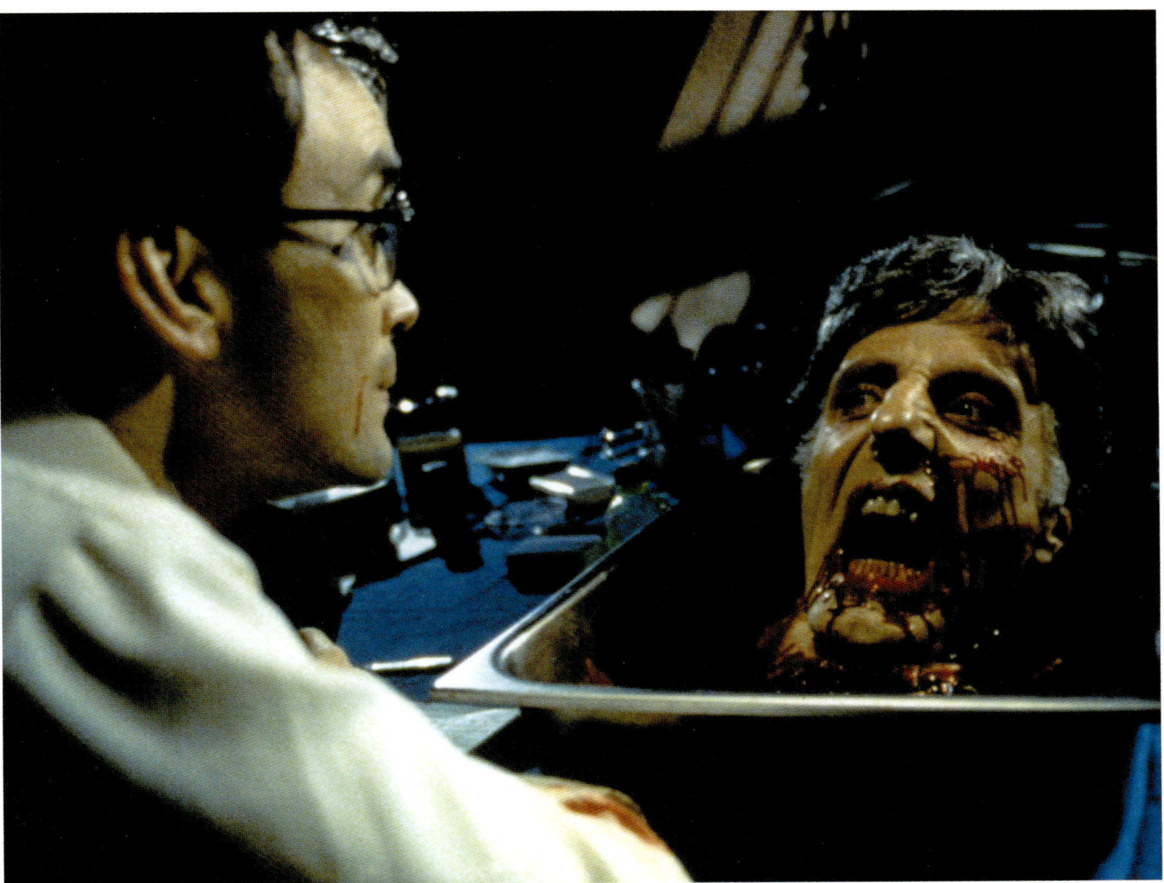

Jeffrey Combs and [the disembodied head of] David Gale in *Re-Animator*.

Demons (1985)

Several Italian *giallo* directors became famous for their bloody murder mysteries and psychological thrillers—see Dario Argento's *Tenebrae* (1982) and *Opera* (1995) for some other good '80s examples. This entertaining splatter film, produced by Argento and directed by Lamberto Bava, is set in a Berlin movie theater where the audience is treated to a free screening and a horrifying, prolonged attack by the forces of hell. A rushed sequel, *Demons 2* (1986), added fun touches like a killer tanning bed and a demon-possessed dog.

The Vanishing (1988)

What's more intense than endless scenes of graphic violence? This psychological drama from Dutch director George Sluizer offers up a hearty dose of existential dread with the story of a young woman (Johanna ter Steege) who disappears while on a road trip in France and the years-long search undertaken by her boyfriend (Gene Bervoets) for her abductor. While the film—which director Stanley Kubrick said was the most terrifying he had ever seen—is a slow burn for much of its running time, it leads to a deeply unsettling conclusion.

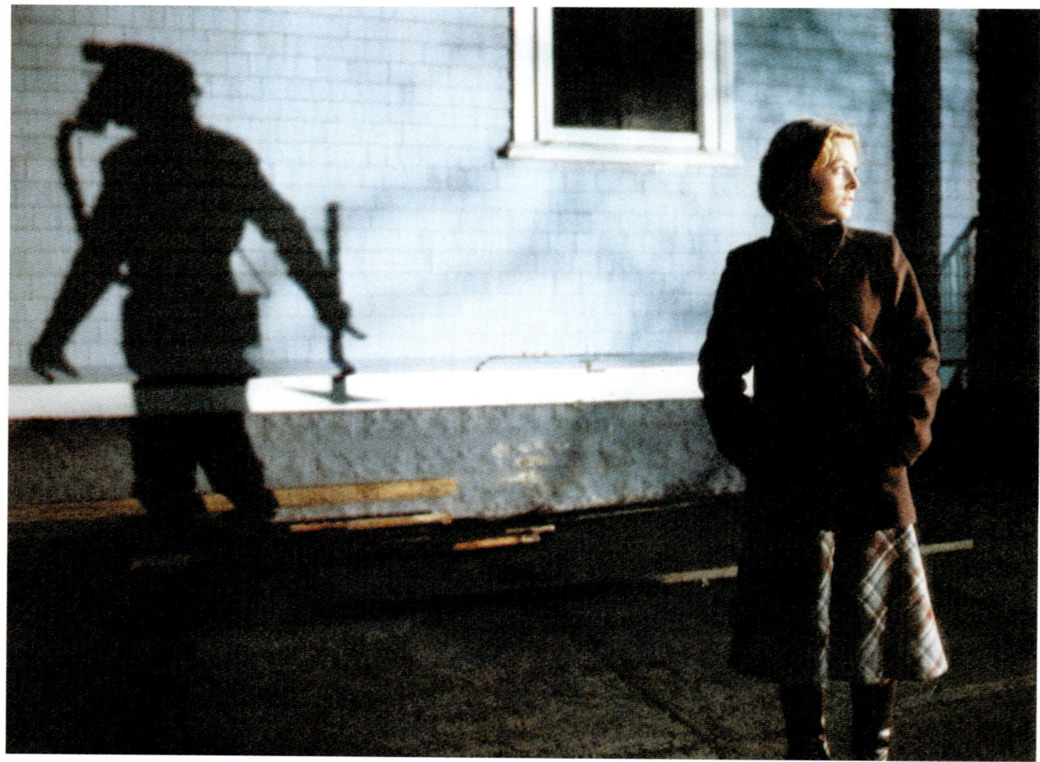

Lori Hallier in *My Bloody Valentine*.

My Bloody Valentine (1981)

This notorious "Canuxploitation" classic is set in the fictional mining community of Valentine Bluffs, which is preparing for its first Valentine's Day dance since a murder spree bloodied up the holiday proceedings twenty years earlier. Tempting fate and recklessly horny, the town's young people enter the mines that night, but few make it back out alive. Because of the incredible gore—multiple gurgling impalements, a head boiled in hot-dog water, a postmortem spin in a laundromat dryer (permanent press?)—the film itself was chopped up for its theatrical release but has since been restored for any strong-stomached viewers out there.

Pet Sematary (1989)

This Stephen King adaptation that takes the grieving process to outrageous extremes was directed by Mary Lambert at the end of the decade and seems like a fitting finale for this journey through '80s horror. Other King books had been made into successful movies—*Christine*, *Cujo*, and *The Dead Zone* all came out in 1983 alone—but none of them tackled the folly of human desire like this story of a family in rural Maine who discover a burial ground near their home that has the power to bring the dead back to life. What follows are some of the most tragic, morally dubious, and sinister scenes imaginable.

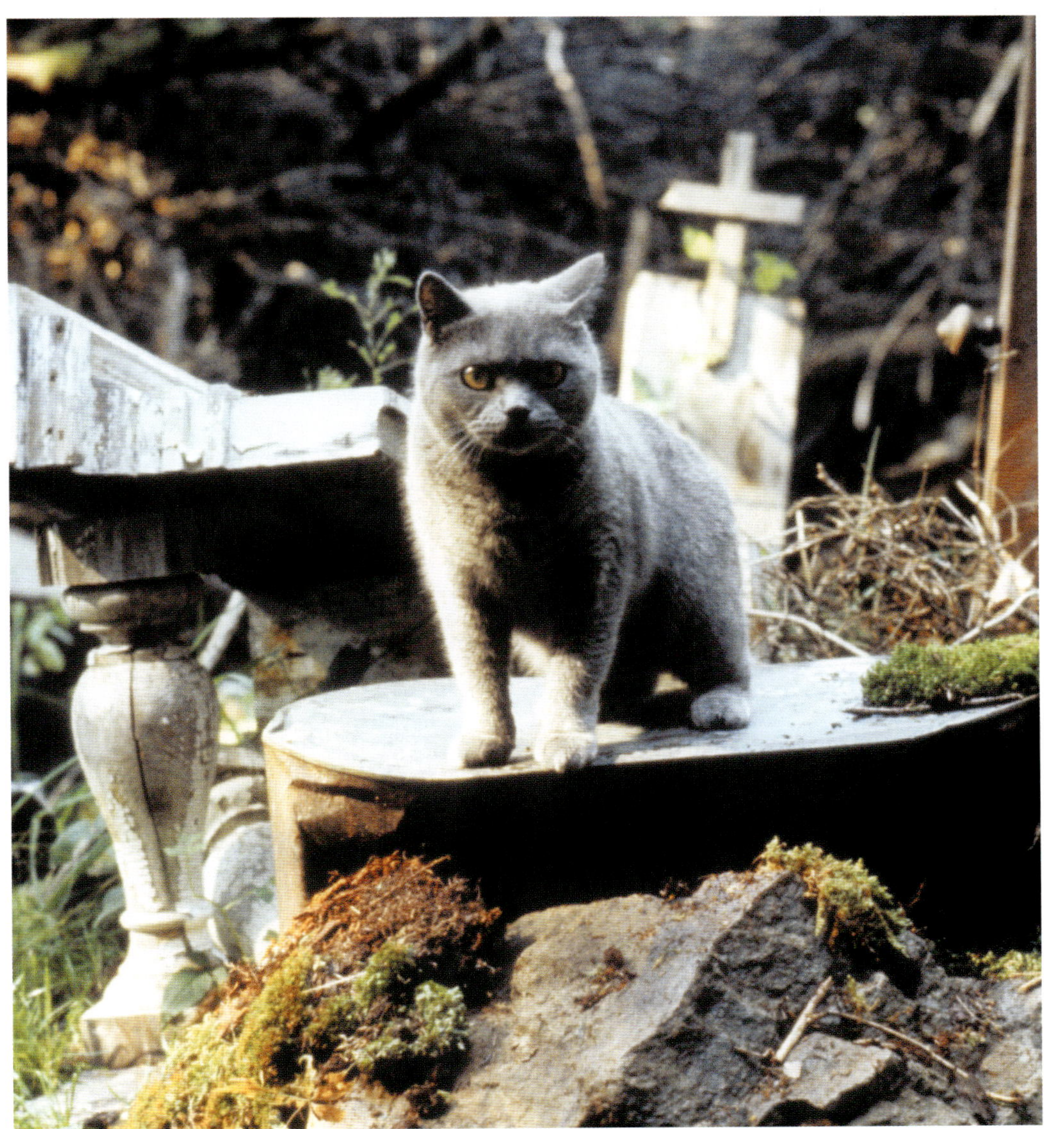

Church the cat in *Pet Sematary*.

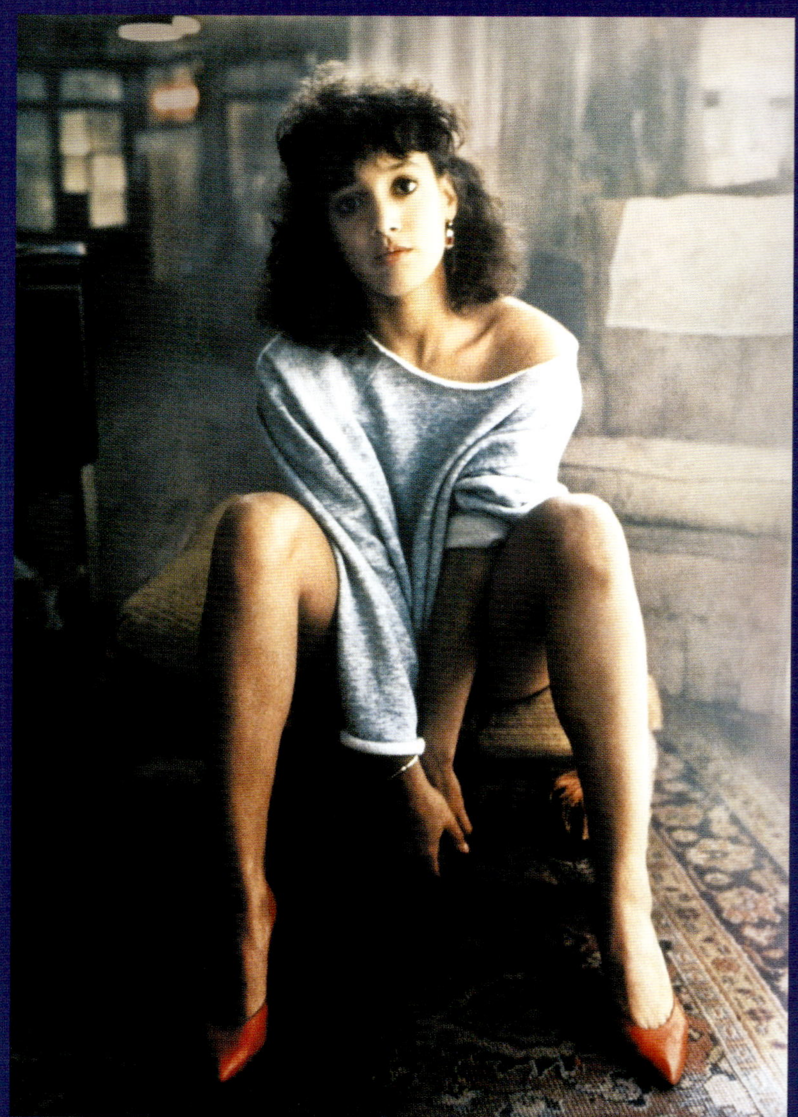

Flashdance

CHAPTER FIVE

MUSIC

THE MOVIES HAVE BEEN SINGING AS LONG AS THEY HAVE BEEN TALKING. When Al Jolson—the biggest recording artist of his day—opened his mouth in *The Jazz Singer* (1927), it was music that came out, in an astonishing moment for Jazz Age moviegoers. Frank Sinatra and Elvis Presley were not just postwar pop stars but A-list film actors, too. Soundtracks—especially for hit musicals—had often been among the biggest-selling albums of their day. By the time the 1980s rolled around, music as a driving force in Hollywood was nothing new.

If anything, the '80s represented a low point for traditional movie musicals. *Saturday Night Fever* (1977) and *Grease* (1978) had shown that there was still an appetite for music on-screen, but the era when *The Music Man* (1962) and *Camelot* (1967) became crossover hits was firmly in the past. In the place of big-budget Broadway adaptations were dance films, compilation soundtracks of New Wave artists, and music videos, thanks to the launch of cable channel MTV in 1981. The emerging world of highly stylized short-form videos, with quick cuts and postmodern storytelling sensibilities, spilled over into mainstream Hollywood productions, influencing cinematic style as much as the reverse.

Classical music biopics, teenage guitarists, and hip-hop anthems all had their day in the sun, and the traditional film composers were still busy as well, with John Williams scoring more than a dozen films like *E.T. the Extra-Terrestrial* (1982) and *Born on the Fourth of July* (1989). But this chapter starts with electronic sounds that, thanks to technologies like the Minimoog analog synthesizer and the Synclavier II sampling system, helped define a new aural landscape in '80s movies.

TANGERINE DREAM

Krautrock pioneer Edgar Froese had left traditional pop music in the rearview mirror. Inspired by the real-world sounds of "musique concrète" and surrealist art, his band adopted a name inspired by trippy Beatles lyrics ("tangerine trees and marmalade skies") and explored synthesized sounds and ambient "space music" on their first albums. Tangerine Dream was based in Berlin but had gotten a call from Hollywood film director William Friedkin to score his 1977 thriller *Sorcerer*.

"I first heard Tangerine Dream while in Munich for the opening of *The Exorcist*," recalled Friedkin, whose 1973 horror masterpiece had famously used the progressive rock song "Tubular Bells." The music for *Sorcerer* was completed before the film was shot, which is unusual, but Froese was undeterred. "It gave us the freedom to do what we wanted to do without being suppressed by a record company," he later said. "Plus, there was the chance to work in one of the most bizarre art forms one could think of."

It turns out Tangerine Dream's synthesizers and Mellotron harmonics worked perfectly in

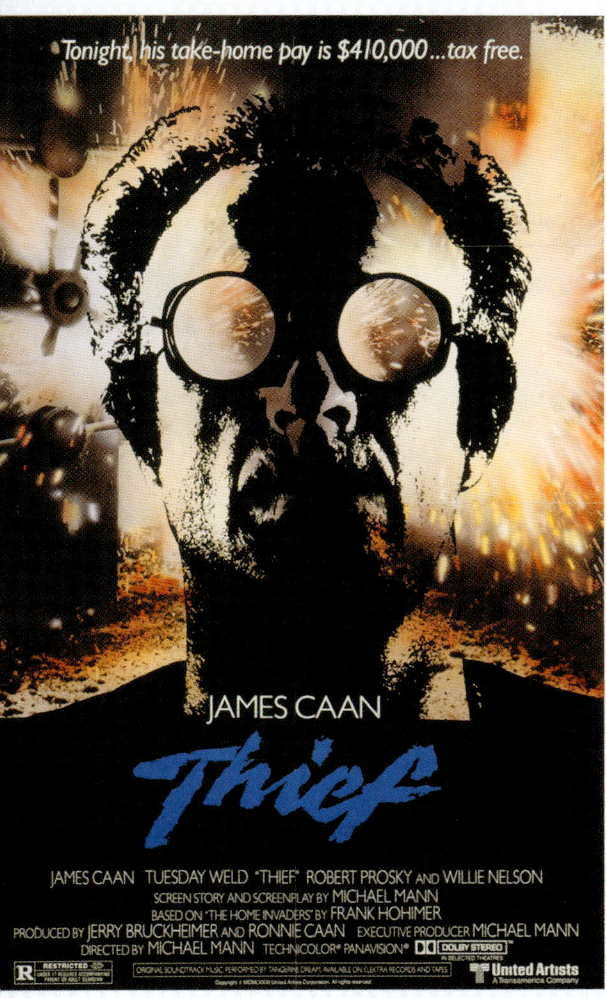

Tangerine Dream composed the music for *Thief* and Michael Mann's follow-up, *The Keep* (1983).

creating mood and elevating tension on-screen, and they would be used in dozens of movie soundtracks during the 1980s. The band's follow-up project was Michael Mann's debut feature, *Thief* (1981), starring James Caan as a burglar for hire. Their electronic score mirrors the cold lone-wolf character at the film's center. "I want the otherness of sound," Mann told keyboardist Johannes Schmoelling. "I want the music to make my protagonist, who's a professional thief, by means of violent pulsing noises, pulsating sequences . . . come across even harder than he already does." The music is especially important in the film's heist sequences, where the music creates and sustains tension, using metallic sounds to imitate drilling and the pulsing rhythms of a ticking clock. When a more melodic sequence appears, such as the vacation sequence shot on a California beach, the style becomes more evocative of a prog-rock band like Pink Floyd. But Tangerine Dream wasn't generally interested in making "popular" music, especially for its movie scores. "Our job was really not just to compose music, but also to develop a sound design," said Schmoelling.

Alongside iconic needle drops like Bob Seger's "Old Time Rock and Roll" and Phil Collins's "In the Air Tonight," the soundtrack for *Risky Business* (1983) was composed of new and existing tracks by Tangerine Dream. These include the opening sequence, "The Dream Is Always the Same," and the evocative single "Love on a Real Train," named after a suggestive line spoken by actress Rebecca de Mornay. The band went on to compose scores to another Tom Cruise film—the fantasy adventure *Legend* (1985)—as well as the Stephen King adaptation *Firestarter* (1984), the high school wrestling drama *Vision Quest* (1985), Kathryn Bigelow's vampire western *Near Dark* (1987), and the nuclear-war romance *Miracle Mile* (1988).

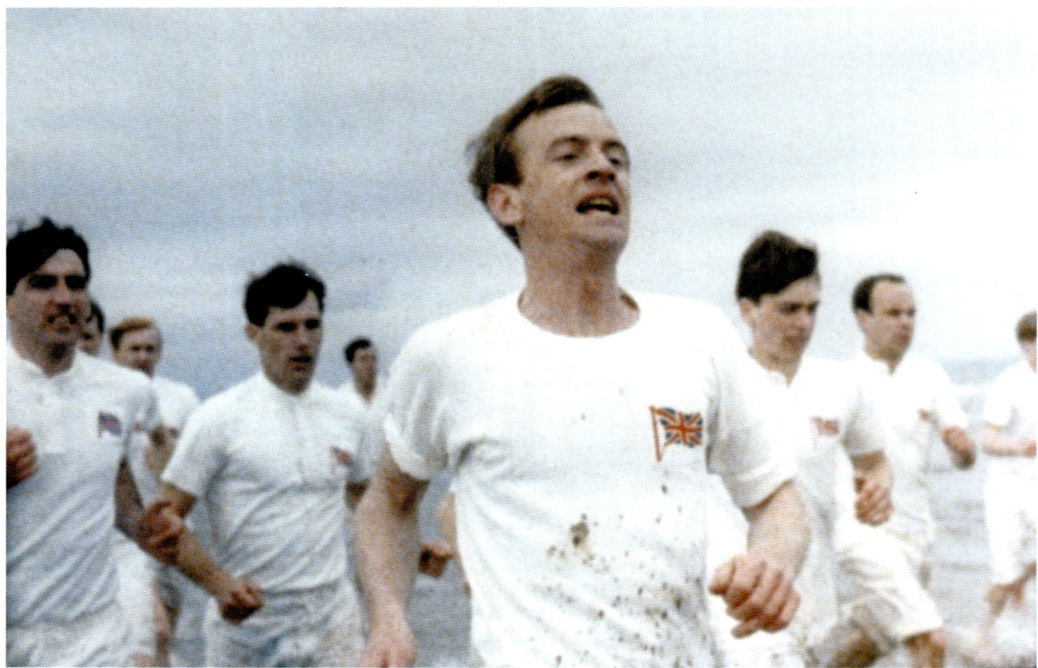

Ian Charleson (center) in *Chariots of Fire*.

VANGELIS

One enduring image of '80s cinema is that of a British running team training on a windy beach, and a key reason is the scene's scoring. *Chariots of Fire* (1981) is set in the 1920s in the lead-up to and during the Paris Olympic Games, but the music is thoroughly modern, composed and performed by Greek progressive rock musician Vangelis Papathanassiou. The heroic opening number and other sweeping musical themes were all recorded personally by Vangelis in his recording studio in central London, which he called Nemo Studios.

Director Hugh Hudson has called the electronic music "perhaps the single most important element in the film," and it was a key factor in the movie's popular success. The famous title track (alternately called "Titles" or "Chariots of Fire") hit number one on the US charts in May 1982 and was nominated for a Grammy for Record of the Year. When *Chariots of Fire* won the Best Picture Oscar, Vangelis took home a statuette himself for the film's music. He was now in great demand and followed up with one of the most iconic sci-fi scores of all time, for Ridley Scott's *Blade Runner* (1982).

Scott and Vangelis had collaborated a few years earlier on a commercial for the fragrance Chanel No. 5, called "Share the Fantasy." For *Blade Runner*, Vangelis combined the electronic hum of the film's neon cityscape with the seemingly eternal nighttime that cloaks Scott's crime thriller in film-noir vibes. The music subtly evokes the existential quandary of the characters played by Harrison Ford and Sean Young—and drops in a saxophone solo for the love theme.

"I never questioned it, but simply loved it," said Scott, describing his first encounter with the music. "Finally, the subtext of sound became a quiet overture to the explosion and wave of music and sound that washed over me, revealing Los Angeles 2019, and I was taken into the future."

GIORGIO MORODER

Italian music producer and film composer Giorgio Moroder had already won an Oscar for his innovative electronic score to Alan Parker's *Midnight Express* (1978) when he created the pop-infused soundtrack to *American Gigolo* (1980). The film famously opens with Blondie's "Call Me," written by Moroder with lead singer Debbie Harry. Similarly, his soundtrack for *Foxes* (1980) features tracks by Cher and Janis Ian, along with the hit single "On the Radio" by Donna Summer. Moroder and the "Queen of Disco" had worked together frequently, as well as with English songwriter Pete Bellotte, to produce many of her hit singles, including "I Feel Love" and "Hot Stuff."

Foxes director Adrian Lyne took as his next project the story of an aspiring ballet dancer who works by day in a Pittsburgh steel mill. In addition to actress Jennifer Beals's off-the-shoulder sweatshirt, *Flashdance* (1983) became famous for Moroder's pop soundtrack, with musical numbers incorporated into the finished film in a series of rhythmically cut sequences that smack of MTV. The lead single and Oscar winner "Flashdance . . . What a Feeling" was written by Moroder and singer Irene Cara, while the other number-one hit single, "Maniac," was produced by singer Michael Sembello and the film's music supervisor, Phil Ramone. "What *Flashdance* did was send the message that contemporary, hard driving music and dance, filmed in short, intense, very colorful bursts, was just the kind of visual jolt that young movie goers, really young movie goers, needed every fifteen minutes or so to hold their attention to the screen," lamented critic Gene Siskel.

Seemingly leaning into the criticism, Moroder joined prolific music video director Steve Barron for his debut feature, *Electric Dreams* (1984), the story of a sentient home computer who seduces its owner's neighbor, a cellist (Virginia Madsen), using its own electronic music capabilities. Barron had directed dozens of videos for artists like Sheena Easton, Toto, Tears for Fears, the Human League, and Michael Jackson. The *Electric Dreams* soundtrack was populated by bands like Culture Club, Heaven 17, and Electric Light Orchestra's Jeff Lynne, and capped with "Together in Electric Dreams" by Moroder and singer Philip Oakey.

Moroder's most audacious project, at least to classic film fans, was his revival of Fritz Lang's silent epic *Metropolis* (1927), which was set to a new electronic score, peppered with tunes by Freddie Mercury, Pat Benatar, Loverboy, and others. Seen today, the film feels more like a kitschy product of 1984 than of the silent era, and critics at the time were unimpressed, despite the significant restoration work that Moroder

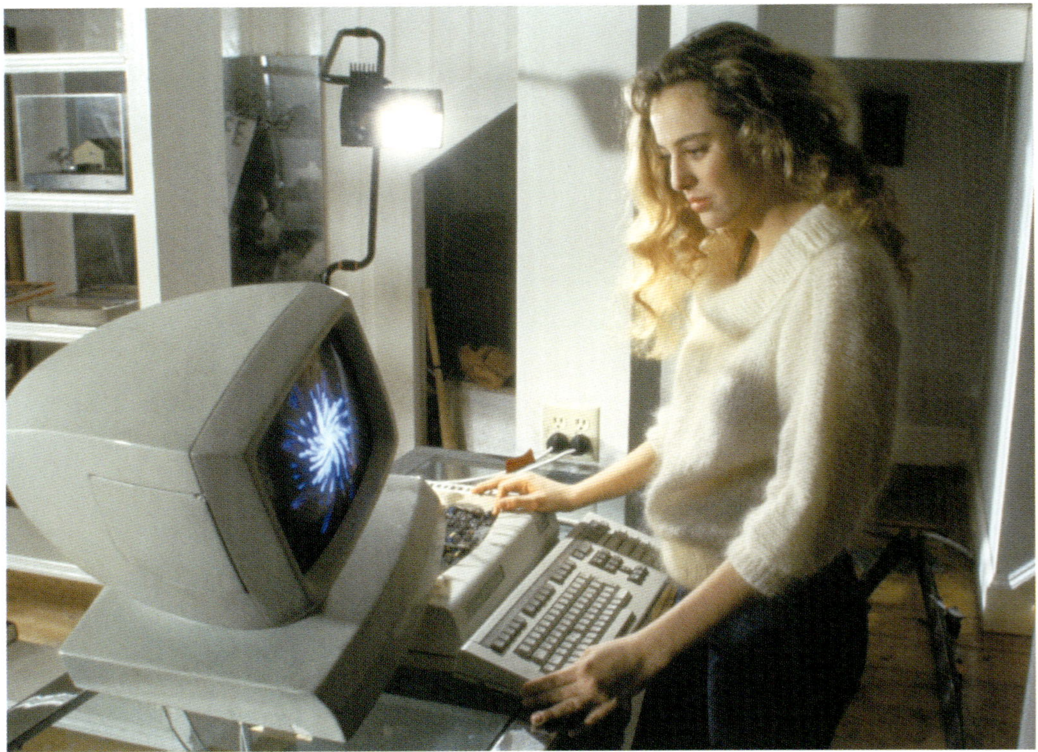

Edgar the computer with Virginia Madsen in *Electric Dreams*.

undertook to reconstruct Lang's masterpiece. "For a movie like *Metropolis*, what's better—to have at least ten different versions locked in museums and be seen by a limited amount of people?" asked Moroder. "Or is it better to have this masterpiece—first of all, closer to Lang's original version—shown to possibly a few hundred thousand people who don't know who Fritz Lang is and probably never saw a silent movie?"

One of Moroder's protégés was German keyboardist and producer Harold Faltermeyer, who assisted on his film scores in the early '80s. His big break as a solo composer came with the Eddie Murphy comedy *Beverly Hills Cop* (1984), which contains one of the premier earworms of the 1980s in the track "Axel F." The now legendary musical cue was composed by Faltermeyer on several synthesizers, but the idea of a stripped-down score in a big-budget comedy—especially one with a giant star like Murphy—made the studio nervous. Director Martin Brest believed in it, though, and the rest is history.

In another twist of fate, the melody of Faltermeyer's famous "Top Gun Anthem" almost became part of his score to the Chevy Chase comedy *Fletch* (1985) until rocker Billy Idol, who was recording nearby, heard the tune and suggested it be used for the Tom Cruise film. Idol's guitarist Steve Stevens wound up playing the soaring guitar solo, to achieve Faltermeyer's goal of portraying the film's pilots as "rock 'n' rollers in the sky." He brought Moroder on board to compose several of the film's songs, including the Kenny Loggins track "Danger Zone" and the Oscar-winning ballad "Take My Breath Away," performed by New Wave band Berlin. The soundtrack album to *Top Gun* (1986) would eventually go nine-times platinum.

Synthesized music would ripple throughout the decade, especially in scores for thrillers and horror films, which tended to benefit from unorthodox music and mechanized sounds. Director John Carpenter, who had personally composed the haunting piano score to *Halloween* (1978), partnered with sound designer Robert Howarth for his '80s films. One of their highlights is their electronic score for the adaptation of Steven King's *Christine* (1983), about a 1958 Plymouth Fury that becomes possessive of its owner. Stanley Kubrick's composer Wendy Carlos famously starts *The Shining* (1980) with a synthesized version of the ominous "Dies Irae" by Hector Berlioz. For David Cronenberg's *Videodrome* (1983), Howard Shore mimicked the film's wild mixing of organic material and technology by using a synthesized orchestral score layered with a live string ensemble. Brad Fiedel's theme for *The Terminator* (1984) suggests cybernetic war drums and a solemn (electronic) horn solo.

MUSIC TELEVISION

The 1980s were, at least for a certain age group, the MTV decade. Music videos transformed the public's way of consuming pop culture and altered the aesthetics of movies in the process; see *Flashdance* for Exhibit A. The network

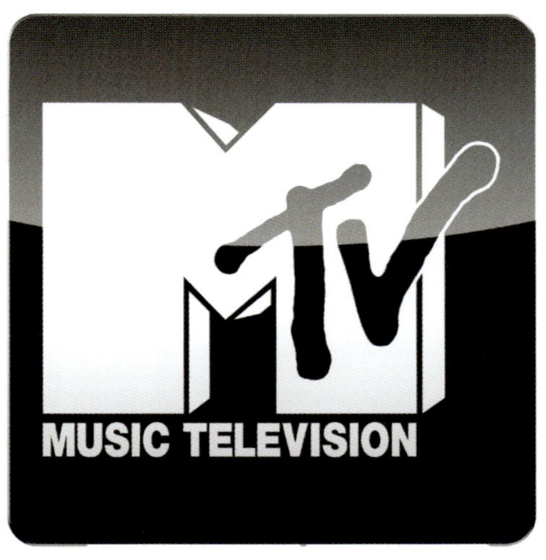

launched on August 1, 1981, with the Buggles' "Video Killed the Radio Star," and America would never be the same. Not only did it provide a platform for a range of bands that otherwise would have flown under the radar, but it also exposed a wide audience to new modes of visual storytelling—often abstract or surreal—and helped break down social barriers by airing, however slowly, a diversity of genres and artists.

MTV ultimately became a lifestyle brand as much as a TV channel. Its personalities articulated the latest slang, its videos dictated the latest fashions, and it excelled at elevating artists with a distinct visual style like Prince, Cyndi Lauper, and Madonna. For once, the *look* of a band and its music became major currency, and behind the scenes came a new crop of young filmmakers to support this emerging industry.

Australian director Russell Mulcahy had made several music videos in England when he directed "Video Killed the Radio Star," which had been originally broadcast on BBC's *Top of the Pops* in 1979. "When people were first asking me to do videos, there was never really a need

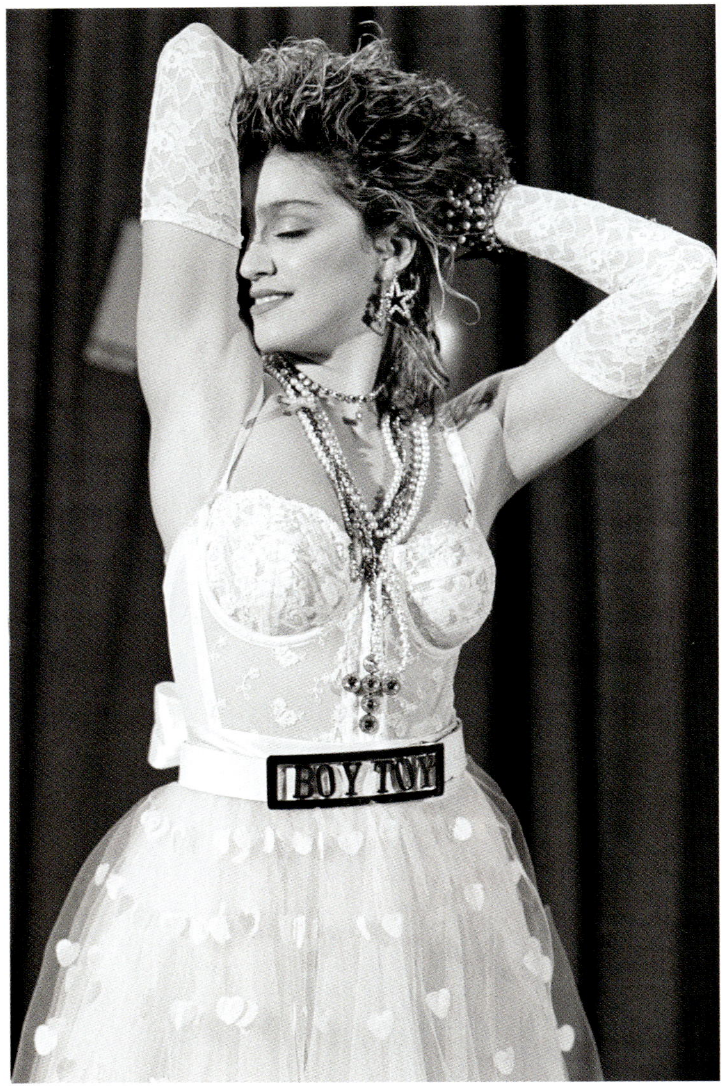

Madonna gave a star-making performance of "Like a Virgin" at the MTV Video Music Awards in September 1984.

or a request for a concept," said Mulcahy. "It was a time of experimentation, both in storytelling and video making. I never wanted to be literal in the videos. I wanted them to be little mini-dramas of themselves." He shot Duran Duran's breakout hit "Hungry Like the Wolf" (1982) in Sri Lanka and made videos for Elton John, Bonnie Tyler, Billy Joel, and Fleetwood Mac before directing the Sean Connery fantasy adventure film *Highlander* (1986).

Electric Dreams director Steve Barron was influential in setting the standard for music videos in the early days of MTV, having directed the Human League's "Don't You Want Me" (1981), Toto's "Rosanna" (1982), Bryan Adams's "Summer of '69" (1984), Michael Jackson's "Billie Jean" (1983), and A-ha's "Take on Me" (1985). His 1985 video for Dire Straits' "Money for Nothing" directly references MTV viewership and uses early computer animation to tell its story—an approach used largely because of frontman Mark Knopfler's resistance to music videos. "Because it was about MTV, it had to be a conceptual video," explained Barron. "And the naivety of the animation was what was cute about it. It was crude and very naïve but at the time it was very different."

Dozens more made careers in the new art form. David Mallet made several iconic videos for David Bowie, including "Ashes to Ashes" (1980) and "Let's Dance" (1983), before shooting Freddie Mercury in drag for Queen's "I Want to Break Free" (1984). Wayne Isham specialized in rock videos like Def Leppard's "Pour Some Sugar on Me" (1988), Mötley Crüe's "Home Sweet Home" (1985), and Bon Jovi's "Livin' on a Prayer" (1986). Dominic Sena made dance-heavy videos for Janet Jackson's "The Pleasure Principle" (1987) and "Rhythm Nation" (1989), while Mary Lambert directed Jackson's "Nasty" (1986) along with several for Madonna, including "Material Girl" (1985) and "Like a Prayer" (1989), which was condemned by the Vatican because of its Catholic iconography.

Some directors colored well outside the lines, like French choreographer and mime Philippe Decouflé, who made surreal videos for New Order's "True Faith" (1987) and Fine Young Cannibals' "She Drives Me Crazy" (1989). Stephen R. Johnson, who directed the first season of *Pee-wee's Playhouse* (1986), used stop-motion techniques for the Talking Heads' "Road to Nowhere" (1985) and the landmark Peter Gabriel video "Sledgehammer" (1986), which was made with Aardman Animation studio and the Brothers Quay.

HOLLYWOOD GOES MTV

In a sign of how aligned the film and music industries were, a number of prominent filmmakers also tried their hand at directing music videos. The first and most popular example is Jon Landis's thirteen-minute video for Michael Jackson's "Thriller" (1983), which is really a short film in the vein of *An American Werewolf in London* (1981). It contains several homages to horror cinema (like 1957's *I Was a Teenage Werewolf*) while rearranging the album track to better fit the video's narrative. It also showcases elaborate makeup by Oscar winner Rick Baker. The red-jacketed pop star transforms first into a werecat and then a zombie, terrifying his girlfriend, and performs one of the great dances of the era. When it premiered on MTV in December 1983, the video was accompanied by a forty-five-minute behind-the-scenes documentary, *The Making of "Thriller."*

Thriller became a sensation and led other directors to join forces with Jackson, including

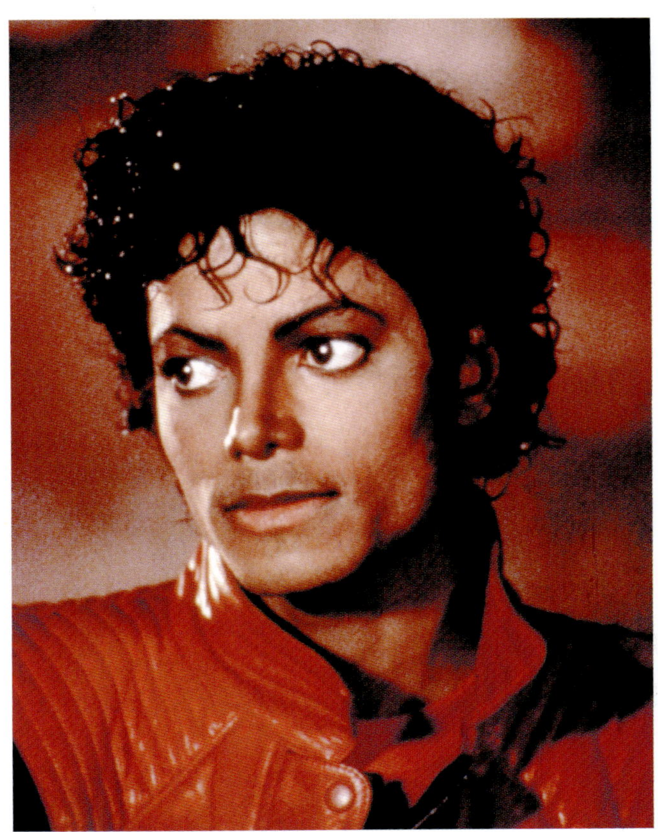

Michael Jackson wore an iconic red jacket in the video for "Thriller."

Francis Ford Coppola and George Lucas, who produced the Disneyland 3-D attraction *Captain EO* (1986). Martin Scorsese's video for "Bad" (1987) aired on CBS the day of the *Bad* album's release. At eighteen minutes, it's even longer than *Thriller* and depicts a talented Black student confronted by an urban gang that attempts to lure him into their life of crime. Inspired by *West Side Story* (1961)—in particular the dance number "Cool"—it was shot on location in a Brooklyn subway station and features another trademark dance from Jackson. "I was in awe of his absolute mastery of movement on the one hand and of the music on the other," said Scorsese.

Brian De Palma filmed the opening night of Bruce Springsteen's Born in the U.S.A. Tour for the video to "Dancing in the Dark" (1984). (That year's film *Body Double* notably contained a sequence in which the band Frankie Goes to Hollywood performs "Relax," which later became a standalone music video.) Three other Bruce Springsteen tunes—"Born in the U.S.A." (1984), "I'm on Fire" (1985), and "Glory Days" (1985)—were filmed by indie director John Sayles. William Friedkin made videos for Laura Branigan's "Self Control" (1984) and Barbra Streisand's "Somewhere" (1985). Veteran director Sam Peckinpah's final works included the video for Sparks's "Funny Face" (1981) and two for Julian Lennon: "Too Late for Goodbyes" and "Valotte" (both 1984). The list goes on: Ken Russell, Tobe Hooper, Gillian Armstrong, Ridley Scott, Kathryn Bigelow, Tony Scott . . .

Music videos occasionally ran long. Roger Waters of Pink Floyd fleshed out the band's 1979 concept album *The Wall* in a screenplay about a musician named Pink who daydreams of war, fascism, and social rebellion, which Alan Parker then directed as a dystopian nightmare, including scenes of surreal animation. Critic Janet Maslin described the resulting rock opera, *Pink Floyd: The Wall* (1982), as "a shameless all-out assault on the senses, rising to crescendos of grandiose fantasy."

ROCKUMENTARIES

A band's visual exposure to its fans wasn't limited to television. Concert films, often incorporating more intimate backstage footage, played on the big screen throughout the decade, and some became classics of the genre. For the feature-length concert film *Stop Making Sense* (1984), director Jonathan Demme shot the Talking Heads' December 1983 shows in Los Angeles using six cameras each night. He captured not just the band's performance and frontman David Byrne's oversize gray suit, but also the stagehands who facilitated the production. "I remember it took a while for the crew and grips and everybody to get used to being onstage and being visible," Byrne recalled. "It seemed like it had kind of a progression to it, a story."

Unlike Demme's film, which revealed the audience only during the final song, *Prince: Sign o' the Times* (1987) showed its attendees throughout. It also showed "the towering percussion section, the synchronized backup singers, the

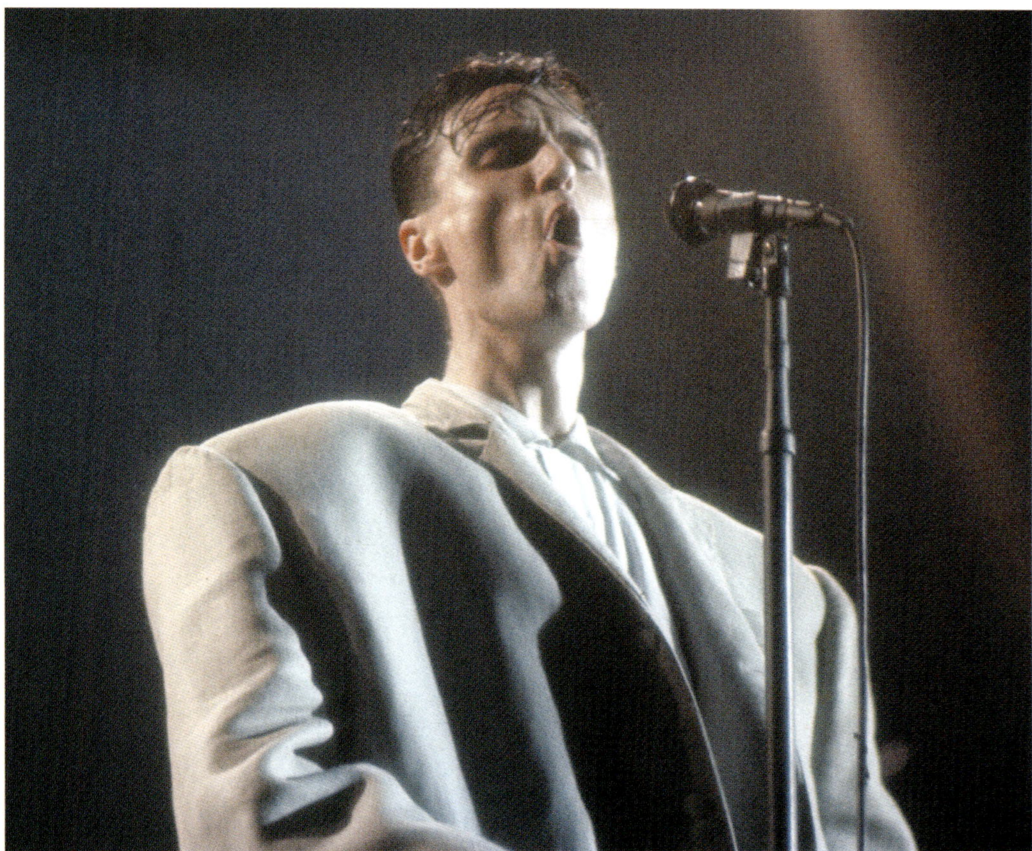

David Byrne in *Stop Making Sense*.

sweating superstar in sexual pantomime," wrote critic Roger Ebert, "and the standard shot of the star leaning forward to tantalize his fans as the first row of the audience surges forward in orgiastic bliss."

U2: Rattle and Hum (1988) was released two weeks after its associated album and documents the Irish band's massively successful 1987 Joshua Tree Tour, using a mix of black-and-white and color footage. For *Depeche Mode: 101* (1989), famed documentarians D. A. Pennebaker and Chris Hegedus followed the English synthpop band to the Rose Bowl, while simultaneously filming a bus of eight young fans who won the chance to meet them at the tour's 101st and final concert.

On a smaller scale but with no less impact is the celebrated *Hail! Hail! Rock 'n' Roll* (1987), which documents rock pioneer Chuck Berry's preparations for a set of sixtieth birthday concerts in St. Louis. Taylor Hackford's camera captures guest artists Keith Richards, Linda Ronstadt, Etta James, and Eric Clapton and interviews famous fans of Berry like Bruce Springsteen, who reminisces on once having been Berry's opening act.

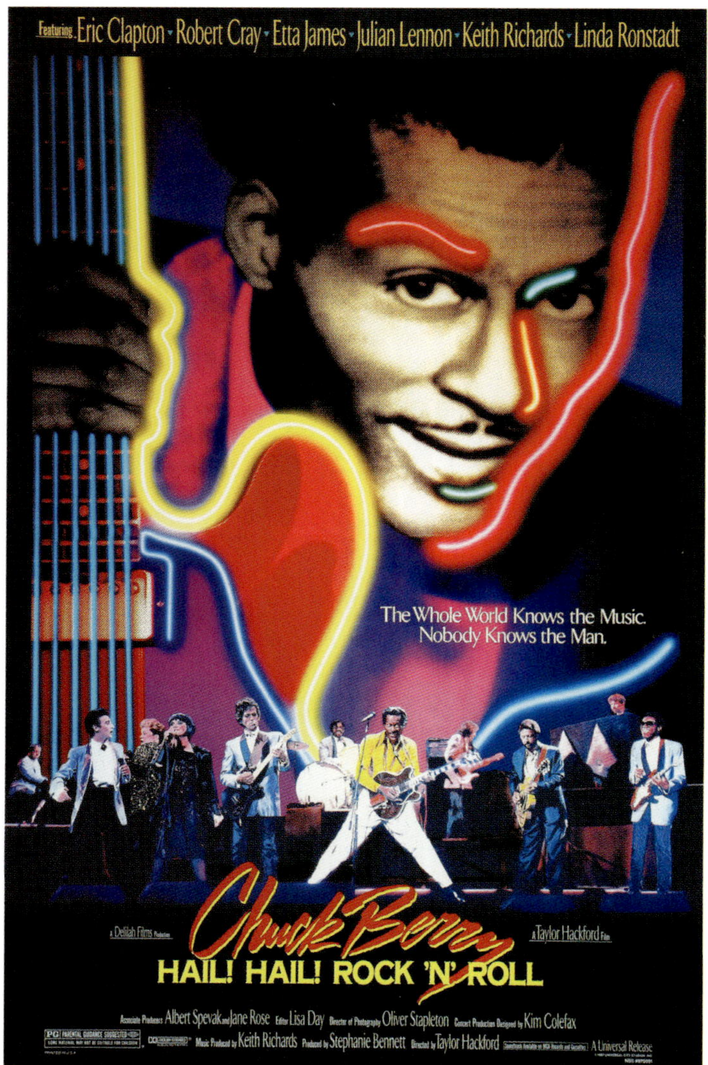

Hail! Hail! Rock 'n' Roll was a revealing portrait of trailblazing musician Chuck Berry.

Beyond rock and roll, the '80s offered an abundance of music documentaries across an array of genres. Fashion photographer Bruce Weber met jazz trumpeter Chet Baker in the mid-'80s and followed the icon in his last years to film the Oscar-nominated profile *Let's Get Lost* (1988). George Nierenberg's vérité film *Say Amen, Somebody* (1982) explores the story of gospel music through two of its legendary figures, composer Thomas A. Dorsey and musician Willie Mae Ford Smith. Director Terry Zwigoff made his feature debut with *Louie Bluie* (1985), a portrait of Black country-blues musician and painter Howard Armstrong. In *From Mao to Mozart: Isaac Stern in China* (1980), accomplished music documentarian Murray Lerner follows one of America's premier violinists as he rehearses with Chinese musicians after the 1976 end of the country's Cultural Revolution, which had banned the performance of Western classic music. Prolific filmmaker Les Blank made a number of short films on American music, such as *In Heaven There Is No Beer?* (1984), which explores the colorful world of polka festivals. ("In heaven there is no beer; that's why we drink it here.")

PUNK CINEMA

Several years after the emergence of bands like the Ramones and the Clash, punk rock began infiltrating the movies. In its rejection of mainstream society, "punk" was an ethos as much as a musical genre, and the films that depicted it were about characters who embraced nonconformity. But culture moves quickly, and as soon as punk was taken seriously, it was declared dead. Many of the films that follow might more accurately be termed "postpunk" in their diversity of style and influence.

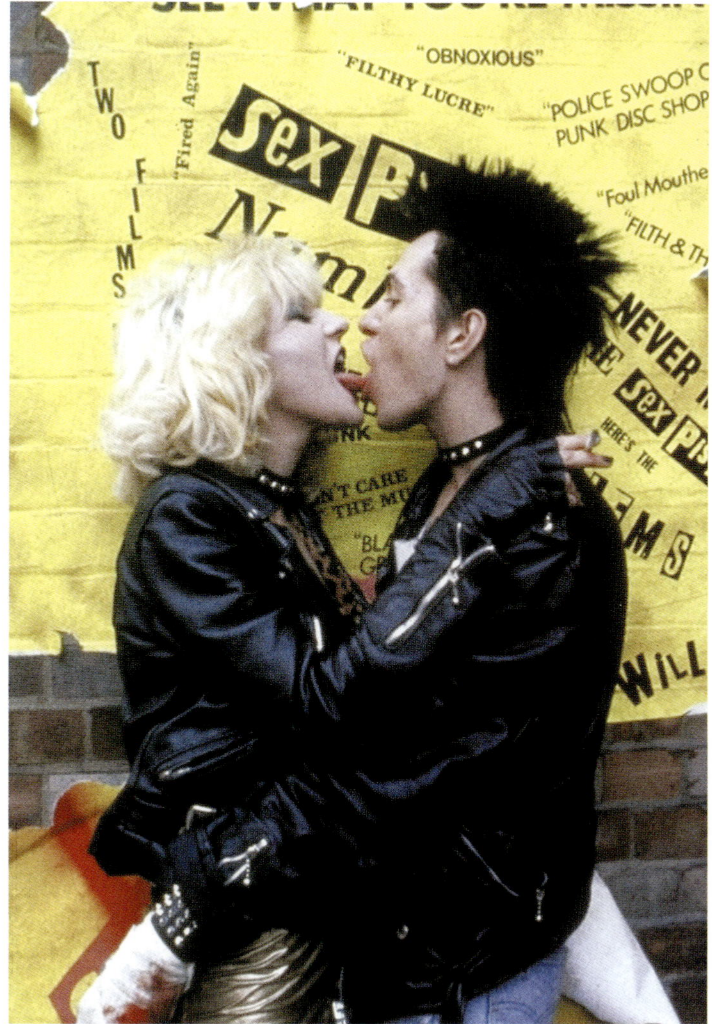

Chloe Webb and Gary Oldman in *Sid & Nancy*.

British director Alex Cox had injected a punk sensibility (and soundtrack) into his 1984 underground sci-fi movie *Repo Man*. He then dove in headfirst with *Sid & Nancy* (1986), a biopic of the volatile, drug-addled Sex Pistols bassist Sid Vicious (Gary Oldman) and his American girlfriend, Nancy Spungen (Chloe Webb), whose suspicious death is used as the film's framing device. Oldman was then an actor at the Royal Shakespeare Company and didn't hide his initial skepticism of the project: "Why make a film about two losers? Who cares about these people?" He was convinced to do the movie by his agent and because of the freedom that Cox offered him to explore the character. "Ultimately, I wanted to capture an essence or a spirit of Vicious, and not completely do an impersonation of him. Because they've already had one Sid Vicious—why give them another?"

The real Sid Vicious can be seen in the documentary *D.O.A.: A Rite of Passage* (1980) by filmmaker Lech Kowalski, which covered the Sex Pistols' 1978 US tour. The band also appear as over-the-top versions of themselves in Julian Temple's mockumentary *The Great Rock 'n' Roll Swindle* (1980), which includes Vicious's punk rendition of Frank Sinatra's classic tune "My Way."

Rude Boy (1980) was a movie about a roadie for the Clash that the band disowned shortly after production (which seems appropriately punk), while *Urgh! A Music War* (1982), *Another State of Mind* (1984), and *X: The Unheard Music* (1985) further documented various bands of the era.

Fictional portrayals of punk culture also emerged in the '80s, starting with *Times Square* (1980) from producer Robert Stigwood, manager of the Bee Gees and producer of *Saturday Night Fever* (1977) and *Grease*. The movie follows the "Sleez Sisters," two teenagers who live on the streets of New York and gain fame through a sympathetic radio deejay (Tim Curry). One subplot involves an attempt to revitalize gritty Times Square, with one man behind the effort asking the public, "Do we want to live in an X-rated city?" Record producer Lou Adler's *Ladies and Gentlemen, the Fabulous Stains* (1982) upped the ante with three teenage girls (Laura Dern, Diane Lane, and Marie Kanter) who start a band and features cameos by several real-life punk rockers.

Arguably the most significant contributions to punk cinema were made by women directors, like NYU film graduate Susan Seidelman, whose indie film *Smithereens* (1982) was shot in 16mm on the streets of New York and retains a handmade aesthetic. "Punk was about redefining the rules and breaking the rules. I think that same held true for punk cinema," she said. "It was so cheap to make movies, and the structure was so loose. . . . It was liberating." Notably, *Smithereens* was the first American independent film selected to compete at the Cannes Film Festival. NYU also graduated Martha Coolidge, who broke out with *Valley Girl* (1983), starring Nicolas Cage as an LA punk who falls in love—for sure, like totally—with a girl from Sherman Oaks.

From the UCLA film school came Penelope Spheeris, who made one of the most enduring punk films, *The Decline of Western Civilization* (1981)—a documentary that focuses on LA-based bands like the Germs, X, and the Circle Jerks. Roger Corman produced her

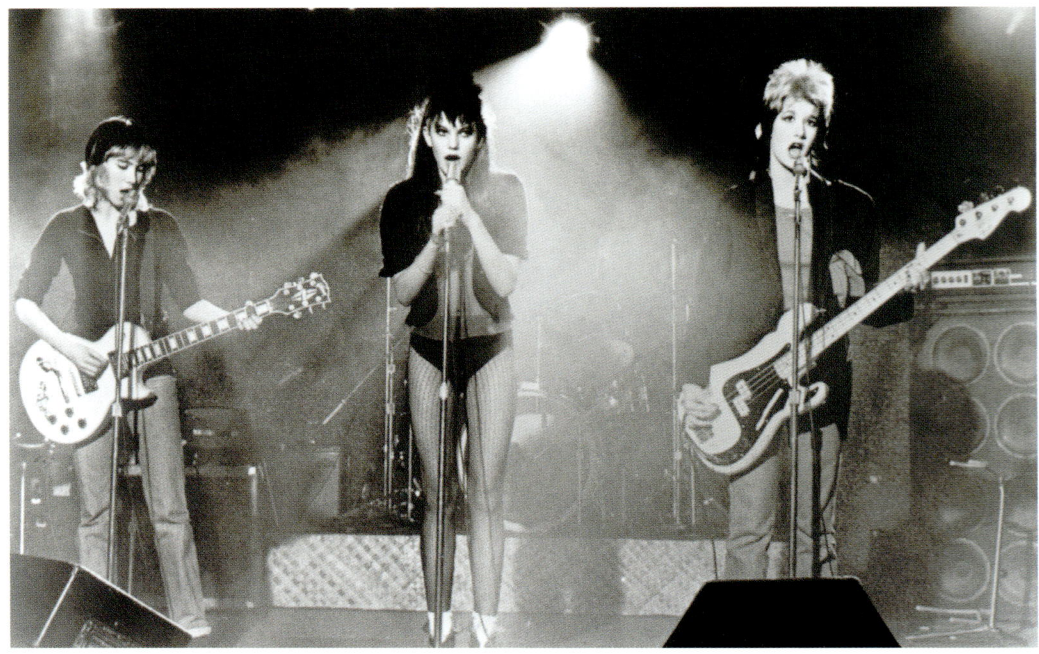

Marie Kanter, Diane Lane, and Laura Dern perform in *Ladies and Gentlemen, the Fabulous Stains*.

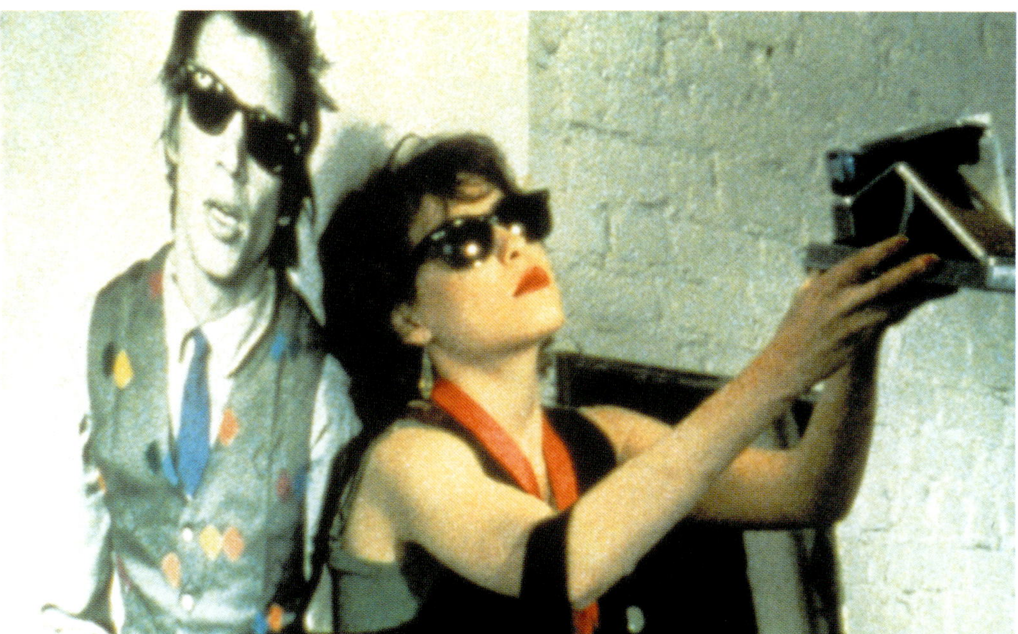

Susan Berman in *Smithereens.*

follow-up, *Suburbia* (1983), about a group of runaway teens who squat in an abandoned home, cast with punk rockers and other non-professional actors. "The reason I did *Suburbia* in the first place, was that I couldn't get any distribution for *Decline*," she explained. "I was told that if I wanted to do a movie about punk rock, I had to write a narrative script. So I did." Another UCLA grad, Allison Anders, made her feature debut as a codirector (with two of her classmates) on *Border Radio* (1987), which concerns a rocker (Chris D.) who flees to Mexico with stolen cash.

HIP-HOP HOLLYWOOD

Another emerging music genre was hip-hop, which burst onto film screens in the early '80s in documentaries and dance-heavy features, often populated with music-industry hitmakers. First out of the gate was Charlie Ahearn's portrait of New York graffiti culture, *Wild Style* (1983), which featured performances by actual street artists Fab 5 Freddy and Lee Quiñones. The documentary *Style Wars* (1983) further explored the racial and class tensions that lurked at the roots of hip-hop, highlighting graffiti as a means of personal expression.

In the era of *Flashdance*, Hollywood never let a good cultural trend go unexploited. Films like *Breakin'* (1984) and its sequels *Breakin' 2: Electric Boogaloo* (1984) and *Rappin'* (1985) were pumped out by studios with diminishing returns. One bright spot was director Michael Schultz's *Krush Groove* (1985), a fictionalized take on the early years of Def Jam Recordings that functions as a showcase for artists like Run-DMC (who also starred in 1988's Rick Rubin–directed *Tougher than Leather*). Schultz later directed rap trio the Fat Boys in the Palm Beach–set screwball comedy *Disorderlies* (1987).

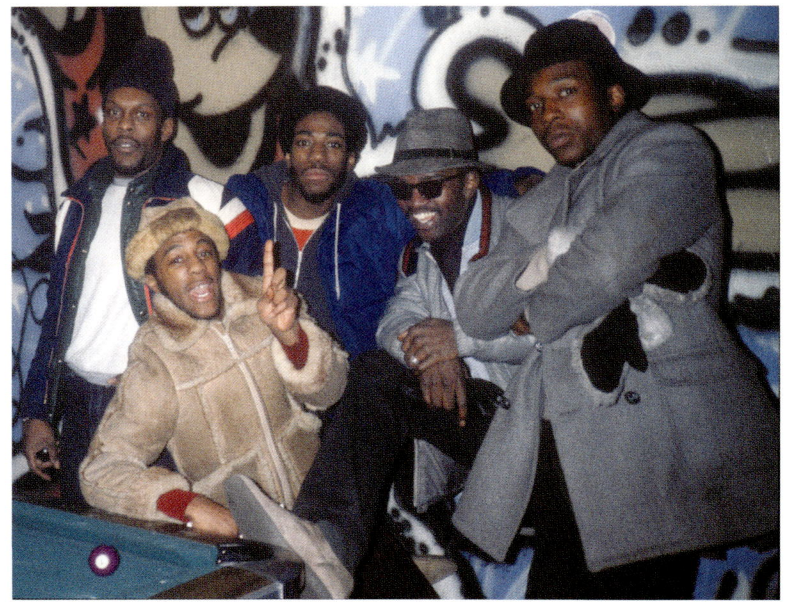

Busy Bee, Kase 2, Fab 5 Freddy, and friends in *Wild Style*.

Enemy's "Fight the Power," to which Rosie Perez dances over the opening credits. (The soundtrack's other hit single, Guy's "My Fantasy," reached number one on the hip-hop charts.) In the film, Samuel L. Jackson plays Mister Señor Love Daddy, the neighborhood deejay who directly references great African American musicians and functions as a modern-day Greek chorus, while Bill Nunn's pivotal character Radio Raheem is perpetually armed with a massive boombox.

Another early landmark was *Beat Street* (1984), starring Guy Davis (son of Ossie Davis and Ruby Dee) as an aspiring MC in the South Bronx. The story centered on the four pillars of hip-hop culture—deejaying, rapping, break-dancing, and graffiti—and was a "labor of love" for producer Harry Belafonte, whose intentions were to make a realistic depiction of the community. "Most people in America think of the South Bronx as . . . a place of violence, a place that is steeped in hopelessness and therefore it is hope-*less*," said Belafonte. "But the ability for the people to survive, to endure, to reach out and to force the universe to focus on it is an awesome tale. It's a hell of a story."

Brooklyn filmmaker Spike Lee, whose *School Daze* (1988) featured a hip-hop soundtrack led by E.U.'s "Da Butt," kicked off his 1989 film *Do the Right Thing* with Public

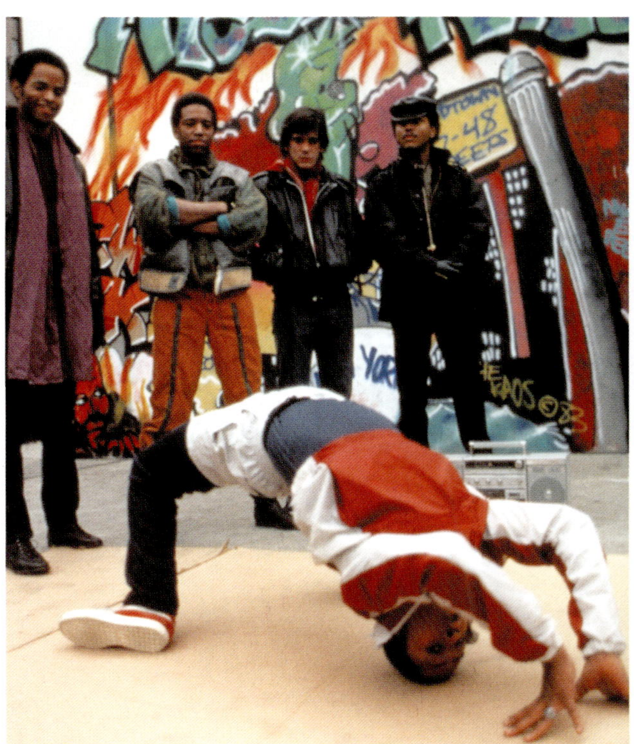

Robert Taylor dances in *Beat Street*.

Oscar-Winning Music

The Academy Awards have a spotty track record when it comes to rewarding great music, but the '80s represent a high point, coming at a time of real synergy between the movie and music industries. Many of the Best Original Songs listed below were legitimate hits, and even winners of the Score awards were sometimes stars in their own right, like Prince (*Purple Rain*), Herbie Hancock (*Round Midnight*), and David Byrne (*The Last Emperor*, with Ryuichi Sakamoto and Cong Su).

1980—"Fame" from *Fame* (performed by Irene Cara), music by Michael Gore, lyrics by Dean Pitchford

1981—"Arthur's Theme (Best That You Can Do)" from *Arthur* (performed by Christopher Cross), music and lyrics by Peter Allen, Burt Bacharach, Cross, and Carole Bayer Sager

1982—"Up Where We Belong" from *An Officer and a Gentleman* (performed by Joe Cocker and Jennifer Warnes), music by Jack Nitzsche and Buffy Sainte-Marie, lyrics by Will Jennings

1983—"Flashdance . . . What a Feeling" from *Flashdance* (performed by Irene Cara), music by Giorgio Moroder, lyrics by Cara and Keith Forsey

1984—"I Just Called to Say I Love You" from *The Woman in Red* (performed by Stevie Wonder), music and lyrics by Wonder

1985—"Say You, Say Me" from *White Nights* (performed by Lionel Richie), music and lyrics by Richie

1986—"Take My Breath Away" from *Top Gun* (performed by Berlin), music by Giorgio Moroder, lyrics by Tom Whitlock

1987—"(I've Had) The Time of My Life" from *Dirty Dancing* (performed by Bill Medley and Jennifer Warnes), music by John DeNicola, Donald Markowitz, and Franke Previte, lyrics by Previte

1988—"Let the River Run" from *Working Girl* (performed by Carly Simon), music and lyrics by Simon

1989—"Under the Sea" from *The Little Mermaid* (performed by Samuel E. Wright), music by Alan Menken, lyrics by Howard Ashman

MUSICIANS CROSS OVER

Hollywood in the '80s offered all sorts of opportunities to musical performers, from major acting roles to producing and directing credits, to—thanks to a new reliance on soundtrack album sales for ancillary revenue—more extensive control over film music in general.

One of the first bands to be handed scoring reins was the British rock group Queen, who wrote an album of mostly instrumental tracks for producer Dino De Laurentiis's whimsical science-fiction film *Flash Gordon* (1980). "We wanted to do something that was a real soundtrack," said lead guitarist Brian May. "It's a first in many ways because a rock group has not done this type of thing before, or else it's been toned down and they've been asked to write mushy background music. Whereas we were given the license to do what we liked, as long as it complemented the picture." Only two tracks had vocals, including "Flash's Theme," which was released as a single and climbed the *Billboard* charts. Queen later contributed several songs to Russell Mulcahy's *Highlander*, including "A Kind of Magic" and "Who Wants to Live Forever."

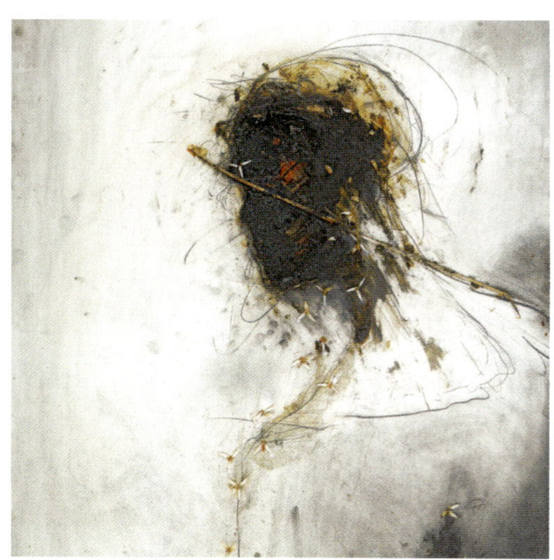

Peter Gabriel's album *Passion*, composed for *The Last Temptation of Christ.*

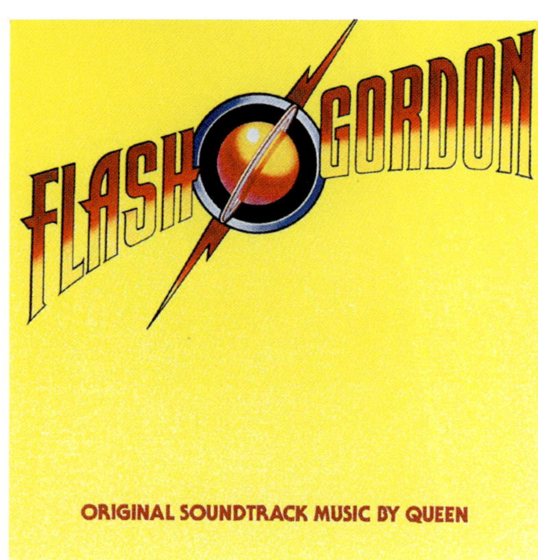

Queen's album for *Flash Gordon* was sparse on vocals.

De Laurentiis produced David Lynch's *Dune* in 1984 and hired rock band Toto to compose the film's original music. That same year, pop duo Eurythmics composed a score for the big-screen adaptation of *Nineteen Eighty-Four* at the request of production company Virgin Films, though their contributions were disowned by director Michael Radford, who claimed their music had been "foisted" on his film. In December, the Alan Parker drama *Birdy* premiered with a score by English singer-songwriter Peter Gabriel, who would later compose the music for Martin Scorsese's *The Last Temptation of Christ* (1988).

More examples followed. Guitarist Mark Knopfler of Dire Straits composed the music for the Scottish film *Local Hero* (1983), including

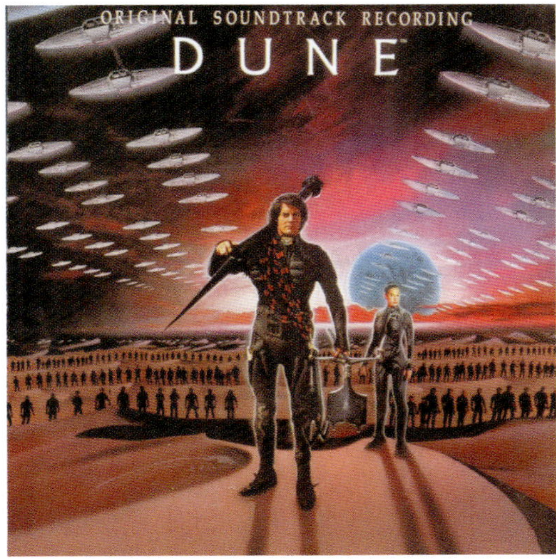

Toto's album for *Dune* also featured Brian Eno.

the popular instrumental theme "Going Home," as well as the fantasy classic *The Princess Bride* (1987). Police drummer Stewart Copeland composed several scores in the '80s, including Francis Ford Coppola's *Rumble Fish* (1983) and Oliver Stone's *Wall Street* (1987). Tom Waits received an Oscar nomination for his song score to Coppola's *One from the Heart* (1982), which he performed with country singer Crystal Gayle. Eddie Van Halen started work on the teen comedy *The Wild Life* (1984), scripted by Cameron Crowe, thinking his contribution would be limited to a track or two. He and music producer Donn Landee "ended up doing just about the whole film," though none of his instrumentals were included on the film's official soundtrack album. William Friedkin recruited British New Wave band Wang Chung to score his crime film *To Live and Die in L.A.* (1985). German jazz saxophonist Klaus Doldinger scored the submarine thriller *Das Boot* (1981) and the children's fantasy *The NeverEnding Story* (1984), both for director Wolfgang Petersen, while American jazz ensemble the Pat Metheny Group scored John Schlesinger's drama *The Falcon and the Snowman* (1985).

Other music stars appeared in front of the camera. British rocker David Bowie, famous for his unconventional stage personae like Ziggy Stardust, had starred in Nicolas Roeg's sci-fi film *The Man Who Fell to Earth* (1976) but did some of his most iconic film work in the 1980s. He played a vampire in *The Hunger* (1983), Pontius Pilate in *The Last Temptation of Christ*, and a POW opposite electronic musician Ryuichi Sakamoto in *Merry Christmas, Mr. Lawrence* (1983). "It's so hard for somebody in music to jump over and do movies," said Bowie. "The idea of them being a rock musician is always at the front of the

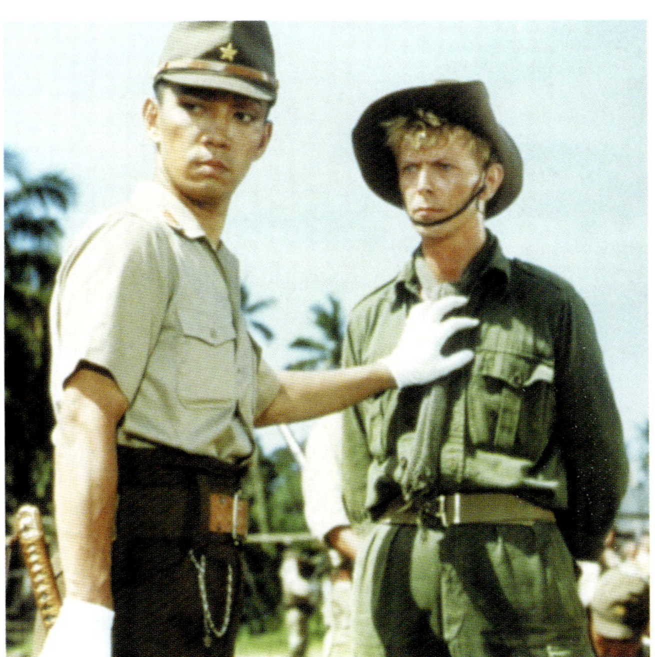

Ryuichi Sakamoto and David Bowie in *Merry Christmas, Mr. Lawrence*.

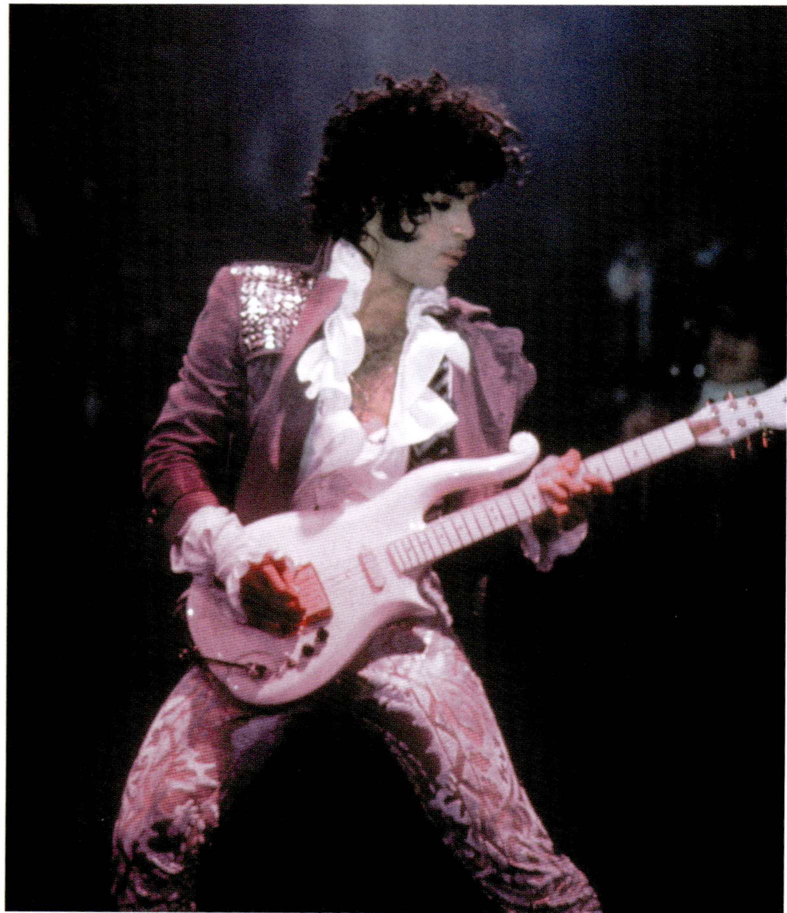

Prince performs in *Purple Rain*.

who becomes interested in two lovers who place notes to each other in newspaper personal ads. Director Susan Seidelman shot the film in New York City in the fall of 1984, during which time Madonna performed "Like a Virgin" at the inaugural MTV Video Music Awards, helping it become her first number-one hit. As a result, *Susan* became "the Madonna movie," significantly raising its profile and ensuring a healthy box office. Further, it caused the film *Vision Quest* (1985), in which she has a cameo role and performs "Crazy for You," to be renamed after the song title in some foreign markets. Her first film, *A Certain Sacrifice*, shot five years earlier on a shoestring budget and never distributed, also got a home-video release that year.

audience's mind. You've got to fight twice as hard and try and work twice as well." His most beloved film may be Jim Henson's 1986 fantasy *Labyrinth*, in which he stars as Jareth, the Goblin King, alongside a young Jennifer Connelly and a variety of puppets from the director's Creature Shop. Though the film disappointed at the box office, it has since become a cult classic.

Before she became a household name, pop singer Madonna was cast as the title character in *Desperately Seeking Susan* (1985), a film about an unsatisfied married woman (Rosanna Arquette)

Her star now shining brightly, Madonna and new husband Sean Penn appeared together in *Shanghai Surprise* (1986), a British-produced comedy set during the Japanese occupation of China, which was roasted by critics. The *L.A. Times* recommended, "Give the film a Shanghai gesture and stay quietly home with a good book," and audiences apparently took the advice to heart. The screwball comedy *Who's That Girl* (1987) didn't fare much better, despite the singer promoting it via her first world concert tour and soundtrack album.

Another major music star of the '80s whose films found wildly different receptions was Prince, whose semiautobiographical *Purple Rain* (1984) was championed by reviewers like Siskel and Ebert. Both Chicago critics placed it on their top-ten lists that year, with Ebert calling it "the best rock and roll film since the Beatles made *A Hard Day's Night*." The film won Prince the Academy Award for Best Original Song Score, and the soundtrack album became one of the all-time bestsellers thanks to tracks like "When Doves Cry" and "Let's Go Crazy."

Prince assumed full creative control over his next film, *Under the Cherry Moon* (1986), which he ultimately directed—after Mary Lambert left two weeks into production, citing creative differences—in addition to tackling the lead role. Filmed in black-and-white in the French Riviera, the story of a pair of gold-digging playboys was designed as a musically driven art film but skewered by critics as a pretentious farce. "For all those out there who can't get enough of Prince," wrote Walter Goodman in the *New York Times*, "*Under the Cherry Moon* may be just the antidote."

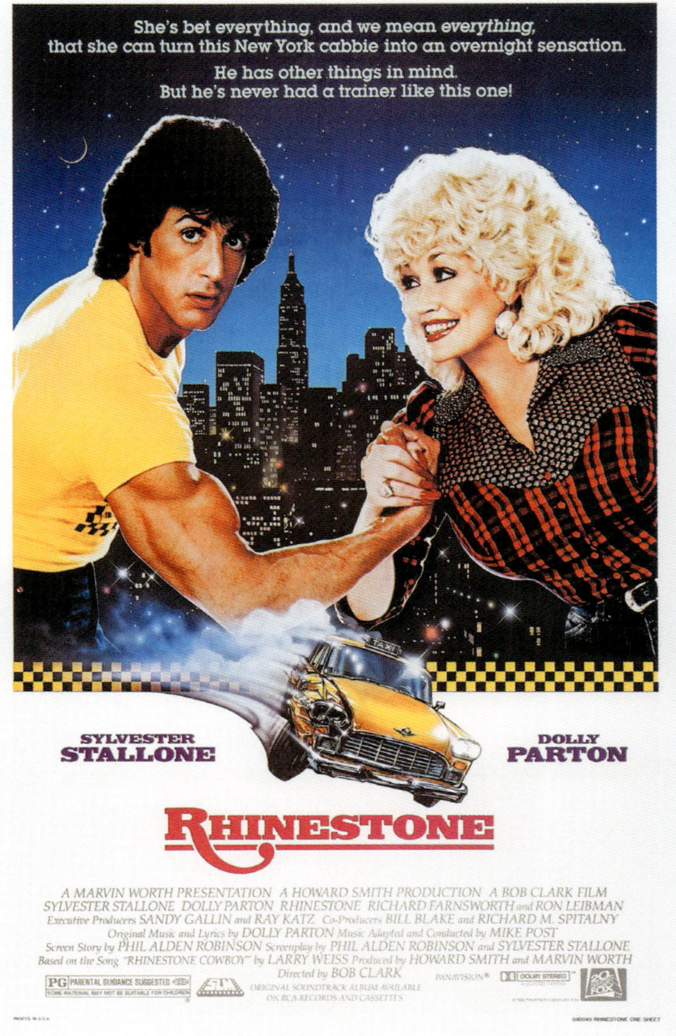

Dolly Parton and Sylvester Stallone, both represented by talent agency CAA, were presented to Fox as a packaged team.

Country star Dolly Parton had been a fixture on television for many years—even hosting her own variety show, *Dolly!* (1976–1977)—before making her big-screen debut in the workplace comedy *9 to 5* (1980) alongside Jane Fonda and Lily Tomlin. Her most famous contribution to the film is probably the title song, a number-one hit in the United States and one of Parton's signature tunes. Her next few roles leaned into her folksy persona as a plainspoken southerner, first as the owner of a brothel in *The Best Little Whorehouse in Texas* (1982), opposite Burt Reynolds as the local sheriff. Next came *Rhinestone* (1984), the Pygmalion story with a Tennessee twist, in which her character is challenged to turn a New York cabbie (Sylvester Stallone) into a genuine country music star. She also had a supporting role in the ensemble drama *Steel Magnolias* (1989), a now classic tearjerker.

When the '80s began, country star Willie Nelson had just kicked off what would be a prolific screen career with a supporting role in *The Electric Horseman* (1979). With *Honeysuckle Rose* (1980), he got the chance to lead a film—and he also had a huge hit with "On the Road Again." He appeared in Michael Mann's *Thief*, Fred Schipisi's western *Barbarosa* (1982), and Alan Rudolph's satire *Songwriter* (1984) with Kris Kristofferson, which was loosely based on events in Nelson's own life. "Plainness, naturalness, that's Willie Nelson's style, and he's a master at it," wrote critic Pauline Kael in her review of *Songwriter*. "Nelson delivers a line so fast that he seems to be brushing it off, but . . . like the exit lines of a matinée idol, they linger in the air."

Though she had dabbled in acting in the late '60s, pop diva Cher's film career began in earnest with the 1982 Robert Altman film *Come Back to the Five and Dime, Jimmy Dean, Jimmy Dean*, for which she had starred in the original Broadway production. Awards recognition followed her throughout the decade, beginning with the Oklahoma-set *Silkwood* (1983), in which

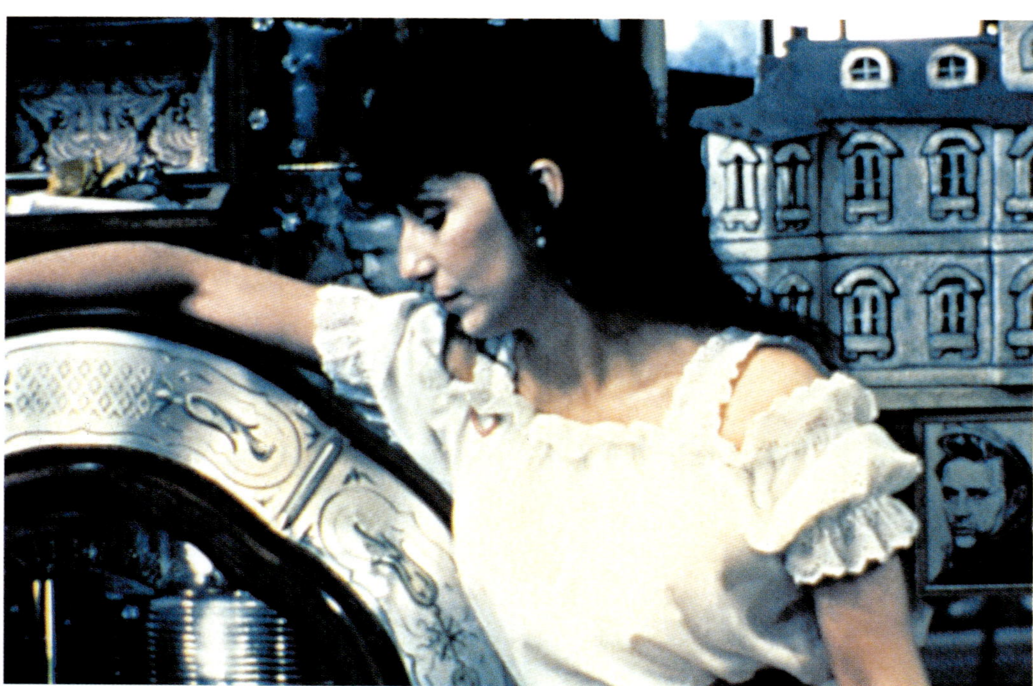

Cher in *Come Back to the Five and Dime, Jimmy Dean, Jimmy Dean.*

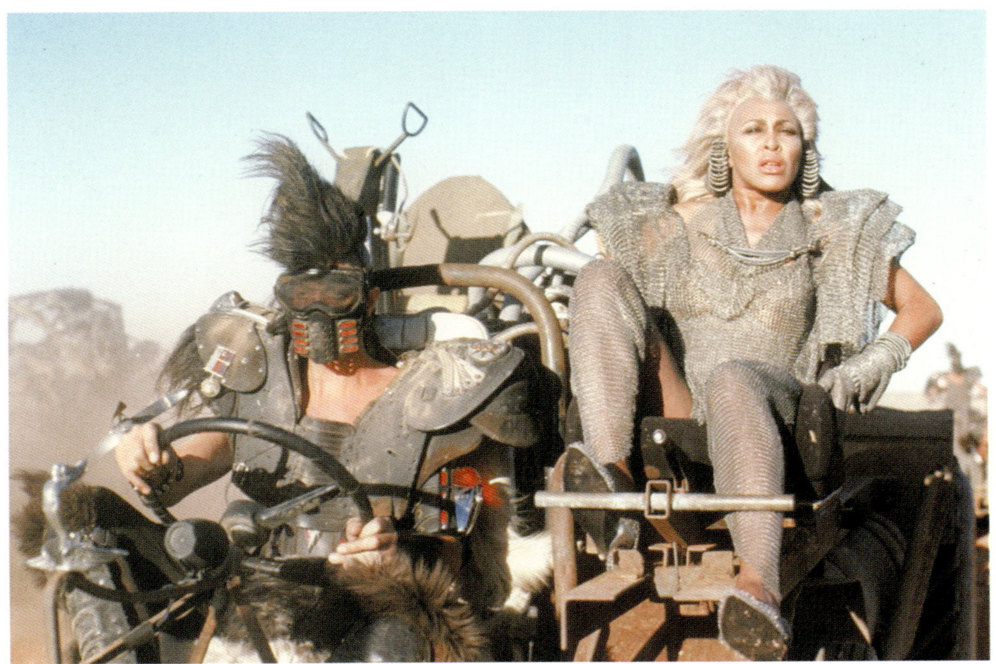

Tina Turner in *Mad Max Beyond Thunderdome*.

she plays a lesbian roommate to Meryl Streep's whistleblower protagonist. Cher was worried that working with Streep "was going to be like having an audience with the Pope." In actuality, they became fast friends, and both wound up with Academy Award nominations. *Mask* (1985) earned her the Best Actress award at the Cannes Film Festival, but it was her role as an Italian American widow who has a whirlwind affair with her fiancé's brother (Nicolas Cage) in *Moonstruck* (1987) that won her the Oscar. "I don't think that this means that I am somebody," she said in her acceptance speech. "But I guess I'm on my way."

Broadway actress and recording artist Bette Midler had been nominated for her 1979 performance as a Janis Joplin–like rock singer in *The Rose*, which opened the door to several major roles for Disney's Touchstone Pictures: a rich but unfulfilled housewife in *Down and Out in Beverly Hills* (1986), a kidnapped Beverly Hills housewife in *Ruthless People* (1986), a woman dating the same man as her acting classmate in *Outrageous Fortune* (1987), and a set of identical twins in *Big Business* (1988). She provided the voice for an animated poodle opposite Billy Joel in the Disney film *Oliver & Company* (1988) and performed her signature hit "Wind Beneath My Wings" for the tearjerker *Beaches* (1988). "I love my work," she told *Entertainment Tonight*. "It's very fulfilling, very creative. You get to pick the clothes, you get to paint the walls. It's all fabulous!"

Other musicians with major film roles include Meat Loaf (*Roadie* [1980]), Sting (*Dune*), Tina Turner (*Mad Max Beyond Thunderdome* [1985]), Debbie Harry (*Videodrome*; *Hairspray* [1988]), Cyndi Lauper (*Vibes* [1988]), Neil Diamond (*The Jazz Singer* [1980]), and Joan Jett

(*Light of Day* [1987]). Performer and model Grace Jones made striking appearances in a pair of high-profile action franchise films: *Conan the Destroyer* (1984) and *A View to a Kill* (1985). Paul Simon wrote the screenplay for and starred in *One-Trick Pony* (1980). Paul McCartney did the same with *Give My Regards to Broad Street* (1984), while Neil Young directed himself (credited as Bernard Shakey) in the apocalyptic comedy *Human Highway* (1982)—alongside the members of Devo as "nuclear garbage men." New York Dolls frontman David Johansen appeared as the Ghost of Christmas Past in *Scrooged* (1988). American saxophonist Dexter Gordon starred in Bertrand Tavernier's ode to jazz, *Round Midnight* (1986), and received an Oscar nomination; Italian tenor Luciano Pavarotti made his film debut with the opera comedy *Yes, Giorgio* (1982) and received a Razzie nomination. (Neither won.)

Behind the scenes, Motown Records founder Berry Gordy produced the cult martial-arts film *The Last Dragon* (1985), which presented a rare mixed-race action hero (played by Taimak), while Quincy Jones served as a producer and composer on Steven Spielberg's *The Color Purple* (1985). "I dropped everything for two years to do this," said Jones. "Shooting a movie is no joke."

MOVIES ABOUT MUSICIANS

The '80s also provided audiences with musical biopics in a wide range of genres and styles. Some were factual or loosely based in real life, others were fictionalized, and many were set decades in the past.

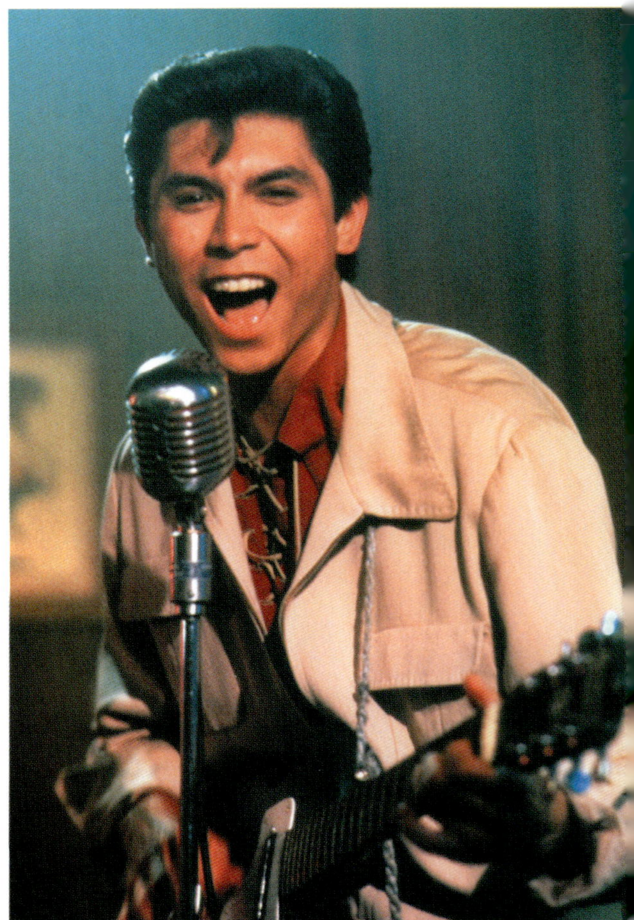

Lou Diamond Phillips as Ritchie Valens in *La Bamba*.

Director Luis Valdez told the story of '50s teen sensation Ritchie Valens in *La Bamba* (1987). The film opens in a California citrus grove in 1957, where the Mexican American Valenzuela family work as farm laborers, and follows the young guitarist (Lou Diamond Phillips) through his rapid rise to stardom and tragic end. Carlos Santana provided the original score for the film—complete with guitar riffs—while the Chicano group Los Lobos recorded Ritchie's songs, per the Valenzuela family's request.

La Bamba was a hit, but others failed to ignite the box office. *Great Balls of Fire!* (1989) starred Dennis Quaid as scandalous piano player Jerry Lee Lewis. "Anyone looking for a true sense of his importance in the history of rock and roll will be let down," reported Caryn James in the *New York Times*. Director Taylor Hackford's debut film, *The Idolmaker* (1980), was a loose portrayal of talent manager Bob Marcucci (Ray Sharkey) who discovered teen idols like Fabian; the singer ended up suing the production for defamation. *Eddie and the Cruisers* (1983), starring Michael Paré as a fictional '60s New Jersey rocker, saw success only after the release of a popular soundtrack album and airings on HBO.

Breaking the mold (while flying under the radar) was indie director Jim Jarmusch's offbeat anthology film *Mystery Train* (1989), a trio of stories about Elvis Presley fans, set in a run-down Memphis hotel. *Streets of Fire* (1984) mixed rock music and biker gangs—"futuristic fantasy meets the Western, gets married and has rock and roll babies," per its director, Walter Hill. *Miami Connection* (1987) featured a college band, "Dragon Sound," who fight a gang of Floridian ninjas with tae kwon do. Others spoofed the genre outright, like 1984's sci-fi comedy *Voyage of the Rock Aliens* and the spy movie *Top Secret!* in which Val Kilmer's '60s pop star visits East Germany.

Two of the most iconic music films of the 1980s also played for laughs—John Landis's action comedy *The Blues Brothers* (1980) and Rob Reiner's mockumentary *This Is Spinal Tap* (1984)—though their production histories couldn't have been more different. The first got its start as a *Saturday Night Live* sketch, with John Belushi and Dan Aykroyd as suited and sunglassed soul performers Jake and Elwood Blues and was handsomely financed by Universal Pictures after the wild success of *Animal House* two years earlier. *Spinal Tap* was a scrappy indie production about a hapless English metal band (led by Michael McKean, Christopher Guest, and Harry Shearer) on tour to promote their new

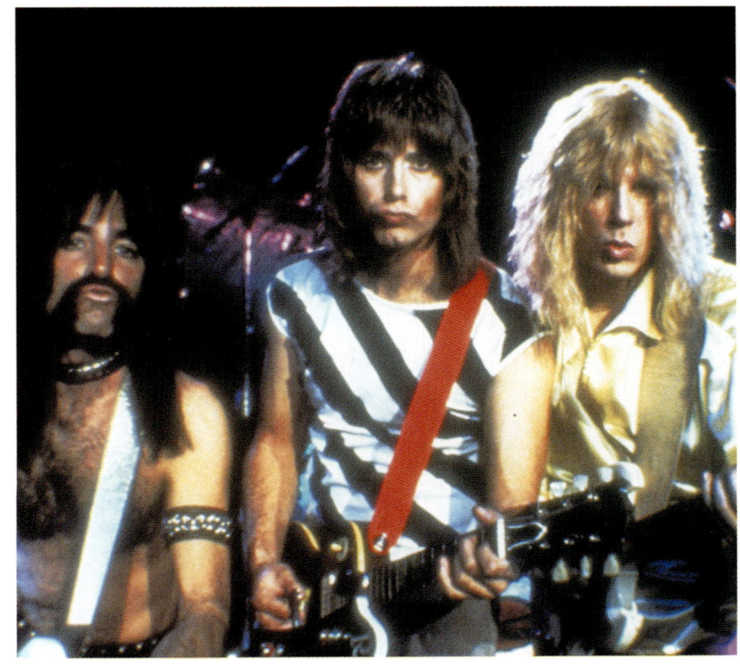

Harry Shearer, Christopher Guest, and Michael McKean in *This Is Spinal Tap*.

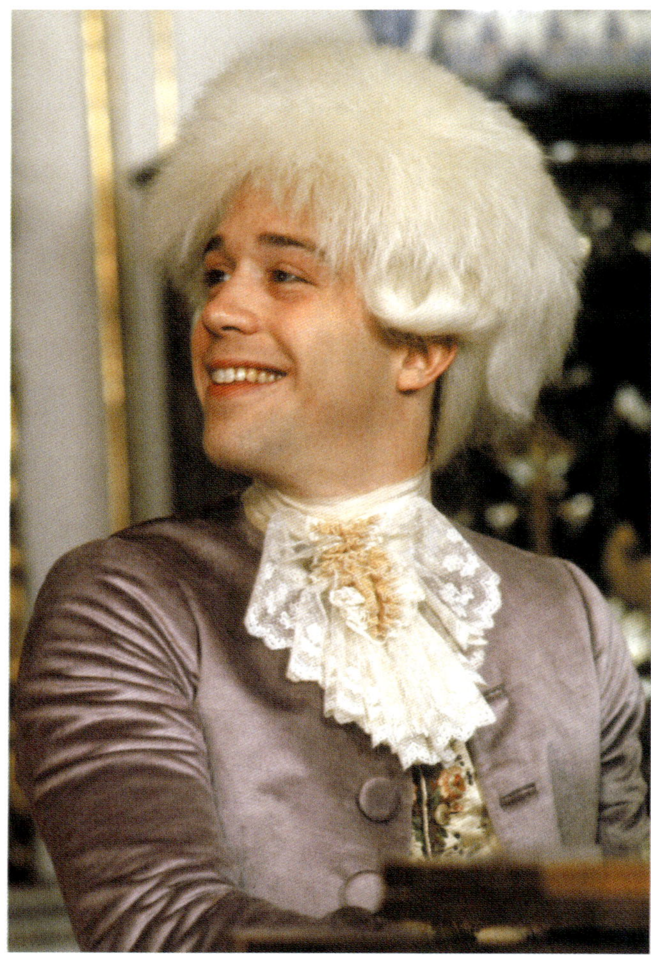

Tom Hulce in *Amadeus*.

album, *Smell the Glove*. "It's a film about love, you know?" said Sting, one of *Spinal Tap*'s mega-fans. "There's so many truths in it. . . . We all recognize ourselves in the parody. It's good for us!" Both films have since been added to the National Film Registry in the Library of Congress.

One of the most unexpected hits of the decade was—at least on the surface—the total opposite of a rock movie. *Amadeus* (1984) was an adaptation of Peter Shaffer's play about the rivalry between young music prodigy Wolfgang Amadeus Mozart (Tom Hulce) and court composer Antonio Salieri (F. Murray Abraham) in eighteenth-century Vienna. With a lot of artistic license, it presents Salieri as an unreliable—but completely relatable—narrator who becomes increasingly jealous of the acclaim and attention heaped upon the vulgar but gifted Mozart, a musical rule breaker as disruptive as any of director Miloš Forman's frequently rebellious protagonists, from *One Flew over the Cuckoo's Nest* (1975) to *The People vs. Larry Flynt* (1996). The film was a box-office success and took home eight Oscars. It also kicked off a minor Mozart frenzy, from an increased interest in his music to Falco's number-one hit single "Rock Me Amadeus."

Classical music also shone in films like *The Competition* (1980), a romance between rival pianists played by Amy Irving and Richard Dreyfuss, and the French thriller *Diva* (1981), about a young man obsessed with an opera star. In the world of jazz, Clint Eastwood's *Bird* (1988) was a loosely structured biopic of saxophonist Charlie Parker (Forest Whitaker). *Crossroads* (1986) starred Ralph Macchio as a guitarist researching blues legend Robert Johnson, while *The Fabulous Baker Boys* (1989) was the story of a pair of brother pianists (Jeff and Beau Bridges) who recruit a lounge singer (Michelle Pfeiffer) to revitalize their act.

Hollywood also found a place for country music on-screen, with lead acting Oscars going to both Sissy Spacek as Loretta Lynn in the biopic *Coal Miner's Daughter* (1980) and

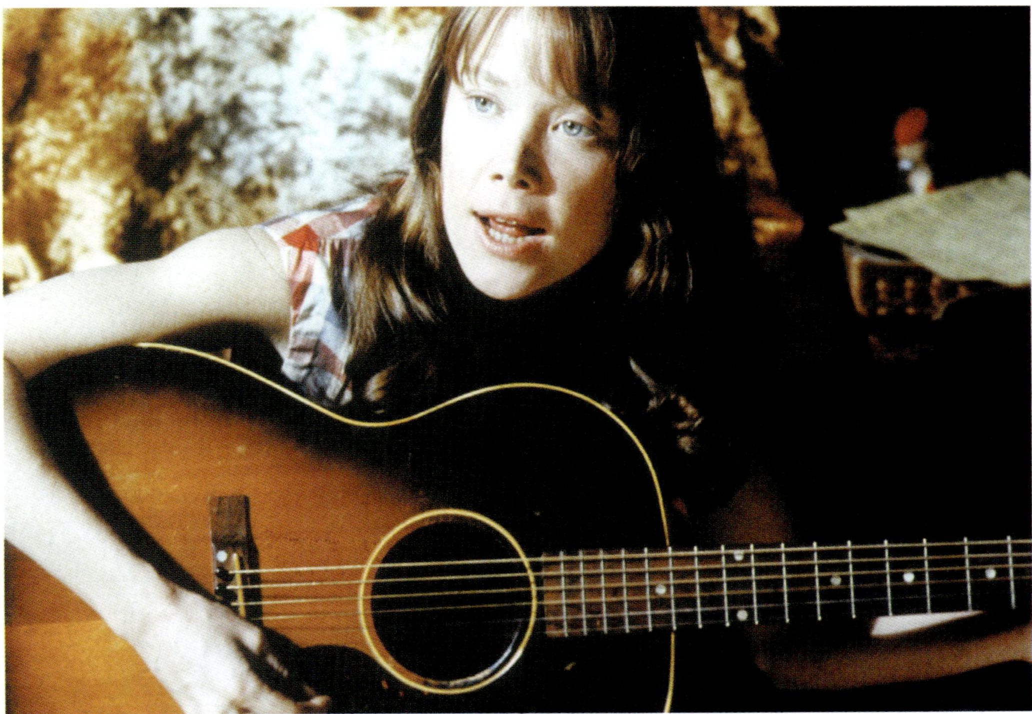

Sissy Spacek as Loretta Lynn in *Coal Miner's Daughter*.

Robert Duvall as an alcoholic singer who seeks redemption in *Tender Mercies* (1983). Jessica Lange appeared as troubled star Patsy Cline in *Sweet Dreams* (1985), while Clint Eastwood directed and starred in the Depression-era *Honkytonk Man* (1982), about a singer with tuberculosis who dreams of performing at the Grand Ole Opry.

CAN'T STOP THE MUSICAL

If there's any aspect of movie music in the '80s that had a tough time, it was the traditional musical. With the commercial success of *Grease* and the acclaimed artistry of *All That Jazz* (1979), Hollywood could have been forgiven for thinking that big-budget productions and Broadway adaptations had a rosy future. That turned out not to be the case.

Columbia's highly anticipated Broadway adaptation *Annie* (1982), directed by John Huston and starring Carol Burnett and Albert Finney, earned a healthy box office but failed to be profitable given its high costs. The critical reaction was mixed. "For a production that means to bring children back to the movies, dragging their parents with them, *Annie* has a dark, dour, mean-spirited tone—*Oliver Twist* as retold by Fagin," wrote Richard Corliss in *Time*. The studio also produced the big-screen adaptation of *A Chorus Line* (1985) with star Michael Douglas, which at the time was the longest-running show in Broadway history, but the film failed to capture the immediacy that had made the backstage musical such a hit onstage. The *New York Times* called it "less a movie than an expensive souvenir program."

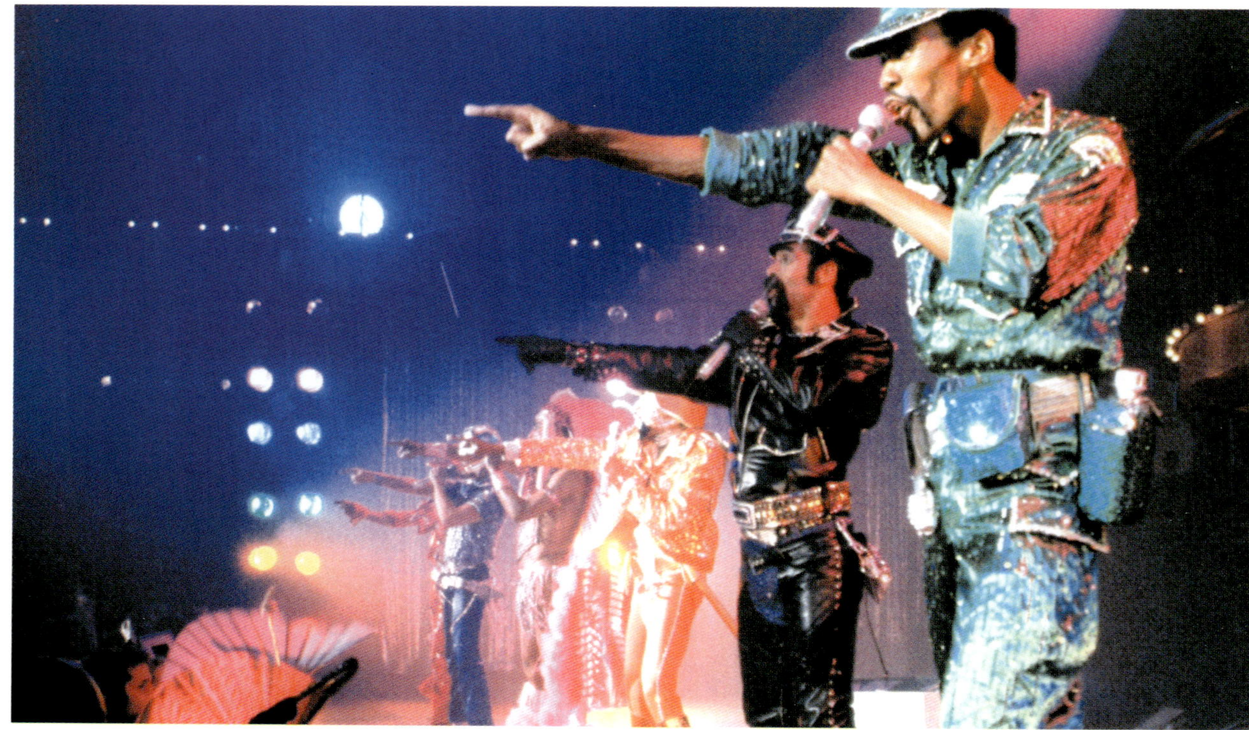

The Village People perform in *Can't Stop the Music.*

Original movie musicals weren't doing much better. The year 1980 alone saw the release of the Village People tribute *Can't Stop the Music*, the dystopian biblical parable *The Apple*, and the mythological roller-skating sugar high *Xanadu*, which today are best appreciated as over-the-top camp classics. "All three of these movies are so bizarre and somewhat misbegotten that they engender strong sentiments," wrote critic and film historian Alonso Duralde. If you love these movies, "you are right. If you hate them, you're also right."

Though a revival of Gilbert and Sullivan's *The Pirates of Penzance* had become a recent hit onstage, *The Pirate Movie* (1982)—a pop fantasy musical made in its wake, starring Christopher Atkins and Kristy McNichol—was only a hit at that year's Razzie Awards.

Studios made a few sequel attempts. *Grease 2* (1982), with Maxwell Caulfield and Michelle Pfeiffer as the romantic leads, flopped at the box office but has since entered cult-classic territory. *Shock Treatment* (1981) was a continuation of *The Rocky Horror Picture Show* (1975) that never came close to becoming a similar midnight-movie phenomenon.

There were a few creative bright spots, however. For the original musical *Victor/Victoria* (1982), which was based on a 1933 German film, comedy auteur Blake Edwards directed his wife, Julie Andrews, as a Parisian cabaret singer pretending to be a female impersonator. Henry Mancini wrote the score, with lyrics provided by Leslie Bricusse, and all of the songs were incorporated naturally into the film's nightclub setting. *Yentl* (1983) was a passion project for its star, Barbra Streisand, who also directed the film. In it, she plays a turn-of-the-century Jewish girl who disguises herself as a boy in order to study at a religious school. The songs, by composer Michel Legrand and lyricists Alan and Marilyn Bergman, are all sung internally by the main character. *Little Shop of Horrors* (1986) was based on an off-Broadway play by songwriters Alan Menken and Howard Ashman (itself based on a 1960 Roger Corman movie) about a florist (Rick Moranis) who discovers that one of his plants is conscious and feeds on human blood. Costar Ellen Greene reprised her Broadway role as Audrey, with comedian Steve Martin in a crucial supporting part as the world's worst dentist. It was directed by Franz Oz, whose previous film *The Muppets Take Manhattan* (1984) was explicitly about the challenges of getting a show produced on Broadway (also with puppets).

Martin had done some of the most challenging and impressive work of his career a few years earlier in Herbert Ross's *Pennies from Heaven* (1981). The film is set during the Great Depression and depicts real-world struggles, but breaks through the drama with a series of ornate fantasy sequences, staged like Busby Berkeley in Technicolor, with actors lip-syncing to recorded voices from the 1930s. The concept was audacious, and the end product was hailed by critics like the *New Yorker*'s Pauline Kael, who called it "the most emotional movie musical I've ever seen."

Ross started his career as a Broadway dancer in the 1940s and had several dance-related films on his résumé, including the ballet drama *The Turning Point* (1977) and the biopic *Nijinsky* (1980). One of his biggest hits was the 1984 teen movie *Footloose*, set in a small God-fearing town where dancing has been banned. Enter city boy Ren (Kevin Bacon) who pushes back on the strict law by proposing a high school prom—while also bopping solo through an empty warehouse and doing the country equivalent of a *Saturday Night Fever* scene on a roadhouse dance floor.

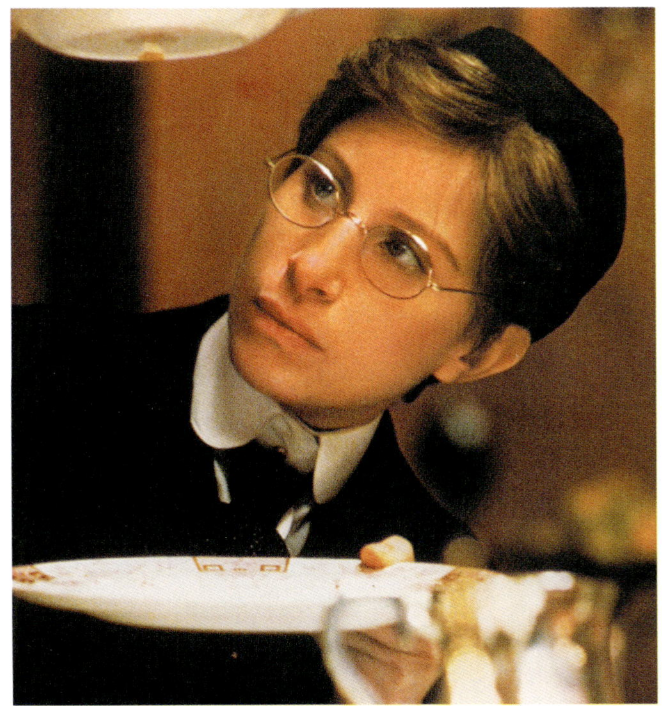

Barbra Streisand directed herself in *Yentl*.

Footloose was one of several high-profile '80s films about teenagers who long to strut their stuff. Beyond the smash hit *Fame* (1980), set in a New York performing arts high school, there was the later pair of comedies *Girls Just Want to Have Fun* (1985) and *Hairspray* (1988), both about girls who dream of being on TV dance shows.

SCORE ONE FOR TRADITION

For all the emphasis placed on radio hits, dance dramas, and pop celebrity in the '80s—driven by a hunger for the ancillary revenue from soundtrack album sales—underscoring was still the most common musical element for most films. Though the styles were changing to fit the era, instrumental scoring continued to provide emotional resonance and tone that was crucial to an audience's experience of a film.

One of the decade's most exciting new talents was Oingo Boingo frontman Danny Elfman, whose scores for Tim Burton's films *Pee-wee's Big Adventure* (1985) and *Beetlejuice* (1988) were full of intricate and playful orchestrations—whimsical, surreal, and manic in equal measure. His score for the blockbuster hit *Batman* (1989) matches that film's darkly creative energy. "Tim just let me go crazy and run amuck," he told *GQ* in 2023. "He's almost never told me that I've gone too far."

After many years writing memorable themes for big Hollywood epics like *The Magnificent Seven* (1960) and serious dramas like *To Kill a Mockingbird* (1962), Elmer Bernstein refreshed his career in the '80s by composing comedic scores for movies like *Airplane!* (1980), *The Blues Brothers*, *Three Amigos!* (1986), and *Ghostbusters* (1984), with rich orchestrations that often play ironically against their films' lack of seriousness. "I think one of the reasons that the scores work is that I do not denigrate the film," he told an interviewer at the time. "I don't try to make the music funny. My theory is that if the comedy is working in the film, let the film do the comedy."

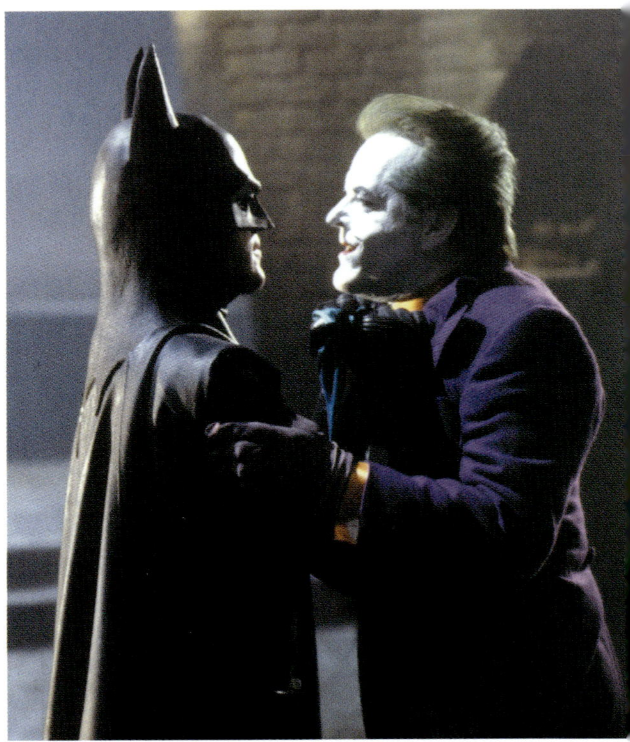

Michael Keaton and Jack Nicholson in *Batman*.

Another veteran composer, John Barry, was most famous for his theme music to the James Bond franchise when he crafted a sultry film-noir score for Lawrence Kasdan's steamy drama *Body Heat* (1981), followed by a suite of yearning, romantic melodies for Sydney Pollack's *Out of Africa* (1985).

Italian master Ennio Morricone worked extensively during the decade—mainly in Europe, but also on American films such as John Carpenter's *The Thing* (1982) and Brian De Palma's *The Untouchables* (1987). His scores for Sergio Leone's gangster epic *Once Upon a Time in America* (1984) and Roland Joffé's South American historical drama *The Mission* (1986) won major industry awards, but his most beloved work may be for Giuseppe Tornatore's nostalgic coming-of-age drama *Cinema Paradiso* (1988), which he wrote with his son, Andrea.

Alan Silvestri, best known for his work with director Robert Zemeckis, developed a soft-rock saxophone solo for *Romancing the Stone* (1984), a soaring sci-fi adventure theme for *Back to the Future* (1985), and a jazz-infused '40s score for *Who Framed Roger Rabbit* (1988).

German composer Hans Zimmer mainly used synthesizers for his scores for the Oscar-winning dramas *Rain Man* (1988) and *Driving Miss Daisy* (1989), which catapulted his career in Hollywood. Meanwhile, minimalist Philip Glass provided the shimmering rhythms for Godfrey Reggio's experimental film *Koyaanisqatsi* (1982), Paul Schrader's *Mishima: A Life in Four Chapters* (1985), and Errol Morris's crime documentary *The Thin Blue Line* (1988).

Songwriter Randy Newman came from a family of famous film composers (his uncle Alfred Newman began writing scores for Samuel Goldwyn in 1930) but was primarily known as a solo recording artist with a bluesy Americana sound. His scores for *Ragtime* (1981) and *Parenthood* (1989) both contain key parts for piano, his primary instrument, while *The Natural*'s (1984) powerful synthesizer theme became a popular anthem for America's pastime. Randy's cousin Thomas Newman also started his film-scoring career in the 1980s with the teen drama *Reckless* (1984).

If anyone can claim the title of king of film composition in the '80s, it is frequent George Lucas–Steven Spielberg collaborator John Williams. He kicked off the decade with *The Empire Strikes Back* (1980) and its ominous "Imperial March," which is now required entrance music for any villainous figure or opposing sports team. Next came an exhilarating march theme for *Raiders of the Lost Ark* (1981), a soaring bike ride melody in *E.T. the Extra-Terrestrial* (1982), and the jaunty "Parade of the Ewoks" in *Return of the Jedi* (1983). "Without question, John Williams has been the single most significant contributor to my success as a filmmaker," Spielberg told an audience in 2012. There's a good argument to be made that Williams's contribution to '80s cinema has made many of the decade's most iconic films the enduring classics they are today.

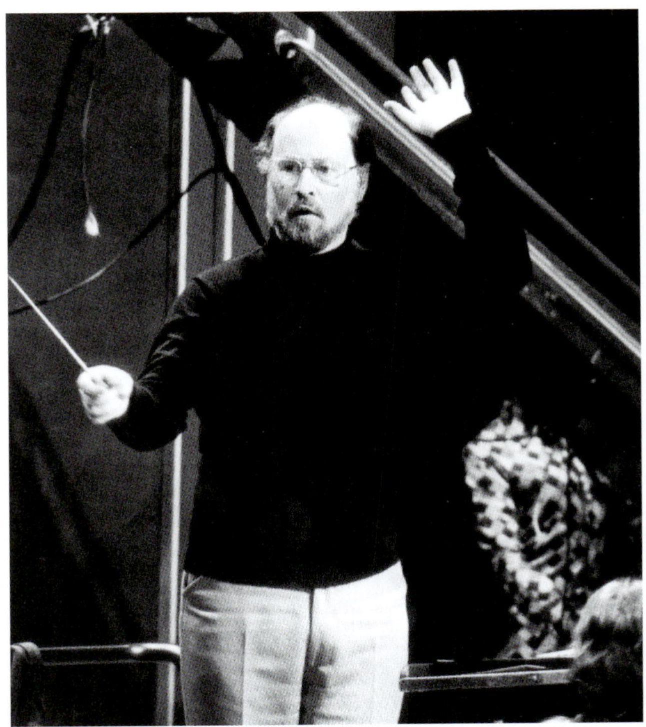

John Williams received twelve Oscar nominations for his work in the '80s.

Beyond Hollywood: India

By the 1980s, the Indian film industry was the biggest in the world. The popular term *Bollywood* is just one piece of the puzzle, as filmmaking stretched far beyond Hindi-language film made in Bombay (now Mumbai). In one of the world's biggest and most linguistically diverse countries, separate infrastructure existed for films made in Bengali, Telugu, Tamil, Assamese, Kannada, Malayalam, and more.

While the '50s and '60s were a postcolonial golden age, the '80s are not remembered as a particularly good time for Indian cinema. The era has been described as "the reign of kitsch," with films that are among the worst in the country's history. If Indian cinema had been on top of the world, by most accounts it now went *over* the top.

Still, film remained the country's most cherished art form, and much of this had to do with its widespread use of music to tell and enhance stories. "Masala" cinema took this up a notch. Referring to the complex spice mixtures in Indian cuisine, Masala films mixed genres, combining comedy with action, romance with musical—often with gaudy sets and costume design. These insanely popular, all-things-for-all-people films were the default in Bollywood cinema of the '80s.

A good early example is *Karz* (The Debt [1980]), directed by Subhash Ghai and starring young heartthrob Rishi Kapoor (son of the famous actor-director Raj Kapoor). *Karz* is a supernatural crime thriller (with music) in which a devious new bride murders her wealthy husband to inherit his fortune. Alas, the man's soul is reincarnated into the body of a young disco star who falls in love with her daughter. One of the film's highlights is the hit song "Om Shanti Om," in which Kapoor spins on a giant turntable, backed by calypso-inspired dancers.

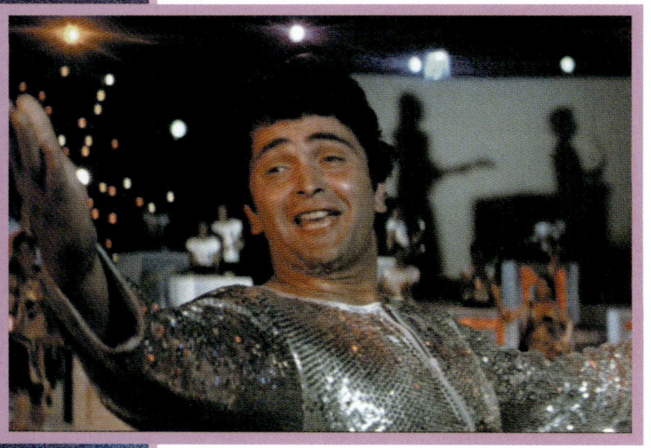

Rishi Kapoor's performance of "Om Shanti Om" in *Karz* was an iconic moment in '80s Bollywood.

Bollywood's disco mania is further revealed in *Disco Dancer* (1982), a so-bad-it's-good film about a young man who becomes a pop star in his quest to avenge his mother's humiliation by a ruthless businessman. Its aspirational view of India made it a major hit at home, and it was even a success abroad. (It became one of the all-time top grossers in the Soviet Union.)

Bollywood actors are often required to dance but not to sing. Since the '40s, they have been dubbed by "playback performers" who often become huge stars in their own right. One example is Kishore Kumar, who performed for both *Karz* and *Disco Dancer*.

In the '80s there was a palpable level of frustration among the country's first postcolonial generation due to a number of social and political factors. This anxiety was being processed in films that depicted politicians as villains, showed gratuitous on-screen violence, and featured vigilante heroes who took on corruption. The film *Mard* (1985) is a good example. *Mard* translates roughly to "real man," and the film opens with the hero (Amitabh Bachchan) lassoing an airplane full of British soldiers who have just looted an Indian fort.

Bachchan had become hugely popular for portraying "angry young men," and his star power threatened to take precedence over his various film roles. In 1982, while filming *Coolie*, his character was meant to die at the finale. When Bachchan suffered a serious intestinal injury performing a stunt and was hospitalized, the outpouring of support from his fans led to a change in the film's script. The hero now survives at the end, and the moment of the on-screen injury is marked by a title card. Bachchan even appears as himself to thank the audience.

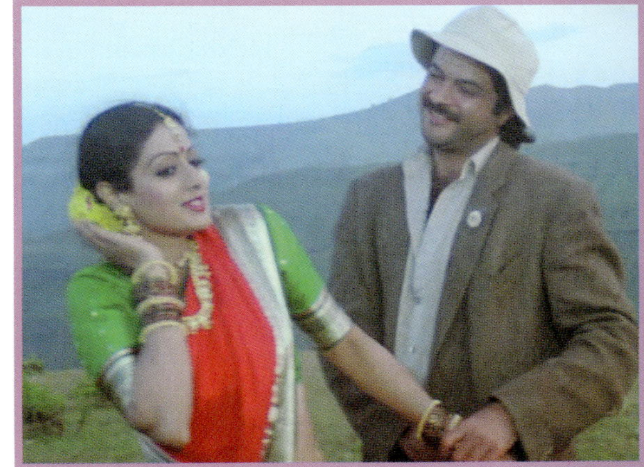

Sridevi and Anil Kapoor fall in love in *Mr. India*.

One part that Bachchan turned down went to Anil Kapoor, a member of the Kapoor film dynasty. His character in the superhero film *Mr. India* (1987) is a humble young man who finds a gadget that makes its wearer invisible. He uses this new power to solve crimes and finds himself pitted against a supervillain (notable Bollywood villain actor Amrish Puri) with plans for world domination. The film was directed by Shekhar Kapur, who would go on to fame in British cinema, with playback music by Kishore Kumar. Anil Kapoor later starred in the gangster film *Parinda* (Bird [1989]), a film that has been compared to Martin Scorsese's *Mean Streets* (1973) because of its

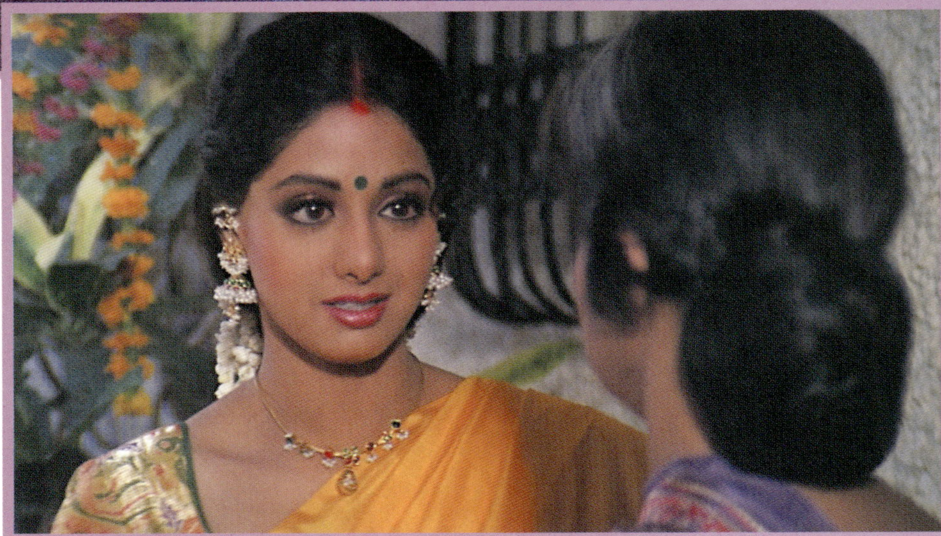

Sridevi as Chandni Mathur in *Chandni.*

conflicted protagonist and expressionist vision of Mumbai as a dark, mysterious city.

The female love interest in *Mr. India* was played by Sridevi, a Tamil star who broke out in Bollywood with the revenge comedy *Himmatwala* (The Brave One [1983]) and performed a famous on-screen snake dance in the romance fantasy *Nagina* (1986). She later starred in the hit romance *Chandni* (Moonlight [1989]), which had the highest-selling soundtrack album of the decade, and the drama *ChaalBaaz* (Trickster [1989]), in which she plays a dual role of identical twins who were separated at birth and raised in different economic conditions—one into a wealthy family, the other into poverty.

Hindi cinema covered a variety of genres. *Chandni* had been directed by Yash Chopra, who was famous for stylish romances like *Silsila* (Continuation [1981]), the story of an extramarital affair that he shot in Amsterdam with Amitabh Bachchan. *Jaane Bhi Do Yaaro* (Just Let It Go, Friends [1983]) was a hit comedy inspired by Michelangelo Antonioni's *Blow-Up* (1966) that satirized bureaucratic corruption in politics, media, and business.

Just as in the United States, teen films had been making a splash since the early '70s, with the template set by director Raj Kapoor's popular *Bobby* (1973). Notable '80s examples are *Rocky* (1981), directed by Sunil Dutt and starring his son, Sanjay Dutt, as a carefree young man who learns the truth about his father's past, and the *Romeo and Juliet*–inspired *Qayamat Se Qayamat Tak* (From Apocalypse to Apocalypse [1988]), known simply as *QSQT*, which starred actual teenagers who fall in love despite their families' sworn animosity.

Women were directing films in Bollywood, too. Writer-director Sai Paranjpye had successes with *Sparsh* (Touch [1980]), about the romance between a blind man and a young widow, and *Chashme Buddoor* (May You Be Saved from the Evil Eye [1981]), a slice-of-life comedy about friends and young romance in Delhi.

More familiar to Western viewers is director Mira Nair, who trained as a documentarian in the United States and was a protégé of D. A. Pennebaker. The Odisha-born Nair frequently returned to her home country to shoot nonfiction films like *India Cabaret* (1984), which explored Mumbai strip clubs and the sexual exploitation of women. *Salaam Bombay!* (1988) focuses on a group of street urchins attempting to survive under harsh conditions in the city slums. It was made as a fiction film so that Nair could stop doing "hit and run" pieces (as she called them) and instead see through a complete story with urban street dwellers, controlling the action, pacing, and emotion. The film screened at the 1988 Cannes Film Festival and won the prestigious Camera d'Or, an award honoring the best debut feature.

The term *parallel cinema* has been adopted to refer to Indian cinema that lies outside the mainstream in both form and subject. Such films are typically nonmusical and depict diverse cultural subgroups. Inspired by Italian neorealism, this movement began in earnest with the 1950s films of celebrated Bengali filmmaker Satyajit Ray, who was still directing in the '80s. His elevated stature meant that his historical drama *The Home and the World* (1984), set during the Swadeshi independence movement, not only played in competition at Cannes, but also received distribution in the United States.

Defining socialist-realist cinema in West Bengal was director Mrinal Sen's *Akaler Sandhane* (In Search of Famine [1981]), about the man-made Bengal famine of 1943. Actress turned director Aparna Sen (no relation) made award-winning films in the 1980s, starting with her debut, *36 Chowringhee Lane* (1981), a primarily English-language drama about a lonely Kolkata woman whose one passion is teaching Shakespeare.

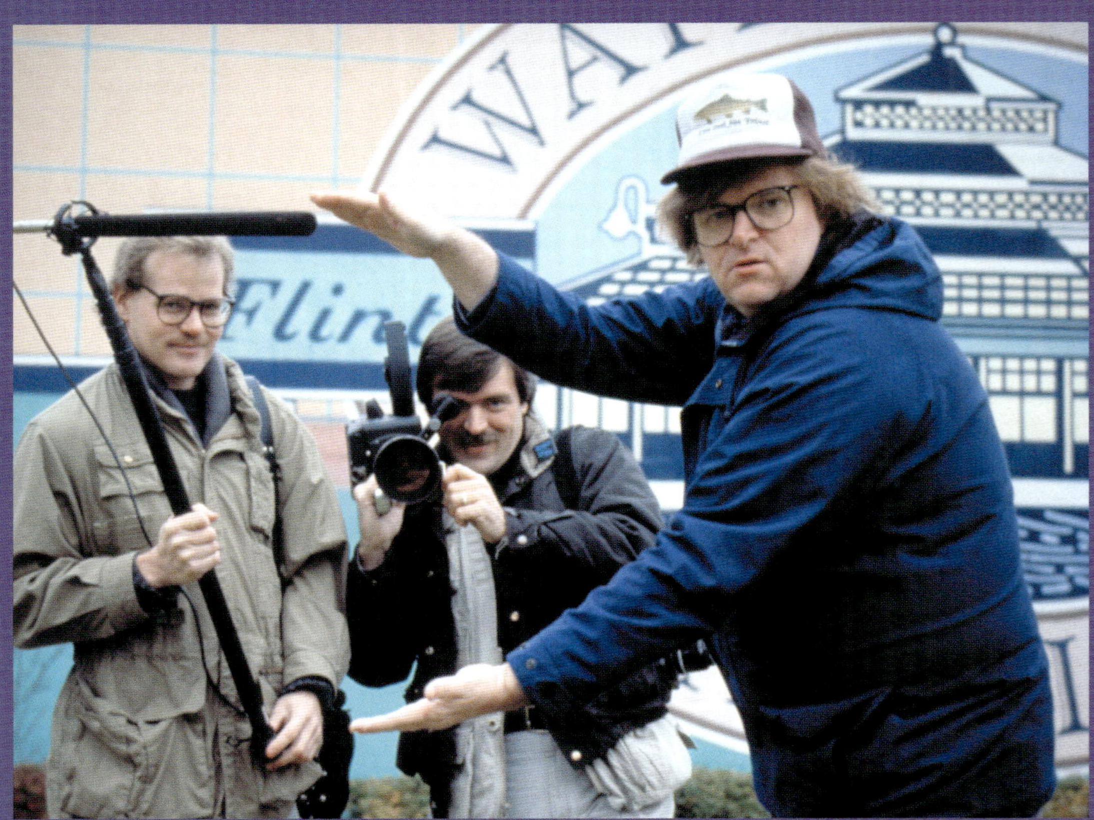

Roger & Me

The DOCUMENTARY SECTION

While fiction filmmakers were navigating new trends in entertainment and a rapidly changing industry, nonfiction filmmaking continued to reveal the world at large through compelling you-can't-make-this-up stories from the past and present. Documentaries of the era spanned a variety of genres, from vérité to found footage, concert films and experimental pieces. (The latter topics are covered in more depth in other chapters.) Some filmmakers doubled as investigators, like Errol Morris or Lee Grant. Some, like Wim Wenders, were in awe of their cinematic subjects. Others were blatantly satirical in the name of public service, like Michael Moore. Many developed personal authorial styles, and a few even became household names, like historian Ken Burns.

The best of these movies united their audience in celebration or remembrance—from programs like the Apollo space missions to humanitarian causes like the AIDS Memorial Quilt—and many pushed for important social changes. The list below is a sample of the most noteworthy nonfiction films of the '80s.

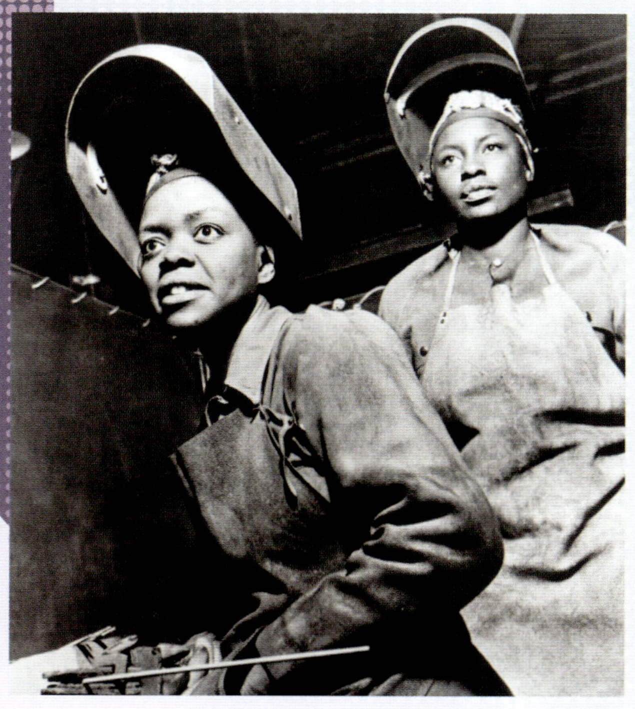

The Life and Times of Rosie the Riveter examined America's progressive workforce during WWII.

The Life and Times of Rosie the Riveter (1980)

This look at women industrial workers during World War II engages in what director Connie Field called the "oral history" tradition of documentary. Made during the heyday of the women's movement in America, it follows five different "Rosies" who recount their service and their return to domestic life after the war, as well as the struggles of racial integration in wartime factories, all of which is contrasted with the official propaganda of contemporary newsreels. Field had received partial funding from the National Endowment for the Humanities, which soon stopped sponsoring politically oriented documentaries in the conservative political climate of the '80s.

Brooklyn Bridge (1981)

Ken Burns, the most popular documentarian of American history, chose as the subject of his first movie this incredible feat of civil engineer-

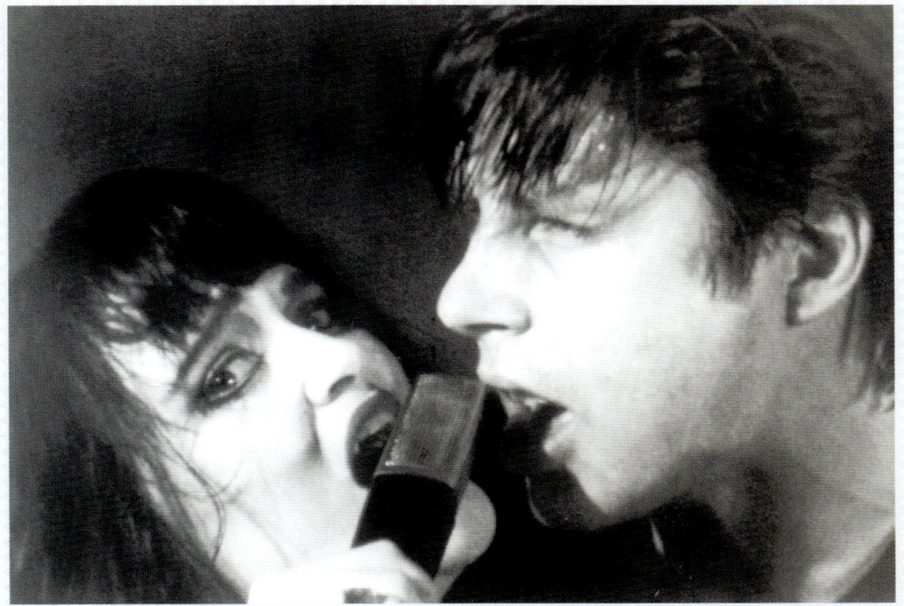

Exene Cervenka and John Doe, members of the band X, in *The Decline of Western Civilization.*

ing. He utilizes what is now a trademark effect of gliding the camera across still photographs, complemented by voice-over narration by historian David McCullough and actors (like Julie Harris) who read primary sources in character. "It was very difficult to convince people that it would be interesting if it was more than ten minutes," said Burns. "And the fact that I was doing an hour, people laughed at me." The film earned an Oscar nomination for Best Documentary Feature, as did his 1985 film *The Statue of Liberty*.

The Decline of Western Civilization (1981)

Self-described "rock and roll anthropologist" Penelope Spheeris set out to explore the musical and social movement known as "punk" in the late 1970s, resulting in this landmark look about the LA rock scene—the first in a trilogy. Her background in music videos (she owned the production company Rock 'n Reel) prepared her to interact with bands like the Circle Jerks and X. The film's distribution was spotty. "Theater owners would laugh at you when you'd call a chain and said 'documentary,'" she explained. After the first screenings in LA caused a public disturbance, the chief of police demanded she stop showing the film. "In good punk rock spirit, I told the man to fuck off and went ahead and did it anyway."

Burden of Dreams (1982)

Documentarian Les Blank followed German director Werner Herzog to the rainforests of Peru to chronicle the troubled shoot of his historical adventure *Fitzcarraldo* (1982). Herzog's film tells the story of an Irish opera lover (Klaus Kinski) who hires the local indigenous population to transport a steamship over a ridge of land to access a valuable parcel of rubber trees.

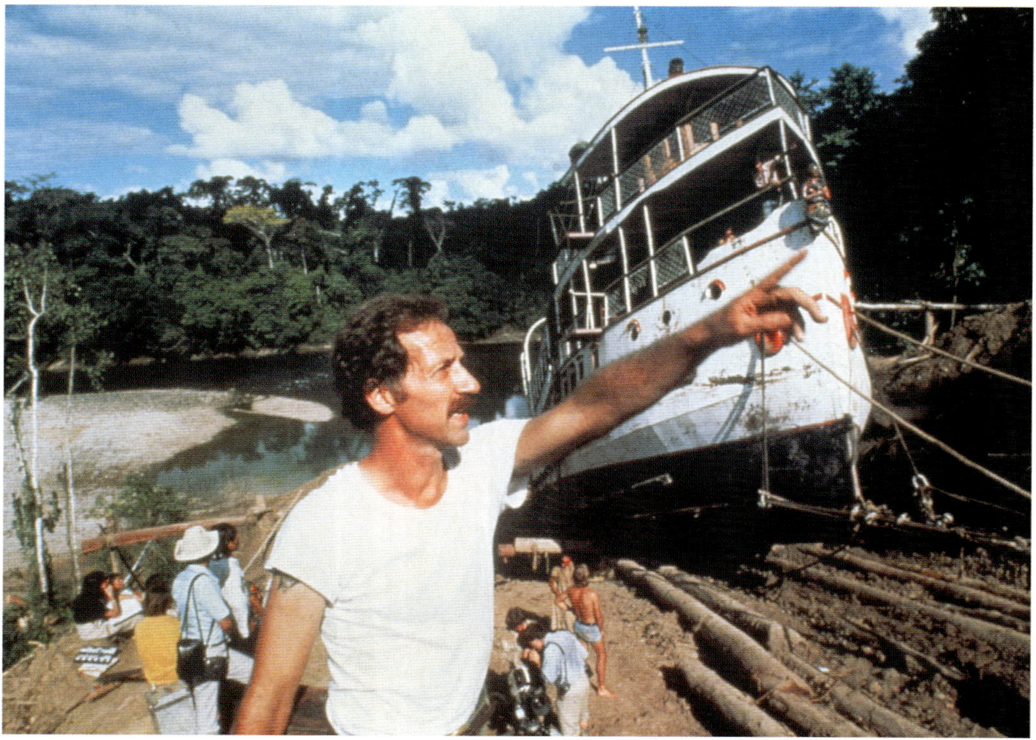

Werner Herzog on location for *Fitzcarraldo* in *Burden of Dreams*.

Problems with filming arose early and often, from hostile natives and bouts of dysentery to historically low water levels. Blank, who made several engrossing vérité-style documentaries in the '80s like *Garlic Is as Good as Ten Mothers* (1980) and *Gap-Toothed Women* (1987), captured indelible footage of Herzog waxing philosophic. "We are challenging nature itself, and it hits back. . . . Nature here is vile and base," he said. "I shouldn't make movies anymore. I should go to a lunatic asylum."

Style Wars (1983)

This early look at hip-hop culture in New York follows several young graffiti artists from a variety of racial and ethnic backgrounds who use subway trains as their own personal canvases. It also charts opposition to graffiti by politicians like mayor Ed Koch, who cites street art as a "quality-of-life offense" punishable by jail time. For a city that not long before had narrowly skirted bankruptcy, beset by rising crime and a crack epidemic, graffiti—along with attendant break-dancing and rap—was a democratizing creative outlet that allowed average citizens to have a voice in their urban jungle.

Marlene (1984)

Legendary actress and singer Marlene Dietrich recorded forty hours of audio interviews for this film about her life and career, resulting in one of the most candid portraits of a movie star ever made. Directed by Maximilian Schell, Dietrich's costar from *Judgment at Nuremberg* (1961), the film draws out blunt pronouncements from the performer about her time in Hollywood ("I was an actress. I made films. Period.") and peers like Fritz Lang ("a monster"). The lasting impression is one of a strong-minded artist, fully in control of her public image.

Streetwise (1984)

Seattle had recently been heralded "the most livable city in America" when photojournalist Mary Ellen Mark went there for a story on homeless youth for *Life* magazine. After befriending several of the kids, she suggested to her husband (director Martin Bell) that they would make compelling subjects for a documentary. The film follows fourteen-year-old Tiny, a victim of a broken home who makes money as a sex worker, and her friend Rat, who explains the ins and outs of street survival like petty theft, blood donations, and squatting in abandoned buildings. The crushing reality of their situation soon becomes clear. "This kind of desperate choice to live on the street, as bad as it may be," said editor Nancy Baker, "is not as bad as being at home."

The Times of Harvey Milk (1984)

San Francisco city supervisor Harvey Milk, the first openly gay elected official in California history, saw himself as part of a movement. His assassination in 1978, along with that of mayor George Moscone, served to galvanize

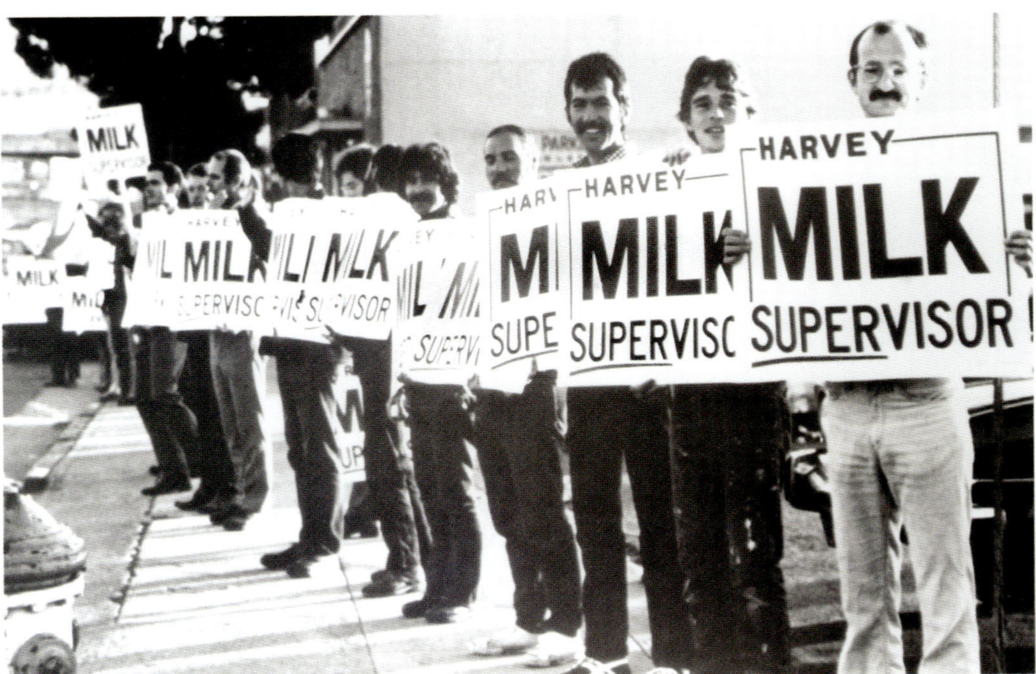

The Times of Harvey Milk explored the legacy of the trailblazing San Francisco politician.

a community who revere him today as a trailblazer and icon. "The film was never intended to be biographical," said director Rob Epstein. "We really saw it as telling Harvey's story for his symbolic value and the fact that he represented something about the times in which he lived." Through moving interviews and archival footage, it documents the heroic struggle of gay Americans for public acceptance and legal protections.

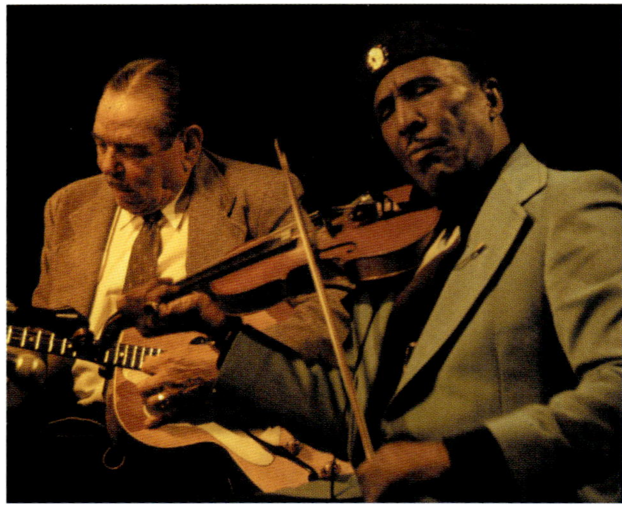

Ted Bogan and Howard Armstrong in *Louie Bluie*.

28 Up (1984)

Michael Apted's *Up* series is an extraordinary documentary project, a decades-long record of the lives of more than a dozen British men and women who—every seven years—sit down for candid check-ins with the director. This fourth installment shows the subjects in their late twenties, after many of them have started careers and begun to raise a family. Their life choices diverged wildly—Paul sold all his possessions and traveled the Australian Outback, Lynn became a children's librarian, and Neil drifted around the United Kingdom—but many had achieved stability. Admirer Roger Ebert found the changes wrought by time deeply thought-provoking. "Do we, even now, contain within us our own personal destinies for the next seven years?" he asked. "Is change possible?"

Louie Bluie (1985)

Long before his breakout films *Crumb* (1994) and *Ghost World* (2001), music lover Terry Zwigoff made this portrait of country-blues string player and folk artist Howard "Louie Bluie" Armstrong and his musical partner, guitarist Ted Bogan. Intending only to write an article about Armstrong, Zwigoff found himself inspired by his subject's charm and salty humor and decided to try his hand at filmmaking instead. "I was very naive about the whole thing," he recalled. The film broke with tradition by discussing the sexuality that flows through music, including a memorable scene with Armstrong's homemade book of pornography. "All the other films about the blues I'd seen tended to be rather sanitized in that way, so I think I sort of over-compensated."

Shoah (1985)

Claude Lanzmann's eleven-year labor of love is one of the most monumental feats of cinema in the '80s, a nine-and-a-half-hour film made up of dozens of interviews with survivors (and some perpetrators) of the Holocaust. Even at its great length, it only scratches the surface of Nazi atrocities at extermination camps in Poland and the Warsaw Ghetto. The film relies fully on eyewitness testimony and modern-day footage, purposefully using no archival images or narration. "Making a history was not what I wanted to do," said Lanzmann. "I wanted to construct something more powerful than that." The completed film, shown theatrically in two parts screened over consecutive days, was quickly heralded as an essential record of a great moral tragedy.

16 Days of Glory (1985)

Bud Greenspan was already an award-winning sports documentarian when he produced his landmark record of the 1984 Olympic Games in Los Angeles—the first of seven official Olympics films he would make during his career. He used multiple crews in the months leading up to the Games to capture footage of the athletes as they trained at home, sparking a deeper emotional investment in viewers. "I'm a storyteller," he explained. "I find the goodness in people, and I present them as people first and athletes second." Highlights include gold-medal wins by American gymnast Mary Lou Retton and British decathlete Daley Thompson. The film *16 Days of Glory* has appeared at various running times, maxing out as a 284-minute miniseries that aired on PBS in July 1988.

Tokyo-Ga (1985)

German director Wim Wenders traveled to the Japanese capital to film this tribute to classical director Yasujiro Ozu. Tokyo was the filmmaker's home city and the setting for a collection of movies that Wenders called "a sacred treasure of the cinema." *Tokyo-Ga* is also part travelogue, a personal diary that explores the diverse culture of the city, from pachinko parlors to driving ranges, to plastic food displays in restaurant windows, and the neon blitz of Shinjuku. Wenders meets with Chishū Ryū, the lead actor of many of Ozu's beloved films, who shares his personal reflections on the director and his working methods. Together they visit Ozu's grave in Kamakura—its headstone inscribed with a single bittersweet message, "emptiness," that suggests the creative potential in everything.

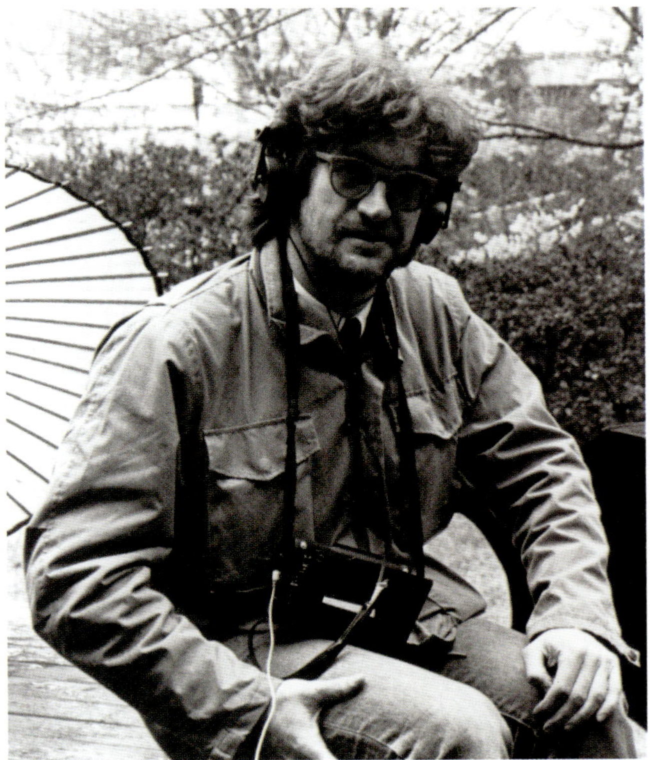

Wim Wenders, director of *Tokyo-Ga*, on location.

Down and Out in America (1986)

Oscar-winning actress Lee Grant directed and narrated this examination of economic disparity in America, which itself won the Oscar for Best Documentary Feature. Visiting with struggling Minnesota farmers and homeless Angelenos living in a makeshift tent city, she identifies the myriad ways in which the nation's promise of a bright egalitarian future isn't living up to its word. For a self-described "city girl" like Grant, the cross-country odyssey she undertook with the film was a revelation. "The making of documentaries. . . . This is what educates me. I feel privileged to have gone on these journeys."

Sherman's March (1986)

Ross McElwee's personal odyssey through history is subtitled "A Meditation on the Possibility of Romantic Love in the South During an Era of Nuclear Weapons Proliferation." Rather than focusing on his ostensive subject—General Sherman's 1864 March to the Sea—the director and North Carolina native soon turns the camera on former girlfriends to investigate why his love life is in shambles (and how that gives him nightmares about nuclear war). What results is a tapestry of contemporary southern culture—replete with would-be matchmakers, Confederate costume balls, and a run-in with Burt Reynolds—told by a filmmaker who can't seem to put down his camera long enough to enjoy himself. "This is not art—this is life!" says an exasperated female friend. "You've got to be more passionate, Ross."

The Emperor's Naked Army Marches On (1987)

This Japanese documentary is part character study, part historical investigation. It follows World War II veteran Kenzō Okuzaki as he tracks down those responsible for the unexplained deaths of two of his fellow soldiers in New Guinea, forty years earlier. Interviewees turn reticent when asked to share details about charges of desertion, execution, and cannibalism. "That I can't do. It was so horrible," says one former soldier. "It would upset everyone." Shown at the

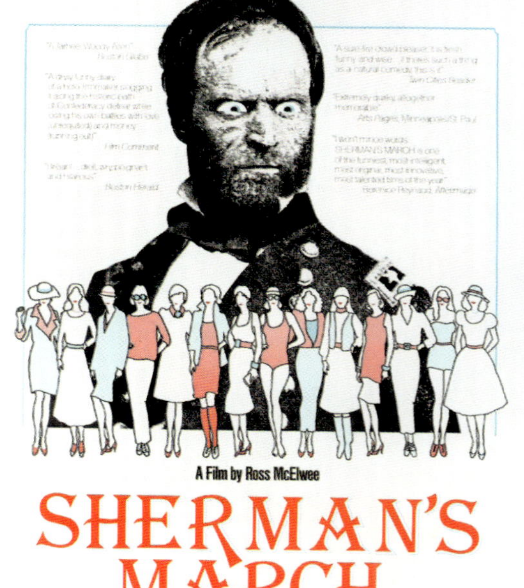

Ross McElwee's revealing documentary *Sherman's March* blazed a trail through his own history.

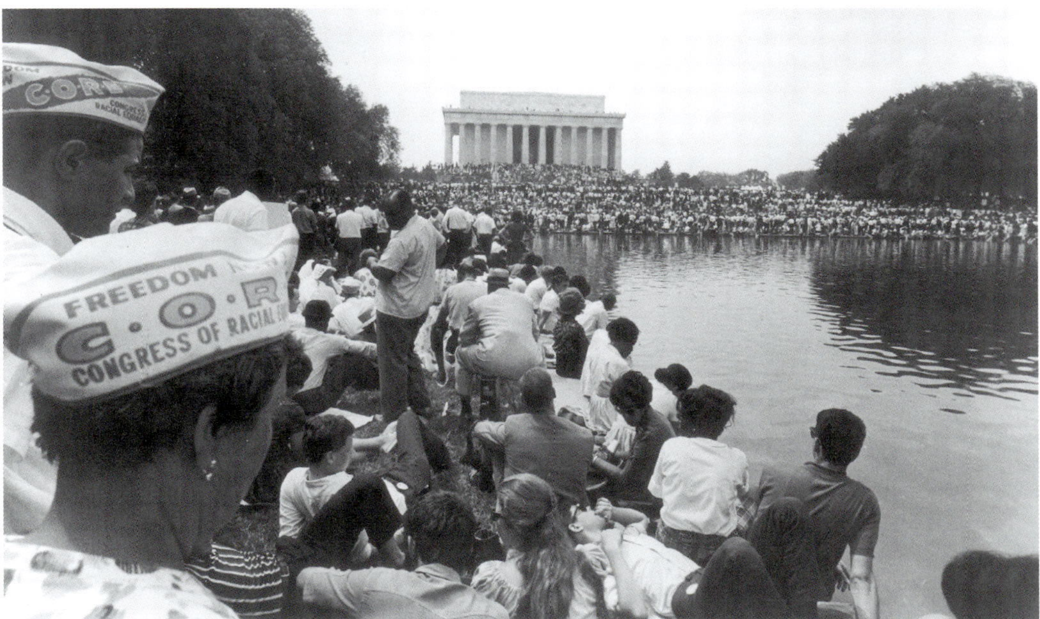

Eyes on the Prize charted the epic story of the civil rights movement in America.

beginning of the film protesting the Japanese emperor, the passionate Okuzaki later gets into physical altercations with some of the participants. He becomes not just a guide through the story, but a subject of the film's thornier examination of the psychological effects of war.

Eyes on the Prize (1987)

Producer Henry Hampton's six-part miniseries on the civil rights era aired on PBS from January to February 1987. Beginning with the 1955 lynching of teenager Emmett Till and ending with the 1965 marches from Selma to Montgomery, the landmark series chronicles the struggle for African American rights over a critical decade. Its production was an enormous undertaking of archival research and oral history, a careful distillation of a voluminous amount of contemporary footage along with new interviews with witnesses and participants, narrated by '60s activist and Georgia state senator Julian Bond. The series' final episode, "Bridge to Freedom," received an Oscar nomination.

Hôtel Terminus: The Life and Times of Klaus Barbie (1988)

French director Marcel Ophuls's epic portrait of a notorious Gestapo officer known as the "Butcher of Lyon" is an involving story of war crimes, corruption, and Cold War espionage. It is the biography of a man said to be personally responsible for the deaths of fourteen thousand people, including major figures in the French Resistance. Barbie was recruited by US intelligence after the war as an anticommunist agent and later shepherded to South America, where he lived under an assumed identity until being tracked down and arrested in 1983. Blessed with a wealth of interview material, Ophuls was able to condense the film down to a

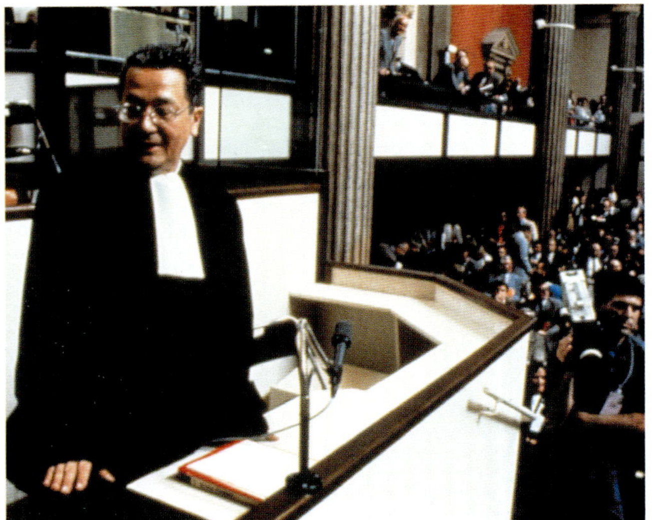

Director Marcel Ophuls put Klaus Barbie on trial in *Hôtel Terminus*.

manageable four and a half hours of sometimes rambling, sometimes infuriating, and often riveting footage.

The Thin Blue Line (1988)

Director Errol Morris set out to make a portrait of the Texas psychiatrist nicknamed "Doctor Death," who often appeared as an expert witness in courtroom trials of dangerous sociopaths. But after interviewing an inmate against whom the doctor had successfully testified, he instead launched into an examination of the crime—the murder of a Dallas police officer—and the man's wrongful conviction. The film exposed holes in the prosecution's arguments and led to the eventual overturning of the case. "Reality is reenacted inside of our skulls routinely—that's how we know about the world," said Morris of the film's controversial use of dramatic reenactments. "I used to be a private detective, years ago. You use everything in an arsenal of tricks to try to figure things out."

Common Threads: Stories from the Quilt (1989)

The AIDS Memorial Quilt was a project launched in 1987 to remember those men and women—both queer and straight Americans—who lost their lives to the epidemic. Rob Epstein and Jeffrey Friedman's moving documentary, narrated by Dustin Hoffman, profiles five individuals who have panels in the quilt through interviews with friends and family. Among them are Olympic decathlete Tom Waddell, intravenous-drug user Robert Perryman, and twelve-year-old hemophilia patient David Mandell Jr. The film also explores the crucial role of activists who raised public awareness and prompted a national response to the crisis, culminating in the unveiling of the quilt on the National Mall in Washington, DC.

For All Mankind (1989)

Texas journalist Al Reinert personally constructed this film over a ten-year period, using official footage shot for NASA's Apollo program and interviews with more than a dozen US astronauts who traveled to the moon between December 1968 and November 1972. Each of the men had been equipped with a 16mm camera during his flight, which led to a cumulative six million feet of film that Reinert discovered in storage at the Johnson Space Center in Houston. He painstakingly enlarged the frames, conducted new interviews, and layered on an atmospheric score by Brian Eno to create a mesmerizing and inspiring story of human endeavor.

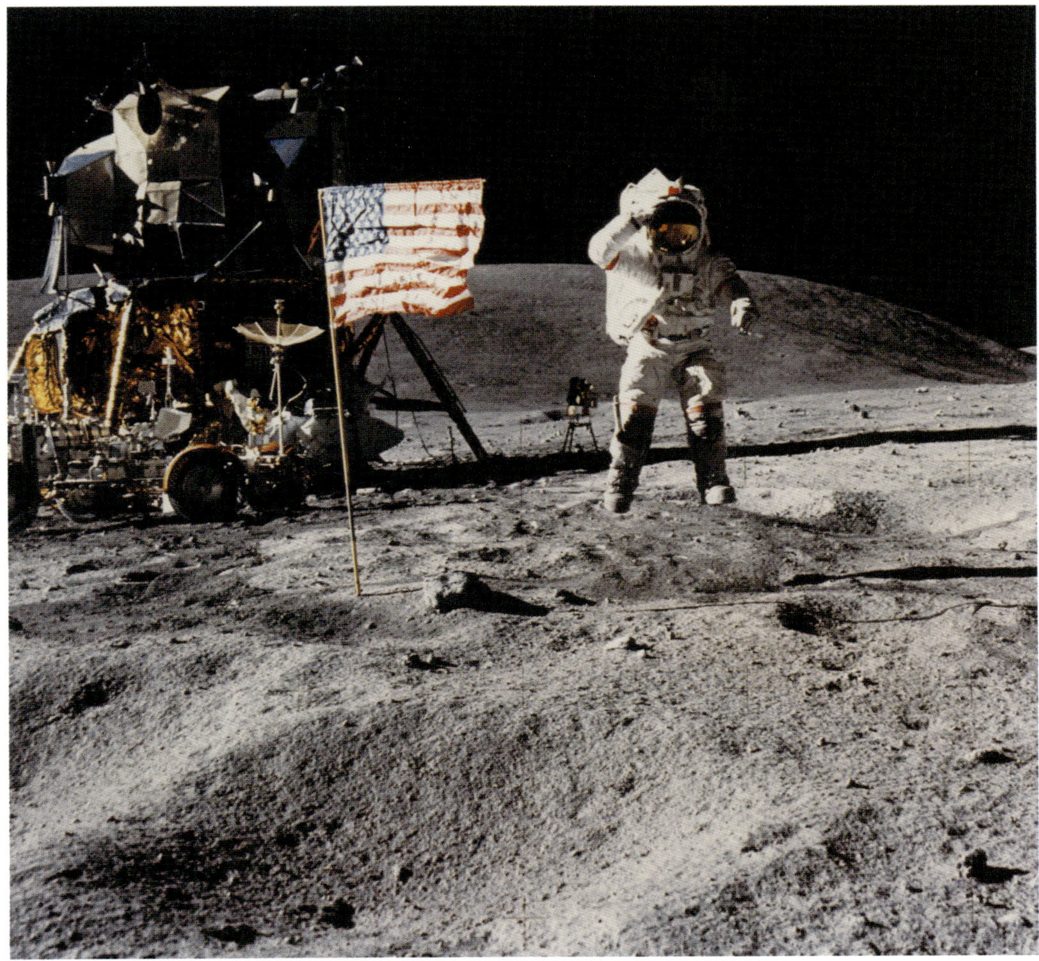

Mountains of archival footage was used to construct *For All Mankind*.

Roger & Me (1989)

In response to the closing of a General Motors plant in Flint, Michigan, local journalist Michael Moore sets off with the goal of interviewing GM chairman Roger Smith about the human toll of the company's business decisions. He never gets the answers he seeks, but along the way he meets an assortment of colorful everyday folks who shine a light on this particular corner of America and how the collapse of domestic manufacturing has drastic ripple effects throughout the economy. Though the film was criticized in some circles for its distortions of fact and chronology, it remains first-rate satire and the opening shot of a career in irreverent muckraking.

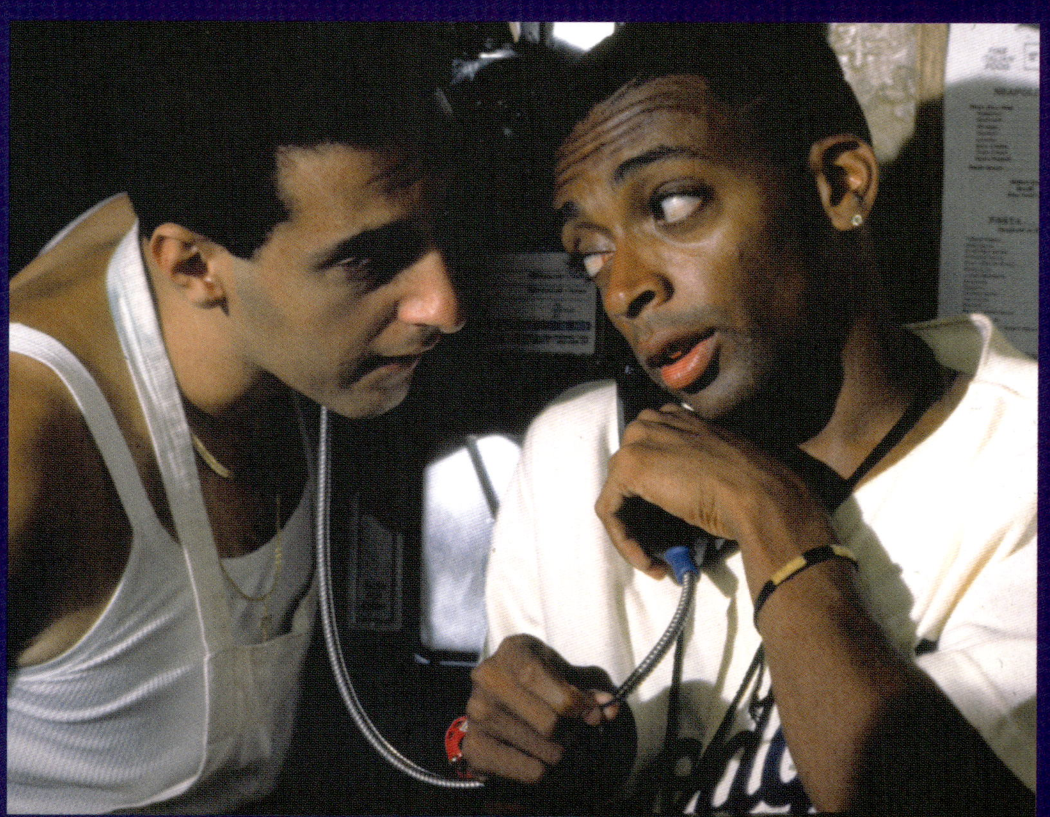

Do the Right Thing

CHAPTER SIX

ALTERNATIVE CINEMA

WHAT HAPPENED TO MAVERICK FILMMAKING IN THE 1980S?

The previous decade had seen a wave of personal stories on-screen, told with urgency and flair, expressing bold opinions on daring subjects—a freedom of expression that was the hallmark of a young generation in the throes of large-scale social change. Now, with Hollywood retreating to the safe harbor of conformity, where a free spirit like Robert Altman could no longer cash a studio check, the baton of cinematic creativity was passed to the lowly, the intrepid, the brave—the independent filmmaker.

Their world was one in which corporate bean counters couldn't suppress originality, where decisions about what to show on-screen were made without regard for sales of Happy Meals or video games, where a tough MPAA rating wasn't a strike against one's potential. It was a parallel industry in which talent didn't answer to studio suits, careers weren't defined by a film's opening weekend, and thinking outside the box was cause for celebration. Independent production wasn't for everyone—many houses were mortgaged in pursuit of dreams—but for those with the skill, the stomach, and a bit of luck, it was the dawn of a new personal cinema.

Yet the term *independent cinema* is imprecise. Industrial independence was nothing new; the classical era saw a lot of small production companies churn out B movies. These included "Poverty Row" operations like Republic and Monogram, where westerns and crime thrillers were made cheaply and quickly, usually with off-brand talent. In the '80s, many movies were still being made separate of major studios, but few would consider, say, *Dirty Dancing* (1987) to be authentically "indie," despite being produced and distributed by Vestron Pictures. In this new era, the idea of an "independent film" conjured up thoughts of aesthetics, not just business models.

The term *alternative cinema* would more aptly describe this broad category of low-budget movies that were thematically and artistically outside the mainstream and represented a diversity of voices and backgrounds. It includes an emerging LGBTQ+ cinema, notable Asian American and African American directors, and even some who rejected narrative filmmaking altogether. Such artists were largely seen as too risky for studio investment—or were themselves opposed to studio interference—and so they forged their own paths.

The '80s were a fertile time for movies that didn't follow the standard Hollywood playbook. A supportive indie-film infrastructure made up of industry groups and film festivals was met with a diversified movie-watching culture that had expanded beyond single-screen theaters to include home video, cable channels, and

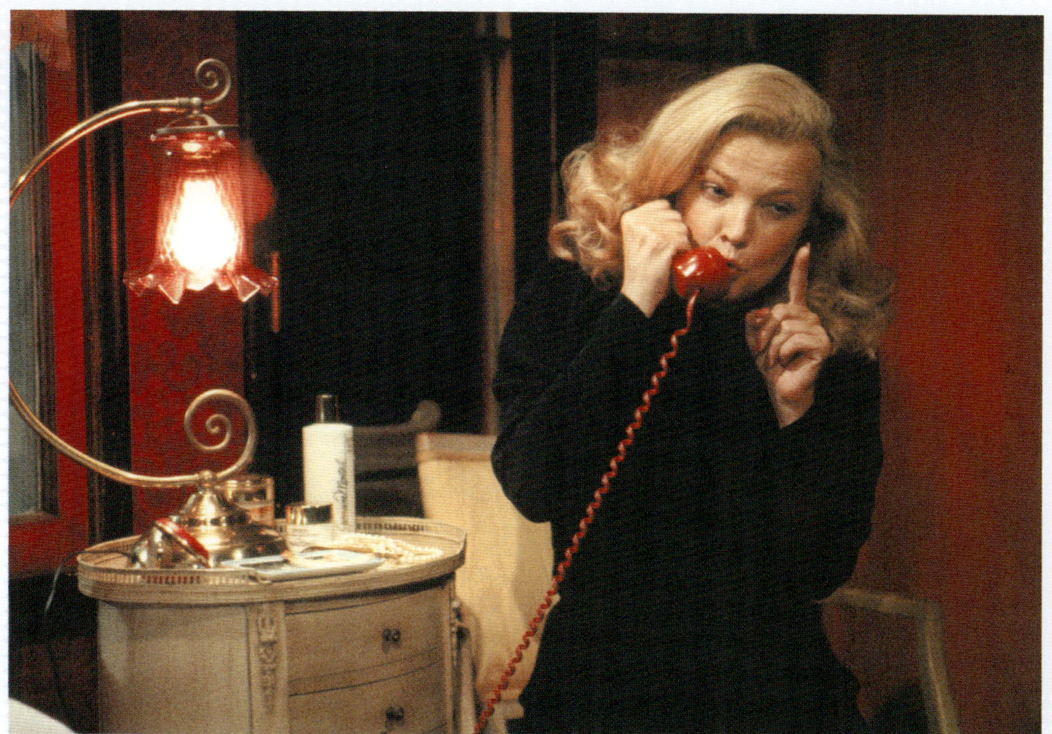

Gena Rowlands in *Love Streams*.

multiplexes that all needed a steady flow of new content. Together, these forces facilitated a rise in alternative filmmaking for audiences hungry for new stories from new storytellers.

Prior to the '80s, only a handful of independent filmmakers had an impact beyond their niche audiences. Most significant of them was writer-director John Cassavetes, whose low-budget films like *Faces* (1968) and *A Woman Under the Influence* (1974) featured compelling dramatic stories about modern relationships. "Referring to John Cassavetes merely as an independent film maker is greatly understating the case," wrote the *New York Times* upon his death in 1989. "He stood as a monument to defiantly single-minded work." He took on acting jobs to fund his filmmaking projects, which he often distributed personally. He answered to no one, and his movies don't fit easily into any defined genre. They are simply his own—the platonic ideal of the American independent film. Ironically, his first film of the '80s—the gangster drama *Gloria* (1980), starring his wife and frequent star, Gena Rowlands—was a Columbia studio project that Cassavetes wrote but hadn't intended to direct. *Love Streams* (1984) was a return to his typical form, the unconventional story of a brother (Cassavetes) and sister (Rowlands) whose tempestuous personal lives lead them to emotional interdependency.

Another filmmaker on the margins of mainstream Hollywood was legendary producer-director Roger Corman, who spent decades making low-budget exploitation films that were purposefully idiosyncratic and iconoclastic. His production companies the Filmgroup and New World Pictures took chances on young directors like Martin Scorsese and Francis Ford Coppola, and later gave rise to '80s auteurs Joe Dante, James Cameron, and Jonathan Demme.

TROUBLES NOW OR LATER

The film career of indie writer-director John Sayles also begins, improbably, with Corman. Sayles was a writer of short stories and novels, like 1975's *Pride of the Bimbos*, who had often envisioned his fiction on the big screen. His first movie gig was the screenplay for Corman's post-*Jaws* (1975) watery horror film *Piranha* (1978), directed by Joe Dante in his solo debut. After a couple more scripts for New World, he was able to save enough money to finance his directorial debut, the ensemble drama *Return of the Secaucus 7* (1980) about a group of old college friends who reunite for a summer getaway. "I had to back up a bit and stop thinking in pictures, as I had been able to do in writing for others, and start thinking in budget," he told the *New York Times*. The Corman films had taught him a core principle of filmmaking: "Talk is cheap, and action is expensive." On *Secaucus 7*, he therefore depended on dialogue to drive the plot forward.

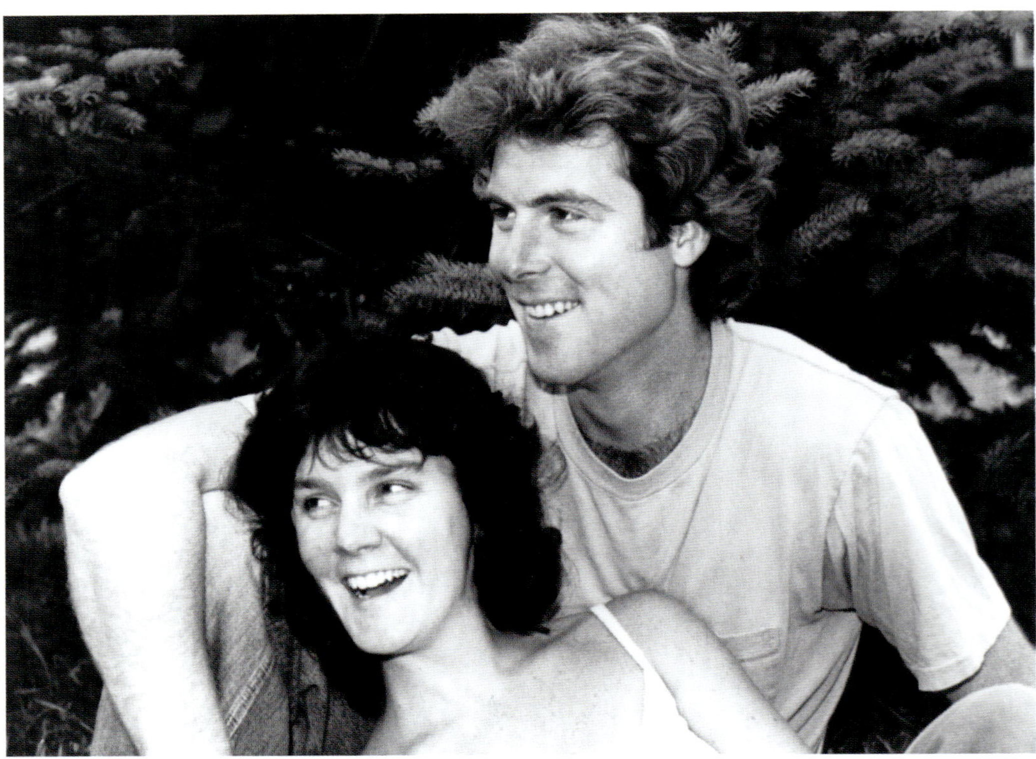

Maggie Renzi and Bruce MacDonald in *Return of the Secaucus 7.*

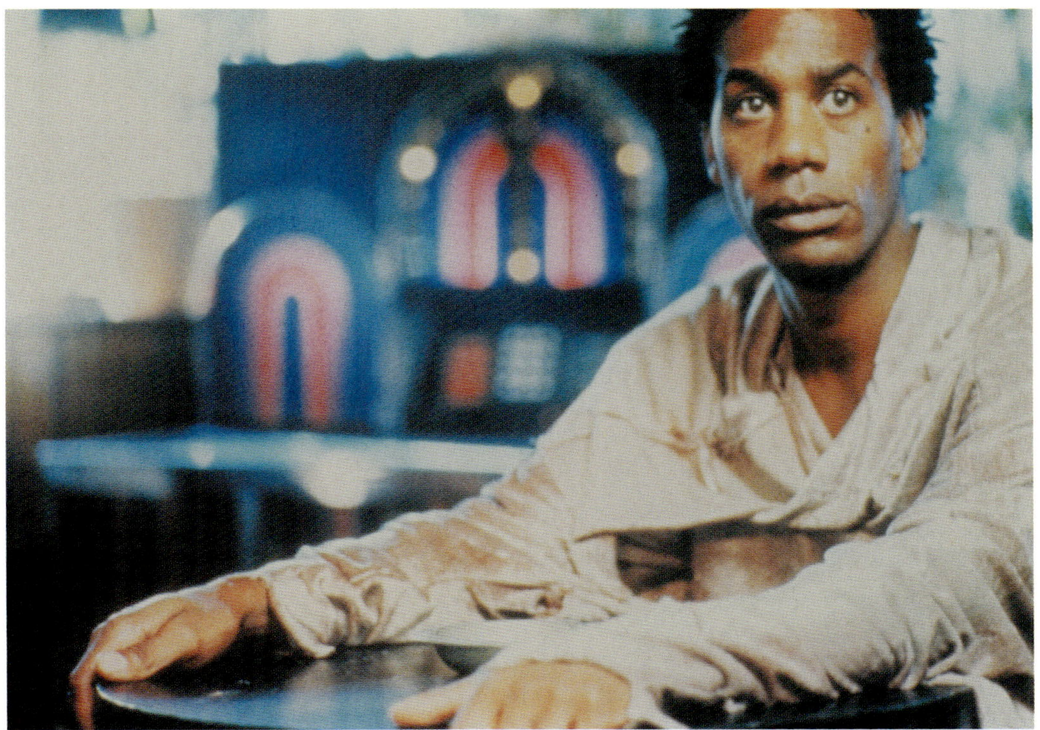

Joe Morton stars in *The Brother from Another Planet.*

Financial limitations led to resourcefulness—like shooting on "short ends," unexposed portions of celluloid at the end of a reel that are discarded when there's not enough length for another take. Sayles was never under the illusion that indie filmmaking would be a walk in the park. Given the choice between full creative control and a studio budget, he saw the choice in simple terms: "Do you want your troubles now or do you want them later?" On the other hand, money sometimes came from unexpected places. In 1983, he was awarded a MacArthur "genius" grant that guaranteed him five years of funding. He also made a trio of music videos for Bruce Springsteen, including "Born in the U.S.A."

The subject matter of his early films is representative of alternative '80s cinema. *Lianna* (1983) depicted a lesbian relationship between a married woman and her college professor, while the sci-fi film *The Brother from Another Planet* (1984) starred Joe Morton as a space alien in the body of a Black New Yorker, a fable of racism. "He may be from another planet, but he's just another immigrant," said Sayles, whose protagonist lands rather pointedly on Ellis Island. Shot in Harlem in March 1984, the white filmmaking team (including producers Maggie Renzi and Peggy Rajski) purposefully hired Black crew members—including cinematographer Ernest Dickerson, who went on to work with Spike Lee. The '60s-set romantic comedy *Baby, It's You* (1983) with Rosanna Arquette was a rare studio-released film that had started life as a project for producers Griffin Dunne and Amy

Robinson, but Sayles's experience with Paramount—which was expecting something akin to a typical teen movie—turned him off from future studio projects.

Perhaps not coincidentally, movies about high-level corruption followed. *Matewan* (1987) dramatized the 1920 coal miners' strike in West Virginia led by a union organizer (Chris Cooper), in which various groups of workers—Italian and Black—were pitted against each other by the mining company. *Eight Men Out* (1988) told the story of the 1919 Chicago White Sox players accused of intentionally losing the World Series while getting exploited by their baseball league. Though the latter film had some high-profile talent—Charlie Sheen, John Cusack, and Christopher Lloyd—and found distribution through Orion, Sayles was experienced enough in the world of filmmaking to keep his ambitions in check. "So many people in film, when they finish one project, they immediately feel they have to do one for more money," he told an interviewer. "I'm glad I'm not hooked into that system. It gives you more freedom."

BUILDING THE INFRASTRUCTURE

The indie scene blossomed in the 1980s thanks in part to the development of organizations designed to nurture talent apart from film schools and studio production. Though mainstream Hollywood was still dominant (a few studios even started their own specialty labels, like Universal Classics in 1983, to distribute indie movies), more and more individual filmmakers were able to find work for themselves and gain recognition outside of the system through the help of upstart institutions. The Independent Filmmaker Project (now the Gotham Film & Media Institute) was founded by producer Sandra Schulberg in 1979 to provide an indie-film market and filmmaker conference alongside the New York Film Festival. "We weren't trying to kill the establishment. We were trying to join the establishment," Schulberg later told the *Hollywood Reporter*.

The Sundance Film Festival dates back to the same era, although it didn't go by that name until 1991. The first "Utah/US Film Festival" took place in September 1978 in Salt Lake City. It had been launched by Sterling Van Wagenen, a Brigham Young University film school graduate, and Utah state film commissioner John Earle with the twin goals of promoting film production in Utah and supporting indie-film talent. Funding was primarily provided by the state film commission, and the inaugural chairman was local Utah resident Robert Redford, who had bought land there in the late '60s. (Redford also happened to be married to Van Wagenen's cousin Lola.) The festival wasn't geared solely toward new films; it also hosted retrospectives and panels about classic American movies.

For its third iteration, the festival dates were pushed to January 1981 to take advantage of ski season in nearby Park City and attract Hollywood types eager for a winter getaway. The festival's increasing focus on independent film was an economic strategy—it was cheaper

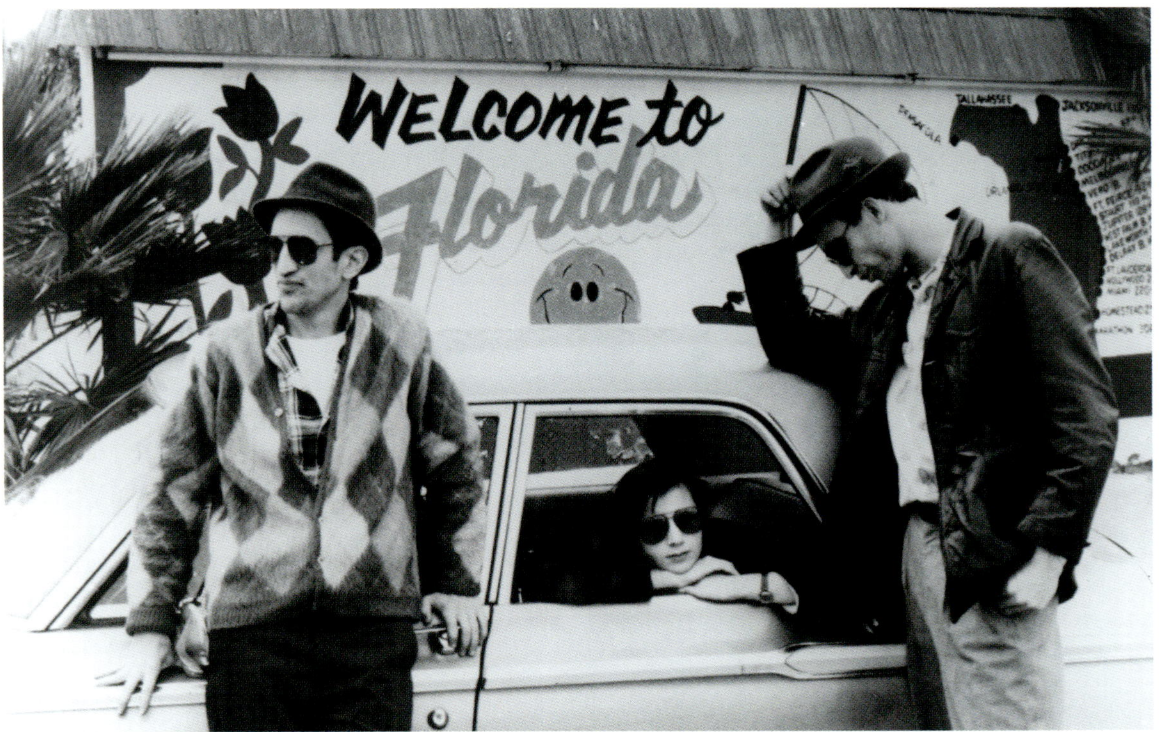

Richard Edson, Eszter Balint, and John Lurie in *Stranger than Paradise*.

to show new movies than to pay rental fees on existing ones. It also experienced a short-lived rebranding as the "US Film and Video Festival" in acknowledgment of the new medium.

Redford's (then unassociated) Sundance Institute was founded in 1981 and featured a "Filmmakers Lab" where aspiring talent would gather each summer to workshop new projects. The institute later took over management of the cash-strapped festival, and the first event under this new arrangement, in January 1985, featured a host of landmark movies: the Coen brothers' *Blood Simple*; Wim Wenders's *Paris, Texas*; the documentary *The Times of Harvey Milk*; Special Jury Prize winner *Stranger than Paradise*; and the opening-night film, *The Trip to Bountiful*, which had been produced by Van Wagenen.

BIG NAMES IN SMALL MOVIES

The beloved filmmaking team Joel and Ethan Coen were Minneapolis-born brothers who studied film (Joel) and philosophy (Ethan) in college before breaking into low-budget film with help from Sam Raimi, whose horror hit *The Evil Dead* (1981) Joel helped to edit. After crafting a screenplay for a crime story, they shot a two-minute trailer that was exhibited to potential investors. By chance, young actor Andrew McCarthy attended one of these fundraising screenings in New York, where he described the novice pair as serious and confident in their work. "A guest asked if something in a particular shot was done on purpose. As Ethan shook his head, Joel looked at him and said, 'There were no accidents.'"

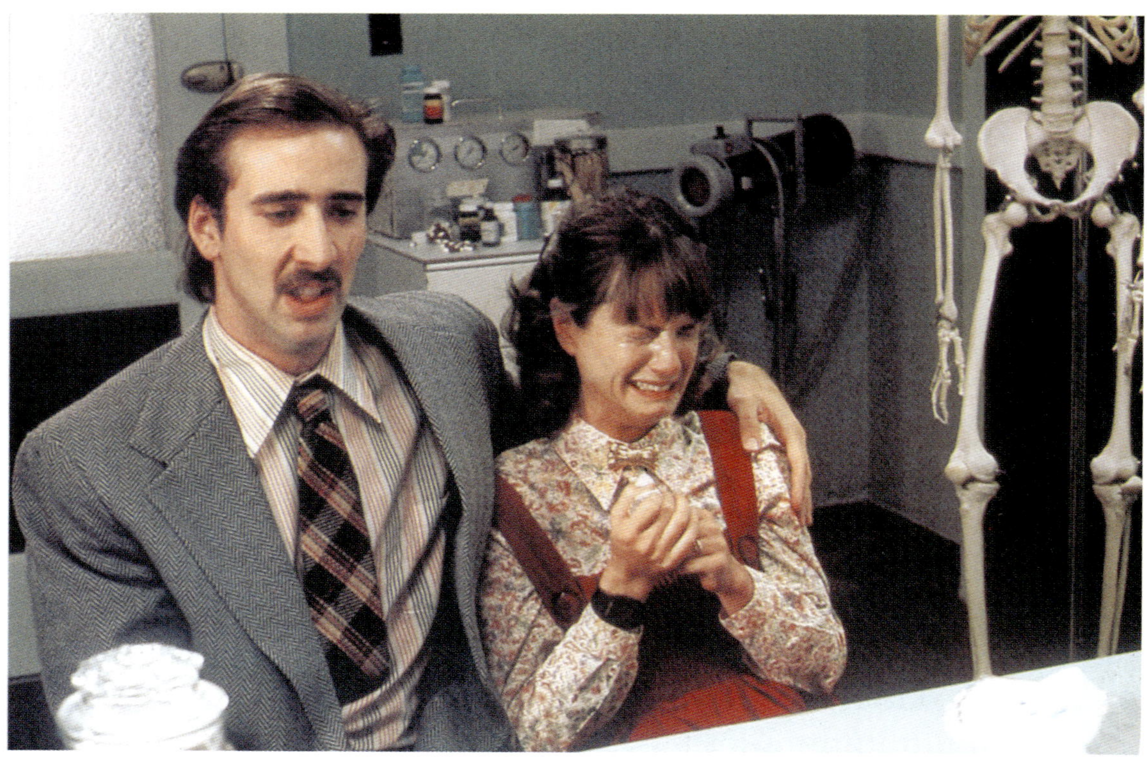

Nicolas Cage and Holly Hunter are desperate for a child in *Raising Arizona*.

They raised the necessary money, storyboarded the entire film in advance, and shot for eight weeks in and around Austin, Texas. *Blood Simple* debuted at the USA Film Festival in Dallas in March 1984, later playing at festivals in Toronto and New York and winning the Grand Jury Prize at Sundance. The brothers signed a three-picture distribution deal with Circle Films, and the film opened in US theaters in January 1985. What these audiences experienced was an indie film that transcended the stylistic limitations that one might have expected from a low-budget film, a gripping and atmospheric neo-noir about a private detective (M. Emmet Walsh) hired to track and murder a Texas bartender (John Getz) and his lover (Frances McDormand), the cheating wife of his boss (Dan Hedaya). In making the detective a villain, the Coens turned a noir trope on its head while playing within the genre's traditions.

Their next film, *Raising Arizona* (1987), was an absurdist comedy and political allegory about poverty, the nuclear family, and the distribution of capital in the Reagan era. It stars Holly Hunter as a prison guard who falls in love with a career criminal played by Nicolas Cage. Unable to have children of their own, they steal and raise one of a rich man's newborn quintuplets—an outrageous premise that fits in well with the film's Road Runner and Coyote vibe.

Another major figure of indie cinema who got his start in the '80s was Jim Jarmusch, whose singular style consisted of a dry wit, collections of offbeat characters, an inclination to dwell in the moment rather than moving the action forward, and an episodic story structure. His early films are evocative of contemporary punk culture, not just in their use of downtown New York music, but in their rejection of storytelling conventions and their lack of pretension. They are notable for their formal simplicity, unhurried pace, and willingness to simmer in traditionally unphotogenic spaces. When asked at the time about his greatest influences, he replied, "the Ramones, because of that sense of purity . . . three chord rock, so simple and minimal."

His New York University film professor, the legendary director Nicholas Ray, brought him along on a documentary being made about his life (*Lightning over Water* [1980]) by Wim Wenders, which resulted in a fruitful relationship with the German filmmaker. (Jarmusch is credited as an "observer.") His time at NYU came to an end when he redirected his scholarship money to make a feature, *Permanent Vacation* (1980), which he tried to submit as a final project. After skipping classes and defaulting on tuition, his registration was canceled and he failed to receive a degree.

Not that it mattered in an industry where "who you know" was paramount. He began shooting his next movie, a short film, with unexposed film stock from Wenders's latest production. Ray had also passed along some noteworthy advice: try to focus on each scene as it's being shot and block out everything else. This suggestion led Jarmusch to design each sequence of what became *Stranger than Paradise* (1984) as a single camera setup—a single shot—thus delineating the work in a helpful way as he was shooting. The film deals with themes of dislocation and alienation, with characters away from home and out of their element, and follows a New Yorker named Willie (John Lurie) whose Hungarian cousin Eva (Eszter Balint) arrives for a brief stay.

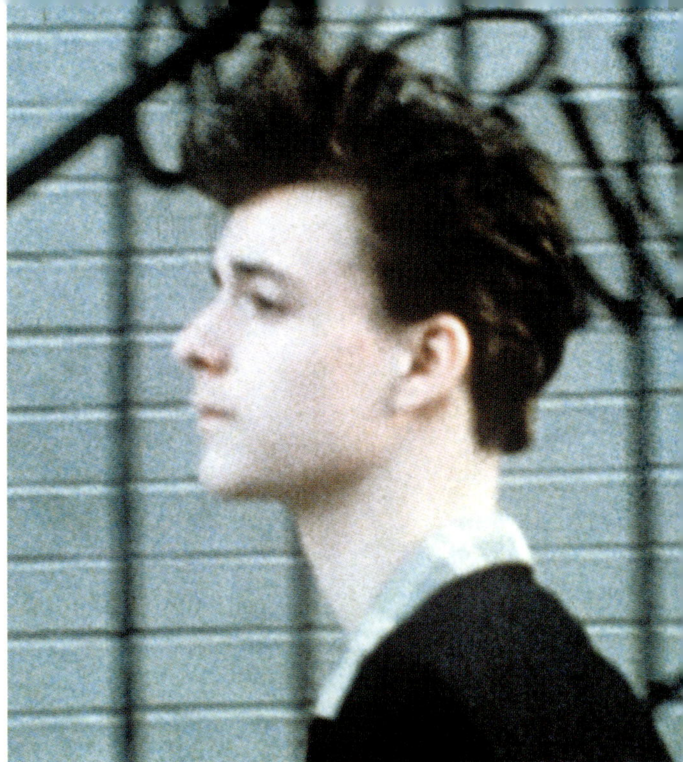

Chris Parker in *Permanent Vacation*.

The short film version of *Stranger than Paradise* played at a few European festivals in 1983 while Jarmusch raised money to expand it into a feature. It ultimately constitutes the first episode (titled "The New World") of a larger three-act structure that sees the characters travel from Brooklyn to Ohio and Florida. Its depiction of the Sunshine State isn't one of picture-postcard beaches but rather bleak black-and-white expanses of sand, ugly

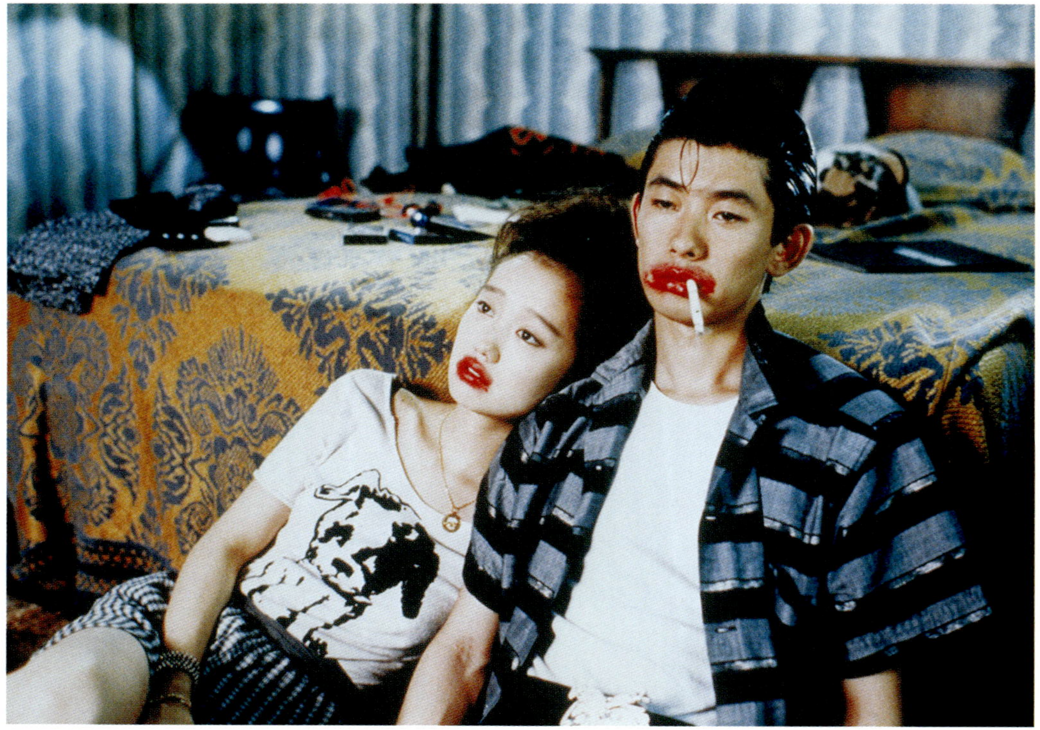

Youki Kudoh and Masatoshi Nagase in *Mystery Train*.

interstate highways, and tacky souvenir shops. "The film has a very kind of pure look or style to it," said the director. "At the time I was really interested in films by Carl Dreyer, or by [Robert] Bresson, or certain filmmakers that did things in a very simple and pure way." The film was a breakthrough with art-house audiences, earning back many times its budget and winning the Camera d'Or at Cannes and the National Society of Film Critics award for Best Film.

His follow-up, *Down by Law* (1986), was also shot in black-and-white, this time by Wenders's collaborator Robby Müller. Set in a New Orleans prison, it stars John Lurie, Roberto Benigni, and Tom Waits as three cellmates who break out together and navigate both the Louisiana bayou and their budding friendship. *Mystery Train* (1989) was another film divided into three parts, with interwoven stories of foreigners—Japanese, Italian, and English—who converge on a rundown Memphis hotel. Though he's clearly a filmmaker at home in low-budget film and possesses a distinct authorial vision, Jarmusch doesn't like putting a label on his work. "I don't know what it means anymore, 'independent films,'" he said years later. "I don't like to be categorized."

One of the decade's biggest indie breakthroughs was *Sex, Lies, and Videotape* (1989) from young director Steven Soderbergh, who had an unsuccessful start in Hollywood before taking a step back and returning home to Baton Rouge, Louisiana. He then wrote a personally resonant screenplay about a couple (Andie MacDowell and Peter Gallagher) who are visited by an old college friend (James Spader), an impotent drifter whose sexual proclivities involve filming women as they describe their erotic experiences. The film was shot in Louisiana and debuted at Sundance, where it won the audience award and ignited a bidding war among distributors. Its appearance at Cannes that May was triumphant: it won the coveted Palme d'Or as well as an acting prize for Spader. "I guess it's all downhill from here," the director quipped during his acceptance speech.

Cult filmmaker John Waters completed two pop culture–related films in the '80s, beginning with the farcical melodrama *Polyester* (1981). The tribute to "women's film" director Douglas Sirk and schlocky showman William Castle was Waters's most elaborate production up to that point—though still budgeted well below $1 million. His frequent star, drag queen Divine, plays unhappy housewife Francine Fishpaw who is married to the unfaithful owner of an adult movie theater and has two disappointing children. She ultimately takes up with the dreamy owner of a local drive-in played by former heartthrob Tab Hunter. The gimmicky appeal of the film was in part due to its use of "Odorama" technology, in which audience members were given scratch-and-sniff cards to use on cue throughout the film. It premiered, appropriately, at a midnight screening at the Cannes Film Festival.

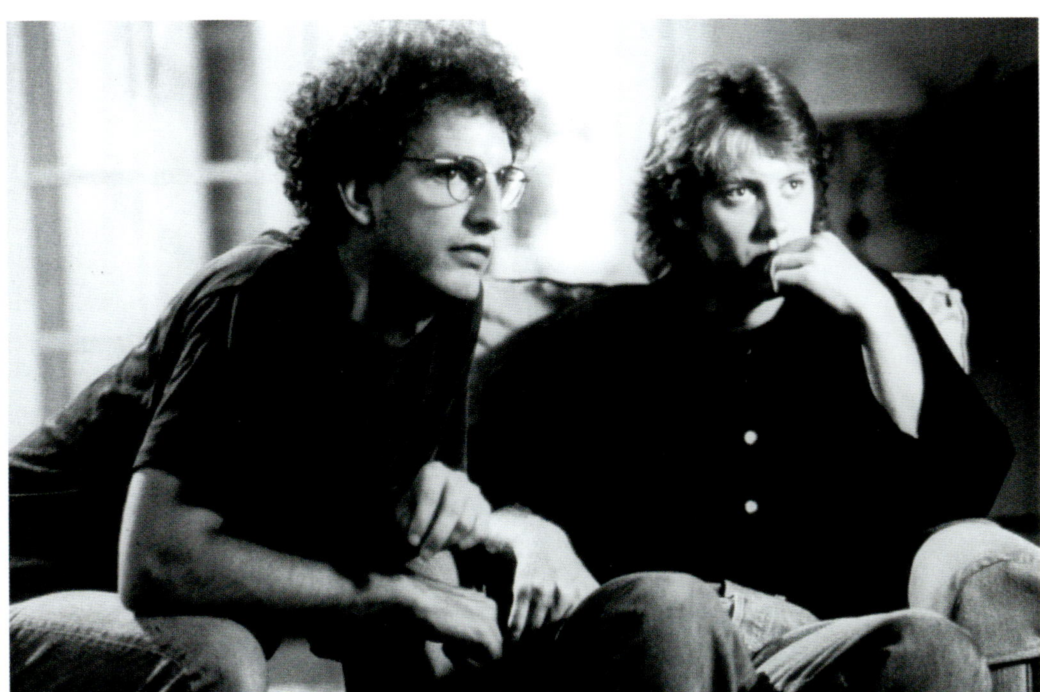

Steven Soderbergh (left) directs James Spader in *Sex, Lies, and Videotape.*

Experimental Cinema

Beyond the world of low budgets, offbeat storytelling, and corrective cultural representation lives a category of cinema that defies all expectations. Experimental film confronts an audience's assumptions of what a "movie" is, often rejecting formal conventions and narrative logic. By doing things differently, they sometimes test our patience and leave us scratching our heads. But several major avant-garde and abstract filmmakers—artists in the truest sense, who don't take the medium's storytelling function as a given—completed major works in the '80s. The selections here barely scratch the surface but are worth seeking out for the adventurous film watcher.

New Orleans–born filmmaker, social activist, and former monk Godfrey Reggio made a pair of wordless documentaries about the imbalance of life on earth. *Koyaanisqatsi* (1982) features fascinating time-lapse photography of modern society set against natural landscapes, while *Powaqqatsi* (1988) mainly uses slow-motion and concerns the developing world—India, Peru, Brazil, Kenya, and Egypt. Both films feature the pulsing rhythms of minimalist composer Philip Glass. (A third film, *Naqoyqatsi*, was released in 2002.) "These films are meant to provoke," said Reggio. "They are meant to offer an experience rather than an idea or information or a story about a knowable or a fictional subject. . . . For some people it's an environmental film. For some people it's an ode to technology. For some people it's a piece of shit. For other people it moves them deeply."

Meanwhile, Ron Fricke—the director of photography on *Koyaanisqatsi*—made the similarly themed *Chronos* (1985), an IMAX film that took a captivating look at the wonders of the world. French filmmaker Chris Marker's essay film *Sans Soleil* (1983) uses letters from a fictional cameraman about his travels in Japan and West Africa as a jumping-off point for an exploration of memory and contemporary society—with detours to the San Francisco of *Vertigo* (1958), an Icelandic volcano, and other locations.

Firmly within the avant-garde world was the celebrated abstractionist Stan Brakhage, who produced indefinable films like the *Arabic Numeral Series* (1981–1982), *The Loom* (1986), and *The Dante Quartet* (1987)—the latter of which involved painting directly onto the celluloid. Jonas Mekas's *He Stands in the Desert Counting the Seconds of His Life* (1986) was a free-flowing portrait of 1960s artists and filmmakers.

Trinh T. Minh-ha's *Reassemblage* (1982) is a collage film about women in Senegal that deconstructs the practice of ethnographic filmmaking. "No Wave" filmmakers Scott B and Beth B made the noir-infused *Vortex* (1982) about a woman (Lydia Lunch) who investigates corporate corruption. James Benning's *American Dreams* (1984) combines a visual series of objects related to baseball legend Hank Aaron with a scrolling narration at the bottom of the screen taken from the diary of the man who shot Alabama governor George Wallace in 1972, forming a conflicting story of masculinity in American culture. Su Friedrich's *The Ties That Bind* (1984) is about her relationship with her German mother, and the sense of transferred guilt that emanates from that nation's role in World War II and the Holocaust. Morgan Fisher's *Standard Gauge* (1985) is a recycled film that shows various strips of 35mm footage collected over the years and serves as a sort of homage to Hollywood filmmaking through its physical material.

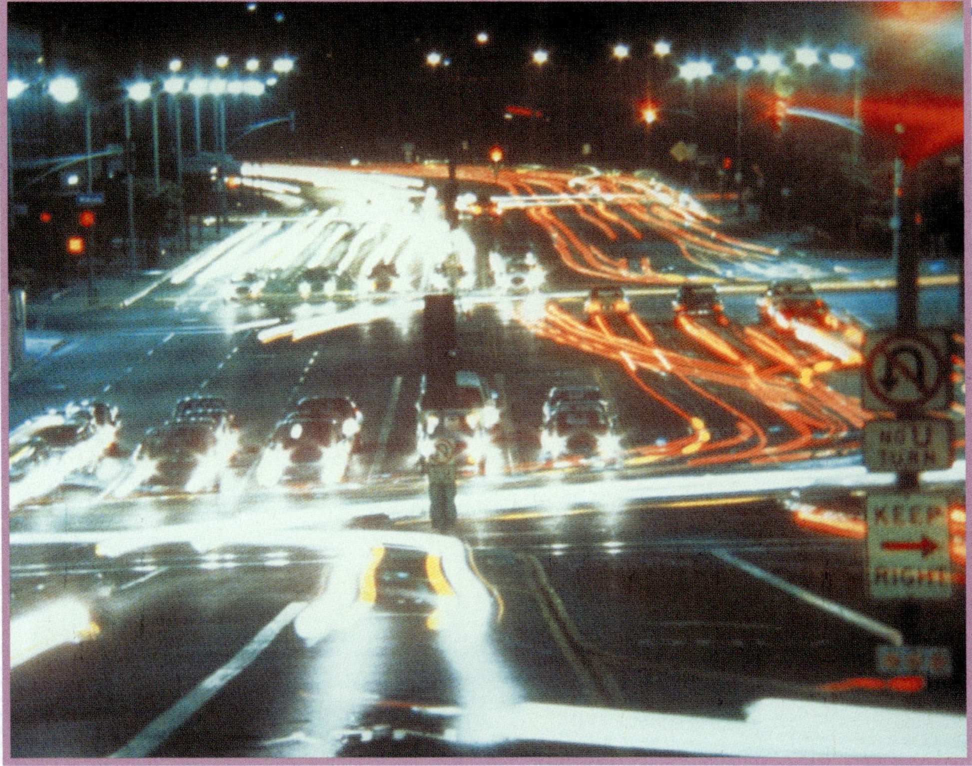

The title of Godfrey Reggio's *Koyaanisqatsi* means "life out of balance" in the Hopi language.

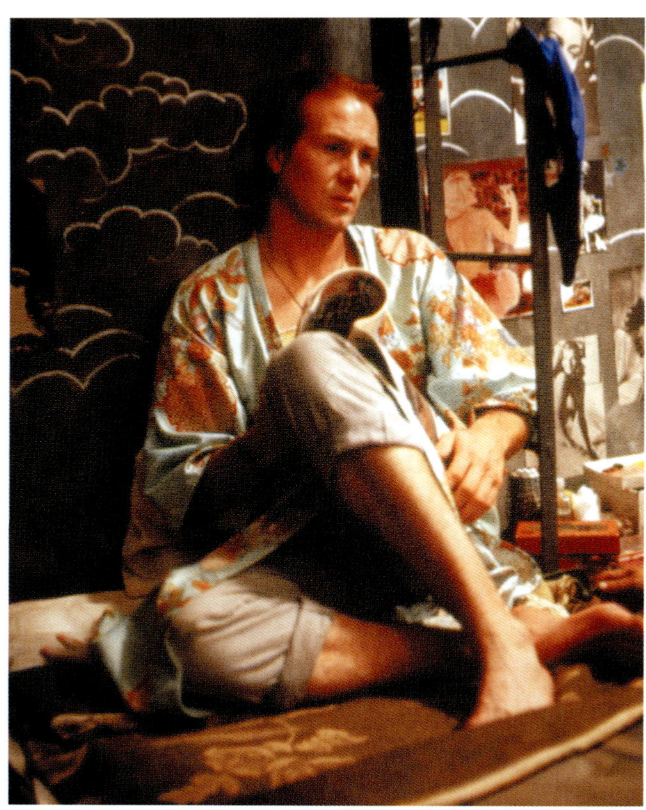

William Hurt in *Kiss of the Spider Woman*.

In *Hairspray* (1988), Divine played the mother of high schooler Tracy Turnblad (Ricki Lake), who dreams of dancing on a popular local-access TV show while also promoting racial equality in 1960s Baltimore. More accessible than Waters's typically outré underground work, it became his most successful movie at the box office; brought him mainstream distribution for his next film, *Cry-Baby* (1990); and was later adapted as a popular Broadway musical (with its own 2007 big-screen version).

Actor and indie filmmaker Paul Bartel had a big hit with *Eating Raoul* (1982), in which he starred with Mary Woronov as an uptight LA couple who attempt to rid their neighborhood of "perverts" by posing as swingers and luring unsuspecting victims to their apartment. The plot devolves—*Sweeney Todd*-like—from serial murder to cannibalism, all wrapped in the blackest of comedies. "The optimistic tale . . . must be an inspiration to anyone who has nagging doubts about the free enterprise system," wrote Vincent Canby, tongue firmly in cheek. "It is full of smiles, punctuated here and there by marvelously unseemly guffaws, but most of the time it works its little wonders quietly."

Hundreds of indie films were distributed in the United States each year, with a few dozen finding distribution through major studios. Nancy Savoca's Bronx-set romantic comedy *True Love* (1989), a Grand Jury Prize winner at Sundance, was picked up by MGM, but a more typical fate befell another Sundance champ, Joyce Chopra's *Smooth Talk* (1985), which got a limited release by International Spectrafilm. Michael Roemer's *Vengeance Is Mine* (1984), with Brooke Adams as a woman torn between her estranged family and neighbors who are similarly fraying at the seams, screened at a couple of film festivals and aired on PBS's *American Playhouse* (where it was retitled "Haunted") but wasn't released theatrically until 2022.

New Yorker Films specialized in foreign fare, including French director Louis Malle's talky English-language film *My Dinner with Andre* (1981). Miramax got its start in the '80s with provocative releases like Lizzie Borden's *Working Girls* (1986); Hal Hartley's debut, *The Unbelievable Truth* (1989); and *Sex, Lies, and Videotape*. New Line Cinema became famous for *A Nightmare on*

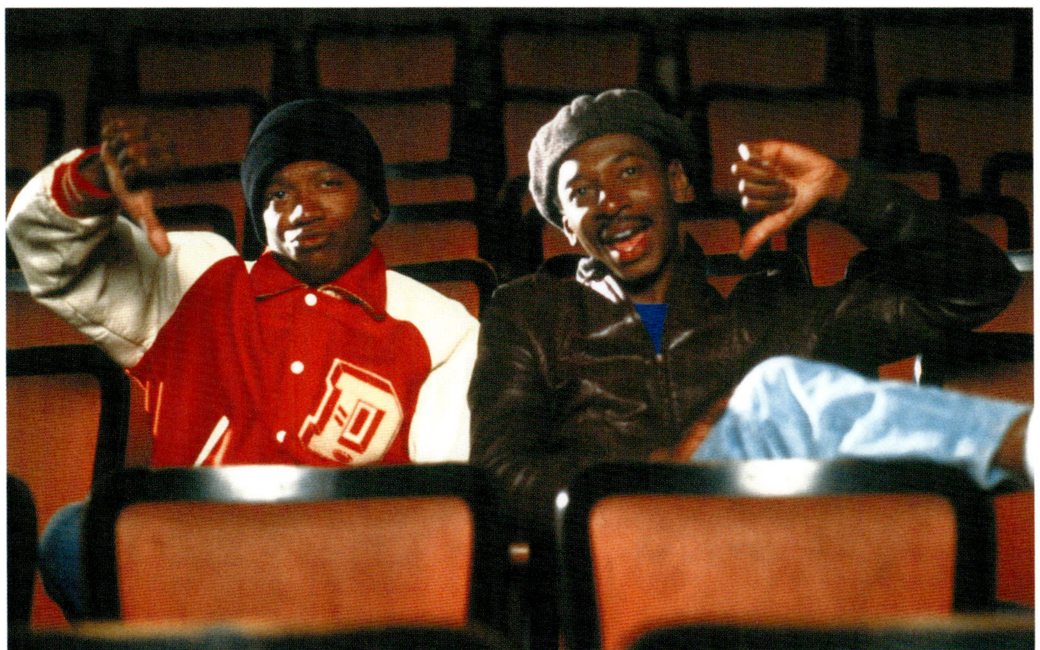

Jimmy Woodard and Robert Townsend parody Siskel and Ebert in *Hollywood Shuffle*.

Elm Street (1984) but also put out Susan Seidelman's *Smithereens* (1982) and both of John Waters's '80s films. Cinecom had Gregory Nava's *El Norte* (1983) and James Ivory's *A Room with a View* (1986), as well as films by John Sayles, Jonathan Demme, Robert Altman, and Paul Bartel. Island Pictures, a film venture of Island Records, distributed Alan Rudolph's *Choose Me* (1984), Hector Babenco's *Kiss of the Spider Woman* (1985), and Spike Lee's *She's Gotta Have It* (1986).

DOING THE HOLLYWOOD SHUFFLE

African American filmmakers in the 1980s were, by and large, not a part of the Hollywood studio system—and on-screen representation wasn't much better. The reality of being Black in the American film industry was memorably parodied by indie filmmaker Robert Townsend in his comedy *Hollywood Shuffle* (1987). The director-writer-producer-star had been a struggling actor for many years (he had small parts in 1975's *Cooley High* and 1984's *A Soldier's Story*), and the film follows an aspiring Black actor—and food-service worker—who finally lands a major role but is disappointed by the stereotype he's asked to portray. The film is peppered with comedic sketches and dream sequences, like a film-noir segment involving Jheri-curl activator and a Siskel-and-Ebert parody called "Sneaking into the Movies." *Hollywood Shuffle*'s existence is a small miracle; it was financed with credit cards, made with leftover film stock cobbled together from other shoots, and shot slowly over two years with borrowed camera equipment. Townsend's cowriter and costar, Keenen Ivory Wayans, went on to make his own movie parody, *I'm Gonna Git You Sucka* (1988),

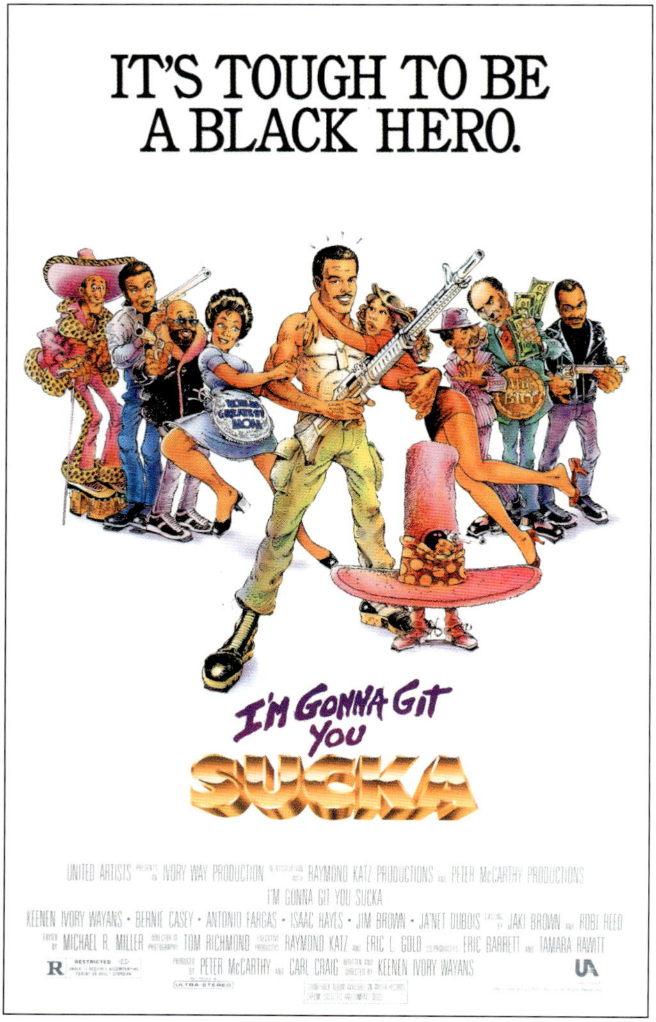

Keenen Ivory Wayans wrote, directed, and starred in *I'm Gonna Git You Sucka*.

which took aim at Blaxploitation. It was distributed by MGM, became a minor hit, and led to Wayans's popular '90s TV series *In Living Color*.

NYU film school graduate Spike Lee similarly scraped together a small budget to make his first feature, *She's Gotta Have It*. Shot in black-and-white in just two weeks, it features a female protagonist (Tracy Camilla Johns) who finds herself torn among three lovers—including a diminutive one played by Lee himself. ("We couldn't afford to pay anybody else," he explained.) The film is notable for both its artistry and its sexual politics, with a story centered around an intelligent and self-determined Black woman whose life avoids easy Hollywood stereotypes. Made for $175,000, it earned more than $7 million and launched Lee's prolific career.

His follow-ups were both distributed by major studios (who saw his talent and revenue potential) but took on subject matter that the establishment wouldn't touch. *School Daze* (1988), released by Columbia, was set at a historically Black college in Atlanta (similar to Lee's alma mater, Morehouse) whose homecoming weekend sees anti-apartheid demonstrations and clashes among various factions of students. *Do the Right Thing* (1989), one of the decade's landmark films, was financed by Universal. Set in Brooklyn over the course of a sweltering summer's day, it again stars Lee as Mookie, a pizza-delivery man who serves as an intermediary between the neighborhood's residents of color and his Italian American boss. As the temperature increases, so do racial tensions, and the film leads to a tragic interaction with the city's white policemen. But perhaps its most noteworthy aspect is its lack of easy answers. "Everyone has their own interpretation of 'what is the right thing?'—not only in the audience, but the characters in the film, too," said Lee. "This film was made to start some discussion, provoke some thought about racism." *Do the Right Thing* played in competition at Cannes, was passed over for major Oscars, and has since been recognized as a major milestone. In 2022, it was the highest-ranking film of the '80s in the prestigious *Sight and Sound* poll of international critics.

On the West Coast, a group of Black film-makers from UCLA's film school—collectively nicknamed the LA Rebellion—emerged in the late '70s and early '80s. The first wave included Charles Burnett, whose Watts-set master's thesis *Killer of Sheep* (1978) was followed by the family drama *My Brother's Wedding* (1983). The Ethiopian-born Haile Gerima directed *Ashes and Embers* (1982), which depicts the struggles and alienation of a Black Vietnam veteran. Other notable directors followed, including Julie Dash (*Illusions* [1982]), Alile Sharon Larkin (*A Different Image* [1982]), and Billy Woodberry (*Bless Their Little Hearts* [1984]).

Euzhan Palcy was born in Martinique and studied literature and film in Paris. Her first film, *Sugar Cane Alley* (1983), was made with a government grant and the support of director François Truffaut, who "believed in me and in that story and told everyone that it should be made," said Palcy. The film, about a young orphan growing up in 1930s Martinique, won awards at the Venice Film Festival and the French César Awards and was screened in the United States in 1984. "When I started out, there were three things that made film people look at me with condescension. I was young, I was Black, and I was female," she said later. "I have won a certain respect, but I think the film community still sees directing as a male job."

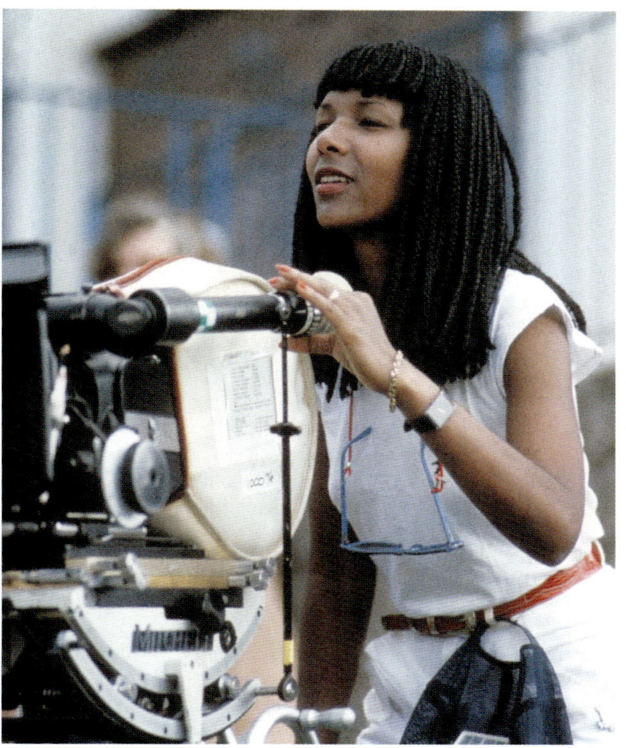

Euzhan Palcy directs *A Dry White Season.*

Her next project was set in South Africa. *A Dry White Season* (1989) was based on the celebrated novel by André Brink and stars Donald Sutherland as a white schoolteacher who investigates the disappearance of his Black gardener. (Marlon Brando, who returned to the screen after almost a decade in retirement, played his lawyer and received an Oscar nomination.) The film expanded the perspective of the novel's Black characters and was championed as an important anti-apartheid statement, but Palcy had not found it easy to get made. "The people who have the money don't care about a film on Black South Africans. They want to do films about Blacks only if they are funny, or if they have star names like Eddie Murphy, Bill Cosby, Prince, or Michael Jackson."

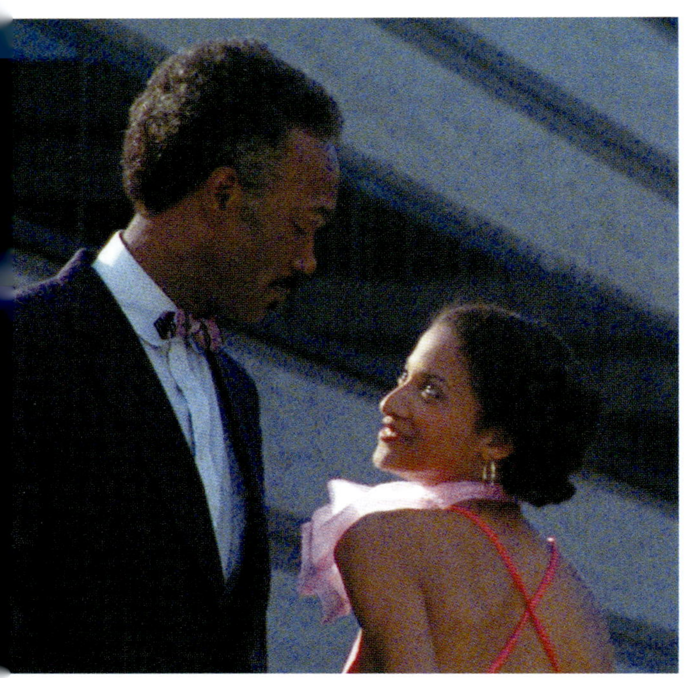

Duane Jones and Seret Scott in *Losing Ground*.

Ultimately picked up by MGM, *A Dry White Season* became the first film from a Black woman director to be released by a major studio. If that fact is shocking, consider this: Kathleen Collins's *Losing Ground* (1982) was the first feature-length movie directed by an African American woman since the silent era. The story of a philosophy professor (Seret Scott) and her painter husband (Bill Gunn) who rent a house in upstate New York for the summer was a lovingly rendered personal statement from an unheralded talent. Collins passed away in 1988, and her film didn't receive distribution outside of the festival circuit until its restoration in 2015.

At the end of the decade, Black directors continued to face production challenges and limited resources, but nonetheless crafted some impressive work. Charles Lane's *Sidewalk Stories* (1989) was a black-and-white homage to silent films like *The Kid* (1921), starring the director, whose Chaplinesque main character lives on the streets and becomes the protector of a young girl. Wendell B. Harris Jr.'s *Chameleon Street* (1989) follows a con artist who impersonates a French exchange student, a civil rights lawyer, and a medical surgeon, among other personae. Queer filmmaker Marlon Riggs made his seminal film *Tongues Untied* (1989) that poetically documents stories of Black men loving other Black men. Riggs's film is "a cannon blast of ideas about blackness and gayness and representation, sure, but also about how to devastate and illuminate and deviate, with a camera, a soundtrack and editing, with finger snaps," wrote film critic Wesley Morris on the film's thirtieth anniversary.

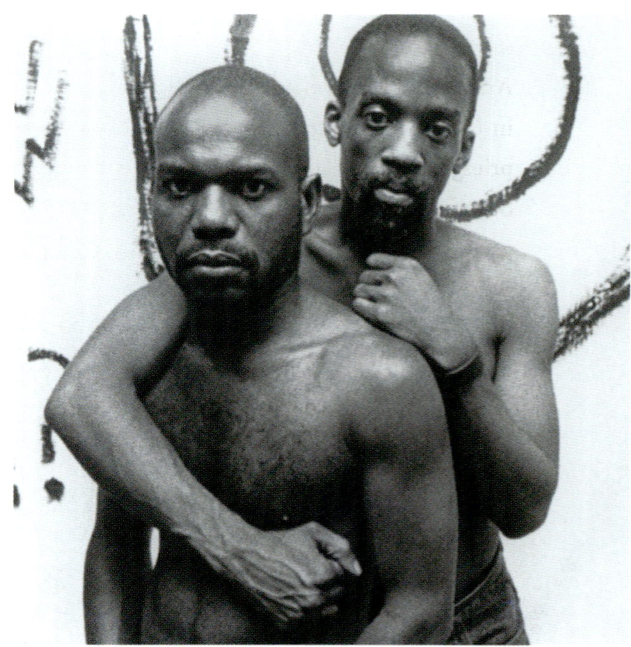

Marlon Riggs and Essex Hemphill in *Tongues Untied*.

QUEER CINEMA

In the early '80s, mainstream Hollywood was continuing to treat queer characters as curiosities or deviants. At best, a film like *Fame* (1980) would include a gay character (Paul McCrane) who was sympathetic but sad. Often the films connected queerness to mental instability or criminality, as in the dark underworld of gay clubs in *Cruising* (1980), the dangerously possessive lesbian in *Windows* (1980), or a psychopathic transgender character in *Dressed to Kill* (1980). In *Zorro, the Gay Blade* (1981), George Hamilton played both the masked hero and his flamboyant twin brother, "Bunny Wigglesworth." *Deathtrap* (1982) featured a pair of jealous homosexual murderers. How did straight characters respond? Perhaps like Arnold Schwarzenegger's brawny title character in *Conan the Barbarian* (1982), who lures a gay priest to a secluded spot where he knocks him out and steals his robe. Positive depictions did exist, as in MGM's *Victor/Victoria* (1982), Warner Bros.' *Personal Best* (1982), and Fox's *Making Love* (1982). But the developing AIDS crisis did nothing to make a wary industry feel more comfortable about depicting authentic gay life.

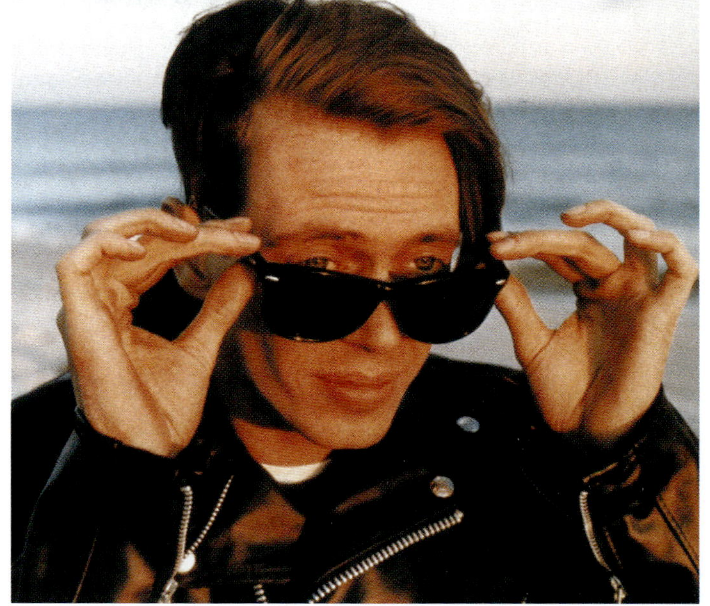

Steve Buscemi in *Parting Glances*.

Enter a wave of queer filmmakers who would tell their own stories. *Desert Hearts* (1985), by lesbian director Donna Deitch, sees a 1950s college professor (Helen Shaver) become drawn to a young Nevada woman (Patricia Charbonneau) while she waits to obtain a divorce. Gus Van Sant's artful debut, *Mala Noche* (1986), is about a convenience-store clerk (Tim Streeter) with an unrequited attraction to a migrant worker (Doug Cooeyate). *Torch Song Trilogy* (1988) starred Harvey Fierstein in an adaptation of his own play about a drag queen who finds true (but tragic) love and takes in a gay teenager. Fierstein also narrated the Oscar-winning documentary *The Times of Harvey Milk* (1984) about the martyred San Francisco politician. Its director, Rob Epstein, subsequently made *The AIDS Show* (1986) and *Common Threads: Stories from the Quilt* (1989).

Narrative features also tackled the AIDS epidemic directly, often by directors who were themselves HIV positive. *Buddies* (1985) was the first to be released, albeit in a very limited theatrical run. The low-budget story of a dying man and his volunteer companion was made by Arthur J. Bressan Jr., best known at that time for his pioneering documentary *Gay USA* (1977). "Artie had to make movies. He did not wait for the film industry to allow us to make queer

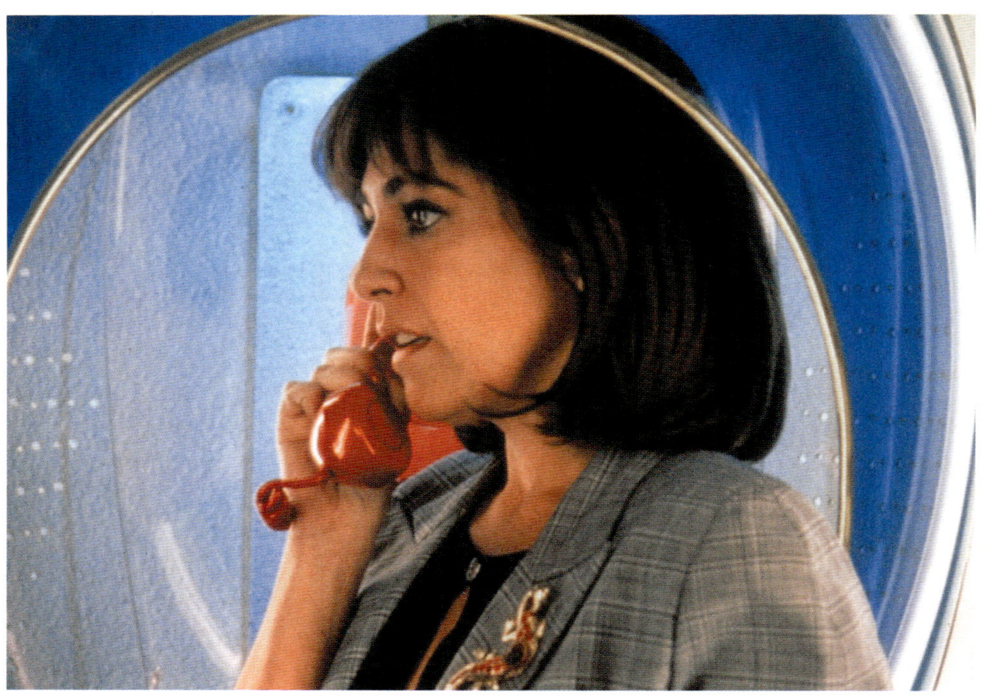

Carmen Maura as voice actress Pepa Marcos in *Women on the Verge of a Nervous Breakdown*.

films," explained fellow director Greta Schiller, who made the documentary *Before Stonewall* (1984). "He grabbed his 16mm camera, formed crews from his friends and a loose network of filmmakers (there were only a handful of them), raised cash for film processing from his friends (including his dentist), and went out into the streets." Already diagnosed with AIDS when he shot *Buddies*, Bressan passed away in 1987.

Later in 1985, NBC aired the television movie *An Early Frost* to high ratings, several Emmys, and a Peabody Award. Gay director John Erman told the story of a young man (Aidan Quinn) who returns home to reveal his sexuality and positive diagnosis to his family. "I just knew in my gut how important this was," Erman said. "Because I had so many friends who not only were dying of AIDS, but whose families were disowning them and who were being thrown out of their apartments and not being able to get a room in a hospital. I just knew that this could be something that would change people's perceptions of gay people." Bill Sherwood's *Parting Glances* (1986), about a couple soon to begin a long-distance relationship, costarred a young Steve Buscemi as a rock musician with HIV. *Longtime Companion* (1989), directed by Norman René, followed a group of friends and lovers throughout the decade. Both filmmakers later died from AIDS complications.

American movies about queer life were supplemented by films from overseas, particularly European art-house fare. Spain's Pedro Almodóvar released a number of provocative, sexually liberated films like *Labyrinth of Passion* (1982), *Law of Desire* (1987), *Women on the Verge*

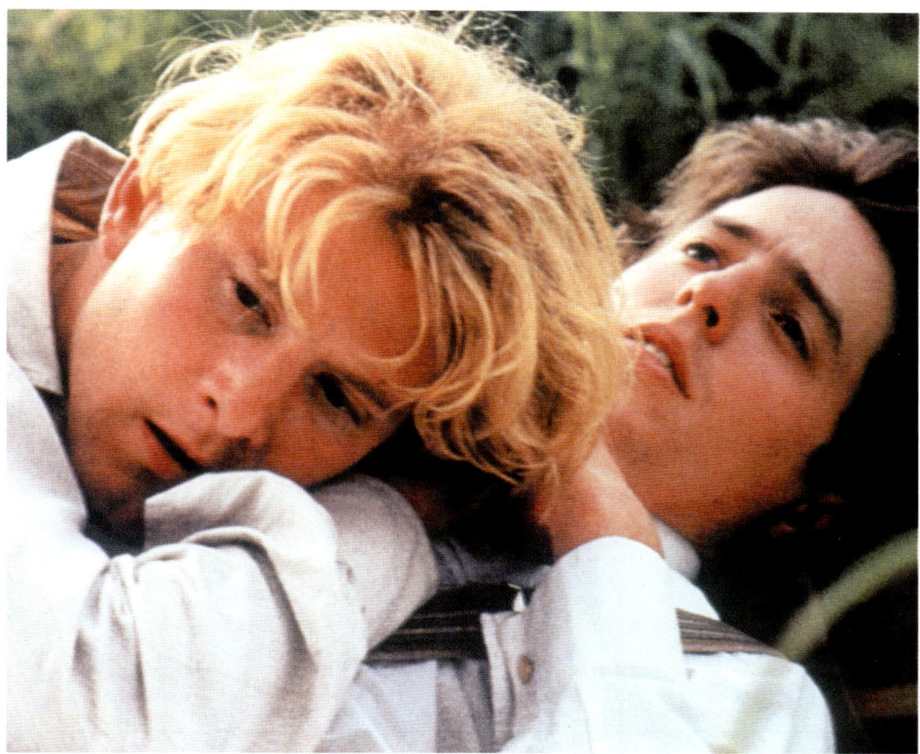

James Wilby and Hugh Grant in *Maurice*.

of a Nervous Breakdown (1988), and *Tie Me Up! Tie Me Down!* (1989), all of which costarred young actor Antonio Banderas and cemented the director's status as a queer visionary. Germany's *Taxi zum Klo* (1980) showed the seedier side of gay Berlin, and director Rainer Werner Fassbinder delivered the outrageously art directed *Querelle* (1982).

Dutch director Paul Verhoeven made the bisexual thriller *The 4th Man* (1983), which Paul Bartel called "the first gay Catholic horror film." Japan's Nagisa Ōshima depicted queer longing in *Merry Christmas, Mr. Lawrence* (1983), while *Beautiful Mystery* (1983) was an early example of a gay "pink" film, which parodied nationalist writer Yukio Mishima. Héctor Babenco's *Kiss of the Spider Woman* starred an Oscar-winning William Hurt as a queer Brazilian prison inmate, while Filipino director Lino Brocka's *Macho Dancer* (1988) follows a gay teenager in Manila's red-light district.

The United Kingdom exported a number of gay-themed films, from Steven Frears's *My Beautiful Laundrette* (1985) and *Prick Up Your Ears* (1987) to the teen thriller *The Fruit Machine* (1988). After the acclaimed TV series *Brideshead Revisited* (1981), several historical films dealt with budding queer relationships, including *Another Country* (1984) and *Maurice* (1987), the latter an E. M. Forster adaptation by life and business partners Ismail Merchant (producer) and James Ivory (director).

Beyond Hollywood: France

Looking back on a stylistic trend that had started in the early '80s, French film critic Raphaël Bassan coined the term *cinéma du look* to categorize a set of films that fused modern pop sensibility with stories of youthful alienation and crime. The foremost example is Jean-Jacques Beineix's debut, *Diva* (1981), a thriller about a young deliveryman who's obsessed with an opera star and gets unwittingly mixed up in a police investigation of the Parisian underworld. A boldly conceived mixture of high art and high energy, it contained a famous motorbike chase in the Métro that seemed to announce a new, kinetic era of French movie-making. "*Diva* is the 1980s by Immaculate Conception," wrote critic Wesley Morris in 2022. "It feels like the 1970s were incinerated and a movie like this is what rose from their ashes, fully formed."

Beineix followed *Diva* with the turbulent romance *Betty Blue*, (*37°2 le matin,* 1986), which appeared alongside similarly forward-looking creations like Luc Besson's *Subway* (1985) and *The Big Blue* (1988) and Leos Carax's *Mauvais Sang* (1986).

Maurice Pialat had critical success with *Loulou* (1980), *À nos amours* (1983), and the Palme d'Or–winning *Under the Sun of Satan* (1987). Bertrand Tavernier made the compelling historical dramas *Coup de Torchon* (1981), *A Sunday in the Country* (1984), and *Life and Nothing But* (1989), as well as the Oscar-winning tale of mid-century jazz, *Round Midnight* (1986). Claire Denis made her directorial debut with *Chocolat* (1988), a coming-of-age story set in colonial French Cameroon.

Meanwhile, the filmmakers of the French New Wave were still delivering major works, twenty years on. Esoteric auteur Jean-Luc Godard returned to form with *Every Man for Himself* (1980) and did the rounds at several US film festivals. (The *Washington Post* reported from Telluride, "Talking to Godard about the new film is rather like communicating with a cloud.") Éric Rohmer captured summertime ennui in *Pauline at the Beach* (1983) and *The Green Ray* (1986). Claude Chabrol made crime stories like *Cop au Vin* (1985) and *Masks* (1987), as well as the wartime *Story of Women* (1988) with Isabelle Huppert. François Truffaut made his final films *The Last Metro* (1980), *The Woman Next Door* (1981), and *Confidentially Yours* (1983) before his death at age fifty-two.

Agnès Varda made a mix of documentaries (*Mur Murs* [1981]), fiction films (*Vagabond* [1985]), and something in between—*Jane B. par Agnès V.* (1988), a freewheeling portrait of her friend actress Jane Birkin. Her husband, Jacques Demy, completed several musical films, including *Une Chambre en ville* (1982) and *Parking* (1985). Fellow Left Bank director Alain Resnais made the celebrated but challenging *Mon oncle d'Amerique* (1980), while Robert Bresson's final film, *L'Argent* (1983), follows a counterfeit 500-franc note and the lives it affects as it is passed among the film's otherwise unconnected characters.

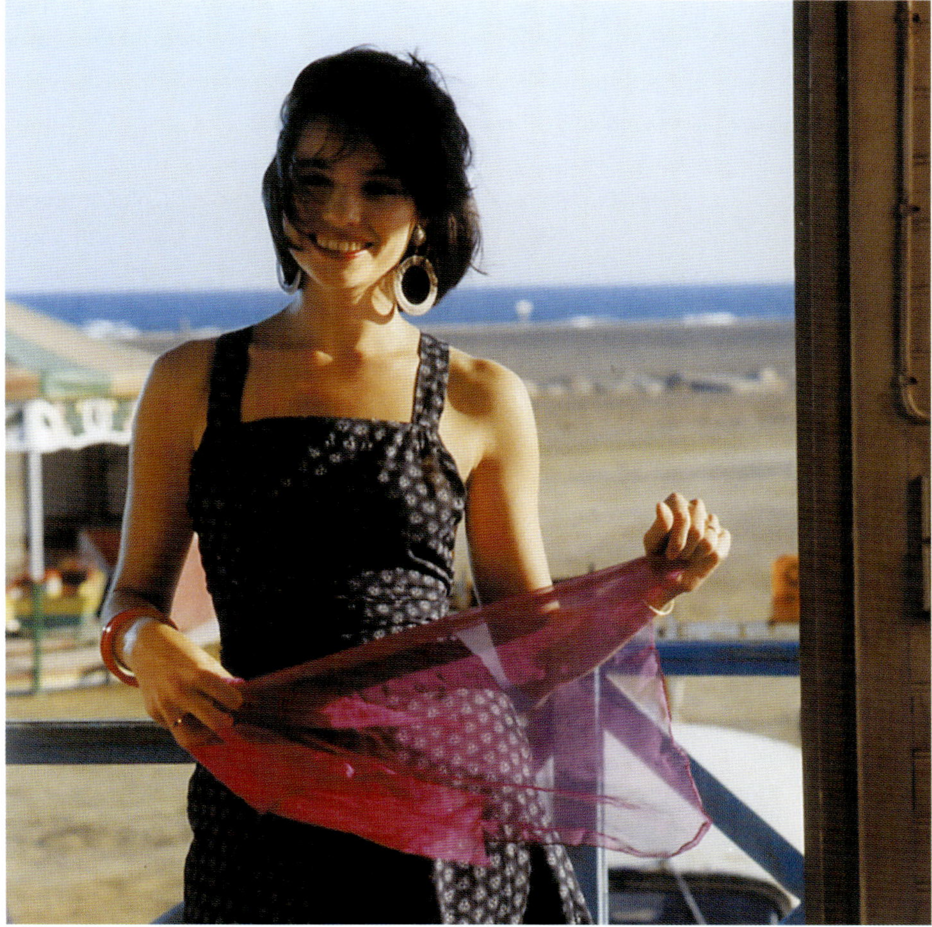

Béatrice Dalle in *Betty Blue (37°2 le matin).*

Todd Haynes's scrappy and original short film *Superstar: The Karen Carpenter Story* (1987) exemplifies alternative filmmaking in the '80s through its defiance of Hollywood storytelling conventions and business practices. Using Barbie dolls in place of actors, the queer filmmaker documents the life of the pop singer who struggled with eating disorders and passed away in 1983, all while parodying the TV docudrama form and drawing attention to unattainable body images that plague modern womanhood. The forty-three-minute film's unlicensed soundtrack meant that the film couldn't be released beyond the film-festival circuit, but its notoriety and good press were enough to guarantee Haynes's future as a filmmaker of ideas, resourcefulness, and creative audacity. His first feature was *Poison* (1991), a queer sci-fi film and AIDS allegory that won the Grand Jury Prize at the Sundance Film Festival and became an important early entry in the New Queer Cinema movement of the 1990s.

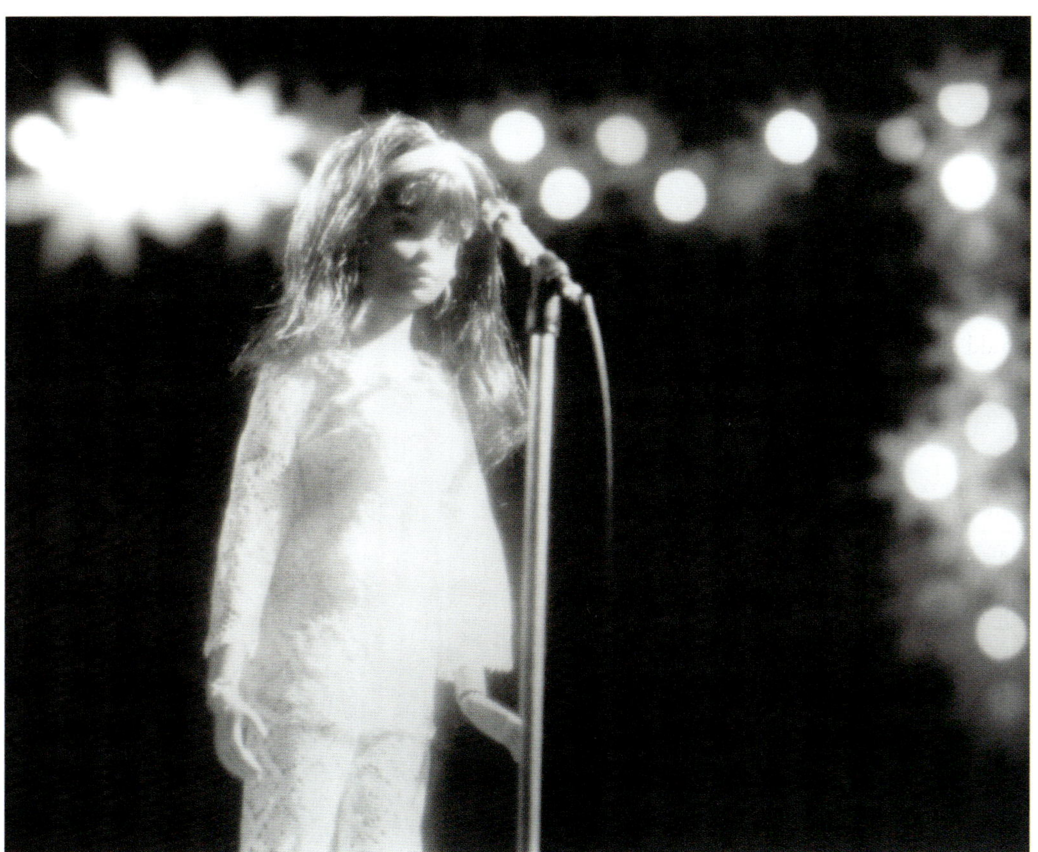

Todd Haynes used a variety of dolls he found at flea markets to portray the characters in *Superstar: The Karen Carpenter Story*.

ASIAN AMERICAN CINEMA

Another group underrepresented in the film industry was the Asian American community, whose depictions in '80s films often consisted of racist stereotypes like the foreign-exchange student Long Duk Dong (Gedde Watanabe) who is the butt of jokes in *Sixteen Candles* (1984) or the wise sensei Mr. Miyagi (Pat Morita) in *The Karate Kid* (1984). Vietnamese-born actor Ke Huy Kwan had roles as cute kids in *Indiana Jones and the Temple of Doom* (1984) and *The Goonies* (1985), but serious adult parts were sometimes reserved for white actors in heavy makeup, like Joel Grey in *Remo Williams: The Adventure Begins* (1985). *Year of the Dragon* (1985), *Big Trouble in Little China* (1986), and *China Girl* (1987) featured white characters dropped into various American Chinatowns. Meanwhile, Hong Kong star Jackie Chan made a couple of unsuccessful forays into Hollywood filmmaking but wouldn't truly bridge the cultural divide until the 1990s. Ditto with action auteur John Woo.

The first Chinese American director to break through was Wayne Wang, whose low-budget film *Chan Is Missing* (1982) was financed with grants from the American Film Institute and the National Endowment for the Arts. It tells of a San Francisco taxi driver and his nephew who are searching for the man who has disappeared with the money for their cab license. "My highest expectation was for it to play festivals and college campuses," said Wang, whose movie-loving father named him after western star John Wayne. "In fact, when seven of us signed a contract saying if the film made back its cost we'd share the profits, everyone laughed." The film did make money, and its success allowed Wang to continue to make authentic films about Asian American life, like *Dim Sum: A Little Bit of Heart* (1985) and *Eat a Bowl of Tea* (1989).

Peter Wang (no relation), an actor in *Chan Is Missing*, later became the first American director to shoot a movie in mainland China with his personal story *A Great Wall* (1986), about a California computer engineer (Wang) who takes his family on a bittersweet visit to his homeland. It predated, by one year, the filming in Beijing of the Oscar-winning historical epic *The Last Emperor* (1987) by Italian director Bernardo Bertolucci, which starred Chinese American actor John Lone as Puyi, the deposed young ruler.

After making the documentary *Unfinished Business* (1986) about Japanese internment during World War II, Steven Okazaki made the rom-com *Living on Tokyo Time* (1987) about a San Francisco dishwasher (Minako Ohashi) who marries a dull musician (Ken Nakagawa) in order to obtain a green card. Michael Toshiyuki Uno directed *The Wash* (1988), which follows an aging Japanese American woman (Nobu McCarthy) who leaves her stubborn husband (Mako) and navigates the widening cultural gap between her upbringing and modern American society.

The documentary *Who Killed Vincent Chin?* (1988) examined the racially motivated 1982 murder of a Chinese auto engineer. It was made by Japanese American director Renee Tajima-

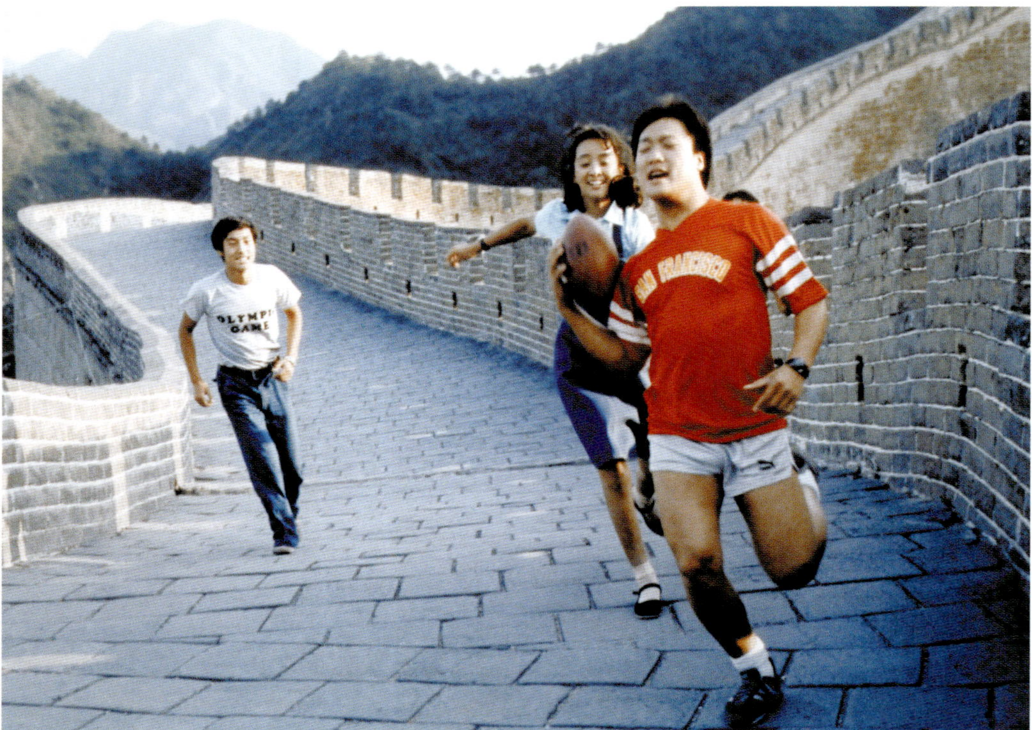

Xiu Jian, Li Qinqin, and Kelvin Han Yee in *A Great Wall.*

Peña and Chinese-born documentarian and activist Christine Choy, who had founded Third World Newsreel, a New York–based distributor and international filmmaking collective. Choy had earlier codirected *Mississippi Triangle* (1984) with Allen Siegel and Worth Long, which depicted the various ethnic communities of the Mississippi Delta, including Chinese Americans. Meanwhile, Arthur Dong's first feature-length documentary, *Forbidden City, U.S.A.* (1989), took a revealing look at the Chinatown nightlife scene in wartime San Francisco. "Did I think that I'm making a film about myself rebelling and being an artist? No," asserted Dong. But it is nevertheless a film dealing with representation, "about being an artist in a country that's mostly white."

That representation speaks to the opportunities the industry gave to new and diverse voices through a supportive infrastructure for independent filmmaking and technological innovation that helped bring their visions to life. "Looking backward, it's obvious that the 1980s was the great primordial swamp out of which the indies crawled, flopped onto land, and slithered off into the jungle," wrote Peter Biskind vividly, in his 2005 book about the rise of independent filmmaking, *Down and Dirty Pictures.* Without the groundbreaking films in this chapter, the indie film boom of the next decade could not have been possible.

Conclusion

THE BEST MOVIES, NO MATTER WHEN OR WHERE THEY ARE SET, SPEAK to the era in which they were made, revealing the social attitudes, political anxieties, and cultural preoccupations of the time. In films as diverse as *First Blood* (1982), *Ferris Bueller's Day Off* (1986), *Wings of Desire* (1987), and *Akira* (1988), the spirit of the 1980s remains well within reach for moviegoers today. The timeless appeal of the decade's films is borne out by the numerous reboots of iconic '80s films—like *Ghostbusters* (1984) and *Road House* (1989)—that have graced theater screens and streaming platforms in the twenty-first century. Eighties movies remain cultural touchstones, part of our modern lexicon, and deserving of a spot in the classic film canon.

"That's all well and good," you might say, "but what about *Bolero* (1984)? *Jaws: The Revenge* (1987)? *Hobgoblins* (1988)?" Sure, every decade has its share of duds. In a June 1980 *New Yorker* article, critic Pauline Kael asked, "Why are movies so bad?" She lamented the state of the film business, from its corporate leadership to the modern star system, to the attitudes of the audience. None of it fared well. "People just want to go to a movie. They're stung repeatedly, yet their desire for a good movie—for any movie—is so strong that all over the country they keep lining up."

It should be noted that Kael typed those words months before *Heaven's Gate* (1980) and other money losers ushered in a supposedly stifled era of top-down studio control. But artists continued to find a way—as they always do—and a new generation of filmmakers entered the business just as the establishment was losing its footing. They brought with them new stories, new styles, and new modes of production that transformed the industry, and we are still living in their shadow. So, hit rewind and let's experience it all over again.

Acknowledgments

THANK YOU, AS ALWAYS, TO ELI ARNOLD (WHOSE FAVORITE '80S MOVIE is *Raiders of the Lost Ark*) for his love, support, and patience. To Sharon Thackston (*The Princess Bride*) for her friendship and horror expertise. To Timo Weidner (*Berlin Alexanderplatz*) for his proofreading, insights, and shrewd criticism and Tabea Höcker (*National Lampoon's Christmas Vacation*) for her constant encouragement. To D.J. Martinez III (*After Hours*) and Grace Martinez (*Little Darlings*) for becoming fast friends and hosting all the movie nights. To my brother, Josh Malahy (*Raising Arizona*), who introduced me to '80s movies. Thanks for always being older than me, Josh.

To my editor, Randall Lotowycz (*Repo Man*), for his shared enthusiasm and excellent advice. And to the team at Running Press: senior vice president Kristin Kiser (*The Terminator*), publisher Shannon Connors Fabricant (*Heathers*), editorial director Cindy Sipala (*Dirty Dancing*), publicity manager Seta Zink (*Cinema Paradiso*), production editor Amber Morris (*Real Genius*), and the book's designer, Amanda Richmond (*Ferris Bueller's Day Off*).

Much gratitude goes to my old colleagues at Turner Classic Movies for signing off on this project: Genevieve McGillicuddy (*Say Anything*), Lindsey Griffin (*The Little Mermaid*), and Mark Wynns (*The Princess Bride*). Thanks as well to Monica Elliott (*Moonstruck*), Yacov Freedman (*Mad Max 2*), Marketa Benson (*Moonstruck*), and Matthew Ownby (*Superstar: The Karen Carpenter Story*). To former TCM colleagues who continue to give me support: Heather Margolis (*Ferris Bueller's Day Off*), Jeanette Gregory (*The Blues Brothers*), Joanna Frankowski (*The Karate Kid*), and Taryn Coleman (*Less than Zero*).

Thanks to Videodrome Atlanta for being such an important part of the local film community, to the Oglethorpe University Library for providing a quiet space to research and write, and to the public library for their vast resources and merciful overdue policies.

And thanks finally to Steven Spielberg for directing my favorite '80s movie, *E.T. the Extra-Terrestrial*. In the fifth grade, I told my class I wanted to be Spielberg when I grew up. I no longer have that goal, which is unachievable anyway, but I continue to be inspired by his creative vision and artistry.

Index

Photo Credits

pages x, xi, 5, 12, 13, 15, 22, 31, 42, 49, 50, 54, 56, 61 (bottom), 67 (top), 68, 88, 89, 90, 93, 94, 95, 97 (top), 113, 119, 124, 125, 131, 132, 133 (bottom), 139, 140, 142, 145, 147, 151, 152, 153, 154, 160, 161, 169, 176, 177 (top), 183, 185, 187, 188, 190, 199, 203, 206 (bottom), 211, 216, 218, 226, 234, 241, 243: courtesy Everett Collection; page 18, courtesy The Walt Disney Company; pages 67 (bottom), 92, 96, 97 (bottom), 98, 120, 163, 166, 189, 235, 256 (bottom), 262, 264: courtesy Photofest; page 135, courtesy Metro-Goldwyn-Mayer; page 149, courtesy Warner Bros.; page 159, courtesy Vox Media; page 197, courtesy Alamy; page 208 (top), courtesy Geffen Records; page 208 (bottom), courtesy Elektra Records; page 209 (top), courtesy Universal Music Group; page 222, courtesy Mukta Arts Ltd.; page 223, courtesy Sujata Films; page 224, courtesy Yash Raj Films; all other photography courtesy Turner Classic Movies, Inc.